A Master's Due

David Herbert Donald

A Master's Due
Essays in Honor of David Herbert Donald

Edited by William J. Cooper, Jr.
Michael F. Holt
John McCardell

Louisiana State University Press
Baton Rouge and London

Designer: *Christopher Wilcox*
Typeface: *Zapf International*
Typesetter: *G&S Typesetters, Inc.*
Printer: *Thomson-Shore, Inc.*
Binder: *John Dekker & Sons, Inc.*

Library of Congress Cataloging in Publication Data
Main entry under title:

A Master's due.

"The principal writings of David Herbert Donald": p.
Contents: Introduction: David Herbert Donald/
Ari Hoogenboom—The election of 1840, voter
mobilization, and the emergence of the second American
party system/Michael F. Holt—"The only door"/
William J. Cooper, Jr.—[etc.]
Includes index.
1. United States—History—Addresses, essays,
lectures. 2. Donald, David Herbert, 1920– —
Addresses, essays, lectures. I. Cooper, William J.
(William James), 1940– . II. Holt, Michael F.
(Michael Fitzgibbon) III. McCardell, John.
IV. Donald, David Herbert, 1920– .
E178.6.M37 1985   973   85-10259
ISBN 0-8071-1260-7

Contents

Acknowledgments

In the making of this book, the editors had substantial assistance from several people. From the inception of this project on through to publication, Aïda DiPace Donald gave her energetic support. Quite frankly, without her willingness to help us this book would never have been published. Eric Walther, a graduate student in history at LSU, had a major part in preparing the bibliography, and Marlene LeBlanc performed critical typing chores.

The editors are delighted to salute their publishers. Leslie Phillabaum early on expressed interest and encouraged us to proceed. Beverly Jarrett's enthusiasm never flagged. We could not have chosen a better editor. Even when dealing with eleven different historians, Barbara O'Neil Phillips maintained her good humor. Because of her, seeing the book through the Press was a pleasure, not a task.

A Master's Due

Introduction

David Herbert Donald: A Celebration

Ari Hoogenboom

"David Donald is coming back!" With the fervor of apostles, students who had taken Donald's courses at Columbia before his 1949 departure for Smith College, proclaimed in the spring of 1951 his imminent return. I was surprised by the unabashed enthusiasm of normally blasé graduate students, and my curiosity grew when I consulted Dumas Malone about a seminar, and he, too, despite his calm spirit, was obviously excited as he told me Donald would be giving a doctoral seminar. That fall during registration I met him. I was struck by his youth (he was about to celebrate his thirty-first birthday), his erudition, and his courtliness. He was of medium height and slight build, appropriately tweedy in dress, with prematurely thinning hair and thick glasses (James G. Randall, his major professor, had worried that Donald would read his eyes out of his head). His manner was friendly, enthusiastic, encouraging, and courteous, and I signed up for "Studies in American Political History in the Reconstruction Period and Beyond," Donald's first doctoral seminar.

As the seminar progressed, its members, including Stanley Hirshson, Irwin Unger, and Grady McWhiney (in the second semester), pieced together Donald's background. We learned from Carl Sandburg's introduction to Donald's first book, *Lincoln's Herndon* (New York, 1948), that he was "born and raised in the State of Mississippi, on a plantation of thousands of acres, with more than a score of Negro field hands." The birthday was October 1, 1920, and the place was Goodman. He graduated from Millsaps College (A.B., 1941), a small Methodist liberal arts college in Jackson, Mississippi, where he studied with Vernon L. Wharton, who later published an influential revisionist study, *The Negro in Mississippi, 1865–1890* (1947). As an undergraduate, Donald considered a career in music and lost a chance to be a high school band director by hitchhiking hatless to the interview ("Young man," he was sternly asked, "where is your hat?").

Lack of a hat did not prevent a career in history. Donald went north, by way of the University of North Carolina, to the University of Illinois, where he earned an M.A. in 1942 and a Ph.D. in 1946. He studied with James G. Randall, the foremost Lincoln scholar, and Randall and his wife Ruth Painter Randall became Donald's "mental godparents." Although his debt to and his affection for the Randalls are great, Donald's views of the Civil War and Reconstruction are closer to those of Wharton than to those of the Randalls. Donald's first publication, "The Scalawag in Mississippi Reconstruction" (*Journal of Southern History*, X [1944], 447–60), is an important revisionist article, antedating Wharton's book by three years, and Donald later handled William H. Herndon's radical antislavery views more sympathetically than Randall could have. Members of the seminar admired Donald's accomplishments and his capacity to subordinate his background and surroundings to the results of scholarship.

We appreciated Donald as a teacher even more than we appreciated him as a scholar. He had much to give, he knew how to give it, and he gave it freely. His lecture course was outstanding. Covering the period from 1828 to 1877, it had an overall hypothesis, the rise and fall of the equal rights principle, and each lecture, though a unit, fitted smoothly into that scheme. During the first half of each meeting, Donald reviewed what historians had said about a problem, then invited class members to suggest solutions and explanations, which he thoroughly discussed before summing up the evening's topic with his own fresh hypothesis, and he timed the whole effort perfectly. His ideas were informed by the latest historiographical insights, but were original rather than simply fashionable. In Donald's huge class of Columbia graduate students, no one had heard a better-organized, more brilliant lecturer. The following year the class proved just as exhilarating to graduate students (including the former editor of the Barnard *Bulletin*, Aïda DiPace), since Donald rethought each lecture and in the process reread portions of a dozen or more books.

Although Donald was stunning in the lecture hall, it was in the seminar room that he became a major force in our lives. Regarding the conventionally taught seminar as useless and boring, he tried to evoke the excitement generated in the 1870s by Henry Adams in his Harvard history seminars. Donald avoided long lectures on how to research and did not waste valuable seminar time reading papers.

We learned by doing. We were to imagine we were writing a monograph on the trial of Andrew Johnson—Donald had suggested several sources—and we were to bring our first paragraph to the next meeting. The following week, Donald discussed them with us, giving close attention to our topic sentences. To our amazement, our returned paragraphs contained more of his characteristic penmanship than our typing. He had analyzed every sentence, phrase, and word, and suggested alternatives for us to consider. None of us, I think, from grade school to graduate school, ever had a teacher who subjected our writing to such critical scrutiny, an experience that all of his students have shared in the years since. In our next assignment we tried to incorporate his suggestions in a 750-word essay evaluating Charles Sumner's Alabama Claims speech of 1869. Donald's unusual effort on our behalf pushed us until we found ourselves (as later Donald students have found themselves) neglecting other courses to meet the requirements of his seminar. He was concerned with our use of evidence, our capacity to form and argue a hypothesis, our organization, our clarity, our form, and our writing style. He was tough, demanded progress, and eliminated those he thought were not progressing. He was fair, and neither personality nor ideology affected his decisions. A "Christian and a conservative" who avowed his philosophical debt to Reinhold Niebuhr, Donald was concerned with the ability, not the beliefs, of his students.

Besides other assignments to determine our strengths and weaknesses, we wrote two papers relating directly to our dissertation subjects. These papers were placed on file in the library a few days before they were to be discussed. We read each paper and one of us, designated chief critic, led the debate. The first paper we considered was an early version of "Toward a Reconsideration of Abolitionists," before Donald gave it at the 1951 American Historical Association convention. Having, at his suggestion, read Gilbert H. Barnes and Dwight L. Dumond on antislavery, we thought our criticism was on a high level (later we smugly thought it better than that of the AHA audience), but Donald, who excelled in debate at Millsaps, demolished our objections. While the debater scored points the scholar was pleased, and during the following week he admitted that our reaction to his view of the abolitionists (as a displaced class) had forced him to recheck and refine some points in his paper. Although we did not relish criticizing each other's papers and dreaded being chief critic, we learned both to criticize and to respond to criticism. After monitoring our efforts, Donald gave his oral critique, ranging from positive to devastatingly negative. (He even dismissed us to discuss one paper privately with its author.) Donald's written critiques of our papers filled the pages' margins and spilled over to their reverse sides. Rather than create a dog-eat-dog environment, mutual criticism encouraged us to cooperate with each other. We were on the lookout for references to all our subjects, including Charles Sumner, on whom D.D., as we called him among ourselves, was working, and he let us use his elaborate notes on Sumner's voluminous correspondence.

A Donald student did more than attend a lecture course or enroll in a year-long seminar. Donald's seminar was a continuing one, and when papers were presented we attended as long as we were in the area. Donald also recognized when we needed help with specific problems. Many of us read books as though they were textbooks, concentrating on data and often missing the theme. Donald taught us how to read. I seemed a particularly hard case. For most of a year he spent an hour each week with me. In his office or over a cup of tea, we discussed what I had read since our last meeting. It is true that Donald occasionally embarrassed me. After one grueling session, perhaps feeling a twinge of guilt for making me squirm, he confessed he felt like a child who had pulled the wings from an insect. Although he sometimes used the stick, he always offered the carrot of help. When Grady McWhiney had difficulties with his qualifying exam in French, Donald looked up McWhiney's examinations, noted his weaknesses, and coached him until he passed.

Donald was available to an extent unheard of at Columbia. Graduate students with other sponsors asked for and received his help, but his own students were the most demanding. His American Civilization colloquium usually adjourned to his apartment for an informal discussion, and he invited members of his continuing seminar to attend. One evening McWhiney and I were too late for the meeting, but Donald graciously asked us in for tea and proceeded to sharpen our wits. In the discussion that followed, Donald and McWhiney, who share a propensity for debate, fell into an argument. I have forgotten its subject, but I remember its inconclusive ending. Knowing that Donald would use his admission to undermine his position,

McWhiney found himself refusing to admit he was sitting on the sofa. Donald attended and enlivened our parties. Often arguing against the field, he entered wholeheartedly into the conversation. When he left, we stayed on for hours analyzing what he had said.

Donald knew how to get the most from us. He noted our short-comings, but he praised us when he thought praise was merited. We sometimes thought that his kicks, interspersed with pats on the head, were more to motivate us than to evaluate us, but despite this suspicion, the kick never failed to jolt us. Shortly after I turned in the first chapter of my dissertation, Donald was hospitalized with mono-nucleosis. He asked me to come to his room to pick up the chapter. Flat on his back, he had nevertheless given it his typical reading (scarcely a sentence was untouched). When he accused me of forgetting everything I had learned in his seminar, I felt that I needed his hospital bed more than he did. Because his criticisms were so sharp, the courtesy and polished manners with which his figurative kicks were administered often seemed incongruous. After a particularly difficult conference, Stanley Hirshson was nonplussed when Donald jumped up like a valet to help him into his coat. Tough standards and frank judgments were often difficult to take, yet Donald's unfailing courtesy, which did not lessen the impact of the critique, told us that his evaluation involved no personal disapproval.

He was concerned with how many books we had read, the number of collections we had searched, the quantity of pages we had written; our personal well-being and our morale mattered to him as well. When Grady and Sue McWhiney arrived in New York, they didn't know anyone and Donald asked us to call on them. When he was out of town, he often wrote chatty letters, telling of his activities. These letters assured us that big brother, despite all those kicks, was our friend and was working extremely hard himself and, as big brother is wont to do, was watching us. From his letters we knew that during July, 1952, he worked eleven hours a day in Washington, finishing the text for his Civil War picture book, and that as soon as he turned in the last of his copy he began receiving proofs. They required an unusual amount of work, since he had to expand or cut the text so it would fit in a specific space. The whole wearisome process took longer than he had calculated, but the result was an eloquent, accurate, and handsome book. The raw materials for *Divided We*

Fought: A Pictorial History of the War, 1861–1865 (New York, 1952) had been in his office the preceding year, and he had involved us in the excitement of his project by letting us peruse the photographs. Donald's tough summer created a text worthy of the pictures. He shrewdly allows the participants at whom we gaze to speak as his brilliantly connected quotations form a smooth narrative of the Civil War.

Donald's work that summer was not limited to *Divided We Fought*. Following a week's vacation in Mississippi, he got on with his Sumner research at the Library of Congress. While he burrowed through the papers of Daniel Webster, Caleb Cushing, Hamilton Fish, and others, Irwin Unger, serving as his assistant, searched the newspapers for references to Sumner. Contemplating the work accomplished and what remained to be done, Donald occasionally jested that it would be so much easier had Sumner not survived Preston Brooks's attack. Although we loved to analyze such remarks, he was obviously being facetious, for at that time nothing mattered as much as his work on Sumner. One weekend, when the Library of Congress was closed, Donald and Unger strolled about and happened on a construction site. A deep hole had been excavated for a foundation, and they approached the barricade for a closer look. The board on which they were standing suddenly gave way. Donald's words, in the harrowing moment before they regained their footing, were "I'll never finish Sumner!" Instilling in us a similar devotion to scholarship was one of his goals.

Donald's accomplishments inspired and shamed us to persevere, as did the knowledge that we must face him when he returned. We were apprehensive about our first meeting after the summer "vacation." McWhiney had gone to the shore only once, but on the way had the bad luck to bump into Donald's office mate. Disappointed that the hardworking McWhiney had not worked even harder, Donald exclaimed, "Come now, Mr. McWhiney, did you spend your entire summer at Jones Beach!"

As we approached the time when we had to leave the nest Donald's concern for our future deepened. Late in the fall of 1952, McWhiney received an emergency job replacement offer from Troy State Teachers College in Alabama, and Donald simply listed the pros and cons of taking it. When McWhiney accepted and left during the weekend, we thought he had made the right decision, but Donald disagreed. He wished McWhiney had remained, and apparently re-solved to give advice in the future. A few years later when Unger con-templated a summer vacation in Europe, he received a letter from Donald, who wrote with reluctance but nevertheless counseled him to stay in the United States and work on his dissertation. Unger stayed, completed his dissertation, and, he notes ruefully at times, has never had his European trip.

Since Donald is a faithful correspondent, his absences from cam-pus scarcely interrupt his interaction with his students. During the summer of 1953, he reported on his latest project from Brunswick, Maine, where he was using the Bowdoin College library. His job of proofreading and annotating Salmon P. Chase's Civil War diaries proved as tedious as his work the previous summer. As usual, he drove himself hard, writing 253 footnotes one day, but he looked for-ward to finishing his task and turning to his work on Sumner. Cor-respondence with his students continued, since Donald spent the 1953–54 academic year as Fulbright Professor of American History at the University College of North Wales. There he busied himself preparing and giving lectures, reading proof for *Inside Lincoln's Cabinet: The Civil War Diaries of Salmon P. Chase* (New York, 1954), whose attractive blue-and-gold jacket especially pleased him, and researching in the Gladstone manuscripts at the British Museum, where he found more important Sumner material than he had antici-pated. He purchased a motorcycle and, protected from injury by his pea-green crash helmet and from the elements by his tentlike mack-intosh, roared up and down the local roads and later toured south-western and central England. Donald's letters and postcards inspired us to keep working, and he responded promptly to our queries. His four-page, single-spaced critique of my dissertation outline was in my hands in less time than it takes for most undergraduates to receive their corrected midterm examinations. In the summer of 1954 before teaching for three weeks in Calabria, Donald toured Italy and joined what appeared to be one and a half million Americans in Rome. That captivating city convinced him, he wrote, that what was wrong with America could be explained by our having been colonized by the En-glish rather than the Italians.

The 1954–55 school year progressed routinely for veterans in the continuing seminar. We sympathized with the recruits going through boot camp, researched our dissertations, and imposed on Donald's time. In 1955 he spent a busy summer in Rochester and at the Henry E. Huntington Library in California. In September when he introduced Aïda DiPace to us as his fiancée, we were stunned. We were happy for Donald—Aïda, a Ph.D. candidate at Rochester, was intelligent and accomplished, vivacious and attractive—but we realized that though we had seemed like his family, we would soon be replaced. After the wedding on October 31, 1955, Donald surprised us by continuing to be generous with his time, and Aïda, who was writing her own dissertation, empathized with us completely. Things were not the same, but they had not changed drastically either, and some of the changes were for the better. Marriage and the birth of Bruce Randall, three years later, made Donald more flexible and tolerant of missed deadlines, though no less exacting in the quality of work demanded.

Donald divided his attention among his students in proportion to the amount they wrote on their dissertations. Chapters presented to the continuing seminar evoked not only the opinions of seminar members but also Donald's detailed critiques. While shepherding his growing flock Donald found time to publish nine provocative essays as *Lincoln Reconsidered: Essays on the Civil War Era* (New York, 1956) and proved that the Lincoln theme had not been exhausted. He also found time to be enormously helpful in finding jobs for his students. In a tight job market, he explored every lead and exploited every contact. His letters of recommendation were carefully crafted and shaded to have the strongest impact. Donald emphasized the candidate's strengths that would appeal to the institution he was writing to, whether it was an urban university, a Bible Belt college, a state university, or an Ivy League school. Rumor has it that his Ph.D. candidates have been hired in preference to applicants with the Ph.D. in hand. In the days when many got jobs through the "old boy" network, Donald's help was indispensable in securing a position, but his aid is scarcely less important in the more open market prevailing today. His training has lost none of its rigor, and his letters of recommendation have retained their individuality and force.

For Donald students, finishing a dissertation while teaching at a remote point was not as disadvantageous as it might have been. Donald's prompt correspondence annihilated distance. Despite his press of work, his comments remained extensive. Although the quality of our chapters varied with how hastily we had written them, the value of his critiques was constant. He was generally pleased with our work, but when disappointed he recognized the pressure we were under and usually was gentle in his criticisms. Aïda and marriage, as well as academic experience, may have mellowed him, but it is more likely that Donald realized he had pushed us as far as he could. We revised our dissertations on the basis of his chapter-by-chapter criticisms, and Donald read the entire manuscript and suggested further revisions. When the time came for us to defend our dissertations, he arranged the strongest possible committees, not only for the criticism his distinguished colleagues could give, but for the weight of their recommendations in the future.

After we secured our doctorates, Donald helped us get on the programs of historical conventions, eased the way to publishing our dissertations and articles based on them, and helped get us jobs at research-oriented institutions. Whenever he sensed a letter would help, he got one off immediately. And the advice he continued to give was always wise and needed, often witty and irreverent, and usually welcome. He impressed upon us that papers at a convention should make only three or four points, should not assume too much knowledge on the part of the audience, should be shorter than the time allotted, and should be carefully rehearsed, since their delivery had as strong an impact as their content. When writing book reviews, he said, we should remember that even a bad book represented an enormous amount of work and, perhaps fearful of the critical monsters he had created, warned us to be kind. When we carved our dissertations into articles for scholarly journals, Donald again read the familiar material and gave us his typical, thorough, and occasionally devastating critiques. When publishers rejected our dissertations, he buoyed up our sagging spirits and usually suggested the strategy that resulted in publication. We all have a thick file of Donald correspondence, alerting us to a job here or telling us he had written there in our behalf. After we found jobs, he advised us to avoid departmental politicking, to remain in ignorance, if possible, about divisions among our colleagues over our future, and, even if we knew who our critics were, to proceed on the assumption that everyone in our department wanted us as permanent colleagues.

Advancing our careers with his criticism, advice, hand holding, job brokering, and faith, Donald was our psychologist, agent, judge, and seer. While he played all these roles in our lives his own career soared. The 1957–58 academic year at the Institute for Advanced Study, despite student demands on his time (he journeyed from Princeton to New York twice monthly to hold office hours at Columbia), enabled him to forge ahead with the Sumner biography. He had planned to spend the following year at the Center for Advanced Study in the Behavioral Sciences at Palo Alto. His plans changed when he was appointed Harmsworth Professor of American History at Queen's College, Oxford, for the 1959–60 academic year. Donald returned to Columbia in the fall of 1958 for what proved to be his last year. We were sad when he left Columbia for Princeton, for to us he was Columbia. We gave him a farewell dinner and a handsome barometer. Never to be outdone in generosity, he gave each of us a copy of *The Enduring Lincoln* (Urbana, 1959), edited by Norman A. Graebner and containing Donald's essay "Abraham Lincoln: Whig in the White House." The barometer was an ideal gift. Its intricacy and fine workmanship appealed to Donald, a complex man ever striving to perfect his own great talents. He confessed he could stare at the instrument for hours, but evidently he did not. Three months after our dinner and after years of prodigious labor, he finished the manuscript on Sumner and the Civil War. Returning to New York for a week of frantic packing, he and Aïda and Bruce sailed on September 9, 1959, on the *Queen Elizabeth*.

The year at Oxford was a pleasant reward for years of hard work. Donald's students there were bright and interested, the meals at the high table were excellent, and the whole experience seemed to come out of a C. P. Snow novel. Donald remained as available to his Columbia students as ever, not only reading their manuscripts and offering them advice, but doing it cheerfully. After all, his main task at Oxford was giving twenty-eight lectures on slavery and secession. Returning to New York in mid-August, Donald and his family then packed and moved to Princeton.

Donald remained there for only two years. The contrast between Columbia, with its throng of graduate students and postdoctoral people vying for attention, and Princeton, where there were hardly enough students for the faculty to cluck over, was sharp and not entirely pleasing. Yet there were compensations. He enjoyed teaching undergraduates, and they idolized him. At the end of each lecture they applauded—until Donald, embarrassed by the accolades, requested they stop. Seniors wrote exceptionally fine and original theses under Donald's direction. Donald had scarcely arrived at Princeton before publication of *Charles Sumner and the Coming of the Civil War* (New York, 1960) brought him critical acclaim and won for him the 1961 Pulitzer Prize for biography. Having associated closely with Donald, we students especially appreciated his meticulous research, his careful weighing of evidence, and his brilliant style, which combined the logic and organization of a mathematician with the capacity of an artist to depict scenes and evoke emotions, not with complex numbers, formulas, or colors, but with simple words. Having been present at the creation, we knew Donald's *Sumner* was a model biography, and, with the sense of camaraderie Donald had developed in us, we rejoiced in the Pulitzer Prize as though we had won it ourselves. In addition, Donald published *Why the North Won the Civil War* (Baton Rouge, 1960), which he edited and to which he contributed the essay entitled "Died of Democracy," his epitaph for the Confederacy. This slender and valuable volume—other contributors are Richard N. Current, T. Harry Williams, Norman A. Graebner, and David M. Potter—grew out of a 1958 conference organized by Donald at Gettysburg College. The book remains the point of departure for any intelligent discussion of the Civil War's outcome.

While at Oxford, Donald also rewrote James G. Randall's classic text *The Civil War and Reconstruction* (Boston, 1961) so completely that he appears as co-author on its title page. Donald preserved intact Randall's treatment of some subjects, such as constitutional problems, where Randall's research remained unchallenged. He thoroughly overhauled other sections and in the process annoyed some historians who were accustomed to Randall's sympathetic portrayal of the Old South, his conviction that the Civil War was a repressible conflict that should have been avoided, his admiration for General George B. McClellan, and his dim view of Radical Reconstruction. By incorporating a generation of scholarship into Randall's text and by bringing out a revised and enlarged edition in 1969, Donald assured the book's preeminence for another generation.

In 1962, Donald went to Johns Hopkins. There he developed a new corps of graduate students, and though they were a decade younger and more numerous than his Columbia crew, they acquired the same hallmarks and scars from his intensive training. There were differences, but they were neither many nor great. He remained unusually committed to and interested in his students, advising and encouraging them. Although to his Columbia students he was big brother or D.D., the one they ran to when they needed help, at Hopkins he was "the master" or daddy. In general, Hopkins students came to him better prepared and needed less of his time. Perhaps the greatest difference was that Hopkins students were financially supported by the university, and it was reasonable to expect them to complete the doctorate in approximately four years; Columbia students had to take odd jobs to keep food on the table.

Donald was pleased with the number and caliber of his Hopkins students and gratified by the progress and activities of his Columbia people. The publication of dissertations, into which he had poured so much effort (Unger spoke for all Donald students when he said, "He has read my manuscript in drafts so numerous as to interfere, I am certain, with his own important work"), made him enormously proud, but none more than Irwin Unger's *The Greenback Era* (Princeton, 1964), which won the 1965 Pulitzer Prize for history. Another pleasing event for Donald was participating in the 1961 symposium on major Civil War controversies, organized at Northwestern by Grady McWhiney. Although he had the flu, Donald, as usual, was a terror in debate. His "Devils Facing Zionwards" appeared in the collection of symposium papers, *Grant, Lee, Lincoln and the Radicals: Essays on Civil War Leadership* (Evanston, 1964), which McWhiney edited. Donald's essay controverted the then classic view, best expressed by T. Harry Williams, that Radical Republicans gave Lincoln his most serious opposition. The influence of Donald's ideas is illustrated in Williams' careful and gracious restatement of his position written for that collection.

Through the 1960s, Donald worked on the second volume of *Sumner* but took time out for other important projects. Aïda Donald and he were the editors of *The Diary of Charles Francis Adams* (2 vols.; Cambridge, Mass., 1964), which dealt with the years from 1820 to 1829 when Adams transformed himself from a carefree boy to a strong-willed man. A Guggenheim Fellowship during the 1964–65 academic year freed Donald from teaching obligations at Johns

Hopkins and enabled him to prepare three essays, delivered as the Walter Lynwood Fleming Lectures in Southern History at Louisiana State University in the spring of 1965 and later published as *The Politics of Reconstruction, 1863–1867* (Baton Rouge, 1965). An artist in his imaginative use of impressionistic evidence, Donald has nevertheless been interested in the methodologies shaped by the behavioral scientists to evaluate hard data. At the University of Illinois, the great sociologist Florian Znaniecki had almost as much influence on him as Randall had. Donald based his earlier essay "Toward a Reconsideration of Abolitionists" on a statistical "recruitment" analysis of approximately one hundred abolitionists, and for his Fleming Lectures he devised a more elaborate analysis of clear-cut data. By tabulating sixteen roll calls on Reconstruction measures, Donald determined the membership of Republican factions. For example, he found that from 1866 to 1867, there were three Radical groups (ultra, Stevens, and independents) in addition to moderates, conservatives, and those who voted so rarely and so inconsistently as to defy categorization. Comparing the degree of radicalism of those Republicans with their margin of victory in elections from 1862 to 1866, Donald discovered that the more comfortable majority a Republican enjoyed, the more radical he was apt to be, and that representing a doubtful district or aspiring to a higher office with a wider (and presumably more diverse) constituency had a moderating effect. Donald capped the 1960s with his election as president of the Southern Historical Association (1969), the publication of *The Nation in Crisis, 1861–1877* (New York, 1969), a by-product of his revision of Randall and Donald, *The Civil War and Reconstruction*, and a year at the Center for Advanced Study in the Behavioral Sciences, where he finished his Sumner biography.

Charles Sumner and the Rights of Man (New York, 1970) achieved Donald's objective "of rediscovering the past." With this work, Donald evoked the Civil War and Reconstruction even more vividly than he had re-created the antebellum period in his first *Sumner* volume. Capturing the drama of the war, the high stakes and high principles involved in it and its aftermath, Donald also conveys Sumner's intense conviction that all people were created equal and that the Civil War was a struggle for freedom everywhere. As readers, we share not only Sumner's thoughts about human rights but, to a remarkable degree, his emotions and feelings. We are elated with

Sumner when the Emancipation Proclamation is announced, weep with Sumner while he holds Lincoln's hand through the night the president lay dying, are humiliated with Sumner as his wife flirts with a young Prussian diplomat, are hurt with Sumner as his influence in the Senate wanes, are pierced with Sumner by the painful symptoms of angina pectoris, and are consumed with Sumner in his desire that his civil rights bill not fail. *Sumner* is more than a book; it is an experience.

After eleven years at Hopkins, Donald moved to Harvard in 1973 as Charles Warren Professor of American History. The following year, reflecting his own broadening interests, Donald assumed the direction of Harvard's American Civilization program. Honors continued to come his way. Before he left Hopkins he had been the American Psychiatric Association's Benjamin Rush Lecturer in 1972, and after arriving at Harvard he was in 1975 Commonwealth Lecturer at University College of London University. Energetically raising a generation of Harvard Ph.D.'s, Donald at the same time continued to publish. He edited *Gone for a Soldier: The Civil War Memoirs of Alfred Bellard* (Boston, 1975) and he joined five other distinguished American historians to write *The Great Republic: A History of the American People* (2 vols.; Lexington, Mass., 1977). Donald's section, "Uniting the Republic, 1860–1890," formed the basis for his next publication, *Liberty and Union* (Boston, 1978). Although his interesting, concise, clear contribution to that collaboration was an example of textbook writing at its best, his students were most intrigued by his use of his middle name. He had never before used Herbert and, after the publication of his Mississippi scalawag article in 1944, had dropped the initial *H*. The elaborate theories his students fashioned illustrate their continuing fascination with their mentor. When confronted, Donald laughed and claimed the explanation was not complicated. He had become incorporated and for legal purposes (to avoid confusion with other David Donalds) had added his middle name. Since he had to sign his full name frequently, he decided life would be simpler if he signed everything David Herbert Donald.

In recent years, in keeping with his involvement in the American Civilization program, Donald has been researching and writing a biography of Thomas Wolfe. He will, we all know, write a book as interesting and as evocative as his *Sumner*. Despite our pride in the bulging David Herbert Donald shelf in our libraries, we did not write this book to celebrate the scholar. His devotion to teaching and his concern for students bind us to him. He did not excuse our failures or make light of our shortcomings but drove us to do our utmost. These essays in his honor express our gratitude.

The Election of 1840, Voter Mobilization, and the Emergence of the Second American Party System
A Reappraisal of Jacksonian Voting Behavior

Michael F. Holt

In 1840 the Whig party won the presidency for the first time in a campaign famous for log cabins and hard cider, a memorable slogan, "Tippecanoe and Tyler, Too," and delightful ditties such as "Van, Van, Van—Van's a Used Up Man." Historians have long mined that colorful election for sprightly lecture material, but the research of Richard P. McCormick has demonstrated that it had substantive significance as well. Voter turnout reached unprecedented heights, jumping from 57.8 percent in 1836 to 80.2 percent in 1840, and the figure was even higher than that in fifteen of twenty-five states. In absolute numbers the total vote increased from 1,505,290 to 2,408,630, or 60 percent. New voters thus cast 37.5 percent of the ballots in the 1840 presidential election, a share never again equaled in American history.[1]

More important, that election was the culmination of the long process during which the second American party system emerged between 1824 and 1840. Since the publication in 1966 of McCormick's pathbreaking account of that process, a number of historians have confirmed even while revising his seminal insight that the Jacksonian party system of Whigs and Democrats did not fully stabilize until 1840, four years after Andrew Jackson left the White House. Recently, excellent studies by Harry L. Watson, William G. Shade, and Ronald P. Formisano, among others, have explicitly argued that the years between the presidential elections of 1836 and 1840 marked a crucial transitional stage in that party system, a shift from what might be called a fluctuating or realigning phase from 1824 to 1836, when voter allegiances had not yet crystalized, to a stable phase from 1840

---

1. Richard P. McCormick, "New Perspectives on Jacksonian Politics," *American Historical Review*, LXV (1960), 288–301. I have used the figures on turnout gathered by Walter Dean Burnham in U.S. Bureau of Census, *Historical Statistics of the United States, Colonial Times to 1970* (2 vols.; 1975), II, 1072.

to 1852, when voter loyalty to the rival organizations was fixed and fierce.[2]

The transition between 1836 and 1840 that ended in the election of the first Whig president involved far more than the hardening of voters' partisan identities and the mobilization of new voters. It was also marked by the elaboration of party machinery and by the emergence of impressively high levels of internal party cohesion and inter-party disagreement or conflict on roll-call votes in both Congress and the state legislatures. For the first time, moreover, the parties articulated coherent and contrasting platforms regarding proper governmental policy at the state and national levels. Both the formulation of platforms and the emergence of party-oriented voting in legislative bodies, in turn, primarily reflected the parties' divergent responses to the panic of 1837 and the subsequent depression that gripped the country for most of the period between 1837 and 1844.[3]

Here those responses can be summarized only briefly. The incumbent Democrats denied culpability for the depression and blamed it instead on bankers, paper money, and excessive credit. Explicitly rejecting any governmental responsibility to provide economic aid to those suffering hardship, they condemned governmental intervention in society as inimical to a moral economic order, equal rights, and personal freedom. Their negative state doctrines were perfectly encapsulated in the Independent Treasury plan of Martin Van Buren that occupied Congress from September, 1837, until July, 1840, when it finally became law in the midst of the presidential campaign. In contrast, the Whigs blasted the Democrats both for causing

2. Richard P. McCormick, *The Second American Party System: Party Formation in the Jacksonian Era* (Chapel Hill, 1966); Harry L. Watson, *Jacksonian Politics and Community Conflict: The Emergence of the Second American Party System in Cumberland County, North Carolina* (Baton Rouge, 1981); William G. Shade, "Political Pluralism and Party Development: The Creation of a Modern Party System, 1815–1852," in Paul Kleppner (ed.), *The Evolution of American Electoral Systems* (Westport, Conn., 1982), 77–111; Ronald P. Formisano, *The Transformation of Political Culture: Massachusetts Parties, 1790s–1840s* (New York, 1983).

3. The literature on these developments is extensive, and I shall not attempt to cite it all here. For a succinct summary, see Shade, "Political Pluralism and Party Development, in Kleppner (ed.), *The Evolution of American Electoral Systems*; see also Michael F. Holt, *The Political Crisis of the 1850s* (New York, 1978), 17–38.

the depression and for refusing actively to end it, and they demanded positive governmental action to spur economic recovery and promote growth. Thus at the state and national levels, sharp interparty legislative battles developed over specific economic policies concerning banking and currency, corporate rights, tariffs, distribution of land revenues to the states, and subsidies for internal improvements. Debates over state and national economic policies, moreover, dominated state and congressional election campaigns from 1837 until 1844. Rarely if ever in American history have political parties provided to the electorate such clear and contrasting alternatives on both concrete policies and general orientations toward the economic role of government.[4]

The concurrence of these developments is significant. In terms of an intensification of voter interest, a widening of issue differences between rival parties, and an increase in ideological polarization, the years between 1836 and 1840 shared most of the characteristics historians and political scientists ascribe to periods of critical voter realignment, such as the 1850s, the 1890s, and the 1930s.[5] Just as severe economic crises sparked the latter two realignments, so apparently did depression and the contrasting party responses to it in the 1830s produce a swing of previous voters and a surge of new voters against the incumbent Democrats, thus accounting for the Whig victory of 1840. Yet few, if any, historians analyze those years in terms of voter

4.   On economic issues in state campaigns after 1837, see James Roger Sharp, *The Jacksonians Versus the Banks: Politics in the States After the Panic of 1837* (New York, 1967); William G. Shade, *Banks or No Banks: The Money Issue in Western Politics, 1832–1865* (Detroit, 1972), 1–111; Herbert Ershkowitz and William G. Shade, "Consensus or Conflict? Political Behavior in the State Legislatures During the Jacksonian Era," *Journal of American History*, LVIII (1971), 591–622; and William J. Cooper, Jr., *The South and the Politics of Slavery, 1828–1856* (Baton Rouge, 1978), 102, 155–66.
5.   Shade makes this same point in "Political Pluralism and Party Development," in Kleppner (ed.), *The Evolution of American Electoral Systems*, 104. On realignment theory, see Walter Dean Burnham, *Critical Elections and the Mainstream of American Politics* (New York, 1970); James L. Sundquist, *Dynamics of the Party System: Alignment and Realignment of Political Parties in the United States* (Washington, D.C., 1973); Jerome M. Clubb, William H. Flanigan, and Nancy H. Zingale, *Partisan Realignment: Voters, Parties, and Government in American History* (Beverly Hills, 1980); and Paul Kleppner, "Critical Realignments and Electoral Systems," in Kleppner (ed.), *The Evolution of American Electoral Systems*, 3–32.

realignment. More surprising, most historians make no connection between the emergence of sharp partisan conflict over economic issues after 1836 and the stabilization of voter loyalties to the respective parties, the mobilization of 900,000 new voters, or the Whig victory of 1840. The central purpose of this essay, therefore, is to argue that previous interpretations of the election of 1840, the emergence of the second party system, and Jacksonian voting behavior have seriously erred in minimizing the role of economic issues and economic conditions. My contention is that they were the most important forces shaping American political development between 1836 and 1844.[6]

Even Shade and Formisano, who argue so perceptively that the second party system reached full flower only between 1836 and 1840, are unwilling to admit that economic issues explain *why* it matured at that time. Formisano, for example, notes that in the first half of the 1830s, Massachusetts was shaken by populistic protest movements that worked outside of and against the major parties. After 1836, however, the energies of those protestors as well as of additional voters were channeled "into two mass parties, whose almost ritualized electoral warfare replaced the creative chaos of the early 1830s." He offers no explicit explanation of how the once repudiated major parties managed to incorporate this support, although he argues that the means of communication upon which mass organization depended had improved and that the parties adopted a crusading style of campaigning that tapped "hopes and fears of public salvation." He admits that the depression after 1837 helped Whigs to mobilize voters,

---

6. Watson, *Jacksonian Politics and Community Conflict*, 245–81, is a decided exception to this generalization, for he not only stresses the centrality of the panic and the economic issues it generated to voting patterns between 1836 and 1840 and to the election of 1840 itself, he sees divergent responses to the evolution of the economy as the key to party formation in the entire period from 1824 to 1840. A more recent study also stresses the centrality of economic issues to political developments after 1837. See Marc W. Kruman, *Parties and Politics in North Carolina, 1836–1865* (Baton Rouge, 1983), 3–28, 55–63. In a sense, therefore, this essay contends that their interpretation of events in North Carolina is applicable to the entire United States. William R. Brock, *Parties and Political Conscience: American Dilemmas, 1840–1850* (Millbrook, N.Y., 1979), 3–70, also recognizes that issue conflict caused the voter mobilization between 1836 and 1840.

but the partisan polarization over economic issues is largely periph-
eral to his analysis. In short, he seems more impressed by the style
than the objectives of the partisan crusades in those years.[7]

Shade is more candid about his uncertainty. "At present," he asserts, "it is nearly impossible for the historian to explain with any
precision why Phase II—the 'normal' or stable phase of the second
party system—appeared when it did." He too admits that the decisive
transition coincided with the panic of 1837, but because he believes
that attempts to establish economic sources of voting behavior have
been fruitless for the South and refuted for the North, he deems the
depression only a background condition, not a cause of party development. In the end, he also cites improvements in communications
as the major reason the party system crystalized in the late 1830s.[8]

Like much of the stimulating recent work on the emergence of
the second party system, almost all previous interpretations of the
presidential election of 1840 ignore or emphatically deny the role of
economic issues in that contest. Most, indeed, argue that "issues [of
any kind] counted for little in the 1840 campaign." Even historians
like Daniel W. Howe and William J. Cooper, Jr., who correctly stress
the importance of the executive tyranny and slavery issues in the
presidential race that year, give short shrift to economic issues, and
Cooper baldly asserts that they had no impact in the South.[9]

Other historians attribute the Whigs' victory in 1840 to the legendary "Log Cabin–Hard Cider" campaign they ran on behalf of General William Henry Harrison, a military hero of great renown and
minimal identification with Whig policies. According to this view,
pragmatic Whig politicos, intent on winning at any cost, engineered
the nomination of the aged Indian fighter rather than their most
prominent congressional leader Henry Clay because they believed

7. Formisano, *The Transformation of Political Culture*, 173–320 (quotations on
245).
8. Shade, "Political Pluralism and Party Development," in Kleppner (ed.), *The Evolution of American Electoral Systems*, 102–105.
9. Paul Murray, *The Whig Party in Georgia, 1825–1853* (Chapel Hill, 1948), 94;
Daniel Walker Howe, *The Political Culture of the American Whigs* (Chicago, 1979),
7–8, 90–92; Cooper, *The South and the Politics of Slavery*, 121–48, esp. 132–33. It
should be pointed out that Cooper argues that economic issues were important in state
and local races between 1837 and 1844, but he specifically denies their significance in
the presidential campaign of 1840.

they could not win on their issues. Refusing to write a national platform and carefully avoiding any mention of issues during the campaign, they instead lubricated voters with generous amounts of strong
drink, stirred them with ingenious slogans, songs, and symbols, and
roused them to a frenzy through the brilliant imitation of Jacksonian
techniques such as parades, mass rallies, and log cabin–raisings.
Excited, dazzled, and befuddled, voters poured out in record numbers to carry Harrison into office. Thus both the unprecedented turnout and the Whig triumph are explained by Whig hoopla.[10]

This analysis possesses a certain logic. After all, if the Whigs
thought they could win by advocating their economic policies, why
did they nominate Harrison rather than Clay? It also comports with
the facts—or at least some of them. Before the Whig nominating convention, many strategists did believe the party could win only by
shunning a platform and nominating a military hero whose fame
might rally the electorate. As one proponent of General Winfield Scott
argued, "Scott's name will bring out the hurra boys. The Whig party
were broken down by the popularity and non-committal character of
old Jackson, and it is but fair to turn upon and prostrate our opponents, with the weapons . . . with which they beat us. . . . The General's lips must be hermetically sealed, and our shouts and hurras
long and loud." After Harrison's nomination the Whigs appeared to
follow this scenario to the letter. They employed flummery and mum-
mery with astonishing effectiveness, and one of their notorious campaign songs openly advised:

> Mum is the word boys,
> Brag is the game;
> Cooney is the emblem
> of Old Tip's fame.[11]

10. For examples, see Robert G. Gunderson, *The Log-Cabin Campaign* (Lexington,
Ky., 1957), 28, 73–74, 96, 115; Walter Dean Burnham, *Presidential Ballots, 1836–
1892* (Baltimore, 1955), 21–22; and Arthur M. Schlesinger, Jr., *The Age of Jackson*
(Boston, 1945), 283–305. Schlesinger asserts that the 1840 election forced the Whigs
"to a concrete choice. Should the campaign be fought once more with the issues and
leaders with which the Whigs had repeatedly gone down to defeat? Or should the past
be forgotten, and the party enter the canvass unencumbered by its former issues and
leaders?" (289).
11. M. Bradley to Thurlow Weed, August 29, 1839, quoted in Gunderson, *The Log-
Cabin Campaign*, 52; for the ditty, see *ibid.*, 115.

Yet there are defects in the logic of this interpretation and obvious facts that it ignores. It assumes that the reasons why Harrison was nominated are identical with the reasons why he won. It does not explain how the carnivallike Whig campaign could have caused the substantial increase in the Democratic vote between 1836 and 1840. It takes the absence of a national platform as evidence of an absence of issues and does not consider other forums in which Whigs articulated differences from the Democrats. Similarly, it drastically minimizes the impact Democratic actions and rhetoric had on defining the choices before the electorate. Proponents of this view, moreover, generally ignore the considerable evidence from Whig sources during and especially after the campaign that Whigs believed they won because of economic issues. Even the supposedly obtuse Harrison noted in the spring of 1840 that "we have many recruits in our ranks from the pressure of the times." Four years later an Indiana editor who anticipated a rematch against Van Buren declared that "the Harrison boys of Hoosierdom will prove in a way that they consider pretty conclusive to Mr. Van Buren that they were neither 'drunk' nor 'mad' in 1840. . . . They will show him that they cast him out because they were opposed to his Sub Treasury—his profligate expenditures—his disregard of the petitions of the people." [12]

Much more important, those who explain the results of 1840 solely in terms of the theatrical Whig campaign for Harrison, or even Van Buren's personal unpopularity, ignore the performance of the Whigs in congressional, gubernatorial, and state legislative races, how that performance varied over time, and how it related to changing economic conditions. Once one adopts a broader and longer perspective, the crucial role of economic conditions and economic issues in causing both voter mobilization and the outcome of the 1840 election becomes palpable.

Proponents of the McCormick thesis do adopt such a perspective, but they are equally emphatic in their rejection of economic causation. According to McCormick, the system was formed "in the successive contests for the presidency between 1824 and 1840. It did not emerge from cleavages within Congress, nor from any polariza-

12. William Henry Harrison to Nathaniel P. Tallmadge, February 22, 1840, quoted *ibid.*, 12; report of Schuyler Colfax in New York *Tribune*, April 8, 1844.

tion of attitudes on specific public issues." Equally important, "the rate at which voters participated was directly related to the closeness of interparty competition rather than to the presumed charismatic effect of candidates or the urgency of particular issues." Specifically, McCormick and others argue that voter turnout jumped in 1840 because highly competitive party organizations that were "for the first time . . . truly national in scope . . . exerted every effort to arouse popular excitement. . . . The result of this competitive situation was an unprecedented outpouring of the electorate."[13]

Party organization did become more extensive after 1836, and it is plausible to contend that the turnout of previous party identifiers was a function of the closeness of party competition—that is, they were more likely to vote if they thought their party needed every vote to win. It is less plausible, however, to maintain that former non-voters could be automatically mobilized simply because parties now competed for their votes. If so, the drop-off in turnout rates after 1840 is inexplicable. Nor does this rather mechanistic behavioral model adequately explain why the Whigs rather than the Democrats captured three-fifths of the 900,000 new voters mobilized between 1836 and 1840. Was it a case, as McCormick asserts, of "the Whigs leading the way in inventiveness and enthusiasm"? It was, after all, the lop-sided surge of new voters to the Whigs, not the close balance between the parties, that produced the Whig victory in 1840. In the states with the largest increase in turnout, moreover, competitive balance was a product not a cause of that voter surge. Since it focuses only on presidential elections, finally, this interpretation, like the traditional accounts of the log cabin campaign, neglects the crucial role of events and elections *between* November, 1836, and November, 1840, in producing the unprecedented voter turnout, forging lasting voter allegiances, and building the coalition that brought the Whigs victory in 1840.[14]

13. McCormick, *The Second American Party System*, 13, 16, 341–42, and "New Perspectives on Jacksonian Politics," 299–301; William N. Chambers and Philip C. Davis, "Party, Competition, and Mass Participation: The Case of the Democratizing Party System, 1824–1852," in Joel H. Silbey, Allan G. Bogue, and William H. Flanigan (eds.), *The History of American Electoral Behavior* (Princeton, 1978), 174–97.
14. McCormick, *The Second American Party System*, 341. For evidence that close party balance was a result rather than a cause of voter turnout, see Table 5.1 in Cham-

Even more surprising, most analysts of Jacksonian voting behavior also underestimate how much the economic crisis of the late 1830s and the contrasting party responses to it determined who voted for whom. This error is especially true of the so-called ethnocultural interpretation of voting, which was first applied to New York in Lee Benson's *Concept of Jacksonian Democracy* and has since been extended to Michigan by Formisano, to Illinois and Pennsylvania by Shade, and to Ohio by Stephen C. Fox. Indeed, I think it accurate to say that for the last twenty years this has been the dominant interpretation of northern voting throughout the nineteenth century. According to this model, ethnic and religious differences were more important determinants of voter cleavages than were the economic characteristics of voters or economic issues.[15]

Virtually all proponents of this interpretation admit that people sometimes have economic reasons for voting. Yet they tend to posit a narrow or rigorous set of conditions that in effect equates economic motivations with class or interest group motivations. They insist that only if one can prove that specific occupational groups or economic interests voted for a particular party because of a specific plank in its platform can a historian speak of economic issues motivating voters. As Formisano says, "Let it be granted that economic policy divided the parties. It must then be shown that parties conveyed these contrasts to voters, that campaigning and communications efficiently disseminated information on formal issues, and that voters saw and acted as members of economic groups. At least all these inferences are necessary if voting is to be seen as motivated by economic interest." Or, as Formisano's mentor Benson argues, "His-

---

bers and Davis, "Party, Competition, and Mass Participation," in Silbey, Bogue, and Flanigan (eds.), *The History of American Electoral Behavior*, 176–77, and note especially the figures for New Hampshire, Maine, Illinois, Michigan, Arkansas, and Tennessee.

15.   Lee Benson, *The Concept of Jacksonian Democracy: New York as a Test Case* (Princeton, 1961); Ronald P. Formisano, *The Birth of Mass Political Parties: Michigan, 1827–1861* (Princeton, 1971); Shade, *Banks or No Banks*, 18–19, 158–67, and "Pennsylvania Politics in the Jacksonian Period: A Case Study, Northampton County, 1824–1844," *Pennsylvania History*, XXXIX (1972), 313–33; Stephen C. Fox, "Politicians, Issues, and Voter Preference in Jacksonian Ohio: A Critique of an Interpretation," *Ohio History*, LXXXVI (1977), 155–70, and "The Bank Wars, the Idea of 'Party,' and the Division of the Electorate in Jacksonian Ohio," *Ohio History*, LXXXVIII (1979), 253–76.

torians must try . . . to specify the conditions under which different types of economic factors are most likely to exercise determining influence upon the voting behavior of specific classes or groups of men."[16]

Largely because of this narrow conceptualization of economic motivation and economic issues and also because they apparently could find no correlation between occupational and class variables and voting behavior, virtually all of the ethnoculturalists insist that economic factors had little or no influence on voting behavior in the 1830s and 1840s. Benson, for example, contends that New York's voting pattern solidified in 1832 and remained the same until 1853. Hence, "party differences over *socioeconomic* issues did not have sufficient impact to alter voting patterns already fixed in 1832; some localized, minor shifts and temporary fluctuations occurred, but the pattern remained essentially unchanged." Fox, who like Shade argues that banking issues often resonated with contrasting cultural values, still asserts that in Ohio, "the financial crisis of 1837 and the banking issues of the early 1840s caused no discernible change in voting habits." Formisano emphatically denies that voters had any issue orientation at all. Economic conflicts, he declares, did not bring Michigan's parties into being in the 1830s or cause different voters to align behind one party or the other in the hard times after 1837. Moreover, he apparently believes that economic issues were insignificant outside of Michigan as well, for elsewhere he maintains that "economic issues at times became quite salient in nineteenth-century politics, though far more in the 1890s than the 1830s."[17]

Let us grant that in the elections the ethnoculturalists have studied, they have demonstrated that there were no clear distinctions between the voting support of the two parties in terms of wealth or occupation. An absence of class polarization, however, is not proof that economic conditions and economic issues do not shape voting behavior. First, one cannot assume that the rich and the poor or bankers and workers react in opposite ways to economic issues. There could

16.   Ronald P. Formisano, "Toward a Reorientation of Jacksonian Politics: A Review of the Literature, 1959–1975," *Journal of American History*, LXIII (1976), 61; Benson, *The Concept of Jacksonian Democracy*, 156.

17.   Benson, *The Concept of Jacksonian Democracy*, 292; Fox, "Politicians, Issues, and Voter Preference in Jacksonian Ohio," 161; Formisano, *The Birth of Mass Political Parties*, 11–12, 31, 48, 55, and "Toward a Reorientation of Jacksonian Politics," 61–62.

be, during a depression, an across-the-board surge toward one party without any correlation between the party's vote and occupational groups or classes appearing. Second, studies of the twentieth-century electorate by political scientists have found that real income, particularly change in real income, is the most salient economic variable influencing voting. Yet this is not measured in any of the economic indexes devised by historians of the nineteenth century.[18] Instead they measure occupation or wealth as signified by the value of real or personal property. Most important, by focusing on individual or group voting behavior, historians have normally ignored fluctuations in party strength or success *over time*, which is what must be used to test the impact of economic variables. Put differently, the ethnoculturalists have little concern for the results of elections—for who won and who lost—and how the pattern of party victory fluctuated over time.

By using time-series analysis, political scientists have generated compelling evidence that economic conditions, as distinguished from individual economic status, do shape changes in voting behavior. More precisely, declining economic conditions depress the vote of the incumbent party and increase that of its rival. Improving economic conditions, on the other hand, have little discernible impact on the vote. Yet historians normally correlate variables from a particular census or tax year with voting returns from a single year or with average party strength over a series of elections. In short, they employ static rather than dynamic variables. If they consider economic change at all, it is usually change over a considerable period of time—the ten years between census returns or the four years between presidential elections. Modern research indicates, however, that only change within the year immediately preceding an election affects voting behavior. Thus in the way they construct both their independent and dependent variables, most historians have made it impossible to measure the impact of changing economic conditions.[19]

18.   Howard S. Bloom and H. Douglas Price, "Voter Response to Short-Run Economic Conditions: The Asymmetric Effect of Prosperity and Recession," *American Political Science Review*, LXIX (1975), 1240–54, esp. 1243.

19.   I have relied heavily on the article by Bloom and Price cited above, but in addition I have used Francisco Arcelus and Allan H. Metzer, "The Effect of Aggregate Economic Variables on Congressional Elections," Saul Goodman and Gerald H. Kramer, "Comments on Arcelus and Meltzer, The Effect of Aggregate Economic Conditions on Congressional Elections," and Arcelus and Meltzer, "Aggregate Economic Variables

To compound matters, the years that most historians have used to test the relative impact of economic versus ethnic and religious variables have been years in which economic conditions were improving rather than declining. They have focused on those times, that is, when modern research suggests economic factors would have had the least impact on voting behavior. To identify the parties' voting bases in New York between 1832 and 1853, for example, Benson studies 1844. Yet 1844 was not only a year of economic recovery but also one in which ethnic and religious tensions were unusually salient because of anti-Catholic riots in Philadelphia, the appearance of the American Republican party, and the presence on the Whig national ticket of Theodore Frelinghuysen, a man who personified evangelical Protestantism and who was consequently anathema to Catholics. Similarly, Formisano examines an average of the party vote for 1848 and 1852. Fox runs most of his tests on returns for 1848; Shade utilizes an Illinois referendum in 1851, when the gold rush and foreign investment were spurring an economic boom. We have, in fact, few close statistical studies of voting in the depression years from 1837 to 1843.[20]

The realignment model adopted by these historians also obfuscates the impact of economic issues on both old and new voters. Ac-

---

and Votes for Congress: A Rejoinder," *American Political Science Review*, LXIX (1975), 1232–69; John R. Hibbing and John R. Alford, "The Electoral Impact of Economic Conditions: Who Is Held Responsible?" *American Journal of Political Science*, XXV (1981), 423–39; and Stephen J. Rosenstone, "Economic Adversity and Voter Turnout," *American Journal of Political Science*, XXVI (1982), 25–46. It should come as no surprise that political scientists do not agree about these matters. I have found the Bloom and Price and the Hibbing and Alford articles the most persuasive.

20.   This point about the unusual intensity of ethnic tensions in 1844 is also made in Donald J. Ratcliffe, "Politics in Jacksonian Ohio: Reflections on the Ethnocultural Interpretation," *Ohio History*, LXXXVIII (1979), 5–35, esp. 10n16, which is a superb critique of the ethnocultural analysis. Both Ratcliffe in this article and Fox in "Politicians, Issues, and Voter Preference in Jacksonian Ohio" do run correlations between economic indexes and returns from 1840, but Fox found no relation between wealth and voting and Ratcliffe (29–31) found that Whigs were stronger in wealthier, more commercially oriented counties while Democrats were stronger in poorer, less commercially oriented counties. Even James Roger Sharp, who attempts to establish an economic division in the electorate in his *Jacksonians Versus the Banks*, distorts the impact of the depression, for he uses as his dependent variable an average of the Democratic vote in the presidential elections of 1836, 1840, and 1844. Economic conditions in the first and the last were far different from those in 1840.

cording to this framework, cleavages in the electorate form during the fluctuating stage of a voting cycle when voters polarize over certain issues. During the following stable phase, those alignments remain constant. Antagonisms engendered by the original polarizing issue persist even after it is resolved, and rival party loyalties themselves become sources of voting behavior. Issues count in the realigning stage, in short, but have minimal impact during stable phases. Instead voters habitually refight old battles. To bolster this interpretation, historians cite two kinds of evidence: high interyear correlations of a party's vote that suggest the same men voted for the same party for the same reasons year after year, and research based on survey data from the 1950s that indicates a low issue awareness among voters and the overwhelming importance of party identification in voting behavior.[21]

This notion of a "standing decision" among voters in most elections is beguiling but dubious. The realignment model ignores new voters who enter the electorate after the realigning stage. At most it assumes that they chose one party or another for the same reasons that motivated those whose allegiance crystalized in the realigning phase. If the years between 1836 and 1840 when the electorate expanded by 60 percent were considered as part of the realignment, this tendency would not be so harmful. But most historians insist that voting patterns froze prior to the panic of 1837 and the articulation of contrasting economic programs. Thus Benson argues that the alignments and motivations of New York's voters remained essentially the same from 1832 to 1853, although the vote increased from 305,649 to 441,692, or 44.5 percent, between 1836 and 1840. Thus Formisano contends that Michigan's cleavage was fixed by battles over alien suffrage between 1835 and 1837, even though turnout jumped by 47 percent between 1837 and 1840.[22]

21.   See, for example, Formisano, "Toward a Reorientation of Jacksonian Politics," 61–62. One of the most frequently cited pieces by a political scientist is Philip E. Converse, "The Nature of Belief Systems in Mass Publics," in David Apter (ed.), *Ideology and Discontent* (Glencoe, Ill., 1964), 206–61.

22.   Benson has argued more accurately that New York's voting patterns stabilized in 1839 rather than 1832, though he does not credit either economic conditions or economic issues for causing that crystalization. See Lee Benson, Joel H. Silbey, and Phyllis F. Field, "Toward a Theory of Stability and Change in American Voting Patterns: New York State, 1792–1970," in Silbey, Bogue, and Flanigan (eds.), *The History of American Electoral Behavior*, 87–91. Formisano, *The Birth of Mass Political Parties*, 134.

High interyear correlations do not necessarily prove stability in voting patterns. Instead they mask the movements of the voters into and out of the participating electorate. Correlation and regression coefficients, like the party percentages on which they are based, conceal changes in the size of the vote and the fact that new voters may have been attracted to a party for reasons that differ from those of its previous supporters. In Ohio, for example, the Whig proportion of the vote increased only from 52.1 to 54.2 percent between 1836 and 1840 and the interyear correlation was $+.888$. In Pennsylvania the arithmetic increment in the Whig proportion of the vote was a microscopic 1.3 percent and the correlation between the 1836 and 1840 returns was approximately $+.95$.[23] Yet 70,000 more men in Ohio and 109,000 in Pennsylvania voted in 1840 than in 1836. How can one assume that habits acquired before 1836 account for the massive mobilization of votes in those two states, New York, and elsewhere or explain why most of those new voters, quite unlike the majority of voters in 1836, preferred the Whigs to the Democrats?

Recent research by political scientists on both aggregate and survey data, moreover, is quite at odds with earlier work based on data from the complacent 1950s. It indicates that voters do respond to issues, especially those who have no previous party identity or low levels of identification with a particular party. In short, new voters are precisely the ones most likely to respond to the issues extant when they cast their first ballot. At the least, people who do not yet identify with a party, those who today might be termed independents, are the most likely citizens to be mobilized to cast a vote against an incumbent party if they form a negative judgment of its performance.[24]

This research has received its most powerful and sophisticated formulation in Morris P. Fiorina's *Retrospective Voting in American National Elections*. Fiorina demonstrates that voter allegiance to a party depends upon evaluations of the party's record in office. "Citizens monitor party promises and performances over time, encapsulate their observations in a summary judgment termed 'party identification,' and rely on this core of previous experience when they assign responsibility for current societal conditions and evaluate ambiguous

23.   The Ohio correlation is given in Ratcliffe, "Politics in Jacksonian Ohio," 14, and that for Pennsylvania in Shade, "Political Pluralism and Party Development," in Kleppner (ed.), *The Evolution of American Electoral Systems*, 85.

24.   Bloom and Price, "Voter Response to Short-Run Economic Conditions," 1240–41.

platforms designed to deal with uncertain futures." More important, "retrospective evaluations" of what a party does in office can change the intensity of party loyalty. "Party ID waxes and wanes in accord with a citizen's evaluations of the recent performance of the party in power . . . with his/her perception of societal conditions, political events, and the performance of incumbent officeholders." A positive evaluation can reinforce identification with a party, but a negative evaluation will weaken it. Negative evaluations may not change the voting behavior of those whose loyalty to a party is strong, but for those with weak partisan identifications—and new voters of course have the weakest attachment of all—such evaluations are likely to cause a conversion to its opponent.[25]

Research by Samuel Kernell on voting in midterm congressional elections supplements Fiorina's findings. He has found that voters with a negative judgment of an incumbent president are far more likely to turn out in such congressional elections than are those who approve his performance, and they will cast their vote against candidates of the president's party. This differential, moreover, is especially true of independents. Members of the president's own party who disapprove of his record support that party's candidates less strongly than do those who approve of his record. Sometimes such disapprovers defect to the opposition but more often they simply abstain. Across all categories, however, disapproval of a party's record has far more impact than does approval in determining whether a potential voter goes to the polls and how he casts his vote once he is there.[26]

These findings, especially those concerning independents or weak party identifiers, are surely relevant to the late 1830s and early 1840s when a fundamental condition—the depression—affected evaluations of incumbent parties. Moreover, the large minority if not the majority of the electorate in 1840 probably had weak party identities. Three-eighths of those voters had not voted in 1836, and, as Shade's research shows, many of the others who entered the electorate prior to 1836 could have developed only a tenuous party identifi-

25. Morris P. Fiorina, *Retrospective Voting in American National Elections* (New Haven, 1981), 83, 96, 102.
26. Samuel Kernell, "Presidential Popularity and Negative Voting: An Alternative Explanation of the Midterm Congressional Decline of the President's Party," *American Political Science Review*, LXXI (1977), 44–66.

cation. That identification might easily have been swayed by the coherent and contrasting party records on economic policy that appeared only after 1836, records that had much greater salience then because economic conditions had changed. Not only were there shifts in party allegiance by previous voters between 1836 and 1840, but vast numbers of new voters were mobilized by both parties during those years. To understand why voters switched parties, why new voters were mobilized, and why most chose the Whigs so that the Whig party triumphed in 1840, therefore, one must look at the party performances and economic and social conditions that shaped voter judgments between 1836 and 1840.

The parties did in fact establish clear records that voters could judge after 1836. Thus the contention that there were no issues in the 1840 election is untenable. In 1837–38 and again in 1840 the rival parties took sharply contrasting stands on virtually every economic issue that came to a vote in Congress. Attention focused primarily on the Independent Treasury bill, which Democrats backed and Whigs opposed, and when Van Buren signed it into law on July 4, 1840, Democrats proudly called it a second Declaration of Independence. Since 1837, Whigs had denounced this measure as precisely the wrong kind of economic remedy. Withdrawing government monies from private banks, they predicted, would reduce bank-note circulation, strangle credit, and thereby drive prices down. That it was passed when prices were already plummeting could only have given these warnings greater resonance among the electorate. The rival parties in Congress and the Democratic president had thus given voters a clear record to evaluate on a concrete issue. The party lines were in fact more sharply drawn than on other issues that historians have traditionally seen as central to elections, such as, say, the Kansas-Nebraska Act of 1854.[27]

27. Schlesinger, *The Age of Jackson*, 261–65. For a particularly good example of a detailed Whig attack on the Independent Treasury bill, see the speech Abraham Lincoln delivered on December 26, 1839, in Springfield, Illinois, in Roy P. Basler (ed.), *The Collected Works of Abraham Lincoln* (9 vols.; New Brunswick, N.J., 1953), I, 159–79. For the partisan dimensions of voting patterns in Congress, see Thomas B. Alexander, *Sectional Stress and Party Strength: A Study of Roll-Call Voting Patterns in the United States House of Representatives, 1836–1840* (Nashville, 1967), 24–36, 137–52. When the House passed the Subtreasury bill in 1840, 97 percent of the Democrats supported the measure and 95 percent of the Whigs opposed it. In contrast in 1854, only 68 per-

Fascination with the folderol of the 1840 Whig campaign has similarly obscured the extent to which its intent was to draw a contrast between the parties, to remind voters of the Democrats' responsibility for the panic and their refusal to do anything to remedy it, and to convince them that only the Whig program of positive governmental action could restore prosperity. Even that notorious piece of demagoguery "The Regal Splendor of the Presidential Palace," a widely publicized speech in which a Pennsylvania Whig congressman denounced the luxury in which Van Buren supposedly lived, had a more serious purpose than arousing the resentment of the poor or proving that Van Buren was a pampered aristocrat compared to Harrison, the fabricated frontiersman with his coonskin cap. In addition it was meant to remind voters that the president who had announced the government could do nothing to help its suffering citizenry was living like a king off the largesse of that same government. So, too, Whig pamphlets such as *The Contrast: William Henry Harrison Versus Martin Van Buren, Harrison and Prosperity or Van Buren and Ruin,* and *The Crisis of the Country* underlined the differences between the results of a Democratic administration and what the results of a Whig administration might be. When Whig speakers announced that wheat would be a dollar a bushel under Harrison and forty cents a bushel under Van Buren, when in many places they promised to repeal the Independent Treasury Act, charter a new national bank, and raise the tariffs, voters learned what the alternatives were, just as they did when Democrats inveighed that the central issue of the election was "SHALL THE BANKS OR THE PEOPLE RULE?"[28]

Much more important than voting records in Congress and campaign rhetoric in framing the issues before the electorate in 1840 were the performances of the two parties at the state level after 1836. Modern political scientists focus almost exclusively on the impact of economic issues on national elections for congressmen and president, perhaps because they assume that only the actions of the national government today can affect economic conditions. In the nineteenth

---

cent of the Democrats supported the Kansas-Nebraska Act while 78 percent of the Whigs opposed it. Even in the North where all Whigs voted against the act, the Democrats were evenly divided for and against it.

28.   Gunderson, *The Log-Cabin Campaign,* 101–105, 149, 194, 211, 228–29; Howe, *The Political Culture of the American Whigs,* 7–8.

century, however, state governments intervened in the private economy much more frequently and actively than authorities in Washington did, and after 1836, most of the battles over banks, paper money, corporate rights, and governmental subsidies occurred in state legislatures rather than in Congress. Since Democrats controlled Congress and the White House between 1836 and 1840, moreover, the only place that Whigs could establish a record for voters to evaluate, other than opposition to Democratic measures, was in the states they controlled. The policies Whigs enacted when in power at the state level, that is, gave voters a clear record to contrast with Democratic actions in Washington and in the states. As a result, people knew what kinds of policies, if not exactly the precise legislation, they could expect should either party win the 1840 election. They hardly needed a national platform to tell where the parties stood as regards the issues. Reactions to state policies, in other words, were as important as, if not more important than, reactions to national issues or to the rhetoric and hoopla of the 1840 campaign in forging voters' allegiances that were reflected in the presidential balloting of 1840.

In most states between 1836 and 1840, indeed, voters were not only presented with sharp differences in the voting records and rhetoric of rival parties. They also gained experience with the actual policies of the two parties as control of state government seesawed back and forth. When the Democrats were in power, they tried to punish banks that had suspended specie payments by forcing them to resume, placing stringent restrictions on note issue, or banning paper money altogether. In addition, they often curtailed expenditures on internal improvements and blocked charters for new corporations. Conversely, when the Whigs came to power, they repealed the anti-banking legislation of Democrats, attempted to expand banking facilities and the supply of paper money and credit, and voted state subsidies for beleaguered internal improvement projects on the grounds that their completion would promote prosperity.

Constraints of space preclude the systematic state-by-state survey necessary to prove this contention, but illustrations from three states suggest the ways in which issue conflict defined choices for the electorate in 1840. In Kentucky, Democrats in 1839 and 1840 attacked the dominant Whig party for incompetence and extravagance in its management of slack-water navigation projects the state had begun in the early 1830s, and demanded an immediate cessation of expenditures on those projects. In reply the Whigs called for an increase in state taxes to pay for their completion and ran on that issue in the 1840 state election. In Massachusetts, where the Democrats had come to power for the first time in November, 1839, Democratic governor Marcus Morton attacked the previous Whig record in his message to the legislature in 1840 and outlined a sweeping plan to impose restrictions on banks, corporate rights, and state subsidies to railroads. Whig legislators vilified the governor's proposals as dangerous to the economic health of the commonwealth in a point-by-point rebuttal. In Pennsylvania the Democrats also gained firm control of the state legislature in 1839, and in 1840 they passed harsh antibanking measures while the Democratic governor was forced to ask for new taxes which Whigs had eliminated in 1836. At the end of the legislative session in March, 1840, the Whigs issued an address denouncing the tax proposal as evidence of Democratic incompetence and the antibanking measures as evidence of Democratic radicalism. The Democrats, Whigs charged, were "breathing nothing but destruction to the banking and credit systems of the Commonwealth." They were "men of no practical experience in the affairs of life—bearded enthusiasts, full of crude and chimerical notions of reform and with no better idea of a banking institution than such as might be picked up in the various but unmeaning vocabulary of a village newspaper." Whigs, they assured the electorate, would succor the banking system to promote prosperity. Apparently voters responded to that message, for the Whigs made substantial gains in the state legislative elections held in 1840 as they also did in Kentucky and Massachusetts.[29]

Throughout the nation, in fact, the Whigs enjoyed sweeping success in the issue-oriented state and congressional elections of 1840, whereas they had suffered defeats in the equally issue-oriented state and congressional contests of 1839. The reason for this reversal of for-

29.   The details of many of these state battles are given in the works listed in note 4. In addition, I have relied on Harry A. Volz III, "Party, State, and Nation: Kentucky and the Coming of the American Civil War" (Ph.D. dissertation, University of Virginia, 1982), 22–25; Arthur B. Darling, *Political Changes in Massachusetts, 1824–1848* (New Haven, 1925), 202–43; Charles McCool Snyder, *The Jacksonian Heritage: Pennsylvania Politics, 1833–1848* (Harrisburg, 1958), 112–50; and Henry R. Mueller, *The Whig Party in Pennsylvania* (New York, 1922), 43–66 (quotation on 63).

tune was not that in the latter year Whig candidates could cling to the coattails of Harrison, for whom the party was conducting such a frenzied campaign. Most state and congressional elections were not held on the same day as the presidential balloting but instead took place earlier in the year. The reason was simply that economic conditions had changed dramatically; 1839 was a year of relative prosperity, and 1840 was a year of deep depression. Voters' reactions to the contrasting party programs and records varied with changing economic conditions.

Throughout the period from 1836 to 1840, party fortunes fluctuated in relationship to oscillating economic conditions. After a period of soaring prosperity from the summer of 1834 to February, 1837, prices began to drop in March and April, and financial panic struck in May, 1837, when banks throughout the nation suspended specie payments. By the end of May, prices had plunged 22 percent from their boom-time high in February, and they remained low for over a year. Then, from about September, 1838, to October, 1839, a period of price and economic recovery set in. In October, 1839, however, prices began to plummet once again after a renewed round of bank suspensions, and they continued to drop throughout 1840, 1841, and 1842, with the next recovery beginning only at the end of 1843.[30]

Changes in wholesale prices come closer to approximating changes in real disposable income than do indexes measuring wealth. In the Jacksonian period the vast majority of Americans were producers who sold the goods they grew, mined, or made, and were not simply wage-earning consumers. Sudden price changes affected the difference between production costs and selling prices. When prices

30. Peter Temin, *The Jacksonian Economy* (New York, 1969), offers the best discussion of economic fluctuations in those years. For the data on monthly wholesale prices, see his Table 3.2 (p. 69). Temin argues that although there was a price deflation after 1837, there was no depression. In the minds of contemporaries, however, the economic hardship was very real. It is difficult to be precise about the date that recovery set in because price figures were for the nation as a whole, and there could have been regional or local variations. Whereas most of the nation's banks did not resume specie payments until August 13, 1838, for example, New York City's had done so in May of that year. I have used September as the start of the recovery not only because most banks did not resume until August but because of price trends. From a bottom of 98 in September, 1837, the wholesale price index reached 100 in May, 1838, 102 in July and August, 107 in September, and 113 in October.

rose, prosperity prevailed; when prices dropped, most people's income dropped.

Fortunately, moreover, price changes can be compared to political trends rather easily. Price data are available by the month. So are election returns since different states held state and congressional elections in different months. Therefore one can plot the relationship between political results and economic conditions over time, without employing the sophisticated multiple regression techniques used by political scientists in time-series analysis. The analysis I have made is not multivariate. I have examined only the relationship between changing price levels and changes in party votes and success in winning office. I recognize that local issues and local constituency characteristics obviously influence voting behavior. Certainly I believe that some voters in all elections are motivated primarily by ethnic and religious or other noneconomic influences. Yet I also assume that if there is a systematic relationship between economic factors and a party's vote across units of widely varying socioeconomic and ethnocultural composition, then economic factors do shape voting behavior and the results of elections. In other words, if slaveholding, staple-crop-producing southern states as well as New England, if the Middle Atlantic and midwestern states, all seemed to respond in the same way to changing economic conditions and issues, those conditions and issues must have had a crucial impact on political behavior.

Between 1836 and the summer of 1841 when the Whigs took control of the presidency and Congress, the parties' fortunes clearly fluctuated with economic conditions. When prices dropped, the Whig vote and the number of offices won by Whigs rose dramatically. When prices climbed, on the other hand, the Whig share of the vote dropped, the Democratic vote grew, and Whigs lost some but not all of the offices they had won during hard times. Table 1 lists the proportion of congressional and gubernatorial seats won by Whigs in different economic conditions from the start of 1836 to the end of 1844, and Table 2 presents the proportion of seats won by Whigs in the lower house of state legislatures from 1836 through 1843.[31] States

31. Virginia's congressional and legislative elections of May, 1837, are included in the boom period in both tables because they were held prior to the bank suspension that month. Even though prices began to drop before May, that is, the most dramatic slump came only after mid-May.

Table 1

Whig Proportion of Congressional and Gubernatorial Seats, 1836–1844

Date of Election and Economic Condition	Congressional Seats	Gubernatorial Seats
January–December, 1836 (boom)	40.4% (N = 151)	46.1% (N = 13)
January–May, 1837 (boom)	23.5% (N = 34)	0% (N = 3)
June–December, 1837 (panic)	67.2% (N = 61)	66.7% (N = 9)
January–August, 1838 (panic)	50% (N = 8)	66.7% (N = 6)
September–December, 1838 (recovery)	50% (N = 130)	42.8% (N = 7)
January–October, 1839 (recovery)	48.4% (N = 93)	14.2% (N = 7)
November–December, 1839 (depression)	0% (N = 2)	33.3% (N = 3)
January–December, 1840 (depression)	62.2% (N = 136)	85.7% (N = 14)
January–December, 1841 (depression)	60.2% (N = 103)	38.5 (N = 13)
January–December, 1842 (depression)	29.2% (N = 65)	27.2 (N = 11)
January–September, 1843 (depression)	28.9% (N = 97)	42.9% (N = 7)
October–December, 1843 (recovery)	48.5% (N = 66)	50% (N = 4)
January–December, 1844 (recovery)	37.9% (N = 145)	58.8% (N = 17)

SOURCES: Congressional Quarterly's *Guide to U.S. Elections* (1975), 566–81, and Joseph E. Kallenbach and Jessamine S. Kallenbach (eds.), *American State Governors, 1776–1976* (3 vols.; Dobbs Ferry, N.Y., 1977–82), I, which lists both the results of elections and the date on which state elections were held.

NOTE: I have included both special and regular congressional elections, so the number of total seats contested occasionally exceeds the number of seats in the House.

Table 2

Whig Share of Seats Won in the Lower House of State Legislatures, 1836–1843

State and Month of Election	1836	1837	1838	1839	1840	1841	1842	1843
New Hampshire (Mar.)	23%	N.A.	46%	37%	38%	35%	27%	36%
Connecticut (Apr.)	35%	35%	73%	59%	66%	67%	32%	41%
Rhode Island (Apr.)	44%	42%	60%	44%	67%	76%	N.A.	73%
Virginia (May)	43%	35%	54%	52%	55%	51%	37%	43%
Louisiana (July)	N.A.	N.A.	35%		46%		57%	
Alabama (Aug.)	51%	51%	41%	33%	49%	45%	33%	38%
Illinois (Aug.)	31%		52%		45%		31%	
Indiana (Aug.)	56%	68%	62%	39%	78%	47%	45%	45%
Kentucky (Aug.)	59%	71%	68%	58%	77%	77%	57%	62%
Missouri (Aug.)	29%		40%		45%		26%	
North Carolina (Aug.)	49%		55%		61%		44%	
Tennessee (Aug.)		64%		44%		52%		53%
Maine (Sept.)	35%	50.5%	39%	39%	54%	30%	22%	34%
Vermont (Sept.)	73%	57%	68%	N.A.	75%	58%	56%	51.5%
Arkansas (Oct.)	25%		44%		34%		30%	
Georgia (Oct.)	44%	N.A.	50%	43%	57%	42.5%	44%	61%
Maryland (Oct.)	76%	60%	53%	41%	76%	47%	43%	58%
New Jersey (Oct.)	38%	68%	62%	62%	77%	60%	55%	40%
Ohio (Oct.)	49%	56%	47%	32%	71%	49%	42%	54%
Pennsylvania (Oct.)	28%	44%	44%	32%	52%	36%	40%	42%

Delaware (Nov.)	67%		67%		100%		67%	
Massachusetts (Nov.)	69%	87%	70%	52%	70%	62%	50%	58%
Michigan (Nov.)	37.5%	44%	40%	71%	61%	11%	11%	11%
Mississippi (Nov.)		50%	52.3%	40%	54%	39%	33%	33%
New York (Nov.)	26%	78%	64%	55%	52%	26%	27%	29%

SOURCES: With the exception of Alabama and Mississippi, these data on the partisan division of state legislatures were made available by the Inter-University Consortium for Political and Social Research. They were originally collected by Walter Dean Burnham. Neither the original source or collectors of the data nor the Consortium bear any responsibility for the analyses or interpretations presented here. For Alabama, I supplemented Burnham's data with information from *Niles' Weekly Register*, LI (1837), 19, and J. Mills Thornton III, *Politics and Power in a Slave Society: Alabama, 1800–1860* (Baton Rouge, 1978), 34–36. For Mississippi, I utilized what I consider the more reliable data in Table III of Melvin Philip Lucas, "The Period of Political Alchemy: Party in the Mississippi Legislature, 1835–1846" (M.A. thesis, Cornell University, 1981).

NOTES: N.A. indicates that Burnham found no data available.

Periods of economic decline are enclosed in blocks.

In 1836 the Anti-Masonic and Whig parties in Vermont still ran separate candidates. Thus the figure given represents the combined total of Anti-Masonic and Whig seats and helps explain the curious fact that the Whig share of seats in Vermont appears to have declined after the outbreak of panic.

are listed in the chronological order in which they held elections, and periods of economic decline are enclosed in blocks. Figure 1 presents a computer-constructed graph of legislative returns in eight states between 1836 and 1840 whose elections were held at different times of the year and whose economies and demographic composition differed widely, and compares the political trend lines with price trends based on the monthly wholesale price index. Table 3, which is constructed in the same way as Table 2, gives the Whig share of the popular vote in gubernatorial and congressional elections between 1836 and 1840. Figure 2 plots the average Whig vote in different months compared to price trends. To clarify the trends still further, Table 4 groups the states by the month or months in which elections were held and shows the mean Whig vote over time. Figure 3 charts those trend lines graphically. Such grouping is undoubtedly artificial. States with vastly different political complexions and economies were grouped together. Yet it is precisely those differences which make the general trend so compelling.

Despite the wide variation in the political preferences, economic structures, and ethnic and religious composition of these states, the figures indicate that with few exceptions the Whigs did substantially better in hard times than during prosperous times. Even the apparent anomalies, moreover, can in large part be accounted for by a more precise economic analysis.[32]

Yet it would be a mistake to infer from these figures that voters reacted to economic conditions alone rather than to the parties' contrasting responses to the economic crisis. If that had been the case, one might expect angry voters to have swung to the Whigs in order to punish the incumbent Democrats in hard times and then during the recovery either to have returned to the Democrats or abstained. Yet such was not usually the case. Unlike most off-year elections in the

32.   To give but one example, Whigs in many southern states did better in the fall of 1838 than in 1837, yet far worse in 1839 than one would predict from wholesale price trends. Mississippi and Georgia are good examples. One reason for this may have been that cotton prices at New Orleans followed an idiosyncratic pattern. In 1837 they did not fall as fast as the general wholesale price index, yet were considerably lower in 1838 than 1837, even though other prices started to rise. In the autumn of 1839, in contrast, cotton prices were high, even though other prices had started to plummet. Compare Tables 3.2 and 3.6 in Temin, *The Jacksonian Economy*, 69, 103, and see his analysis of cotton prices, pp. 152–54.

Figure 1

Wholesale Price Trend and Whig Legislative Strength

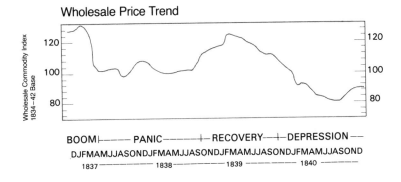

Wholesale Price Trend

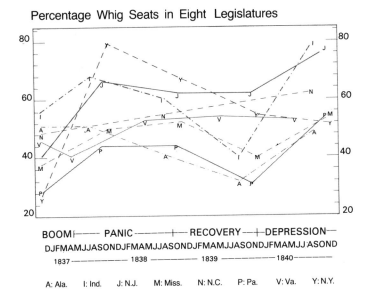

Percentage Whig Seats in Eight Legislatures

A: Ala.   I: Ind.   J: N.J.   M: Miss.   N: N.C.   P: Pa.   V: Va.   Y: N.Y.

Table 3

Whig Proportion of the Popular Vote Related to Economic Condition, 1836–1840

State and Month of Election	1836 P	1837	1838	1839	1840	1840 P
New Hampshire (Mar.)	25.0%	2.2% G	46.9% G	43.9% G	40.8% G	44.5%
Connecticut (Apr.)	49.3%	47.5% G	54.1% G	52.6% G	53.9% G	55.5%
Rhode Island (Apr.)	47.2%	56.8% C		52.5% C	58.4% G[1]	61.3%
Virginia (May)	43.6%	N.R.		48.2% C		49.4%
Louisiana (July)	48.3%		52.8% G		56.5% C	59.7%
Alabama (Aug.)	44.7%	46.3% G		49.6% C[2]		45.6%
				10.0% G		
Illinois (Aug.)	45.2%		49.2% G			48.9%
			40.7% C			
Indiana (Aug.)	55.9%	55.5% G		49.3% C	53.7% G	55.8%
Kentucky (Aug.)	53.0%	63.9% C		N.R. C	57.2% G	64.3%
Missouri (Aug.)	39.4%		42.3% C		42.8% G	43.2%
North Carolina (Aug.)	46.9%	44.1% C[3]	64.2% G	45.5% C[3]	55.0% G	57.5%
	53.1% G					
Tennessee (Aug.)	58.0%	60.7% G		49.0% G		55.7%
		68.9% C		51.5% C		
Maine (Sept.)	39.9%	50.1% G	47.9% G	45.9% G	49.9% G	50.1%
Vermont (Sept.)	60.0%	55.7% G	56.4% G	52.5% G	62.7% G	63.9%
	55.7% G		54.7% C			
Arkansas (Oct.)	36.0%		39.0% C		42.4% C	43.7%
Georgia (Oct.)	51.8%	50.6% G	51.5% C	48.5% G	52.2% C	55.8%
Maryland (Oct.)	53.7%	53.8% C[4]	49.7% G	48.8% C		53.8%

New Jersey (Oct.)	50.5%		49.9% C		51.7% C	51.8%
Ohio (Oct.)	52.1%		48.6% G		52.9% G	54.2%
Pennsylvania (Oct.)	48.8%		48.9% G		46.0% C[5]	50.1%
Delaware (Nov.)	53.2%		49.7% C		53.8% G	55.0%
Massachusetts (Nov.)	54.4%	60.3% G	54.9% G	49.7% G	55.6% G	57.6%
Michigan (Nov.)	45.6%	48.8% G	49.6% C	51.8% G	51.2% C	52.1%
Mississippi (Nov.)	48.2%	53.6% G[6]		45.7% G		53.4%
				45.7% C		
New York (Nov.)	45.4%	68.8% C	51.4% G	50.6% L[7]	50.3% G	51.2%

SOURCES: Burnham, *Presidential Ballots*; Kallenbach and Kallenbach (eds.), *American State Governors, 1776–1976*; and the Congressional Quarterly's *Guide to U.S. Elections*.

NOTES: Those returns contained in lined blocks represent elections held during times of depression.

The initials C (congressional), G (gubernatorial), and L (legislative) denote the type of election.

[1] Although Rhode Island held gubernatorial elections annually, 1840 is the first year for which the Kallenbachs list the party affiliation of candidates.

[2] The percentage for the Alabama congressional elections of 1839 is based on the popular vote in only three of five districts. It inflates Whig strength statewide, for the Whigs did not contest the other two races.

[3] These percentages are based on the popular vote in only nine of thirteen congressional districts in 1837 and eleven of thirteen in 1839. In 1837 the Whigs elected six of thirteen congressmen as they had in 1835 and four of thirteen in 1839. In these elections the *Guide* lists Augustine H. Shepperd as a Whig. I have considered him a Democrat, for he was a Conservative Democrat who only converted to the Whig party after the 1838 session of Congress. In 1839 he ran as a Whig and lost. See Jean E. Friedman, *The Revolt of the Conservative Democrats* (Ann Arbor, 1979), 131.

[4] The percentage in the Maryland congressional elections of 1837 is based on popular returns for six of seven districts.

[5] This percentage is based on the popular vote in only twenty-one of twenty-five congressional districts. It was not reported in the other four. Two of these were multimember districts in which the Whigs elected a total of five members. The Democrats carried the other two.

[6] This represents the combined share of the vote polled by two Whig candidates. Their division of the vote allowed the Democrat Alexander G. McNutt to win the Mississippi governorship in 1837.

[7] The New York returns in 1837 and 1839 are for statewide totals of the votes for state legislative candidates. The returns can be found in the *Tribune Almanac*.

Figure 2

Wholesale Price Trend and Whig Percentage of Popular Vote

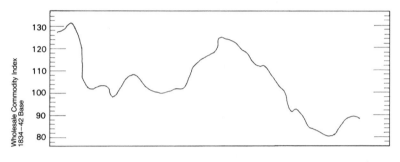

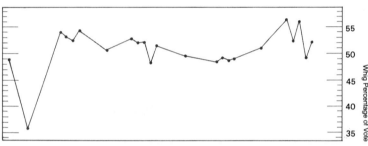

The Whig percentage of the vote in the lower graph represents the mean vote for states in which elections were held in the different months. The price trend is based on the monthly wholesale price index in Temin, *The Jacksonian Economy*, Table 3.2, p. 69.

Table 4

Mean Whig Share of the Vote in State and Congressional Elections, 1836–1840

Month	1836 P	1837	1838	1839	1840	1840 P
March-April (N.H., Conn., R.I.)	40.5%	35.5%	50.5%	49.6%	51.0%	53.8%
July-August (La., Ala., Ill., Ind., Ky., Mo., N.C., Tenn.)	48.9%	54.1%	52.1%	48.3%	53.1%	53.8%
September (Maine, Vermont)	50.0%	52.9%	52.1%	49.2%	56.3%	57.0%
October (Ark., Ga., Md., N.J., Ohio, Pa.)	48.8%	52.2%	47.9%	48.7%	49.0%	51.6%
November* (Del., Mass., Mich., Miss., N.Y.)	49.4%	54.2%	51.4%	49.1%	52.7%	53.9%

SOURCES: Burham, *Presidential Ballots*; Kallenbach and Kallenbach (eds.), *American State Governors, 1776–1976*; and the Congressional Quarterly's *Guide to U.S. Elections*.
NOTES: Where gubernatorial and congressional returns existed for the same year, I used the gubernatorial return, unless the turnout in the congressional election was bigger. The figures represent averages of the Whig percentage of the vote in different states, not of the raw vote. Thus they are not weighted by population. Clearly states of widely varying political complexions are grouped together, but the mean does allow a clearer picture of the impact of economic fluctuations on Whig fortunes.

Those figures enclosed within blocks again represent returns from elections when the economy was slumping.

Virginia, the lone state to hold elections in May, is not included because of insufficient data, but the figures on the proportion of legislative seats won there are generally congruent.

*Neither this table nor the chart computed from it includes the New York Whig percentages in 1837 and 1839, which I discovered after constructing the graph on the computer. Inclusion of those figures would change the November average for 1837 to 53.8% and that for 1839 to 49.4%.

Figure 3

Wholesale Price Trend and Whig Popularity

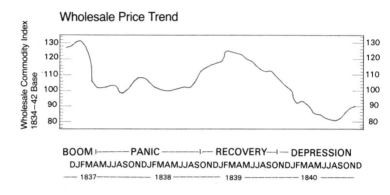

Wholesale Price Trend

BOOM ⊢————PANIC————⊣—— RECOVERY—⊣— DEPRESSION
DJFMAMJJASONDJFMAMJJASONDJFMAMJJASONDJFMAMJJASOND
——1837—————— 1838 —————— 1839 —————— 1840 ———

Mean Whig Percentage by Election Date

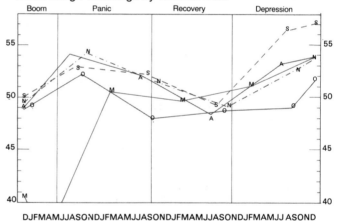

DJFMAMJJASONDJFMAMJJASONDJFMAMJJASONDJFMAMJJ ASOND
——1837—————— 1838—————— 1839—————— 1840 ———

Month of election   M: Mar.-Apr.   A: July-Aug.   S: Sept.   O: Oct.   N: Nov.
The 1836 elections are shown in the first column and the 1840 presidential elections
are shown in the last column.

twentieth century and most in the nineteenth century after 1840, voter turnout in fact continued to increase with each subsequent state or congressional election between 1836 and 1840.

Table 5 presents the change in the absolute vote of each party after the presidential election of 1836. It also indicates the proportion of each state's increase in turnout, between the presidential elections of 1836 and 1840, achieved in state and congressional elections. These figures indicate, among other things, that the remarkable turnout in 1840 was not simply a product of the Whigs' log cabin campaign or of the fact that party organizations competed for the first time on a national scale. Prior to 1840, at least two-thirds of the total increase in turnout had been achieved in ten states, and Pennsylvania almost reached that mark in 1838. Although the excitement engendered by the presidential campaign surely contributed to the additional turnout in 1840, moreover, the size of the vote in the state and congressional races in the spring, summer, and early fall of that year often exceeded the total in November. It is equally noteworthy that in most states which held elections prior to November in 1840, the Whigs gained the majority of their total increment that year in the issue-oriented congressional and gubernatorial elections, not in the presidential balloting. Something more than hard cider and hoopla was bringing these voters to the polls to elect Whig legislators, Whig congressmen, and Whig governors.

The figures on the change in each party's vote between successive elections also suggest that different voters were responding to the parties' contrasting programs in different ways during different economic conditions. Although there were some defections and abstentions from the Democrats during depression periods and from the Whigs during the recovery of 1838–39, the fluctuation in the party vote and success rate over time was caused primarily by a kind of leapfrogging pattern of voter mobilization. In the panic period of 1837–38, that is, the Whigs gained the larger share of new voters joining the electorate. Then, in the recovery elections of 1838–39, they retained most of those new voters and even added more newcomers to their ranks. Still, their share of the vote and of offices declined because the Democrats brought out even more new voters than the Whigs had earlier mobilized. Finally, in 1840, the pattern reversed again and considerably more new voters swung to the Whigs than to the Democrats in most states.

Table 5

Change in the Whig and Democratic Vote, 1836–1840

State		1836 P	1837	1838	1839	1840	1840 P
New Hampshire (Mar.)	W	6,228	− 5,671	+ 25,008	− 1,640	− 3,225	+ 5,597
	D	18,697	+ 3,664	+ 6,380	+ 1,725	− 997	+ 3,332
	T		− 1.5% G	86.0% G	86.0% G	75.5% G	
Connecticut (Apr.)	W	18,798	+ 7,819	+ 498	+ 3,589	− 344	+ 1,238
	D	19,294	+ 10,075	− 7,880	+ 6,156	− 1,863	− 499
	T		95.0% C	63.7% G	107.5% C	96.9% G	
Rhode Island (Apr.)	W	2,711	+ 1,571	N.A.	− 232	+ 747	+ 416
	D	3,036	+ 225		+ 399	− 242	− 155
	T		65.0% C		71.0% C	89.0% G	
Virginia (May)	W	23,361	N.A.	N.A.	+ 7,284	N.A.	+ 11,992
	D	30,263			+ 2,542		+ 10,952
	T				30.0% C		
Louisiana (July)	W	3,583		+ 4,005		+ 1,561	+ 2,147
	D	3,842		+ 2,934		+ 267	+ 573
	T			60.4% G		76.3% C	
Alabama (Aug.)	W	16,658	+ 3,947		− 7,767	+ 8,718	+ 6,959
	D	20,638	+ 3,264		− 1,221	+ 13,056	+ 4,894
	T		28.6% G		−30.6% C*	53.0% L	
Illinois (Aug.)	W	15,240		+ 14,482		+ 8,580	+ 7,274
	D	18,459		+ 12,209		+ 12,904	+ 3,871
	T			44.8% G		81.0% L	

State		Votes					
Indiana (Aug.)	W	41,221	+ 4,846		+ 3,569	+ 13,334	+ 2,337
	D	32,478	+ 4,437		+ 14,136	+ 3,246	− 6,567
	T		21.0% G		62.0% C	100.4% G	
Kentucky (Aug.)	W	36,762	+ 8,195		N.A.	+ 9,945	− 3,705
	D	32,762	− 7,410			+ 13,808	− 6,567
	T		4.6% C*			117.6% G	
Missouri (Aug.)	W	7,377			+ 9,814	+ 5,014	+ 671
	D	11,342			+ 12,068	+ 6,246	+ 373
	T				64.0% C	96.9% G	
North Carolina (Aug.)	W	23,643	− 5,524	+ 20,000	− 11,405	+ 17,800	+ 1,015
	D	26,810	− 3,869	− 1,786	+ 10,806	+ 4,819	+ 615
	T		− 18.6% C*	47.0% G	43.1% C*	105.0% G	
Tennessee (Aug.)	W	36,058	+ 19,404		− 3,672		+ 8,404
	D	26,120	+ 9,789		+ 18,268		− 6,231
	T		55.0% G		94.0% G		
Maine (Sept.)	W	15,239	+ 19,119	+ 8,539	− 8,148	+ 10,848	+ 1,015
	D	22,990	+ 10,889	+ 12,337	− 5,448	+ 4,819	+ 615
	T		55.0% G	94.0% G	68.0% G	96.8% G	
Vermont (Sept.)	W	20,951	+ 1,306		+ 875	+ 9,032	− 1,208
	D	13,962	+ 3,760		+ 2,621	+ 744	− 4,991
	T		32.0% G		75.4% G	118.0% G	
Arkansas (Oct.)	W	1,339		+ 2,989		+ 1,460	+ 628
	D	2,380		+ 4,391		+ 1,105	− 1,220
	T			91.0% C		122.8% C	

Continued on next page

Table 5 (*Continued*)

State	1836 P	1837	1838	1839	1840	1840 P
Georgia (Oct.)	W 24,481	+ 9,697	− 900	− 563	+ 6,584	+ 1,045
	D 22,778	+ 10,639	− 2,147	+ 3,418	+ 1,291	− 3,996
	T	81.0% G	69.1% C	80.3% G	111.8% C	
Maryland (Oct.)	W 25,853	− 5,902	+ 7,458	− 2,679		+ 8,803
	D 22,269	− 5,173	+ 10,626	− 1,765		+ 2,802
	T	−23.0% C*	49.0% G	18.0% C		
New Jersey (Oct.)	W 26,137		+ 2,289		+ 4,916	+ 9
	D 25,592		+ 2,900		+ 2,646	− 97
	T		41.0% C		100.7% C	
Ohio (Oct.)	W 105,809		− 3,663		+ 43,298	+ 2,599
	D 97,122		+ 10,762		+ 21,428	− 5,368
	T		10.0% G		102.7% G	
Pennsylvania (Oct.)	W 87,233		+ 35,088		N.A.	+ 21,702
	D 91,233		+ 36,592			+ 15,848
	T		65.5% G			
Delaware (Nov.)	W 4,736		− 337		+ 1,446	+ 122
	D 4,154		+ 297		+ 633	− 212
	T		− 0.5% C		100.9% C	
Massachusetts (Nov.)	W 42,247	+ 8,318	+ 1,077	− 917	+ 20,159	+ 1,990
	D 35,721	− 2,734	+ 8,808	+ 9,239	+ 4,135	− 3,215
	T	12.5% G	33.0% G	50.0% G	101.8% G	

Michigan (Nov.)	W 5,545	+ 9,339	+ 1,215	+ 2,970	+ 3,772	+ 92
	D 6,607	+ 8,711	+ 1,042	+ 1,350	+ 3,754	− 368
	T	58.0% G	64.0% C	77.0% G	100.9% C	
Mississippi (Nov.)	W 9,820	+ 4,992		+ 1,074		+ 3,629
	D 10,294	+ 2,529		+ 6,057		− 1,870
	T	46.0% G		89.0% G		
New York (Nov.)	W 138,765	+ 17,340	+ 37,042	− 9,287	+ 38,416	+ 1,002
	D 166,884	− 26,355	+ 42,422	− 3,182	+ 37,447	− 3,990
	T	− 2.9% L	51.0% G	49.7% L	99.8% G	

SOURCES: The Congressional Quarterly's Guide to U.S. Elections; Burnham, Presidential Ballots; Kallenbach and Kallenbach (eds.), American State Governors, 1776–1976; and the Tribune Almanac.

NOTES: The figures listed in the left column, 1836 P, are the total votes for each party in the presidential election of 1836. Other columns list the change in the popular vote measured from the total in the immediately preceding election. For 1840 the figures under the presidential election column represent changes from the state and congressional elections held earlier in the year. For states which held congressional or gubernatorial elections in November simultaneously with the presidential election, the figures in column 1840 P represent the difference between the presidential vote and the gubernatorial or congressional vote.

The initials C (congressional), G (gubernatorial), and L (legislative) denote the type of election used in the table.

Where more than one election was available, I used the returns for the election with the highest voter turnout.

The row marked T for each state gives the proportion of the total increase in turnout between the presidential elections of 1836 and 1840 achieved in the state or congressional elections. For example, if the presidential vote increased by 100,000 in a state between those two years and the vote for governor in 1838 in that state was 60,000 larger than the presidential vote in 1836, then the T for that state in 1838 would be 60%.

*These are incomplete congressional returns—i.e., where the popular vote was given for some but not all congressional districts—and hence the statewide total was usually smaller than votes for governor or president. In most cases the reason for partial returns was that some congressional seats were uncontested by one party or the other.

Contemporary research by political scientists helps explain this pattern. They have found that bad economic conditions hurt an incumbent party far more than good conditions help it. People who disapprove of a party's record are much more likely to vote against it than people who approve of that record are likely to vote for it, especially among independents, who for our purposes can be equated with previous nonvoters. Finally, those most directly hurt by bad economic conditions are more likely to turn against the party they blame than are voters less affected by hard times.

If this modern research is applicable, it seems likely that during the panic period of 1837–38 those voters who suffered most from declining prices, who blamed them on Democratic hard-money programs, and who found the Whig program more likely to restore economic recovery, swung to the Whigs. During the recovery period, most of those men continued to vote Whig because they attributed the recovery to Whig actions in the states. Still, the Democrats rebounded because they mobilized tens of thousands of new voters who regarded the Whigs' probanking legislation of 1838 and 1839 as a threat to equal rights. At the same time, during that brief period of relative prosperity, many potential new voters who approved of the Whig effort did not vote because the Whig program did not seem as necessary to them as it once had. Once prices plummeted in 1840, however, the Whigs again attracted tens of thousands of additional supporters from men who suffered economic hardship, who resented the refusal of Democrats to help them, and who found the Whig program of governmental activism once again necessary in changed economic conditions.

Such a scenario is consistent with the growing evidence that Whigs and Democrats attracted supporters from different kinds of economic constituencies, if not from different classes. That is, the Whigs were far stronger than Democrats in areas that were closely involved in the commercial economy. Because these areas were most likely to be hurt by financial stringency, bank suspensions, and price declines, their residents would respond most positively to the Whig message. In contrast, Democrats received their strongest support from groups and areas that were at once most immune from price fluctuations, most impervious to Whig promises of economic recovery, and most likely to respond instead to Democratic warnings that Whig programs would create a privileged aristocracy subversive of republicanism. In much of the nation, Democratic voting strength was concentrated among subsistence farmers in the most remote and economically underdeveloped regions of states and counties. Such voters feared becoming ensnared in precisely the kind of commercial-monetary network the Whigs hoped to foster. New Democratic voters, that is, were not responding to economic conditions. They came to the polls to punish the Whigs for their actions at the state level.[33]

It is possible, in sum, that the parties recruited their new voters between 1836 and 1840 from different economic constituencies and that, as economic conditions changed, new voters were more likely to turn out in one kind of constituency than the other. It is beyond my purpose here to attempt to test that hypothesis. Preliminary research on Ohio, Mississippi, and Virginia, however, demonstrates that Whigs significantly outpaced Democrats among new voters in wealthy, commercially oriented counties between 1836 and 1840 and that a far larger proportion of new Democratic voters than of new Whig voters came from the poorest counties in those states.

Whatever the source of the parties' new voters, the tables and especially the graphs presented here clearly refute the notion that the Whigs won the election of 1840 because of hullaballoo and snappy slogans. Whig strength surged during the panic period of 1837–38, they retained most of those gains during the recovery of 1838–39, and their fortunes soared once again almost as soon as depression set in at

33. Watson, *Jacksonian Politics and Community Conflict*, 246–81, makes this point explicitly and even provides statistical evidence (p. 279) that the two parties' votes in Cumberland County grew in different areas—the Whigs' in wealthier, more commercially oriented sections and the Democrats' in the remote areas hostile to the urban commercial sector. For additional evidence on this difference in the economic orientation of Whig and Democratic constituencies, see Ratliffe, "Politics in Jacksonian Ohio," 29–31; Kruman, *Parties and Politics in North Carolina*, 16–17; Thornton, *Politics and Power in a Slave Society*, 39–45; Thomas B. Alexander *et al.*, "The Basis of Alabama's Antebellum Two-Party System," *Alabama Review*, XIX (1966), 243–76; Donald B. Cole, *Jacksonian Democracy in New Hampshire, 1800–1851* (Cambridge, Mass., 1970); Charles G. Sellers, *James K. Polk: Jacksonian 1795–1843* (Princeton, 1957), 374; and Shade, *Banks or No Banks*, 158–63. That concrete probanking measures by Whigs could incite Democratic voters was demonstrated in Pennsylvania in 1836. In 1835 the Whigs won sixty-eight of the one hundred seats in the Pennsylvania house, and in 1836 they used that power to give a state charter to the Bank of the United States. Attacking that action, Democrats won seventy-two of the one hundred seats in the house in October, 1836, even though Van Buren won only 51 percent of the state's vote a month later.

the end of 1839. Their striking gains in the spring and summer of 1840 before the presidential election simply repeated the pattern set in 1837–38. Presidential coattails cannot account for triumphs that occurred months before the presidential balloting. Once prices fell again, Whig victory in 1840 was assured because depression made their program salient and attractive to new voters who yearned for recovery. Their victory in 1840, moreover, was emphatically a triumph of the Whig party as a whole—legislators, gubernatorial candidates, and congressmen—and not just of "Tippecanoe and Tyler, Too." In short, Henry Clay's famous lament when he learned that he had been denied the Whig nomination for 1840—that he was "always run by my friends when sure to be defeated, and now betrayed for a nomination when I, or any one, would be sure of an election"— was correct. No matter whom the Whigs ran for president in 1840, he was going to win because the presidential victory was simply a single facet of a genuinely sweeping party victory.[34]

Why, then, did the Whigs nominate Harrison instead of Clay? The answer to that question lies largely, though not exclusively, in the timing of the Whig national convention that met in early December, 1839. Since 1836, Clay's prospects for the nomination had risen and fallen with the record of the Whig party in off-year elections, that is, inversely with economic trends. Prior to the panic many Whig strategists believed the party needed Harrison to win, but during the Whig surge of 1837–38, Clay became the front-runner because it seemed that the party could triumph with the economic issues that Clay championed. When the Whigs suffered reverses at the end of 1838 and in 1839, however, Clay's chances were crippled. A military hero who might lure voters away from the Democrats once again seemed necessary.

The Whig convention met after economic recovery had dealt the Whigs a series of losses in the summer and fall of 1839 and before the real impact of the price slump that began late in 1839 had been felt.[35] Hence the Whigs shunned a national platform, opted for a military

34. The statement was originally attributed to Clay by Henry Wise in his memoirs, *Seven Decades of the Union*, and is quoted in Gunderson, *The Log-Cabin Campaign*, 68.

35. In 1839 the Whigs lost state or congressional elections in Maine, Ohio, Indiana, Pennsylvania, Massachusetts, Maryland, Georgia, North Carolina, Tennessee, Mississippi, and Alabama, and their hold on New York was precarious.

hero, and planned a "hurra" campaign. Even they, however, could not have anticipated that the disdainful Democratic response to Harrison's nomination would give them their most memorable symbols, log cabins and hard cider. Had the Whigs convened in May, 1840, when the Democratic national convention met, the results would probably have been very different. Then prices would have been 16 percent lower than they were in December. Then the Whigs would have been coming off a string of victories in Rhode Island, Connecticut, and Virginia, which pointed as they surely did to triumph in the fall. In those conditions, Clay, who had considerable support even in December, might well have received the prize he so hungered for. By May, 1840, in sum, it would have been clear that the Whigs did not need a noncommittal general to win.

Why Harrison received the Whig nomination and why he won the election, therefore, are different questions that have different answers. Yet, ironically, changing economic conditions explain his triumph in both cases.

The economic roller-coaster ride between 1837 and 1843, indeed, was clearly the predominant influence shaping American political development in those years. Not only did it spur the parties for the first time to formulate clear and contrasting economic policies, but it also molded officeholders in the respective parties into disciplined phalanxes who supported their rival programs in state and national legislative bodies in order to establish contrasting records to take to the electorate.[36] Because economic conditions gave salience to those records, moreover, men with different levels of involvement in

---

36. Referring to Congress, Donald Stokes has argued that the solidarity of a party behind its program is partially a function of the members' "perception of forces on their constituents' voting behavior. . . . If the member of the legislature believes, on the one hand, that it is the national party and its leaders which are salient and that his own electoral prospects depend on the legislative record of the party as a whole, his bonds to the legislative party will be relatively strong. . . . But if the legislator believes, on the other hand, that the public is dominated by constituency influences and that his prospects depend on his own or his opponent's appeal or on other factors distinctive to the constituency, his bonds to the legislative party will be relatively weak." Donald E. Stokes, "Parties and the Nationalization of Electoral Forces," in William N. Chambers and Walter Dean Burnham (eds.), *The American Party Systems: Stages of Political Development* (New York, 1967), 184. In other words, party became a much more important determinant of roll-call voting behavior after 1836 because Whig and Democratic officeholders believed voters responded to the parties' records on specific issues.

and attitudes toward the commercial economy joined the electorate in record numbers and gave their respective allegiance to the rival parties. Hence it was in the state and congressional elections between November, 1836, and November, 1840, that voter loyalties crystalized, new voters were mobilized, and the Whigs built a coalition that gave them control of most state governments, both houses of Congress, and the White House in 1840.

The period between 1836 and 1840, in short, witnessed a realignment that should have made the Whigs the majority party during the stable phase of the second party system. Yet, as recent research has made clear, permanent realignments are not simply products of the voter movements that replace one party in power with another. Rather, they are products of the policies passed by the new "in" party once it gains power.[37] To cement the allegiance of the new voters gained in 1840 and effect a permanent realignment, the Whigs had to pass the programs for economic recovery they had promised, just as they had at the state level in 1838 and 1839. After 1840, however, state legislation would not be enough to hold those voters, for the Whigs now controlled the White House and Congress, and expectant Whig voters looked to Washington for action. For that reason, the Whigs failed to remain the majority party during the stable phase of the party system. As is well known, John Tyler, who succeeded Harrison a month after his inauguration, vetoed crucial parts of the Whig program in the summer of 1841 during a special session of Congress and again in the summer of 1842. As a result, disillusioned and frustrated Whig voters dropped out of the electorate almost as fast as they had joined it in 1840. They could not support the Democrats, but neither would they turn out for a party that had so disappointed them. The upshot was that the majority Whigs had built in the off-year elections between 1836 and 1840 melted away in the off-year elections between 1840 and 1844.

Perhaps no better evidence exists that voters responded to issues and party records, indeed, than what happened to the Whigs in the elections of 1841, 1842, and 1843. The congressional and gubernatorial results set forth in Table 1, for example, reveal not only a dramatic decline in Whig fortunes in 1842 and 1843, at least while the depression lasted, but a striking disparity between Whig fortunes

37. See Clubb, Flanigan, and Zingale, *Partisan Realignment*, 11–45.

in congressional and gubernatorial elections in 1841. The reason for that disparity is that all elections for Congress in 1841 were held before May 31 when a special session of Congress convened, and many of the gubernatorial elections were held in the fall of the year, after Tyler had wrecked Whig plans for a new national bank. The special session of Congress lasted from May 31 to September 13, 1841, and Tyler cast his major vetoes on August 16 and September 9. Of the five gubernatorial elections held before the first veto, the Whigs won three; of the eight held between September and November when the extent of the Whigs' programmatic failure had become clear, they lost six. To a remarkable extent, indeed, even the results of the state legislative elections listed in Table 2 reflect the impact of the Whigs' failure in Washington. In 1841, with the exception of Indiana, the Whigs did as well in states voting before September as they had in 1840. Beginning with the elections of September, 1841, on the other hand, the Whigs suffered disastrous declines in their legislative strength everywhere, and those declines continued in 1842 and 1843.

The reason for this reversal of Whig fortunes was clear to Whigs and Democrats alike. Prior to September, 1841, voters responded to the promise that the Whig program would bring economic recovery just as they had in 1840. In the words of a defeated Democrat, before September "the people acted in view of the liberal promises of *relief and reform* which had been made to them." Once Congress adjourned, however, they were "disappointed and dissatisfied. They now find that they have been deceived." Throughout 1841 and 1842, indeed, both Whig congressmen and their constituents warned that people had elected Whigs because of their program. If they did not enact it in its entirety, the Whigs would suffer disaster at the polls because disillusioned voters would no longer support them. It was fear of such a reaction that caused congressional Whigs to pass measures they knew that Tyler might veto. The consequences of those vetoes and the ruin of the Whig program were precisely what they had predicted—substantial and one-sided abstentions that allowed the Democrats to recover the offices they had lost in 1840 and the first half of 1841.[38]

38. James K. Polk to John C. Calhoun, February 23, 1842, in J. Franklin Jameson (ed.), "Correspondence of John C. Calhoun," *Annual Report of the American Historical Association for 1899, Volume II* (Washington, D.C., 1900), 844–45.

Thus the Whigs failed to remain the majority party during the stable phase of the second party system. They failed, not because of antiparty sentiment among the voters or defections to the Liberty party, as some historians have maintained. Rather, they failed because the new voters they mobilized by promising to pass an economic program before 1841 stayed at home once they did not enact it.[39] Between 1841 and 1843, in sum, economic issues and contrasting party records were the central determinants of voting behavior just as they had been between 1836 and 1840 when the electorate expanded, the party system crystalized, and the Whigs won their first presidential election.

39.   Benson (*The Concept of Jacksonian Democracy*, 133) states that the Whigs failed to remain the majority party in New York because of defections to the Liberty party; Formisano (*The Birth of Mass Political Parties*, 57–58) says that antiparty sentiment and vulnerability to the Liberty party explain why Whigs became the minority party in Michigan after 1840. Yet abstentions far outnumbered defections to the Liberty party in the North, and they wrecked the party in the South as well. I have found popular voting returns from forty-nine state and congressional elections in twenty-five states in 1841, 1842, and 1843. Of those forty-nine elections, the Whigs suffered drop-off in forty-seven, and in all but three of those forty-seven, Whig drop-off was greater than Democratic drop-off and usually substantially greater.

"The Only Door"
The Territorial Issue, the Preston Bill, and the Southern Whigs

William J. Cooper, Jr.

"The inevitable dissolution of the Confederacy"—in February, 1849, those ominous words rang through the United States Capitol.[1] That cry was no lonesome wail. In the winter of 1848–49, calculations on the longevity of the Union were legion and loud. The second session of the Thirtieth Congress, which ran from December 4, 1848, to March 4, 1849, witnessed the bursting of sectional tensions that had been festering for almost two years. These tensions were directly related to slavery and its future in the nation, especially in the lands newly acquired from Mexico.

In the second session a vigorous, though little-known, attempt was made to resolve the territorial issue. It proposed to do so with a finality that would have removed the vexed territorial question from the political arena. This endeavor included almost all the ingredients associated with mid-nineteenth-century politics—inventiveness, ingenuity, boldness, caution, fear, partisanship, bipartisan cooperation, sectionalism, nationalism, slavery, freedom. But, after all the politicking, the rhetoric, the voting, it failed. This is the story of that effort and why it failed.

The question of the new relationship between slavery and the United States had been brought to the fore by the Wilmot Proviso. Introduced in the House of Representatives during the summer of 1846, the proviso prohibited slavery in any territory gained from the Mexican War. The proviso readily passed the House, but never made it through the Senate. More important, during 1847 and 1848 it assumed major political importance; in the South it became the chief issue. When the Mexican War ended in 1848, theoretical propositions about slavery in the territories quickly became matters for practical

---

1. *Congressional Globe*, 30th Cong., 2nd Sess., Appendix, 175; hereafter cited as *CG*. All citations are to this Congress and session.

decision. Formally ratified by the Senate in March, 1848, the treaty concluding the two-year-old conflict added to the American domain California and the Southwest, more than 500,000 square miles. With the acceptance of the treaty, the slavery issue focused on what stance Congress would adopt toward slavery in the Mexican Cession, permit or prohibit it. Slavery, Vice-President George M. Dallas prophetically recorded in his diary, "will agitate the whole of the session."[2]

From both sides of the Mason-Dixon Line, thunderbolts crashed about the halls of Congress. Resolutions from Florida demanding that Congress recognize the rights of slavery were matched by equally vehement pronouncements from other southern states. The Virginia legislature declared that passage of the Wilmot Proviso would necessitate "determined resistance . . . at all hazards and to the last extremity" by every Virginian. The great sentinel of the South, John C. Calhoun, insisted that the aggression of the North upon the South should be resisted and that the time had come for action. Democrats and Whigs alike spoke the same language. To the Virginia Democrat James McDowell, nothing less than "national safety" was at stake. Henry Hilliard, Whig of Alabama, proclaimed to his fellow congressmen that before he would "surrender one jot or one tittle of the rights or the honor or the glory of the South, 'my right hand shall forget its cunning and my tongue cleave to the roof of my mouth.'"[3]

Northerners did not back away. The legislature of New York passed and forwarded to Congress resolutions urging the imposition of the Wilmot Proviso as well as the abolition of the slave trade in the District of Columbia. The preamble castigated slavery as "revolting to the spirit of the age." Senator John P. Hale of New Hampshire presented to the Senate "a very large number of petitions" demanding passage of the proviso along with abolition of both slavery and the slave trade in the District of Columbia. The Illinois legislature told its state congressional delegation never to permit the extension of slavery into the cession. To many northerners, such resolutions originated in the conviction that slavery "forever lusts for conquests and expan-

2.   George M. Dallas Diary, December 12, 1848, in Roy F. Nichols, "The Mystery of the Dallas Papers," *Pennsylvania Magazine of History and Biography*, LXXIII (1949), 485–86.
3.   *CG*, 33, 440, 456, Appendix, 105, 175, 213; William J. Cooper, Jr., *The South and the Politics of Slavery, 1828–1856* (Baton Rouge, 1978), 270.

sion." For these northerners, fundamental issues were at stake. On the Wilmot Proviso the cry went out—"The question cannot be compromised."[4]

The territorial issue had become critical. To southerners and northerners alike, the territories represented the future; they ensured the prosperity and permanence of republican government, of the United States. Geographical expansion had been central to the American experience since the colonial period, and during the first four-and-a-half decades of the nineteenth century the United States was a nation on the march, a march in which southerners and northerners had energetically participated. Southerners viewed the Mexican Cession as a national treasure dearly purchased by blood and money during the Mexican War, much of both theirs. Access to the cession, which meant no restriction on slavery, they demanded as Americans. In their mind the proviso, an attempt to bar them officially from the cession, branded them as unpatriotic and castigated them as un-American.[5]

Whether southerners expected or even wanted slavery to expand into the cession is a difficult question. Southerners both opposed and supported such expansion, but the evidence does not permit a conclusive answer. Among southern Whigs in the late 1840s, however, the dominant view was that slavery would not become established in the territories. Most southern Whigs believed that natural forces, chiefly the climate, effectively barred the growth of slavery in the cession. But all southerners, opponents as well as supporters, were adamant about southern rights in the territories. They could never accept the absolute prohibition of slavery during the territorial phase. The proviso was anathema to all southerners.

By the mid-1840s, more and more northerners began to perceive the South almost as an errant child, certainly as a section that really did not fit in the new, burgeoning nation. Many saw the South as economically backward and morally deficient, all because of the un-American institution, slavery. Paradoxically, however, in the northern perception the blemished South wielded vast and unjustified political power, a contradiction that mocked American ideals while

4. *CG*, 181, 309, 347, Appendix, 101; Albany *Evening Journal*, February 23, 1849.
5. On the South and the territories, see Cooper, *The South and the Politics of Slavery*, 238–44.

it restricted legitimate northern power. For those who so described the South their responsibility was clear: to guarantee national moral and economic progress and simultaneously to bridle southern political power necessitated the restriction of slavery. This outlook had a long history; its birth antedated the nineteenth century, and it was clearly articulated during the Missouri crisis (1819–1821). But after the annexation of Texas and the Mexican War it loomed increasingly large in northern society.[6]

These divergent northern and southern territorial views had profound political implications. With two great parties competing for votes in North and South, each actively pursued sectional protection as an appropriate political issue. In the South, it gave legitimacy to parties. It was widely employed in the North, especially by the Whigs, and in 1848 it became the keystone of the new Free-Soil party. This political reality meant that even those not ideologically concerned about the extension of slavery found themselves caught up in the politics of the territories. Practically no one, certainly not active, ambitious politicians, could stand back and look upon the territorial question as just another political topic. For almost everyone, the meshing of ideology and politics made the territorial issue a powerful, explosive force.

Although Democrats and Whigs as well as antiparty zealots were deeply involved in this territorial crisis, the Whigs had special concerns. Almost every Whig was painfully aware that the proviso had created a broad, deep chasm in the party. The double question of the proper policy toward expansion and a united party front on the issue had plagued the Whigs since the presidential campaign of 1844 and the furor over Texas. Then northern Whigs adamantly opposed bringing Texas into the Union while southern Whigs ranged across the spectrum of opinion, from outright opposition to enthusiastic support. Attempting to find a safe island in this political torrent, the party's paladin Henry Clay pleased few and helped defeat himself. After that disorienting and dispiriting experience all Whigs became alert to dangers posed to their party by territorial expansion. Their deep internal division convinced Whigs that the country could not stand the strain if slavery and expansion became one. In this sense,

6.   The most complete treatment of the northern perception of the territories is in Eric Foner, *Free Soil, Free Labor, Free Men: The Ideology of the Republican Party Before the Civil War* (New York, 1970).

Whigs saw their party as a laboratory testing unity and disunity for the nation.

After the annexation of Texas most Whigs stood foursquare against any more territorial expansion. The Democrats differed totally; they galloped on their steed of expansion. Opposing what they called an offensive policy, Whigs could find little positive in President James K. Polk's ambition for the Southwest and California. When that drive led to war with Mexico, the Whigs protested the president's culpability, though most in Congress felt compelled to vote additional troops and money as long as American soldiers were in combat. But the onset of war did not change the Whig attitude toward expansion; the party generally urged that additional territory not become a spoil of war. Such booty, Whigs feared, would mean desperate trouble for their party and their nation. With the treaty ending the war, Whig opposition to more territory became academic. The Mexican Cession was a reality, and Whigs had to confront what they had so vigorously fought and deeply feared—the merging of slavery and expansion.

The initial consideration of this potent combination occurred in the long first session of the Thirtieth Congress, which lasted from December, 1847, all the way into the hot summer of 1848. The result, however, was not a confrontation. The first major effort to avoid a North-South showdown on imposing the Wilmot Proviso in the cession originated with the Democrats and enjoyed the strong support of President Polk. Even though most Democrats were willing to extend the hallowed Missouri Compromise line from its original western boundary on out to the Pacific Ocean, they could never muster the votes to gain passage. When the Missouri option faltered, a select Senate committee devised another formula. Carrying the name of the Delaware Whig senator John M. Clayton, the Clayton Compromise proposed to turn the question of slavery in the Mexican Cession over to the federal judiciary. The striving of Senator Clayton and other border and southern Whigs, along with the backing of President Polk and many Democrats, enabled the compromise to pass the Senate by a narrow margin. But in another close vote, it failed in the House. Thus, when Congress adjourned in August, 1848, it had not found a way around the Wilmot Proviso. As a result, all of the Mexican Cession remained unorganized.[7]

7. David M. Potter, *The Impending Crisis, 1848–1861* (New York, 1976), 69–76.

From the failure of the Missouri extension and of the Clayton Compromise, from all the debate and votes surrounding their legislative history, one clear message emerged for the Whig party. Although a substantial majority of southern Whigs were willing to accept either the extension or the compromise, every northern Whig opposed both. On the key issue of solving the Wilmot Proviso, the party was stumped.

Already well underway when Congress disbanded, the presidential campaign did not aid Whig unity. Most Whigs, southern as well as northern, lined up behind Major General Zachary Taylor, a hero of the Mexican War. For the southerners, Taylor was something special, a slaveowning cotton planter who called Baton Rouge, Louisiana, home. That particular southern identity, coupled with his heroic wartime service, caused southerners to flock to his banner. Few northerners felt the same joy about Taylor, but by a variety of routes and for a number of reasons, most supported his candidacy. Only the extreme antislavery men refused to join Taylor's political army. Appalled that a slaveowner headed the ticket, they bolted and helped form the Free-Soil party, which made the Wilmot Proviso a political article of faith. General unity on Taylor did not mean, however, that the Whigs had discovered a solution to their territorial puzzle. The party simply dodged the entire question by not adopting a platform expounding principles and goals. This underscored Whig division on the territorial issue, a wide gap already seen in the Congress.[8]

During the campaign, there seemed to be two Taylors. Southerners presented him as a native son who would never act against the interests of the South or of slavery. Of course most southerners did not and could not separate the two. In contrast, northerners depicted him as a nationalist and a good Whig who would surely abide by the will of Congress. If the Congress passed the Wilmot Proviso, they insisted that Taylor as president would sign it into law. Although Taylor kept his own counsel throughout the furor, only one valid conclusion can be drawn. On the territorial issue, two different Taylors were presented by Whig enthusiasts on opposite sides of the Mason-Dixon

8. *Ibid.*, 78–82; Cooper, *The South and the Politics of Slavery*, 244–53; Michael F. Holt, "Winding Roads to Recovery: The Whig Party from 1844 to 1848," in Stephen E. Maizlish and John J. Kushma (eds.), *Essays on American Antebellum Politics, 1840–1860* (College Station, Tex., 1982), 122–65.

Line. This truth was never more forcefully put than by an angry Democratic correspondent to the Washington *Daily Union*. Notwithstanding the partisan passion of the accusation, it carried a powerful truth: "Louisiana and Massachusetts have joined hands. One urged that safety to the South demanded the election of General Taylor; while the other, with equal vehemence, declared that protection to the North from the encroachments of the slave power imperiously required the same result. A very great fraud has unquestionably been perpetrated by the friends of General Taylor, either in one section of the Union or the other. Somebody has been cheated and grossly deceived." Thus on the territorial front, the Taylor victory did not at all signify that the Whigs had overcome their cleavage of two years. But with Taylor's great win, the party would have to govern, which meant it would have to devise a territorial policy or face possible ruin.[9]

That possibility quickly jumped from theoretical to practical. The discovery of gold in California caused great excitement. Throughout the country, newspapers were filled with features on California, discussions of the best ways to reach the new El Dorado, stories about individuals or groups striking out for the goldfields. Few locales escaped or wanted to escape the California fever. Describing attitudes in Washington for former president Martin Van Buren, an experienced political hand underscored that "California occupied every body's thoughts . . . to the exclusion of every thing else." This consuming interest had a most practical political manifestation. California had no civilian government; it was run by the military. To organize the area officially and to set up a civilian government required congressional action, so the question of slavery in the Mexican Cession would have to be confronted—in some fashion.[10]

The solution to the pressing territorial problem was crucial for the nation and for the Whig party. Thoughtful Whigs knew full well the extent of their difficulties. They also recognized that the interregnum—the five months between Taylor's election and his inauguration—comprised a critical time for them, one simultaneously filled with danger and opportunity. Throughout those weeks the

9. Washington *Daily Union*, December 9, 1848.
10. H. D. Gilpin to Martin Van Buren, December 21, 1848, in Martin Van Buren Papers, Library of Congress. Every newspaper that I looked at for this essay carried numerous California stories.

Democrat Polk would still occupy the White House, and during most of them the second session of the Thirtieth Congress would be meeting. Two old facts were known: the first session of the Thirtieth had failed utterly to resolve the territorial dispute; James K. Polk would veto any bill containing the Wilmot Proviso. But there was also a new fact. On March 4, 1849, a Whig, not a Democrat, would become president. This new situation did not, however, clarify the territorial issue—nobody knew where Zachary Taylor actually stood. Assumptions abounded, but concrete knowledge was scarce. Thus absolute certainty about what President Taylor would or would not do could not substantially influence Whig congressmen and senators.

When the second session opened on December 4, 1848, the Whigs were no more unified than they had been during the first session or in the presidential campaign. All Whigs recognized that it was "of the first importance to [them] to 'start right.'" But few agreed on the direction. Ardent Free-Soilers had their platform for the newly elected administration: "We declare that there shall be no more Slavery and no more Slave States." The Albany *Evening Journal*, whose editor Thurlow Weed, the kingpin of the Whig organization in New York, had been a mainstay in the Taylor campaign, announced that the election signaled "a boundary line had been fixed for Slavery. The next Congress, with the assent of the president, will carry out the wishes of the People." In contrast, Virginia Congressman Jonathan Pendleton wanted to come up with a plan that would attract southern Democrats. He was looking for "something that will carry with us the Southern people." Noting this basic difference, thoughtful party leaders who saw Taylor's victory "not as a temporary triumph but one which if wisely and prudently directed is to . . . the remotest time a decisive and salutary influence in the destinies of our country" were indeed anxious.[11]

None exhibited more concern than John J. Crittenden and John M. Clayton. Crittenden had relinquished his Senate seat to become governor of Kentucky. The protégé of Henry Clay, Crittenden had broken with his mentor to back his old friend Zachary Taylor for the

11.   William B. Preston to William C. Rives, December 6, 1848, and Jonathan Pendleton to Rives, December 28, 1848, both in William C. Rives Papers, Library of Congress; Charles Francis Adams to John G. Palfrey, December 12, 1848, in Adams Family Papers, Massachusetts Historical Society, Boston; Albany *Evening Journal*, December 15, 1848.

Whig nomination. Viewed as wise and reasonable as well as a confidant of Taylor, Crittenden maintained a correspondence that kept the postal service active between Frankfort and Washington. And no one wrote to him more frankly and thoughtfully than Clayton, the senator from Delaware, who had given his name to the ill-fated Clayton Compromise. Both men were joyous over Taylor's triumph. They believed it augured a brilliant future for both the Whig party and the nation, and they did not separate the fate of one from the other. They also perceived a common danger. "The great [threat]," wrote Clayton in early December, "is the slavery question." Responding, Crittenden agreed, "This question of slavery is the only one that seriously threatens us." Each a moderate, border-state man trying to balance ardent proslavery spokesmen with zealous antislavery crusaders, they sought to control emotion and find a middle way. In Crittenden's careful formulation the slavery issue "ought therefore to be dealt with, always, with the utmost coolness and discretion." But the great puzzle remained, "Now upon the slave question what can be done?"[12]

While Whigs wrestled with their dilemma, the Democrats moved. In the aftermath of their defeat in the presidential election a number of Democrats, in the words of Vice-President Dallas, wanted "to try hard to do nothing:—leaving all unsettled questions and especially the free soil one, to harrass [*sic*] Genl. Taylor next winter." Aware of the Whig division, Democrats of this inclination just wanted to let their political enemies sweat. But President Polk did not want to leave the territorial issue to Zachary Taylor; he did not want to wait at all. Concerned about the ultimate fate of what he saw as the great prize of his administration, Polk was both eager for and anxious about the formal organization of the Mexican Cession. He feared that congressional inaction might lead to any one of several possible disasters such as an independent California, or the reversion of much of the cession back to Mexico, or a frightful, sectional division in the United States.[13]

In his final annual message to Congress on December 5, 1848,

12. John M. Clayton to John J. Crittenden, December 13, 1848, in John J. Crittenden Papers, and Crittenden to Clayton, January 7, 1849, in John M. Clayton Papers, both collections in Library of Congress; Alexander Stephens to Crittenden, December 6, 1848, in Crittenden Papers.
13. George M. Dallas to his wife, December 7, 1848, in Nichols, "The Mystery of the Dallas Papers," 477.

Polk did not minimize the gravity of the issue. He urged the assembled congressmen and senators "at your present session to approach the adjustment of the only domestic question which seriously threatens, or probably ever can threaten, to disturb the harmony and successful operation of our system." Lecturing the lawmakers, he professed that "it is our solemn duty to provide with the least practicable delay for New Mexico and California regularly organized territorial governments." Keenly aware of the powerful reactions engendered by the territorial question, Polk called on "the spirit of compromise," which had "overcome" the slavery-related difficulties of earlier times, all the way back to "the adoption of the Constitution."[14]

The president did not content himself with either platitudes or generalizations. He pointed to the Missouri Compromise line of 36°30' as a possible solution. "Upon a great emergency," Polk reminded the Congress, a previous deal had been struck to eliminate a menace to the Union. Congressional action to extend the line westward to the Pacific Ocean would receive his blessing, for he was confident that would cause "peace and harmony [to] again fill our borders." But Polk was not a one-solution man. Should Congress instead "prefer to submit the legal and constitutional questions which may arise to the decision of the judicial tribunals," he and "all parts of the Union should cheerfully acquiesce." That reference to the once rejected Clayton Compromise indicated that Polk was willing to support any feasible compromise plan. Concluding this portion of his message, he "earnestly invoked" the Congress "for the sake of the Union, its harmony, and our continued prosperity as a nation, to adjust at its present session this, the only dangerous question which lies in our path, if not in some one of the modes suggested, in some other way which may be satisfactory."[15]

Another way became the Democratic solution. After the failure back in the summer of both the extension of the 36°30' line and the Clayton formula, few in Congress felt either could become a legislative success, despite Polk's hopes. The territorial issue was simply

14. James D. Richardson (comp.), *A Compilation of the Messages and Papers of the Presidents, 1789–1897* (10 vols.; Washington, D.C., 1896–99), IV, 633–43 (quotations on 639–40).
15. *Ibid.*, 641–42.

too explosive. Minds were set, and the realities of politics in both North and South made practically impossible the legislative give-and-take required to turn either approach into acceptable legislation. President Polk saw only one aspect of the territorial issue when he described it as "a mere political question on which demagogues and ambitious politicians hope to promote their own prospects for political promotion." But he was surely right when he condemned them for "disturbing the harmony if not dissolving the Union itself." The issue simultaneously excited and paralyzed. Realistically, there was no chance for a true territorial compromise.[16]

Polk's wishes seemed doomed, but a young Democratic senator from Illinois was determined to prevail. Thirty-five-year-old Stephen A. Douglas was just emerging as a major Democratic and national figure, a position he would occupy for the next dozen years. Convinced that territorial expansion was necessary for national greatness, and especially that the immediate organization of California was essential, Douglas strove to find some legislative path that the country and the Congress could safely follow through the political minefield created by the Wilmot Proviso. On the first day of the session he indicated his strategy—the prompt admission of California as a state. Then on December 11 he staked out his path. Acknowledging the political impossibility of territorial action, Douglas declared it unnecessary. Taking another tack entirely, he presented a bill that would bring in all of the Mexican Cession as one state, California. Because California was so huge, Douglas' bill reserved for Congress the right to create later additional states from the area that lay east of the Sierra Nevada. Douglas argued that passage of his bill would simultaneously guarantee American control of the cession, meet the critical need for governmental organization in California, and destroy the proviso as a dangerous political issue. His was a bold initiative, and absolutely unprecedented.[17]

Douglas' new thrust did not generate an overwhelmingly positive response. Even among fellow Democrats doubt was widespread,

16. Milo Milton Quaife (ed.), *The Diary of James K. Polk During His Presidency, 1845–1849* (4 vols.; Chicago, 1910), IV, 251.

17. *CG*, 1, 21. For a full account of Douglas' activities, see Robert W. Johannsen, *Stephen A. Douglas* (New York, 1973), 241–48.

and outright opposition was present. Some argued that such a giant state as Douglas' California would be impossible to govern. Others asserted that Mexicans living in the cession were unfit to become immediate members of the American congregation; they needed a period of tutelage, not provided for in Douglas' plan. Then, certain senators raised procedural points over the proper committee to consider the bill. Douglas wanted it assigned to his own Committee on the Territories, which was dominated by friendly colleagues. Several southerners insisted that the bill be referred to the Committee on the Judiciary, chaired by Andrew P. Butler of South Carolina and unfriendly to Douglas' plan. These senators argued that statehood bills had always been sent to Judiciary. Douglas replied that policy had been followed only because no Committee on the Territories had existed; it was relatively new. This contest involved both policy and rules. And Douglas failed. By a margin of one, the Senate sent his California bill to Judiciary. The vote was sectional, not partisan. Every senator voting in favor of Judiciary was from a slave state while all but one for Territories were from free states.[18]

This lack of enthusiasm was symptomatic of the major negative reaction among Democrats. Butler was a disciple as well as a colleague of the other senator from South Carolina, John C. Calhoun. And Calhoun opposed Douglas' statehood scheme. Calhoun and his followers blasted the plan as the Wilmot Proviso under another rubric. "The object [of immediate statehood]," they declared, "is manifestly to exclude slavery" just as surely as Wilmot's proviso would have. As the Calhounites interpreted the issue, "it is a matter of little importance . . . practically, how we are deprived of the common conquest and purchase." They vehemently denounced Douglas' initiative as "a sneaking, crawling expedient, to surrender every thing to the North."[19]

This attack prefaced Calhoun's major initiative during the ses-

18.   *CG*, 37, 46–49; Dallas Diary, December 18, 1848, in Nichols, "The Mystery of the Dallas Papers," 487.
19.   *CG*, 49; Louis T. Wigfall to John C. Calhoun, January 4, 1849, in Chauncey S. Boucher and Robert P. Brooks (eds.), *Correspondence Addressed to John C. Calhoun, 1837–1849* (Washington, D.C., 1930), 494; Charleston *Mercury* quoted in *Niles' National Register*, LXXV (February 28, 1849), 139.

sion. Calhoun sensed that the genuine rage southerners felt about the proviso could provide the foundation on which he could build the southern unity he had cherished for so long. Among southerners in Congress that rage deepened when on December 21 the House passed New Yorker Benjamin Gott's resolution instructing the House Committee for the District of Columbia to report a bill outlawing the slave trade in the District. On the very next evening some eighteen senators and fifty-one congressmen representing both parties and every slave state but Delaware met in the Senate chamber. To Calhoun this conclave offered the opportunity he so wanted and believed essential for southern unity. He planned a published address specifying southern grievances and calling for a southern convention, which would present the southern position—perhaps even an ultimatum—to the North.[20]

At this dramatic moment Calhoun recognized that his success depended upon nonpartisan support. He had to bring both Whigs and Democrats to his banner. His personal strength among southern Democrats and the close ties many of his lieutenants maintained with the party prompted substantial Democratic backing. In fact, when Calhoun's Southern Address was formally adopted in January, 1849, the signers included every southern Democratic senator except the two Texans and more than two-thirds of the southern Democratic congressmen, an impressive achievement indeed. The southern Democrats who failed to participate were notable in their solitude.[21]

Calhoun also united the southern Whigs but not quite as he had hoped. Southern Whigs shared the distress of Calhoun and the southern Democrats over the militant antisouthern stance taken by numerous northerners, many in their own party. But at the same time they perceived Calhoun's move as a threat to the bright political future they envisaged with Zachary Taylor. From the southern Whig vantage point, the Calhoun–southern Democratic combine was attempting to undo the Whig presidential victory. That alliance, as the prominent Georgia Whig congressman Robert Toombs put it, had mounted "a

20. *CG*, 83–84. For Calhoun's movement, see Cooper, *The South and the Politics of Slavery*, 269–70, 287–88; and Charles M. Wiltse, *John C. Calhoun: Sectionalist, 1840–1850* (Indianapolis, 1951), 378–88.
21. These totals exclude the border states.

bold stroke to disorganize the Southern Whigs and either destroy Genl. Taylor in advance or compel him to throw himself in the hands of a large section of the democracy of the South."[22]

Determined to prevent what they saw as a poorly disguised campaign to sabotage their actual and potential success, southern Whigs torpedoed Calhoun's hopes for unity. Initially many attended the southern caucus, and some actively participated. The southern Whigs, however, were not there to help the caucus but "to control and crush it." And with various techniques they succeeded. Despite vigorous attempts to attract the Whigs, Calhoun failed. His long-cherished unity went aglimmering. A saddened Calhoun wrote that "the [southern] Whigs . . . are opposed to any activity; they rely on General Taylor."[23]

Calhoun's failure had not been for want of trying. He strove to woo the southern Whigs. "We have done all we could do here to unite the South," he informed a South Carolina friend. Even so, Calhoun "found it impossible to draw in the supporters of Genl. Taylor beyond a very limited extent." "I conversed freely with them," Calhoun reported, "and gave every assurance that our object was to support [Taylor], if he would support the South, by rallying with his supporters and uniting the whole South in support of him and his administration." "But," as Calhoun lamented, "it all proved in vain."[24]

Rejoicing over Calhoun's failure, the southern Whigs congratulated themselves on their political prowess and lauded their hero, Zachary Taylor. Their faith was in the future, not the present. They "did not expect an administration which [they] had brought into power would do any act or permit any act to be done which it would become necessary for our safety to rebel at." Because of Taylor, southern Whigs feared neither the antislavery North in general nor the internal Whig conflict over sectional issues in particular. The dimin-

22.   Robert Toombs to John J. Crittenden, January 3, 1849, in Ulrich B. Phillips (ed.), *The Correspondence of Robert Toombs, Alexander H. Stephens and Howell Cobb* (Washington, D.C., 1913), 139. Also see Alexander Stephens to [unknown], December 27, 1848, in Alexander Stephens Papers, Library of Congress.

23.   Toombs to Crittenden, January 3, 1849, in Phillips (ed.), *Correspondence*, 139; John C. Calhoun to James Edward Calhoun, January 17, 1849, in John C. Calhoun Papers, William R. Perkins Library, Duke University, Durham.

24.   John C. Calhoun to Henry W. Conner, February 2, 1849, in Henry W. Conner Papers, South Carolina Historical Society, Charleston.

utive, forceful Alexander Stephens captured this mood exactly—we "feel *secure* under General Taylor."[25]

Although supremely confident, indeed overconfident, about Taylor, the southern Whigs were under no delusion about their northern comrades. Many believed with a North Carolina congressman that the northerners had "a fixed determination" on the territorial issue as well as other slavery-related matters. After all, the spark that led to the specific timing of the southern caucus was lit by a northern Whig, Benjamin Gott of New York. Northern Whigs voted overwhelmingly for Gott's resolution, an action that helped prompt southern Whigs to join the southern caucus. By moving toward Calhoun, the southern Whigs had more in mind than influencing the outcome of the caucus; they also wanted to use that affiliation to press northern Whigs to pull back on Gott's resolution. They succeeded on the latter front as well as on the former. Only six days after passing the resolution, the House refused to lay on the table a motion to reconsider. Although the vote on December 27 did not specifically defeat Gott's resolution, it did block any positive action. This effective revocation of the resolution angered certain northern Whigs who criticized their comrades for supporting reconsideration. Even among those who stood by Gott some believed that northern Whigs "[were] not acting wisely on the slavery question." Men like Nathan K. Hall of New York felt that too often northern Whigs were "improperly & unnecessarily offensive" to the southerners.[26]

That attitude along with the reversal on Gott's resolution prompted one important southern Whig to think that the party could find unity on slavery. Robert Toombs believed that his northern comrades "[would] come up to safe ground." As he viewed intraparty relations, "the temper of the North is good & . . . I think we can work out of present troubles, preserve the Union & disappoint bad men &

25. Robert Toombs to John J. Crittenden, January 22, 1849, in Phillips (ed.), *Correspondence*, 141; Alexander Stephens to John J. Crittenden, January 17, 1849, in Alexander Stephens Papers, Perkins Library, Duke University.

26. David Outlaw to Emily Outlaw, December 14, 1848, in David Outlaw Papers, Southern Historical Collection, University of North Carolina, Chapel Hill; *CG*, 83–84, 105, 216; New York *Tribune*, January 7, 1849; Nathan K. Hall to Millard Fillmore, December 30, 1848, in Millard Fillmore Papers, State University of New York, Oswego.

traitors." Referring to what he called "these legacies of Polk's administration," Toombs foresaw "nothing desperate in settling [them] . . . unless we have treason in our ranks."[27]

Toombs's optimism augured well for the party and for the country, if he and his colleagues could turn it into reality. That would not be easy. Just as the southern Whigs would not and could not accept the Wilmot Proviso, many northern Whigs had adopted it as their issue. Early in the session an important Cincinnati editor urged Indiana Congressman Caleb B. Smith "to push it to an issue at once." Thomas B. Stevenson wanted the proviso forced in the House even if it was destined to fail in the Senate or to be vetoed by Polk. Should failure or veto occur, Stevenson was sure "it will raise such a storm in the north that it *must* go hereafter and add to the inducements to Taylor and the South to acquiesce in the bill in the following session." A close congressional friend of the vice-president elect Millard Fillmore told his fellow New Yorker that Taylor and the southern Whigs must "submit to the prohibition of slavery in the territories [or] his administration will be in a minority in Congress & with the people." And the zealous pro-proviso northerners who inclined toward the Free-Soil party wanted nothing more than "to arouse public sentiment at the North" behind the proviso.[28]

If an open battle took place over the proviso, the Gott reconsideration would evaporate in the heat of vicious intraparty fighting. Many southerners tried to assure their northern comrades that they did not demand or expect slavery to migrate to the cession, though certain northerners still feared "a plot" to plant slavery in the new lands. A key southern Whig editor told Fillmore that "not the first slave will go there, if no such proviso or restriction is enacted." The proviso, he went on, "is needless as a practical matter and will certainly place the Southern Whigs in a hopeless minority." Daniel Lee's prescription was: "Let the Northern Whigs evince their good sense by forbearance on so excitable a topic and all will be peace, harmony, and continued success." Congressional southerners echoed the sentiment that slav-

---

27. Toombs to Crittenden, January 3, 1849, in Phillips (ed.), *Correspondence*, 140.
28. Thomas B. Stevenson to Caleb B. Smith, December 12, 1848, in Caleb B. Smith Papers, Library of Congress; N. K. Hall to Millard Fillmore, January 8, 1849, in Fillmore Papers; John G. Palfrey to Charles Francis Adams, December 7, 1848, in Adams Family Papers.

ery could never flourish in the cession. Do not wreck the fortunes of the party on the abstraction of the proviso, they implored their northern colleagues. "Why in the name of common sense," asked the Louisville *Daily Journal*, "do [northern Whigs] insist upon the actual Congressional prohibition of slavery?" According to the *Journal*, the South was "willing" to let the territories "follow their destiny," but southerners would never consent to the congressional violation of their rights by the enactment of the proviso.[29]

It seemed, then, to many perceptive, moderate Whigs that room did exist for party rapprochement on the crucial territorial issue. Experienced politicians such as Crittenden and Clayton believed that agreement on the territorial question was not only opportune but essential. They feared that the longer the delay in settlement the greater the likelihood that the issue would tear apart the Whig party. They, along with others, concluded that a solution ought to be found before Taylor's inauguration on March 4, 1849. To postpone or to avoid or to neglect dealing with the territories would leave a potentially dangerous threat to the success of the Taylor administration and, thus, to the well-being of the Whig party.

These Whigs moved directly. Although the evidence does not permit a precise charting of the course they followed, it is clear where they landed—Douglas' California bill. Before the end of 1848 the Richmond *Whig* found Douglas' statehood bill the best chance to provide "equality and justice to all the States." Even those who really cared little for Douglas' proposal thought it had to be carefully considered, given the serious difficulties presented by expansion and slavery. As early as December 13, Senator Clayton had assured Crittenden that "Taylor shall have no trouble with [the proviso]." Clayton was confident that "we will saw round that knot." Acknowledging the failure of his own compromise proposal back in the summer, Clayton insisted, "But now I have another project which I think will succeed." Douglas' specific bill Clayton called "a failure," but, he went on, "if any chance should offer, we will use it to settle the matter at once." By the words "any chance" Clayton obviously meant the fashioning of a Whig agreement. By marking his letter "confidential"

29. Palfrey to Adams, December 7, 1848, in Adams Family Papers; Daniel Lee to Millard Fillmore, January 25, 1849, in Fillmore Papers; *CG*, Appendix, 223; Louisville *Daily Journal*, January 18, 1849.

and by telling Crittenden that he would not use his franking privilege because he feared the envelope might be opened, Clayton underscored the delicacy of his position and the fragility of his hopes. Crittenden himself believed that co-opting Douglas' approach would bring to the Whig party and to the country "certain success."[30]

With Whig unity, a reasonable hope for success did exist. Whigs controlled the House by a narrow margin, 117 to 111. But that majority had a gross sectional imbalance; there were twice as many northerners as southerners. Clearly, the party rapprochement that Toombs described was critically important. The Democrats enjoyed considerably more sectional balance; free-state men outnumbered their slave-state colleagues by only 5. In the Senate the Democrats dominated, 36 to 22.[31] In Democratic ranks the southerners edged out northerners while the Whigs broke evenly along sectional lines. If the Whigs could forge any kind of unity and attract Democratic support, there was indeed an opportunity for the Clayton-Crittenden approach to succeed. Success, however, would require Democratic backing, which did not at all appear impossible.

Douglas' bill certainly had not died. The energetic Illinois senator never slackened in his determination to push it to a vote. And during December, President Polk made a slightly different version of Douglas' original bill an administration measure. After repeated conversations with Douglas, his cabinet, and other influential senators, Polk decided the statehood plan was the safest way around the proviso and the surest way to organize the Mexican Cession before he left the presidency. The cabinet, however, believed that the entire cession was simply too large for one state. As a result, Polk urged Douglas to alter his bill so that it called for two states—California, and the land east of the Sierra Nevada organized as New Mexico. After some thought, Douglas agreed to modify his bill.[32]

30.   Richmond *Whig*, December 22, 1848; Louisville *Daily Journal*, December 21, 1848; Clayton to Crittenden, December 13, 1848, in Crittenden Papers; Crittenden to Clayton, January 7, 1849, in Clayton Papers.

31.   These totals include two Democratic senators from Iowa who took their seats in late December and one Democratic congressman from South Carolina who did not arrive in the House until early February.

32.   Quaife (ed.), *Polk Diary*, IV, 231, 233, 235, 236–37, 238, 254–55, 257–58, 279, 286–87, 293, 299–300, 302–303, 312–13, 316; Johannsen, *Stephen A. Douglas*, 244–45.

This new plan became Douglas' proposal as well as the administration's way around the noxious Wilmot Proviso. And Polk put all of his effort and authority behind it. In his mind it took on the character of a compromise solution in the manner of both the Missouri extension and the Clayton bill. No one pushed harder for passage than Thomas Ritchie, editor of the administration's newspaper voice, the Washington *Union*. A major Virginia Democratic leader who had edited the Richmond *Enquirer* for four decades before going to Washington to take charge of the *Union*, Ritchie focused considerable attention on the southern Whigs. Warning that Zachary Taylor would not protect them from the Wilmot Proviso, Ritchie urged the southern Whigs to work with their Democratic counterparts to eliminate forever the threat of the proviso. He told them that Taylor's friends in the House had the power to settle the cession issue. He challenged them to meet "the great duty which now calls upon [you] to act in behalf of the South, or rather in behalf of the Union." And he assured them that the Democrats stood ready to cooperate in the critically important cause of southern safety and national unity. Ritchie argued that the strength of proviso sentiment in the Congress made the statehood alternative "all that is left." He warned southern Whigs that if they refused to support statehood and brought on the proviso, "how *then* can [you] excuse [yourselves] to [your] indignant constituents?" No idle threat this—in southern politics accusations that a party failed to guard zealously southern rights could easily mean political disaster.[33]

The advocacy of Douglas, Polk, and Ritchie had two crucial meanings for southern Whigs. First, it indicated that the votes might be there to pass some kind of statehood plan, if the southern Whigs could unite behind it. Second, general support among southern Democrats would provide assurance that the statehood solution would not end up haunting the Whigs. The southern Democrats could never attack them for giving away the possibility of slavery in the cession. Both parties would have joined forces behind a measure that everyone knew would preclude the introduction of slavery. No one doubted that California would enter the Union as a free state. Calhoun and his loyalists would surely cry foul, but with the Whigs and Democrats marching arm in arm, the Calhounites would cry in vain.

33. Washington *Daily Union*, December 9, 10, 1848, January 16 (quotation), 21, 28, February 4, 8 (quotation), 15, 1849.

For both southern Whigs and southern Democrats, immediate statehood also guaranteed that southern honor could escape the territorial tangle unscathed. Everyone agreed that a state could make its own decision on slavery. Thus, southern rights would not be threatened or disregarded should California and possibly New Mexico request admission to the Union as free states. Southern rights, which ultimately meant southern honor, only became involved with proposals to shut slavery out of the common national possessions, the territories. That potential outcome, of course the goal of the Wilmot Proviso, the South could not and would not accept. Southerners saw the proviso as an assault on their Americanism and an insult to their honor.

The Whigs behind the Clayton-Crittenden strategy went on the offensive in the House. Their majority made this move logical. Besides, despite Douglas' energy and determination, his bill was still bottled up in the Senate. William B. Preston took the lead, introduced the bill, and made the key speech. A forty-three-year-old Virginian, Preston was serving his first term in Congress. He was neither a major force in the Whig party nor even a widely known southern Whig. Although the evidence is unclear on why Preston took or was assigned his primary role, his specific proposal was too close to the designs of Clayton and Crittenden for mere coincidence. Clearly he represented the border and moderate southern Whigs who wanted to solve the territorial issue with statehood prior to Taylor's inauguration. Preston's bill harked back to Douglas' original proposal; it would bring in all of the cession as one state, California.[34]

There are several possible reasons for the choice of Preston. From early in the talk of presidential candidates, he had been a vigorous Taylor man. Using Preston could easily imply that the president-elect himself favored the statehood approach, which might bring in some wavering Whigs. Nothing concrete indicates precisely where Taylor stood in early February, though he did adopt a variation of the statehood approach when he became president. Then, Preston hailed from Virginia, not a border slave state, but also not a deep southern state. An appeal from a reasonable Upper South man might entice

---

34. *CG*, 477; Toombs to Crittenden, January 22, 1849, in Phillips (ed.), *Correspondence*, 141. Toombs indicated that Preston would "move," but he gave no indication of why Preston was chosen.

some moderate northerners and could undoubtedly be·counted upon to attract substantial votes from the lower slave states, Whigs for sure and possibly even some Democrats.

William B. Preston addressed his fellow representatives on February 7.[35] In his speech Preston made a valiant and largely successful effort to omit nothing pertinent. He announced that he intended to propose a remedy for "the great question of the age." He would shun discussing "the merits or demerits of our peculiar system in the South, or the merits of those principles which gentlemen of the North propose to lead in by Congressional legislation here upon us." He maintained that he advocated solution, not argument. Acknowledging that others had pursued a similar goal, he noted Douglas' bill. With his praise for Douglas as "very patriotic and determined," Preston angled for Democratic support. Time and time again through the long speech he stressed the nonpartisanship of his bill, and he called for help from "the good men and the calm men and the wise men of all parties." He defined his proposal as "a bill under which neither party is victorious, and neither party overcomes." He described his purpose as embracing the "spirit of republicanism, [which] is but the spirit of the Revolution." Asserting that Washington was no closer to California than England was to the colonies, he called on Congress to uphold the sacred American tradition of letting the people govern themselves. For Preston that was the supreme principle, not the presence or absence of the institution of slavery.

In Preston's depiction this loyalty to the greatest American virtue would spare the country "perpetual agitation" over the territorial issue. He argued that his bill was "*no compromise at all.*" Possible compromises, like extending the Missouri line, Preston asserted, only guaranteed future battles. Those contests would occur, he predicted, each time a new state carved from the cession asked for admission to the Union. Thus in his scenario the sectional dispute took on a quality of endlessness, precisely what Preston wanted to preclude. "I want the question ended," he announced. In his mind his bill would provide just that. Echoing the call of many moderate Whigs, certainly those troubled by events since 1844, Preston cried out, "I want repose." And as he put it, "*The bill now offered gives finality to the question.*"

35. For Preston's speech, see *CG,* 477–80.

Preston also turned his attention to zealous supporters of the proviso, many of whom claimed allegiance to the Whig party. In an attempt to win their support or at least quiet their opposition to his statehood proposal, Preston repeated the moderate southern Whig refrain that slavery would never flourish in the cession or in his new state. According to Preston, the forces of nature decreed against the success of slavery. That reality, Preston insisted, made pressing for the Wilmot Proviso at best unnecessary and at worst dangerous. The result, freedom in the cession, would come from either approach. Why, then, he questioned the provisoists, demand something so bitterly and deeply opposed by the South when the goal could be achieved without such animosity?

But Preston hurried to declare that his legislative initiative in no way violated the honor of the South. Emphasizing the "great, abiding, solemn question of honor that every southern man, who does not stand up to, is recreant to himself and forgetful of his ancestors," Preston thundered, "Now, I yield to no man on these points." To Virginia, with "my eyes full upon her," and to his fellow southern congressmen he declaimed, "I do not, as a southern man, surrender anything to [the North]." Because southerners as well as northerners agreed that a state had the authority, in fact it rested nowhere else, to decide about slavery for itself, Preston did not believe there could be any possibility of blemished honor or bartered rights.

In conclusion Preston invoked the good sense and patriotism of all Americans. Calling his proposal "the only door" through which the new territories could safely be incorporated into the Union, he urged his listeners to think solely about the benefits of its passage—benefits that, he assured the House, could be gained in no other way. He reiterated this claim along with all that went before in a florid peroration: "Recognize this principle—adopt the remedy imbodied [*sic*] in this bill, and it will come over this House and over this nation like the sweet breath of spring to the chamber of disease—healing, strengthening, renovating all of us, so that we shall take up our beds, like the man of old, and run the great and glorious republican course which lays so full before us."

In the immediate aftermath of Preston's impassioned oratory the inner circle of planners expressed pleasure and optimism. Toombs informed Crittenden that Preston's speech "was a very good one and its effect happy." Reprinted in a national periodical such as *Niles' National Register*, the speech itself was carried far beyond Capitol Hill. An inveterate optimist on the party-sectional issue throughout the session, Toombs pronounced "the question for all practical purposes as now settled." He reached that conclusion even though he knew that both the Calhounites and the antislavery extremists were dead set against Preston's proposition. He also noted that New York and New England Whigs wanted to hold off passing Preston's bill until the Thirty-first Congress. In Toombs's interpretation that hesitancy was politically, not ideologically, motivated. "Their object," he reported, "is unmistakably to make themselves necessary to the [Taylor] adm. in carrying it, and demanding terms for their service." Despite that possible barrier Toombs exuded confidence: "We shall bring them in I think, but if not we can carry it without them."[36]

Toombs had good reason for his buoyant mood. In Preston's native state his effort brought forth lavish praise. Calling his plan the proper solution and printing the speech, the Richmond *Whig* congratulated Preston for proposing a measure which "compromises neither the honor nor the interests of any portion of the confederacy." According to the *Whig*, it would "restore tranquility to the country and peace to the national councils." Both Democrats and Whigs cheered Preston. To one senior Virginia Whig, former United States senator William C. Rives, Preston's performance "look[ed] like the revival of the glories of our earlier history, when the statesmen and the patriots of Virginia were also the statesmen and patriots of the Union." Governor John B. Floyd, a Democrat, added his accolades. In Congress, Preston's Democratic colleague James McDowell called the statehood plan one "of mediation and peace." In McDowell's mind, all other considerations paled beside "what [statehood] may fairly hope to accomplish—the pacification and perpetual union of more than twenty million of freemen!"[37]

In the House, McDowell's was not an isolated response. Border-state Whigs were emphatic in their support. Preston's bill called for

36. Robert Toombs to John J. Crittenden, February 9, 1849, in Phillips (ed.), *Correspondence*, 147; *Niles' National Register*, LXXV (February 28, 1849), 133–37.
37. Richmond *Whig*, February 13, 16, 1849; William C. Rives to William B. Preston, February 13, 1849, and John B. Floyd to Preston, February 19, 1849, both in William B. Preston Papers, Virginia Historical Society, Richmond; *CG*, Appendix, 213.

an unusual state, a Marylander admitted, but critical times overrode conventional thinking. Alabama Whig Henry W. Hilliard insisted that statehood would preserve southern honor. He underscored his loyalty to the Union and to the South: "I will cling to both." Preston's effort even gained congratulations and tentative support from Deep South Democrats. Albert G. Brown of Mississippi viewed statehood as a possible way to preserve the "harmony and peace of the Union." He would consider voting for it, provided he saw northern backing. He was ready, he told the House, but "I want to know whether our opponents [the provisoists] are ready to meet us in a corresponding spirit." Certainly the House allies of Stephen A. Douglas were, but, then, they had never been vigorous crusaders for the proviso. Ominously, this chorus of enthusiastic or, even, qualified support for Preston's bill included no northern Whigs.[38]

Not everyone liked Preston's bill. Some Democrats, North and South, saw grave difficulties in it, though from dramatically opposite perspectives. A close observer of Georgia politics wrote to his state's most prominent Democratic congressman, Howell Cobb, that the statehood idea simply "[would] not suit the present state of the public mind in the South." In his view both Douglas' and Preston's bills "[were] founded upon a mere quibble." To accept either would be "a fatal indication" of southern weakness. To North Carolina Congressman Abraham Venable, Preston's bill gave away too much: "To vote for this bill is to seal forever the question against the South." In opposition certain northern Democrats pictured statehood as a ruse for "the safe introduction of slavery into the free states." A congressman from Douglas' Illinois condemned his colleagues for supporting statehood "for the purpose of avoiding this vexed question of slavery." He wanted to meet it head on, "boldly and fearlessly."[39]

Although Preston did not persuade all Democrats, the most vigorous opposition arose within his own party, among his northern colleagues. Congressman Horace Greeley of New York denounced Preston's proposal as "contrived" to deliver the cession to slavery. As such, Greeley announced he would oppose it to the utmost. His newspaper, the popular and widely read New York *Tribune*, rarely missed

38. *CG*, Appendix, 106–107 (quotation), 120–21 (quotation), 157, 220–21, 241, 247.
39. Hopkins Holsey to Howell Cobb, February 13, 24, 1849, both in Phillips (ed.), *Correspondence*, 148–55 (quotation on 154); *CG*, Appendix, 101, 162, 220.

an opportunity to excoriate anything or anybody opposed to free soil. Thurlow Weed's Albany *Evening Journal* wanted the proviso attached to any California bill. Condemning slavery as "insidious," the *Evening Journal* declared, "Better that the whole of government should be stopped—better re-cede the Territories acquired, or permit them to be formed in an independent Republic—than that the majority in the popular branch of our National legislature should again succumb to the chicanery or threats of the South." John Gorham Palfrey of Massachusetts thought the entire statehood scheme "a plot" to slip slavery into the cession, but he felt sure that Preston's bill could get nowhere in the House "as a distinct proposition."[40]

Events on the Senate side of the Capitol certainly gave credence to Palfrey's opinion. To no avail Douglas had tried through January and into February to get his revised California bill brought to a vote. Then on February 20, John Bell, a Whig from Tennessee, attempted to push California statehood before the Senate. He, like Preston, emphasized the disastrous potential of the proviso, of the unending battle over slavery in the territories. He asserted that Congress must make an "irrevocable" decision, statehood, in order to "close up this breach forever." "Cut off the head of the hydra," Bell pleaded. Despite the similarity to Preston's approach, not a shred of evidence even suggests that Bell was the Senate spearhead of a two-front Whig advance on California. The outcome of Bell's effort also implies that he acted on his own. When the Senate on February 21 buried his proposal by 39 to 4, Bell was the lone Whig voting aye. None of his southern Whig colleagues joined him. He was supported only by Douglas, ever willing to back any statehood initiative, along with two of his Democratic friends, a northerner and a southerner. Of the other slave-state Whig senators, 5 voted with the majority and 5, including Clayton, did not vote. Although Bell's location in the Crittenden-Clayton design cannot be pinpointed, the Senate decision did not augur well for Preston, who was awaiting House action on his bill.[41]

In the House the northern antagonism toward any substitute for

40. *CG*, Appendix, 248; New York *Tribune*, January-February, 1849, *passim*; Albany *Evening Journal*, February 23, March 2, 1849; John G. Palfrey to Charles Francis Adams, December 7, 1848, and February 18, 1849, both in Adams Family Papers.
41. *CG*, 340–41, 435, 552, 553, 562–66, 573; Washington *National Intelligencer*, February 21, 1849 (quotation).

the proviso had a tangible impact. On February 27 the House resolved itself into the Committee of the Whole to consider California.
Congressman Preston moved the adoption of his bill, technically a
substitute for a territorial bill. George Ashmun, Massachusetts Whig,
and William Collins, New York Democrat, proposed amendments.
Collins' specifically added the Wilmot Proviso to the bill; the Collins
amendment forbade slavery in the proposed state of California. Preston had anticipated the possibility of a proviso-type amendment.
During his major speech he argued that his bill precluded the proviso
because Congress could not dictate to a state. Evidently the members
felt that all had been said that needed saying because no debate followed the introduction of Collins' amendment. Immediately tellers
were appointed, and the question was called—91 congressmen voted
for the amendment; 87 voted no. The Wilmot Proviso now adorned
the proposal that was designed to avoid it. And the adoption of the
Collins amendment killed the Preston bill. In the vote on the bill with
the proviso attached, not a single aye vote was cast. With no ayes reported, the noes were not even counted. The Preston bill was dead.[42]

Exactly who would have voted for the pristine Preston bill, the
bill without the proviso, is impossible to ascertain. A vote on it never
occurred. Whether or not Toombs had carefully counted votes or exaggerated wildly, we will probably never know, though the second
possibility seems likely. It is even impossible to be precise about either the sectional or the partisan division on Collins' amendment.
Neither the *Congressional Globe* nor the *House Journal* provides a
roll call for the 91 to 87 tally. It is a reasonable assumption, however,
that almost every southerner voting was in the minority, for later on
the same day 87 congressmen, including every slave-state representative voting but two Kentuckians, opposed unsuccessfully a California territorial bill with the proviso included. And without question
the 91 congressmen favoring the Collins amendment included both
Democrats and Whigs, though possibly more northern Democrats
than Whigs did not cast a ballot. That surmise rests on the support
initially provided to Preston by certain northern Democrats.[43]

The shutting of Preston's "door" ended any possibility of solving
the territorial problem during the Thirtieth Congress. Provisoists re-

---

42. *CG*, 607–608.
43. *Ibid.*, 609. Nor did any of the newspapers I consulted have a roll call.

joiced over Preston's failure, but they kept up their guard lest some legislative trick be played against free soil at the very end of the session. An attempt was made to permit President Polk to appoint territorial officials without formal organization, but it went nowhere.[44]

In the South the voice of opposition to Preston's statehood strategy became louder and louder. Southern Democrats took the lead in denouncing immediate statehood as no more than the proviso by another name. Building through the late winter and spring, this attitude attracted widespread support. The result even affected the relentlessly sanguine Robert Toombs. Back in Georgia after Congress had adjourned, Toombs took stock of public opinion. He was surprised. In mid-May he informed his friend William Preston, by then a member of Zachary Taylor's cabinet, "It is an undeniable fact that the public feeling in the South is much stronger than many of us supposed. It is now my deliberate opinion," he went on, "that the passage of the Wilmot Proviso would lead to civil war." Toombs said he did not base his somber conclusion on excitement or emotion but on "something infinitely more dangerous, a settled[,] resolute determination in all classes not to submit to it." According to Toombs, the admission of California as a state would be accepted only "with bitterness of feeling & without cordiality, if slavery was in turn excluded."[45]

The increasing southern Democratic campaign against statehood made it more and more unlikely that statehood could remain a viable political platform in the South. Responding to the southern Democratic cry and to the unyielding northern Whig stance, southern Whigs backed away from statehood. By the autumn of 1849 a meaningful southern constituency for statehood had disappeared. When President Taylor in December proposed his version of statehood to the Thirty-first Congress, he found practically no support among southern Whigs for a plan most had been willing to accept ten months earlier. Taylor's insistence led to a fundamental break between him and those who had so lauded and counted upon him. Vigorous animosity replaced enthusiastic friendship.[46]

---

44. *Ibid.*, 561–62, 573–74, 664–65, 666, 668, 682–91; New York *Tribune*, February 28, March 1, 1849; John G. Palfrey to Charles Francis Adams, March 2, 1849, in Adams Family Papers; Francis P. Blair to Martin Van Buren, March 5, 1849, in Van Buren Papers.
45. Robert Toombs to William B. Preston, May 18, 1849, in Preston Papers.
46. Cooper, *The South and the Politics of Slavery*, 275–76, 283–87.

Preston was right. His plan provided "the only door" through which the territorial problem could be solved; statehood would have eliminated the proviso as a political issue. The ungainly size of Preston's California would have undoubtedly led to future questions, but they would not have possessed the emotional and political force of the proviso. And politicians could probably more easily have dealt with them. The supporters of Preston's bill saw a moment of political opportunity and tried to capitalize on it. They failed. They were unable to withstand the force of the territorial issue, which the Compromise of 1850 would check only briefly. The issue became more and more furious until it could be neither managed nor put off. Cataclysm resulted.

American Historians and Antebellum Southern Slavery
1959–1984

Peter Kolchin

Twenty-five years ago, Stanley M. Elkins published a short book that helped revolutionize the study of antebellum southern slavery. In *Slavery: A Problem in American Institutional and Intellectual Life*, Elkins presented two distinct but interrelated theses that quickly elicited historical debate. Although neither of them has survived close scrutiny, both were instrumental in redirecting the focus of studies on slavery and in reshaping our understanding of the "peculiar institution."[1]

Most immediately controversial was the "Sambo thesis," in which Elkins offered a sweeping reinterpretation of the slave personality. Antebellum slavery, he argued, was such a brutal, "closed" institution that it transformed its victims into docile, childlike "Sambos." Torn from their African homeland, stripped of their native culture, deposited in an alien society that regarded them as little more than animals, deprived of any meaningful cultural life of their own, southern slaves came to identify with the only "significant other" they had—their masters. Because the master's authority and influence over his slaves were total, the individual slave, "for his very psychic security, had to picture his master in some way as the 'good father'"; southern slavery created a dependent population of depersonalized "Sambos."[2]

Less noted at first, although in the long run equally thought-provoking and significant, was Elkins' second thesis. Sambo's habitat, he argued, was solely the southern United States. Strongly influenced by

1.   Stanley M. Elkins, *Slavery: A Problem in American Institutional and Intellectual Life* (Chicago, 1959).
2.   *Ibid.*, 120, 128–29.

Frank Tannenbaum's suggestion that Latin American race relations were far more flexible than were North American, Elkins maintained that in Spanish and Portuguese America the Church and Crown came between master and slave, acting to protect the sanctity of slave marriage and limiting the severity of slave treatment; in the individualistic United States, by contrast, where "the dynamics of unopposed capitalism" reigned supreme, nothing protected the slave from the master's arbitrary authority. As a consequence, slavery was far harsher in the capitalistic United States, he insisted, than in "quasi-medieval" Latin America.[3]

During the past twenty-five years, in part as a response to Elkins' theses and in part as a consequence of new interest in the lives of the obscure and oppressed, a vast outpouring of historical works has radically altered our understanding of antebellum slavery. Although all fields of history are subject to revision, few—perhaps none—have been the targets of such sweeping reinterpretation. This development justifies an effort to take stock, to assess where we have come, where we now stand, and where we might well venture in the future. Here I seek to provide this kind of assessment, outlining and evaluating the major trends in recent interpretations of antebellum slavery. I make no attempt to list all, or even most, works on the subject, a task that would require a far lengthier essay than this; rather, my aim is to analyze broad patterns of historical investigation, and to offer a critique of dominant interpretations in three separate but related areas of slavery studies.

The most prevalent single theme in recent work on antebellum slavery is an emphasis on slave culture and community. In the 1960s, historians increasingly stressed slaves' rebelliousness, participation in subtle forms of day-to-day resistance, and conscious use of role playing to get their own way. Although these themes were not entirely new, they received fresh emphasis as early critics of Elkins sought to rebut the notion of slave docility, and in the process found it necessary to focus on the slaves more as subjects in their own right than as objects of white treatment. The effort to test—and usually to repudi-

3.   *Ibid.*, 37, 67. See Frank Tannenbaum, *Slave and Citizen: The Negro in the Americas* (New York, 1946).

ate—the Sambo thesis thus brought the slaves themselves to center stage in the drama of slavery.[4]

This new focus came to full fruition during the 1970s as scholars produced an increasing number of works seeking to rediscover the slave experience. These scholars invariably found that exploring new questions required extensive use of previously little used black sources, which offered a perspective on slave life very different from the plantation records, diaries, and travel accounts that had provided the basis for traditional studies of slavery. Relying on slave autobiographies, interviews with former slaves, black folklore, and less often statistical data culled from census reports and plantation records, historians probed diverse areas of slave life, dissecting family patterns, religious beliefs, folklore, resistance, and communal behavior. The emerging picture of southern slavery was radically new and exciting.[5]

In the 1970s, leading revisionist authors differed widely in ideology, methodology, and approach to slavery. Eugene D. Genovese offered a Marxist view of the slaves' world, a view that strongly empha-

4. See, for example, the essays in three collections: Ann J. Lane (ed.), *The Debate over Slavery: Stanley Elkins and His Critics* (Urbana, 1971); John H. Bracey, Jr., August Meier, and Elliott Rudwick (eds.), *American Slavery: The Question of Resistance* (Belmont, Calif., 1971); and John Henrik Clarke (ed.), *William Styron's Nat Turner: Ten Black Writers Respond* (Boston, 1968); for a thoughtful evaluation of some of this literature, see Kenneth M. Stampp, "Rebels and Sambos: The Search for the Negro's Personality in Slavery," *Journal of Southern History*, XXXVII (1971), 367–92. For earlier emphases on slave resistance, see Raymond A. Bauer and Alice H. Bauer, "Day to Day Resistance to Slavery," *Journal of Negro History*, XXVII (1942), 388–419; Herbert Aptheker, *American Negro Slave Revolts* (New York, 1943); and a book that remains in many respects unsurpassed as an overall introduction to antebellum slavery, Kenneth M. Stampp, *The Peculiar Institution: Slavery in the Ante-Bellum South* (New York, 1956), esp. 86–140.

5. On the use of, and sometimes the problems associated with, these black sources, see C. Vann Woodward, "History from Slave Sources," *American Historical Review*, LXXIX (1974), 470–81; John W. Blassingame, "Using the Testimony of Ex-Slaves: Approaches and Problems," *Journal of Southern History*, XLI (1975), 473–92; George P. Rawick, "General Introduction," in Rawick (ed.), *The American Slave: A Composite Autobiography, Supplement Series 1* (12 vols.; Westport, Conn., 1977), I, ix–li; Paul D. Escott, *Slavery Remembered: A Record of Twentieth-Century Slave Narratives* (Chapel Hill, 1979), 3–17; David Thomas Bailey, "A Divided Prism: Two Sources of Black Testimony on Slavery," *Journal of Southern History*, XLVI (1980), 381–404; and Marion Wilson Starling, *The Slave Narrative: Its Place in American History* (Boston, 1981).

sized the centrality of religion to antebellum black life; whereas Robert W. Fogel and Stanley L. Engerman presented a two-volume econometric study in which they attempted through quantification to achieve a "scientific" evaluation of the slave experience. Herbert Gutman used plantation records to explore slaves' family relations, while Lawrence W. Levine studied folktales and music to probe blacks' social attitudes and aspirations. Among students of the slave community, John W. Blassingame, a black liberal, relied primarily on slave autobiographies, whereas George P. Rawick, a white radical, used the Federal Writers' Project interviews with former slaves.[6] Most of these scholars were also exceptionally critical of each others' work, deploring grave methodological errors and ideological shortcomings. Thus, Fogel and Engerman insisted that their scientific "findings" rendered obsolete the "traditional interpretation" put forth by virtually all previous historians of slavery; Gutman derided Fogel and Engerman's book as "old-fashioned" scholarship based on "an archaic historical model"; Genovese and Elizabeth Fox-Genovese, meanwhile, blasted Gutman as well as Fogel and Engerman—along with most other scholars—for subscribing to the same flawed "bourgeois" interpretation of history.[7] In short, historians appeared to be far from any general consensus concerning what slavery meant for the antebellum slave.

Nevertheless, a common thrust—emphasis on the independent lives of the slaves themselves—gave unity to much of the revisionist work of the 1970s. Some historians stressed slave religious behavior,

---

6. Eugene D. Genovese, *Roll, Jordan, Roll: The World the Slaves Made* (New York, 1974); Robert William Fogel and Stanley L. Engerman, *Time on the Cross: The Economics of American Negro Slavery* (2 vols.; Boston, 1974); Herbert G. Gutman, *The Black Family in Slavery and Freedom, 1750–1925* (New York, 1976); Lawrence W. Levine, *Black Culture and Black Consciousness: Afro-American Folk Thought from Slavery to Freedom* (New York, 1977), Chaps. 1–2; John W. Blassingame, *The Slave Community: Plantation Life in the Antebellum South* (1972; rev. and enl. ed., New York, 1979); George P. Rawick, *From Sundown to Sunup: The Making of the Black Community* (Westport, Conn., 1972).

7. Fogel and Engerman, *Time on the Cross*, esp. I, 3–12, and II, 168–248; Herbert G. Gutman, *Slavery and the Numbers Game: A Critique of Time on the Cross* (Urbana, 1975), 169, 165; Elizabeth Fox-Genovese and Eugene D. Genovese, *Fruits of Merchant Capital: Slavery and Bourgeois Property in the Rise and Expansion of Capitalism* (New York, 1983), 90–178.

seeing black Christianity, related to but in important respects distinct from the Christianity of southern whites, as the central, unifying feature of slave life.[8] Others showed that slaves' family ties were stronger than most historians had previously believed, and argued that the family was the principal purveyor of common values among slaves.[9] Still others focused on slave folklore,[10] slave resistance,[11] and the slave community as a whole.[12] But they shared a commitment to the argu-

8. Genovese, *Roll, Jordan, Roll*, 161–324; Milton C. Sernett, *Black Religion and American Evangelicalism: White Protestants, Plantation Missions, and the Flowering of Negro Christianity, 1787–1865* (Metuchen, N.J., 1975); Albert J. Raboteau, *Slave Religion: The "Invisible Institution" in the Antebellum South* (New York, 1978); Mechal Sobel, *Trabelin' On: The Slave Journey to an Afro-Baptist Faith* (Westport, Conn., 1979).

9. Gutman, *The Black Family*; see also Richard H. Steckel, "Slave Marriage and the Family," *Journal of Family History*, V (1980), 406–21; Cheryll Ann Cody, "Naming, Kinship, and Estate Dispersal: Notes on Slave Family Life on a South Carolina Plantation, 1786 to 1833," *William and Mary Quarterly*, 3rd ser., XXXIX (1982), 192–211; and John C. Inscoe, "Carolina Slave Names: An Index to Acculturation," *Journal of Southern History*, XLIX (1983), 527–55. But for a thoughtful critique of the dominant new approach to slave families, in which the author argues that slave women did not play the traditional female role as it was defined in nineteenth-century America, see Deborah G. White, "Female Slaves: Sex Roles and Status in the Antebellum Plantation South," *Journal of Family History*, VIII (1983), 248–61.

10. Levine, *Black Culture and Black Consciousness*, Chaps. 1–2; Sterling Stuckey, "Through the Prism of Folklore: The Black Ethos in Slavery," in Lane (ed.), *The Debate over Slavery*, 245–68; Dickson D. Bruce, Jr., "The 'John and Old Master' Stories and the World of Slavery: A Study in Folktales and History," *Phylon*, XXXV (1974), 418–29; Michael Flusche, "Joel Chandler Harris and the Folklore of Slavery," *Journal of American Studies*, IX (1975), 347–63; Dena J. Epstein, *Sinful Tunes and Spirituals: Black Folk Music to the Civil War* (Urbana, 1977).

11. Stephen B. Oates, *The Fires of Jubilee: Nat Turner's Fierce Rebellion* (New York, 1975); Vincent Harding, *There is a River: The Black Struggle for Freedom in America* (New York, 1981); Peter Kolchin, "The Process of Confrontation: Patterns of Resistance to Bondage in Nineteenth-Century Russia and the United States," *Journal of Social History*, XI (1978), 457–90; Michael P. Johnson, "Runaway Slaves and the Slave Communities in South Carolina, 1799–1830," *William and Mary Quarterly*, 3rd ser., XXXVIII (1981), 418–41.

12. Blassingame, *The Slave Community*; Rawick, *From Sundown to Sunup*; Leslie Howard Owens, *This Species of Property: Slave Life and Custom in the Old South* (New York, 1976); Escott, *Slavery Remembered*; Thomas L. Webber, *Deep Like the Rivers: Education in the Slave Quarter Community, 1831–1865* (New York, 1978); Charles Joyner, *Down by the Riverside: A South Carolina Slave Community* (Urbana, 1984).

ment that slaves were generally able in the quarters to develop their own culture far more than had been recognized, and to lead far more autonomous lives.

They also led, historians emphasized, far more varied lives. Not only did slave experiences differ on the basis of geography, economy, size of holding, and character of owner, but there was a broad range of slave occupations—from field hand to house servant, artisan, preacher, driver—on given holdings as well. Further, many slaves, through sale, hire, or plantation reorganization, experienced a wide variety of different "slaveries."[13] The consequence of this autonomy and diversity, almost all historians agreed, was to prevent the slaves' infantilization in the manner suggested by Elkins.

Indeed, although emphases differ from historian to historian, and although many of the details remain to be filled in, it is clear that a new orthodoxy has emerged among scholars of slavery. Southern slaves, they maintain, were by no means simply passive victims of white oppression. Although antebellum slavery was brutal, it was not a closed institution, and slaves were able in many ways to help shape their own lives. In the slave quarters they were able to develop a culture that differed in important respects from that of their masters, to lead semi-autonomous lives built around their families and churches, and consequently to resist becoming Sambos. As George P. Rawick put it: "While from sunup to sundown the American slave worked for another and was harshly exploited, from sundown to sunup he lived for himself and created the behavioral and institutional basis which prevented him from becoming the absolute victim."[14]

The effect of this new literature has on the whole been highly salutary. We now know far more about an inexcusably ignored subject than we did but a few years ago, and the themes of independence, community, and culture have represented major historical advances. At the risk of challenging a newly establish consensus,

13.   Virtually all recent studies of slavery insist on the wide variety of slave experiences. For two very different views of slave stratification, see Fogel and Engerman, *Time on the Cross*, I, 148–52; and John W. Blassingame, "Status and Social Structure in the Slave Community: Evidence from New Sources," in Harry P. Owens (ed.), *Perspectives and Irony in American Slavery* (Jackson, Miss., 1976), 137–51.
14.   Rawick, *From Sundown to Sunup*, xix.

however, I would like to suggest that there are increasing signs the argument is being pushed too far—far beyond what the historical evidence will sustain. Thus, in an effort to get away from the slaves-as-passive-victims approach, many historians virtually deny the harmful impact of slavery on the slaves, who *were*, after all, objects of dreadful oppression as well as subjects in their own right. For example, Herbert Gutman, whose work on slave families has been pathbreaking, opines that historians have paid "too much attention . . . to slave 'treatment'" and insists that focusing on the negative effects of slavery leads people to "blame the victim." Similarly, John W. Blassingame, who has sensitively explored slave culture, maintains that "the social organization of the quarters was the slave's primary environment" while "the work experience which most often brought the slave in contact with whites represented his secondary environment and was far less important." To these and other authors, it almost seems as if the slave community was able to flourish independently, little scathed by slavery.[15]

Such an approach is especially problematical in that in general there was little economic basis for the slave community's autonomy. With the exception of isolated areas—most particularly the low-country rice estates of South Carolina and Georgia, where under conditions of widespread owner absenteeism slaves worked on the "task" system and developed a significant "internal economy" of their own—most slaves received the bulk of their sustenance from resident masters, who went to great lengths to discourage independent economic activity on the part of their bondsmen. Most lived, by international standards, on extremely small holdings, where whites impinged on their lives on a daily basis. Unlike slaves in Jamaica, for example, who typically lived on large estates of over fifty and rarely saw their absentee owners, three-quarters of all southern slaves were held in units of under fifty, the vast majority by masters who personally presided over their agricultural operations. Emphasizing the independence of these slaves too often seems to require the slighting of this

15. Gutman, *The Black Family*, 303, and *Slavery and the Numbers Game*, 176; Blassingame, *The Slave Community*, 41. For a critique of recent work for ignoring injury to slaves, see Stanley M. Elkins, "The Two Arguments on Slavery" (1975), reprinted in his *Slavery* (3rd ed.; Chicago, 1976).

socioeconomic reality and indeed of the very essence of slave relations—the exploitation of slave labor.[16]

Many revisionist works on slavery exhibit a celebratory tone that comes close to suggesting life as a slave was an enviable experience. Strong and loving families, a compassionate religion, a true folk culture, and group solidarity seem to have rendered the slave community an idyllic place in which to work and raise children. As Thomas L. Webber concludes in his book that pushes the argument to its logical extreme, "To understand the nature of education in the slave quarter community is to come to grips with the paradox of the 'free slave.' . . . By passing their unique set of cultural themes from generation to generation, the members of the quarter community were able to resist most of white teaching, set themselves apart from white society, and mold their own cultural norms and group identity. While still legally slaves, the black men, women, and children of the quarter community successfully protected their psychological freedom and celebrated their human dignity."[17]

Perhaps, but I would submit that in order to present a balanced view of slave life, historians will need to take account more fully of *slavery*, which after all did impose certain constraints on those whom it touched—including the slaves. Revisionist historians deserve our thanks for sensitively probing the slaves' lives and insisting that they were active beings with a vital culture of their own. At the same time, these historians have too often gotten away from a central truth that Elkins, for all his faults, fully recognized: slavery was not only a brutal but also a brutalizing experience. If slaves were able to help make their own world, that world was not nearly so independent of outside

16.   On the "internal" slave economy of the rice lowlands, see especially the interesting articles by Philip D. Morgan, "Work and Culture: The Task System and the World of Lowcountry Blacks, 1700 to 1800," *William and Mary Quarterly*, 3rd ser., XXXIX (1982), 563–99, and "The Ownership of Property by Slaves in the Mid-Nineteenth-Century Low Country," *Journal of Southern History*, XLIX (1983), 399–420. For the international comparison, see Peter Kolchin, "Reevaluating the Antebellum Slave Community: A Comparative Perspective," *Journal of American History*, LXX (1983), 579–601.

17.   Webber, *Deep Like the Rivers*, 261–62. This celebratory tone is perhaps most pronounced in Harding, *There is a River*. For a major exception to this trend, see the sensitive but hardheaded essays by Willie Lee Rose in *Slavery and Freedom*, ed. William W. Freehling (New York, 1982), 1–72.

influences as many recent scholars have implied. Slaves were indeed subjects, but they were also objects of an oppression that even under the best of circumstances was degrading to its victims.

A second major focus of recent historians has been antebellum slavery as a system. Here, too, scholars have brought new approaches and methodologies to bear and have reached some striking new conclusions. Although the interpretive unity provided by recent studies of the slave community has been less in evidence among those dealing with the slave system, something approaching a new orthodoxy has taken shape. Curiously, this new orthodoxy's most salient implication is remarkably similar to that of the community studies: both sharply play down the importance of slavery in shaping southern life.

Much of the new work has centered on the economics of slavery. This is a subject on which historians had long differed, with their interpretations usually based more on impressionistic evidence such as contemporaries' observations than on systematic analysis of economic data. If most (but not all) concurred in the judgment of nineteenth-century free-labor advocates that slavery was a backward labor system that impeded southern economic development, some, such as Kenneth Stampp, maintained that slaveowners reaped healthy profits from their exploitation of slave labor, whereas others, including Ulrich B. Phillips and Eugene D. Genovese, argued that antebellum slavery was increasingly unprofitable. Then, beginning in 1958, with Alfred H. Conrad and John R. Meyer's article "The Economics of Slavery in the Ante Bellum South," and accelerating during the 1970s with the work of Robert W. Fogel and Stanley L. Engerman and their disciples, economic historians used sophisticated econometric models and computer technology to study the late-antebellum southern economy, relying primarily on statistics derived from census reports and plantation records.[18]

18. Alfred H. Conrad and John R. Meyer, "The Economics of Slavery in the Ante Bellum South," *Journal of Political Economy*, LXVI (1958), 95–130, and *The Economics of Slavery* (Chicago, 1964); Robert William Fogel and Stanley L. Engerman, "The Economics of Slavery," in Fogel and Engerman (eds.), *The Reinterpretation of American Economic History* (New York, 1971), 311–41. On the early debate over the economics of slavery, see Harold D. Woodman, "The Profitability of Slavery: A Historical Perennial," *Journal of Southern History*, XXIX (1963), 303–25; Fogel and Engerman,

They reached two basic conclusions. First, they arrived at a general consensus that antebellum slavery was a highly profitable institution in which slaveowners could expect to earn 10 percent annual returns on their investment, a figure that compared favorably with profits reaped in contemporary nonslaveholding ventures. Investing in slaves was therefore rational from an economic point of view, and explaining slavery's persistence did not require exploration—or even postulation—of particular social values among the masters. Second and more remarkable, slavery was also beneficial to the southern economy as a whole. If the South failed to match the North in urbanization and industrialization, this was primarily because of the "comparative advantage" of the section's agriculture, and was but another indication of rational choice on the part of profit-maximizing southern businessmen. The southern economy was so far from stagnating that between 1840 and 1860, measured in terms of per capita income, it was growing at a faster rate than that of the North: 1.7 percent annually versus 1.3 percent. Indeed, Fogel and Engerman insisted that "economies of large-scale operation, effective management, and intensive utilization of labor and capital made southern slave agriculture 35 percent more efficient than the northern system of family farming."[19]

Although the claim that slave agriculture was *more* efficient than was the free system elicited widespread skepticism, the broader revisionist argument—that slavery did not retard southern economic development—seemed once again to suggest that slavery's impact on the South was minimal. Just as other historians were discounting the harmful impact of the peculiar institution on the blacks, arguing that the slave community was able to flourish because "the social organi-

Time on the Cross, II, 168–247; and Hugh G.J. Aitken (ed.), *Did Slavery Pay? The Economics of Black Slavery in the United States* (Boston, 1971).

19. Fogel and Engerman, *Time on the Cross*, I, 5. See also Stanley L. Engerman, "A Reconsideration of Southern Economic Growth, 1770–1860," *Agricultural History*, IL (1975), 343–61; and Claudia Dale Goldin, *Urban Slavery in the American South, 1820–1860* (Chicago, 1976). For non-econometric works arguing that slavery was not inconsistent with urbanization and industrialization, see Robert S. Starobin, *Industrial Slavery in the Old South* (New York, 1970); David R. Goldfield, *Urban Growth in the Age of Sectionalism: Virginia, 1847–1861* (Baton Rouge, 1977); and Ronald L. Lewis, *Coal, Iron, and Slaves: Industrial Slavery in Maryland and Virginia, 1715–1865* (Westport, Conn., 1979).

zation of the quarters," not slavery, was their primary environment, so too students of the slave economy were insisting that slavery had little adverse effect on the southern economy. Although econometricians and community scholars constituted two distinct groups, they unwittingly combined to minimize the significance of slavery as a distinctive labor system.

This view that there was little especially distinctive about antebellum slavery has received its most forceful and self-conscious recent expression in James Oakes's widely acclaimed book *The Ruling Race*. Agreeing with Fogel and Engerman—and many others before them—that slaveowners were best seen as acquisitive capitalists whose goals differed little from those of northern businessmen, Oakes generalized that "in . . . fundamental ways, the slaveholding experience coincided wth the American experience at large. Except for its defense of bondage, the slaveholders' ideology was strikingly similar to the Republican party ideology of the 1850's." Not only the southern economy but southern society, thought, and way of life were preeminently American. Slavery was simply one variant of the broad current of American capitalism.[20]

Numerous historians developed further elements of the thesis that slavery did not sharply set the antebellum South off from the North. Thus, George Fredrickson, although conceding the existence of paternalistic arguments in behalf of slavery, maintained that most defenders of the peculiar institution were democratic-racists who adhered to the basic tenets of Jeffersonian egalitarianism—for whites only; their ideology was therefore not fundamentally different from that of most other Americans. Oakes vacillated between the view that the proslavery argument was "at base racial" and the view that it "focused upon the profitability of slavery and the white man's right to make money and accumulate property," but in either case defenders of slavery were expressing American, rather than distinctly southern, doctrine. J. Mills Thornton portrayed Alabama politics as characterized not by planter domination and elitism but by a democratic pandering to popular prejudices. And Edward Pessen insisted that despite slavery, antebellum North and South were fundamentally alike: "Without being replicas of one another, both sections were relatively

20. James Oakes, *The Ruling Race: A History of American Slaveholders* (New York, 1982), 227.

rich, powerful, aggressive, and assertive communities, socially strati-
fied and governed by equally—and disconcertingly—oligarchic internal arrangements." He concluded: "That they were drawn into the
most terrible of all American wars may have been due, as is often the
case when great powers fight, as much to their similarities as to their
differences." Other historians, though contending that the Old South
was different from the North, have dismissed *slavery* as a cause of
this difference. In a curious way, then, recent scholars have pushed
the peculiar institution back to where it stood for Frank Owsley—
a relatively unimportant institution on the periphery of southern
society.[21]

   This general downgrading of slavery's importance, while representing the dominant trend among recent scholars, has not gone unchallenged. Indeed, the argument that slavery had relatively little impact on the white South has met with rebuttal on several fronts. And
properly so, I believe, for the argument in general goes well beyond
what the evidence will support. Although its critics are not united in
precisely what slavery did to southern society, they have succeeded in
showing that in the years preceding the Civil War, slavery did increasingly set the South off from the rest of the country.

   If the revisionists have established to virtually everyone's satisfaction slavery's profitability to slaveowners, they have been far less
successful in producing a consensus with respect to slavery's impact
on the southern economy as a whole. Some econometricians have
challenged the assertion that slave agriculture was more efficient
than free, and others have suggested that slavery did in fact impede
southern industrialization and urbanization, whether by providing
sufficiently high returns in agriculture to discourage investment in
manufacturing or by producing a planter class largely inimical to
manufacturing and urban life. Other historians have gone further,

21.   George M. Fredrickson, *The Black Image in the White Mind: The Debate on Afro-
American Character and Destiny, 1817–1914* (New York, 1971), 43–70; Oakes, *The
Ruling Race*, 34, 134; J. Mills Thornton III, *Politics and Power in a Slave Society: Alabama, 1800–1860* (Baton Rouge, 1978); Edward Pessen, "How Different Were the Antebellum North and South?" *American Historical Review*, LXXXV (1980), 1148. See, for
example, Bertram Wyatt-Brown, *Southern Honor: Ethics and Behavior in the Old
South* (New York, 1982); and Forrest McDonald and Grady McWhiney, "The Antebellum Southern Herdsman: A Reinterpretation," *Journal of Southern History*, XLI
(1975), 147–66. Frank L. Owsley, *Plain Folk of the Old South* (Baton Rouge, 1949).

questioning many of the economic revisionists' basic assumptions, from the notion that slaveholders' behavior was prompted by economic rationality to the contention that per capita income growth is the best index of socioeconomic development. If the southern economy was expanding rapidly before the Civil War, much of that expansion resulted from an enormous growth in the world demand for cotton, a growth that could not long have been sustained at antebellum rates. Furthermore, although the southern economy was clearly not stagnating, it was growing along lines increasingly different from the northern, failing to undergo the same kind of qualitative transformation. Virtually every major index of modernization except per capita income growth—population growth, absolute level of per capita income, industrialization, mechanization, scientific endeavor, education—indicated what most contemporaries recognized: the South was lagging further and further behind the North.[22]

On a broader level, the portrait of slavery as simply another variant of capitalism is open to serious challenge. This portrait is based on the tacit assumption that the mode of *exchange* is most important in shaping a society's character, for the South was obviously part of the world capitalist system through which slaveowners sought to maximize their income by selling staple agricultural products. At the same time, however, as a mode of *production*, slavery bred relations between master and slave that were fundamentally different from those between employer and employee. The most forceful and prolific exponent of the thesis that antebellum southern slavery constituted a distinctive labor system that created a distinctive kind of society has been Eugene D. Genovese, most recently in collaboration with Eliza-

22.   See, for example, Paul A. David (ed.), *Reckoning with Slavery: Critical Essays in the Quantitative History of American Negro Slavery* (New York, 1976); Heywood Fleisig, "Slavery, the Supply of Agricultural Labor, and Industrialization of the South," *Journal of Economic History*, XXXVI (1976), 572–95; Gavin Wright, *The Political Economy of the Cotton South: Households, Markets, and Wealth in the Nineteenth Century* (New York, 1978), 4, 44–55, 74–88, 90–127; Fred Bateman and Thomas Weiss, *A Deplorable Scarcity: The Failure of Industrialization in the Slave Economy* (Chapel Hill, 1981), 118–27, 157–63; and especially Harold D. Woodman, "Economic History and Economic Theory: The New Economic History in America," *Journal of Interdisciplinary History*, III (1972), 323–50. For a still largely persuasive exposition of the basic conflict between slavery and urban life, see Richard C. Wade, *Slavery in the Cities: The South, 1820–1860* (New York, 1964).

beth Fox-Genovese. Although slaveowners were businessmen in that they produced for a world market, slavery as a productive system entailed social relations antithetical to those of free-labor capitalism: "The Old South emerged as a bastard child of merchant capital and developed as a noncapitalist society increasingly antagonistic to, but inseparable from, the bourgeois world that sired it." Not only the South's economy, but its whole way of life, was a reflection of its slave-labor system: southern society was planter-dominated and infused with precapitalist values.[23]

Central to Genovese's interpretation of slavery is the much misunderstood concept of planter paternalism. In contrast to Oakes, who insisted that their acquisitive character "destroyed for most slaveholders whatever remained of the elemental principle of the paternalistic ethos," Genovese maintained that antebellum planters showed strong paternalistic tendencies. In doing so, he was not, as some of his critics charged, reviving the discredited notion of a benign slavery, but rather arguing that the particular nature of antebellum slave relations bred feelings in the masters that differentiated them from employers interested in their employees only as instruments of profit. Southern slaveholders were, with some exceptions, resident owners who played a major role in running their own holdings, knew their slaves personally, took an interest—often far too much interest—in their lives, and sought to perpetuate their utter dependence by providing for their material (and often their spiritual) comfort. Planter paternalism was predicated on the nonmarket relationship between master and slave.[24]

23.   Eugene D. Genovese, *The Political Economy of Slavery: Studies in the Economy and Society of the Slave South* (New York, 1965), and *The World the Slaveholders Made: Two Essays in Interpretation* (New York, 1969); Genovese, *Roll, Jordan, Roll*, 1–158; Fox-Genovese and Genovese, *Fruits of Merchant Capital*, 1–60, 90–171, 337–414 (quotation on 5).

24.   Oakes, *The Ruling Race*, 22; Genovese, *The World the Slaveholders Made*, 95–102, 165–244; Genovese, *Roll, Jordan, Roll*, 3–158; see also Willie Lee Rose, "The Domestication of Domestic Slavery," *Slavery and Freedom*, 18–36. Of course, emphasis on planter paternalism has sometimes gone hand in hand with a view of slavery as a benign institution. See, for example, Ulrich B. Phillips, *American Negro Slavery: A Survey of the Supply, Employment and Control of Negro Labor as Determined by the Plantation Regime* (New York, 1918); and for a less extreme version, William K. Scarborough, "Slavery—The White Man's Burden," in Owens (ed.), *Perspectives and Irony in American Slavery*, 108–10.

Although Genovese may have exaggerated the degree of planter paternalism—according to Oakes, he "ignores . . . the profound impact of the market economy on the nature of slavery"—he is surely right that slavery represented more to most masters than simply the easiest way to make money, that it shaped their lifestyle and world view as well. A number of historians have seen in the proslavery cause, for example, a broadly conservative movement designed to defend a whole way of life that had come under attack by free-labor spokesmen. While recognizing that proslavery ideologues often used racial arguments, these scholars have stressed the degree to which they were defending a social system, not just black racial subordination. It was no accident that these polemicists linked slavery with order, morality, religion, tradition, and social harmony, while associating abolitionism with all the other "isms" spawned by free labor—from socialism, trade unionism, and excessive individualism to divorce, free love, and crime in the streets.[25]

In short, there is abundant evidence that slavery served to set the South off from the rest of the country. A wide range of recent works, not all focusing directly on slavery, testify to the distinctiveness of antebellum southern society and strongly suggest the predominant role of slavery in producing this distinctiveness. Thus, scholars have established that ownership of wealth was much more concentrated in the rural South than in the rural North, with slaveowners the clear beneficiaries: "The average slaveowner was more than five times as

25. Oakes, *The Ruling Race*, xiii; Genovese, *The World the Slaveholders Made*; William McKee Evans, "From the Land of Canaan to the Land of Guinea: The Strange Odyssey of the Sons of Ham," *American Historical Review*, LXXXV (1980), 15–43; Peter Kolchin, "In Defense of Servitude: American Proslavery and Russian Proserfdom Arguments, 1760–1860," *American Historical Review*, LXXXV (1980), 809–27; Dickson D. Bruce, Jr., *The Rhetoric of Conservatism: The Virginia Convention of 1829–1830 and the Conservative Tradition in the South* (San Marino, Calif., 1982). For efforts to establish a middle position, see Robert E. Shalhope, "Race, Class, Slavery and the Antebellum Southern Mind," *Journal of Southern History*, XXXVII (1971), 557–74; and Thomas Virgil Peterson, *Ham and Japheth: The Mythic World of Whites in the Antebellum South* (Metuchen, N.J., 1978). For two recent, and differing, surveys of the proslavery argument, see John McCardell, *The Idea of a Southern Nation: Southern Nationalists and Southern Nationalism, 1830–1860* (New York, 1979), 49–90; and Drew Gilpin Faust (ed.), *The Ideology of Slavery: Proslavery Thought in the Antebellum South, 1830–1860* (Baton Rouge, 1981), 1–20. See also David Donald, "The Proslavery Argument Reconsidered," *Journal of Southern History*, XXXVII (1971), 3–18.

wealthy as the average Northerner," Gavin Wright found, and "more than ten times as wealthy as the average nonslaveholding Southern farmer."[26] Authors such as William J. Cooper, Jr., have shown the degree to which southern whites were conscious of the centrality of slavery to their society, and hence the degree to which slavery dominated southern politics.[27] Still others have explored the distinctiveness of antebellum southern law, lifestyle, and the position of women.[28] As a result of these works, the burden of proof now rests squarely on the shoulders of those who would minimize slavery's influence, for too much of what we know points to its pervasive impact on southern life.

If the degree to which slavery differentiated the South from the rest of the country has produced considerable disagreement, another subject—the third major area of concentration by recent slavery schol-

26.   See, for example, Gavin Wright, "'Economic Democracy' and the Concentration of Agricultural Wealth in the Cotton South, 1850–1860," *Agricultural History*, XLIV (1970), 63–93, and *The Political Economy of the Cotton South*, 35; Randolph B. Campbell, "Planters and Plain Folk: Harrison County, Texas, as a Test Case, 1850–1860," *Journal of Southern History*, XL (1974), 369–99; and Randolph B. Campbell and Richard G. Lowe, *Wealth and Power in Antebellum Texas* (College Station, Tex., 1977).

27.   William J. Cooper, Jr., *The South and the Politics of Slavery, 1828–1856* (Baton Rouge, 1978); see also William W. Freehling, *Prelude to Civil War: The Nullification Controversy in South Carolina, 1816–1836* (New York, 1965); William L. Barney, *The Secession Impulse: Alabama and Mississippi in 1860* (Princeton, 1970); Michael P. Johnson, *Toward a Patriarchal Republic: The Secession of Georgia* (Baton Rouge, 1977); Steven A. Channing, *Crisis of Fear: Secession in South Carolina* (New York, 1970); and McCardell, *The Idea of a Southern Nation*. But for a very different view of southern politics, see Thornton, *Politics and Power in a Slave Society*; and Michael F. Holt, *The Political Crisis of the 1850s* (New York, 1978).

28.   Mark V. Tushnet, *The American Law of Slavery, 1810–1860: Considerations of Humanity and Interest* (Princeton, 1981); Michael Stephen Hindus, *Prison and Plantation: Crime, Justice, and Authority in Massachusetts and South Carolina, 1767–1878* (Chapel Hill, 1980); David Bertelson, *The Lazy South* (New York, 1967); Dickson D. Bruce, Jr., *Violence and Culture in the Antebellum South* (Austin, 1979); Steven Hahn, "The Yeomanry of the Nonplantation South: Upper Piedmont Georgia, 1850–1860," in Orville Vernon Burton and Robert C. McMath, Jr. (eds.), *Class, Conflict, and Consensus: Antebellum Southern Community Studies* (Westport, Conn., 1982), 29–56; Catherine Clinton, *The Plantation Mistress: Woman's World in the Old South* (New York, 1982).

ars—has been the degree to which peculiarly American conditions set antebellum southern slavery off from that of other slave societies. Like studies of the slave community, comparative work on slavery received its major impetus from Elkins' controversial book; unlike them, however, it has dealt mainly with slave treatment, not slave life. Much of this work has therefore suffered from serious limitations of focus, even as it has proved extremely fruitful in answering certain historical questions. Ultimately, however, the comparative approach to slavery promises to provide a way to bridge the gap between community and systemic studies of slavery, while yielding new insights in both areas.

During the past two decades, comparative historians have in general refuted Elkins' thesis of a contrast between a harsh North American and a mild Latin American slavery. Although Iberian law did serve to provide slaves with more protection than did English and American, nowhere was law automatically translated into fact, and actual slave treatment depended far more on concrete socioeconomic conditions than on legal or religious tradition. The substantial excess of males over females that prevailed in many slave societies, for example, proved more important than pronouncements by either Church or Crown in shaping the nature of slave families. As a rule, slaves were driven more relentlessly during boom times than during periods of economic stagnation, but numerous other factors, from the slave trade to plantation size, residence of owners, and the ratio of slave to free populations, influenced the nature of specific slave systems.[29]

During the 1960s and 1970s, many historians found that southern slavery, rather than being set off by its peculiarly capitalistic and closed nature, as Elkins had claimed, shared essential features with slavery elsewhere. As David Brion Davis put it, "Negro bondage was

---

29. See, for example, Marvin Harris, *Patterns of Race in the Americas* (New York, 1964), Chap. 6; David Brion Davis, *The Problem of Slavery in Western Culture* (Ithaca, 1967), Chap. 8; Carl N. Degler, *Neither Black nor White: Slavery and Race Relations in Brazil and the United States* (New York, 1971), Chap. 2; and most of the essays in Laura Foner and Eugene D. Genovese (eds.), *Slavery in the New World: A Reader in Comparative History* (Englewood Cliffs, N.J., 1969). For a book supporting the Elkins thesis, see Herbert Klein, *Slavery in the Americas: A Comparative Study of Virginia and Cuba* (Chicago, 1967).

a single phenomenon whose variations were less significant than underlying patterns of unity." Thus, Genovese suggested that Sambo, far from being a product of peculiarly American conditions, was a function of slavery itself: "For reasons common to the slave condition all slave classes displayed a lack of individual initiative and produced the famous Lazy Nigger, who under Russian serfdom and elsewhere was white." Other scholars found common themes in slaveholders' ideology, even in societies with widely varying cultural traditions.[30]

As comparative research continued, it became clear that far from being uniquely harsh, American slavery was in some respects actually milder than variants to the south. Carl Degler argued that "the physical treatment of slaves in Brazil may well have been harsher than that in the United States." More startling, Genovese inverted Elkins' system of categorization, suggesting that the resident character of southern slaveownership created a peculiarly paternalistic, pre-bourgeois master class that stood in stark contrast to the more capitalistic regime of absentee Caribbean proprietors. Assault on the thesis that American slavery was unusually severe was thus linked to assault on the view that American slavery was preeminently capitalistic; in comparative perspective, southern planters appeared among the least capitalistic of New World slaveowners. Although not all historians accepted Genovese's concept of planter paternalism, few challenged his contention that on a purely material level the treatment of southern slaves compared favorably with that of most bondsmen elsewhere. The most basic of all the contrasts was especially telling: of the major New World slave societies, only the United States saw its bound population grow through natural reproduction, with the number of slaves approximately tripling after African imports were outlawed in 1808. Historians have not entirely agreed on the reasons for this remarkable development; some have stressed the higher material standard of living in the United States, others the more equal sex ratios that prevailed there, and still others differences in disease systems between the temperate South and the tropical environment of the Caribbean, Central America, and Brazil. Signifi-

30. Davis, *The Problem of Slavery in Western Culture*, 229; Genovese, *The World the Slaveholders Made*, 5; Evans, "From the Land of Canaan to the Land of Guinea"; Kolchin, "In Defense of Servitude," 810–19.

cantly, however, each of these explanations tends to imply a slavery harsher elsewhere than in the United States.[31]

Recent research has thus established that southern slavery was indeed unique, but in a way quite different from that postulated by Elkins. As Genovese pointed out in an important essay, in evaluating the relative severity of different slave systems one must distinguish clearly among the slaves' material conditions, quality of life, and access to freedom. In the first of these—and in some respects in the second as well—slaves in the Old South fared better than most did elsewhere, whereas in the third they often fared substantially worse. Comparison has thus made clear the need to distinguish sharply between slave conditions and race relations, for if scholars have demolished the notion that American slavery was uniquely harsh, they have rarely quarreled with the view set forth by Tannenbaum and Elkins that American race relations were unusually rigid. Not only was manumission more restricted and acceptance of freed slaves and their descendants into society more grudging than elsewhere, but Americans generally adopted a "two-color" system of categorizing people, with the tiniest admixture of black "blood" making one black, rather than the three- or multicolor systems prevalent in other countries. A "mild" version of slavery did not necessarily produce correspondingly "mild" race relations.[32]

31. Degler, *Neither Black nor White*, 67; Genovese, *The World the Slaveholders Made*; Philip D. Curtin, *The Atlantic Slave Trade: A Census* (Madison, Wis., 1969), Chaps. 2, 3; C. Vann Woodward, "Southern Slaves in the World of Thomas Malthus," in *American Counterpoint: Slavery and Racism in the North-South Dialogue* (Boston, 1971), 78–106. For an interesting demographic comparison, see Richard S. Dunn, "A Tale of Two Plantations: Slave Life at Mesopotamia in Jamaica and Mount Airy in Virginia, 1799 to 1828," *William and Mary Quarterly*, 3rd ser., XXXIV (1977), 40–64.
32. Eugene D. Genovese, "The Treatment of Slaves in Different Countries: Problems in the Application of the Comparative Method," in Foner and Genovese (eds.), *Slavery in the New World*, 202–10. The subject of race relations is largely beyond the scope of this essay. See Harris, *Patterns of Race in the Americas*, Chap. 7; Degler, *Neither Black nor White*, 93–264; Winthrop Jordan, "American Chiaroscuro: The Status and Definition of Mulattoes in the British Colonies," *William and Mary Quarterly*, 3rd ser., XIX (1962), 183–200; Laura Foner, "The Free People of Color in Louisiana and St. Domingue: A Comparative Portrait of Two Three-Caste Societies," *Journal of Social History*, III (1970), 406–30; Harry Hoetink, *Slavery and Race Relations in the Americas: An Inquiry into Their Nature and Nexus* (New York, 1973); and George M. Fredrickson, *White Supremacy: A Comparative Study in American and South African History* (New York, 1981), 94–135.

In studies that compare slavery, then, as in those that focus on the antebellum slave community, recent historians have reached a broad consensus rejecting a hypothesis put forth by Elkins. Their work has on the whole been persuasive and highly beneficial, dispelling much of the parochialism that for so long surrounded the study of southern slavery, which was, after all, only one of numerous unfree labor systems existing in the modern world. If a comparative awareness put southern slavery in a new light, rigorous comparison of different slave systems both destroyed old assumptions and led to the posing of significant new questions.

Nevertheless, comparative slavery studies suffered, I believe, from two major limitations that served by the mid-1970s to bring them close to a dead end. One was a product of success: because so much of the comparative work was aimed at destroying Elkins' thesis of a uniquely oppressive American slavery, once that goal was accomplished it was less clear precisely why slave systems should be compared. It is not surprising, then, that after the early 1970s, there occurred a marked decline in the number of comparative works on slavery.

The second limitation was even more problematical. If recent students of antebellum slavery have exaggerated the autonomy, cohesion, and felicity of the slave community, students of comparative slavery have tended to ignore it altogether. It is striking that at a time when slave life became the most important focus of historical research on antebellum southern slavery, slave treatment—together with race relations and owner ideology—remained the primary subject of comparative historians. As a result, the comparative work seems curiously out of touch with the historical mainstream. One reason for this disjunction may be the paucity of sources available for the study of slave life outside the southern United States, for there exist elsewhere few slave autobiographies and no equivalent to the Federal Writers' Project interviews. As I suggest in the next section, however, creative comparison can tell us much about the slaves as well as the masters, and to create a well-rounded portrait of slavery, historians will have to turn in this direction.[33]

33.   For comparative works that focus on the slaves rather than on the masters, see Eugene D. Genovese, *From Rebellion to Revolution: Afro-American Slave Revolts in the Making of the Modern World* (Baton Rouge, 1979); and Kolchin, "The Process of Confrontation," and "Reevaluating the Antebellum Slave Community."

An evaluation of the past quarter-century's writings on antebellum slavery inevitably suggests a need for new directions. This is less a criticism of these works than an acknowledgment of their significant contribution to our understanding of the past: because of their achievements, their potential has been largely fulfilled and it is time to move on. Since most of the recent revisionist works have been on the "middle level," avoiding sweeping survey and detailed case study alike, I believe that the most constructive approach for the next few years will involve simultaneously narrowing our focus to examine in greater depth topics that have received insufficient attention and broadening it to ask new questions and gain new perspectives.

On the "micro level," we need to learn a great deal more about numerous topics, some of which have been treated in generalizing works but require more specialized focus for full elaboration, and others of which have been largely ignored. A good example of the former is slave resistance. Most of the community studies have had something to say about slave protest—usually stressing the extent to which the bondsmen struggled against their dehumanization and in the process gave the lie to the Sambo stereotype—and specific events, such as the Nat Turner revolt, have been the subjects of considerable scholarly endeavor.[34] But there has been little progress, either substantive or conceptual, in our knowledge of slave resistance as a whole. Historians continue to generalize on the subject without an adequate basis, in part because there has been little work aimed at answering basic questions pertaining to the types, causes, consequences, and prevalence of slave resistance. Under what circumstances, for example, were slaves most likely to run away? Why did some fugitives seek to escape to the North while others engaged in temporary local truancy? Did variations in the treatment of slaves significantly affect their rate of flight? What led most slaves to run away by themselves while a smaller number cooperated with other fugitives? What can we learn from these patterns about the slaves' values

---

34. The modern controversy on the Turner revolt was provoked by William Styron's historical novel *The Confessions of Nat Turner* (New York, 1967). For reactions to it, see Clarke (ed.), *William Styron's Nat Turner*; Henry Irving Tragle (ed.), *The Southampton Slave Revolt of 1831: A Compilation of Source Material* (New York, 1971); and John B. Duff and Peter Mitchell (eds.), *The Nat Turner Rebellion: The Historical Event and the Modern Controversy* (New York, 1971). The best account of the revolt is Oates, *The Fires of Jubilee.*

and attitudes? What impact did flight have on those who remained behind? These and many other questions on resistance can be satisfactorily answered only by work that focuses on them rather than dealing with them in passing. Given the extraordinary profusion of writings on slavery, it is surprising that we still lack comprehensive studies of slave resistance, flight, and violence short of rebellion—let alone any of these on a local or regional level. Better knowledge of slave resistance, encompassing both detailed empirical work and a more sophisticated analytical framework, is crucial to understanding the slaves' mentality, and thus slavery itself.[35]

An example of a topic that has been curiously neglected is slave stratification. Although it is a commonplace that slaves performed a wide variety of tasks, which conferred differing levels of status, we have learned remarkably little about the social structure of the slave community. How widespread was slave stratification? Where was it greatest, and why? Did it vary with the size of holdings? Did it increase over time? Is John W. Blassingame correct in his interesting but highly speculative suggestion that slaves ranked themselves according to totally different criteria from those applied to them by their masters? Did slave stratification lead to significant divisions within the quarters that might have served to undermine the slave community's sense of unity? What can be said, for example, about slaves' violence against other slaves? Surely, what we know of humanity suggests that slaves must have had enemies among their fellow bondsmen as well as among their masters. How, then, did they take out their hostilities on each other, and what do such patterns suggest about their world view and social order? Answering such questions will require careful mining of plantation records and slave narratives, but will also necessitate coming to grips with the relationship between objective stratification (based on occupation or material standing) and subjective status, whether ascribed by masters or by slaves.[36]

35. For a pioneering venture, see Johnson, "Runaway Slaves and the Slave Communities in South Carolina."

36. Blassingame, "Status and Social Structure in the Slave Community," in Owens (ed.), *Perspectives and Irony in American Slavery*; for the interesting but highly speculative argument that slaves displaced their hostility against owners onto other slaves, see Lawrence T. McDonnell, "Slave Against Slave: Dynamics of Violence Within the American Slave Community" (Paper delivered at American Historical Association meeting, December 28, 1983, San Francisco).

Many other topics cry out for similar attention, from house servants and elite slaves to master-slave relations and plantation management.[37] Often, such subjects can most profitably be investigated at the local level, where sources can be intensively mined and a comprehensive view gained that is impossible when dealing with the South as a whole.[38] Studies of individual plantations or collections of plantations seem to offer especially fruitful possibilities, facilitating examination of selected topics both in greater depth and over a longer span of time than usually essayed, although this approach has so far been rare.[39]

At the opposite extreme, on the "macro level," two needs are most apparent. Although it has become something of a cliché that historians of slavery should deal more than they have with change over time, the vast majority of slavery studies remain "snapshots" depicting conditions at a given moment, and thus fail to come to grips with the essential historical process. We know that antebellum slavery differed in important respects from southern slavery a century earlier; as only one example among many, the slaves' conversion to Christianity was largely a result of the religious revivals that swept much of the South during the late eighteenth and early nineteenth centuries, and to the extent that black Christianity became a central feature of the slave community during the half century before the Civil War, slave life underwent fundamental alterations. Similarly, important changes ensued in slave family life, acculturation, and

37. Existing work on the subject includes William L. Van Deburg, *The Slave Drivers: Black Agricultural Labor Supervisors in the Antebellum South* (Westport, Conn., 1979); James Herbert Stone, "Black Leadership in the Old South: The Slave Drivers of the Rice Kingdom" (Ph.D. dissertation, Florida State University, 1976); James M. Clifton, "The Rice Driver: His Role in Slave Management," *South Carolina Historical Magazine*, LXXXII (1981), 331–53; and William Kauffman Scarborough, *The Overseer: Plantation Management in the Old South* (Baton Rouge, 1966).

38. For local studies, see Morgan's important articles "Work and Culture" and "The Ownership of Property by Slaves." See also the essays in two collections: Elinor Miller and Eugene D. Genovese (eds.), *Plantation, Town, and Country: Essays on the Local History of American Slave Society* (Urbana, 1974); and Burton and McMath (eds.), *Class, Conflict, and Consensus.* For two state studies, see Joe Gray Taylor, *Negro Slavery in Louisiana* (Baton Rouge, 1963); and Julia Floyd Smith, *Slavery and Plantation Growth in Antebellum Florida, 1821–1860* (Gainesville, 1973).

39. Important exceptions include Drew Gilpin Faust, *James Henry Hammond and the Old South: A Design for Mastery* (Baton Rouge, 1982), 69–104; and Cody, "Naming, Kinship, and Estate Dispersal."

treatment, as well as in master-slave relations, owner ideology, and the southern economy. Late-antebellum conditions were in many ways atypical of those that prevailed during the two and a half centuries of southern slavery. We still lack, however, works showing the development of slavery—or even of particular features of slavery— over several generations. If the study of slavery is to regain its historical dimension, it must address the central historical phenomenon: change.[40]

Second, we must broaden the comparative perspective that has been directed so fruitfully at the masters and race relations, by applying it to the slaves themselves. In a sense, this suggestion parallels that of the need to examine the evolution of slavery, for just as considering change over time implies a temporal comparison, examining the South in a broader geographical context implies a spatial comparison. The purpose of both is to provide a wider perspective, for by studying the slaves in historical isolation, historians have lost an opportunity to grasp certain insights and have reached conclusions that an expanded view might render questionable.

Although the slave experience everywhere in the New World had certain important constants—labor exploitation and subjection to the slaveowners' arbitrary authority, adjustment to a new environment, creation of an Afro-American culture, resistance to dehumanization—these developed differently in different countries, depending on specific historical conditions. For example, as we have seen, antebellum southern slaves lived, by international standards, on relatively small holdings, came in frequent contact with their owners, and enjoyed good material conditions. Their lives, consequently, differed in important respects from those of other New World slaves. American slaves in general ate better, lived longer, had more children, and maintained more stable family relations than did most others; at the same time, they faced greater owner interference in their lives and consequently had more difficulty achieving economic independence, cultural integrity, and communal autonomy. Indeed, I believe that

40.   For recent works that do explore change over time, see Rose, "The Domestication of Domestic Slavery"; Ira Berlin, "Time, Space, and the Evolution of Afro-American Society in British Mainland North America," *American Historical Review*, LXXXV (1980), 44–78; John B. Boles, *Black Southerners, 1619–1869* (Lexington, Ky., 1983); and, at the local level, Morgan, "Work and Culture."

applying a comparative focus to antebellum slave life will lead to a significant reevaluation of the nature of the slave community.[41] Such an approach would also serve to provide a bridge between studies of slave life, which usually have focused on the antebellum South in isolation from the rest of the world, and studies of the slave system, which have often examined the South within the broader world context but ignored the slaves themselves.

The history of antebellum southern slavery remains a field in flux. The past twenty-five years have seen an extraordinary profusion of scholarship that has altered almost beyond recognition our understanding of the "peculiar institution." Although the pace has now slowed somewhat, there is no sign that this process of historical revision is nearing completion. If we have learned much, much remains to be learned, and it is a virtual certainty that twenty-five years from now some of our widely held assumptions will have been overturned while others will be under attack. It is unlikely, however, that our understanding of antebellum slavery will change as much in the next quarter-century as it has in the last. Much remains to be done, but a rough outline of our basic map exists; the task now is to refine and perfect it, filling in gaps and correcting false leads, not to begin from scratch. For this we have to thank the recent generation of scholars who have served as pioneers, exploring virtually uncharted territory. They have inevitably made mistakes, but despite specific criticisms that may legitimately be leveled against them, they have reason to congratulate themselves, for their accomplishments have been extraordinary.

41. See Kolchin, "Reevaluating the Antebellum Slave Community."

Ethnic Roots of Southern Violence

Grady McWhiney

Visitors from Europe and the North to the Old South often described white southerners as a "*heathen* race" of "barbarians" who were "more savage than the Indians." One foreigner complained that in Louisiana killings which "would be called murder[s] in France" were as common as "quarrels followed by fist fights." A dispute in Texas between Methodists and Presbyterians became so furious, explained a stranger, that "the president of the Presbyterian University was shot down on the street." Some men in Kentucky reportedly "roasted to death, before a large log fire, one of their friends, because he refused to [take a] drink. They did it thus: Three or four of them shoved and held him up to the fire until they themselves could stand it no longer; and he died in 20 hours after. No legal inquiry took place," claimed a visitor from England, "nor, indeed ever takes place among *Rowdies*, as the Backwoodsmen are called." Travelers elsewhere in the antebellum South were appalled by what they saw. "Horrible," announced a northerner who witnessed several violent encounters, "I would not live in [the South] . . . for a mine of gold."[1]

Stories of southern exorbitance were commonplace. As a joke, a playful Alabama "boy" bit off a piece of a man's ear. On another occasion, several young Kentuckians rode "down to Savannah, with a

1. Charles Fenno Hoffman, *A Winter in the West* (2 vols.; New York, 1835), II, 231; George Hanger Coleraine, *The Life, Adventures, and Opinions of Col. George Hanger*, ed. William Combe (2 vols.; London, 1801), II, 404–405; Victor Tixier, *Tixier's Travels . . .*, ed. John Francis McDermott (Norman, 1940), 40; Frederick Law Olmsted, *A Journey Through Texas . . .* (rpr. New York, 1969), 69–70; William Faux, *Memorable Days in America: Being a Journal of a Tour to the United States . . .* (London, 1823), 179; W. Stuart Harris, "Rowdyism, Public Drunkenness, and Bloody Encounters in Early Perry County," *Alabama Review*, XXXIII (1980), 19; Henry Benjamin Whipple, *Bishop Whipple's Southern Diary, 1843–1844*, ed. Lester B. Shippee (Minneapolis, 1934), 40. See also George William Featherstonhaugh, *Excursion Through the Slave States . . .* (2 vols.; London, 1844), II, 42–69.

drove of horses and mules . . . and, having sold them, they were spending the effects of the sale to suit their taste." These young men attracted attention by throwing "three, heavy, cut-glass tumblers, [a] large platter, [some] plates, and knives and forks, and small articles of furniture" from their hotel room window. When the manager went up to investigate, the roisterers threatened to shoot him if he came into their room. The next morning they uncomplainingly paid seventy dollars in damages in addition to their regular fare. A Yankee who witnessed these events expressed "astonishment that those young men would spend so large a sum of money for such a foolish gratification." He was told "that that was a small amount, compared with what is frequently paid for such 'busts' by young men at the South." More typical, he learned, was a young man from the Georgia backcountry who on a Sunday morning drove his carriage on the sidewalks, creating havoc among the pedestrians, and then rode into the saloon at Savannah's largest hotel, where he shot at the bartender. Captured by the police and fined five hundred dollars, the man replied: "Cheap enough! I have had a good frolic."[2]

Good frolics appealed to southerners, even such dangerous affairs as the race of two boats down the Mississippi River. On board one boat "was an old lady, who, having bought a winter stock of bacon, pork, &c., was returning to her home on the banks of the Mississippi." Fun lovers on board both boats insisted upon a race; cheers and drawn pistols obliged the captains to cooperate. As the boats struggled to outdistance each other, excited passengers demanded more speed. Despite every effort, the boats raced evenly until the old lady directed her slaves to throw all her casks of bacon into the boilers. Her boat then moved ahead of the other vessel, which suddenly exploded; "clouds of splinters and human limbs darken the sky." On the undamaged boat, passengers shouted their victory. But above their cheers could "be heard the shrill voice of the old lady, crying, 'I did it, I did it—it's all my bacon!'"[3]

Southerners seemed all too addicted to such extravagant and deadly activity. A European visitor reported that it was "absolutely

2. Charles G. Parsons, *Inside View of Slavery: Or, a Tour Among the Planters* (Cleveland, 1855), 29–31.

3. Henry Anthony Murray, *Lands of the Slave and the Free* . . . (2 vols.; London, 1855), I, 227–29.

necessary to carry arms in the South." Houses in Grand Gulf, Mississippi, another man claimed, "show the most conclusive proof of outward violence in broken windows, splintered doors, etc. . . . Several suspicious characters have been hanged and 1 whipped to death. Here every man carries a cane that illy conceals a poniard & from the bosom of everyone the silver handle of a dagger peeps out." A Texan told a Swiss traveler: "We in Texas don't need so much quiet and orderly people, we need restless minds, men that have a noose around their necks and sparks in their bodies, who don't value their lives more highly than a nutshell and are handy with their rifles." Southerners typically exaggerated their tales and often "put on" outsiders, but a visitor was correct when he said that in the South, a "bowie-knife was a universal, and a pistol a not at all unusual, companion." And incidents were bound to occur. "Yesterday a gentleman, drunk, in the stage, drew his dirk," reported a traveler. "He had the stage stopped, jumped out and fought the other passengers, myself excepted. They dressed him soundly, disarmed him, and with the unanimous consent of the screaming ladies, left him behind, on the road, to fight and spit fire at the trees."[4]

One observer mentioned several specific encounters that he claimed were characteristically southern. The first was an enraged diner "deliberately shooting at another in the dining saloon." Next was the case of a man, "hard pressed by creditors, who . . . seized a bowie-knife in each hand, and rushed among them, stabbing and ripping right and left, till checked in his mad career of assassination by a creditor, in self-defence, burying a cleaver in his skull." A third incident involved one Levi Tarver, who met another man on a public road and exchanged "high words" with him; the man "drew a bowie-knife, and completely severed, at one blow, Levi's head from his body." The final affair occurred when two gentlemen began kicking each other at a "respectable evening party" after one stepped on the

4. William Kingsford, *Impressions of the West and South* . . . (Toronto, 1853), 53; Barton Griffith, *The Diary of Barton Griffith, Covington, Indiana, 1832–34* . . . (Crawfordsville, Ind., 1932), 13; Charles Sealsfield, *America: Glorious and Chaotic Land; Charles Sealsfield Discovers the Young United States* . . . , trans. E. L. Jordan (Englewood Cliffs, N.J., 1969), 151; Olmsted, *A Journey Through Texas*, 20; Faux, *Memorable Days in America*, 200.

other's toe; a borrowed bowie knife brought the dispute to a bloody end. The man who reported these events did not consider all southerners to be "blood-thirsty"; indeed, he thought that many were "the most kind, quiet, and amiable men I have ever met; but, when taken in connexion with the free use of the bowie-knife, they afford strong evidence that there is [in the South] a general and extraordinary recklessness of human life."[5]

The southerner's propensity to fight surprised and disturbed many observers. "The darkest side of the southerner is his quarrelsomeness, and recklessness of human life," wrote a wayfarer. "The terrible bowie-knife is ever ready to be drawn, and it is drawn and used too, on the slightest provocation. Duels are fought with this horrible weapon, in which the combatants are almost chopped to pieces; or with the no less fatal, but less shocking rifle, perhaps within pistol-distance." In the matter of duels, one traveler said that a colonel in the South Carolina militia introduced him to several "young gentlemen . . . who, with the young colonel, had all there met as gay proud birds of a feather; men, I mean, who, in duels, had killed their man each!" Some encounters were especially gruesome. A man described what he called "one of the bloodiest duels ever fought in this section of the country. The arrangement was that each [antagonist] should be armed with a double barrelled gun loaded with buck shot, with a pair of pistols & a bowie knife. At the word they were to advance towards each other and fire at such time as they pleased. If the guns failed to kill they were to use the pistols & then finish with bowie knives & fight until one or the other was killed. They fought until both were very badly mutilated and then the seconds separated them."[6]

Various writers have attempted to account for southern violence, but with little success. The usual explanation that slavery made southerners violent is far too simplistic; so is the assertion that the antebellum South was a frontier and therefore a violent society. Some of the most violent parts of the South had few slaves; nor were all frontiers in America and abroad tumultuous places. The South was

5.   Murray, *Lands of the Slave and the Free*, I, 243–46.
6.   Philip Henry Gosse, *Letters from Alabama* . . . (London, 1859), 250–51; Faux, *Memorable Days in America*, 45; Whipple, *Southern Diary*, 32–33.

and still is a violent society because violence is one of the cultural traditions that southerners brought with them to America.[7]

Their Celtic ancestors were, authorities agree, characteristically violent. "Their propensity to fight led them into hostilities on very slight occasions," one writer explained. "The whole race was warlike and fierce, and ready to fight with the greatest ardour . . . but accompanied with a rashness and temerity not very compatible with military discipline." Proud and contentious Scots, Irish, Welsh, and other Celtic people—touchy about their honor and dignity—were ever ready for either mass combat or individual duels.[8]

7. The influence of culture on southern violence is noted in such important recent studies as Sheldon Hackney, "Southern Violence," *American Historical Review*, LXXIV (1969), 906–25; Raymond D. Gastil, "Homicide and a Regional Culture of Violence," *American Sociological Review*, XXXVI (1971), 412–27; Dickson D. Bruce, Jr., *Violence and Culture in the Antebellum South* (Austin, 1979); John Shelton Reed, "Below the Smith and Wesson Line: Southern Violence," in *One South: An Ethnic Approach to Regional Culture* (Baton Rouge, 1982), 139–53; Bertram Wyatt-Brown, *Southern Honor: Ethics and Behavior in the Old South* (New York, 1982); and Edward L. Ayers, *Vengeance and Justice: Crime and Punishment in the 19th-Century South* (New York, 1984). Wyatt-Brown and Ayers also emphasize the importance of honor as well as cultural continuity, and Wyatt-Brown further recognizes the Celtic influence (among others) in shaping the Old South, but none of these works trace the emphasis on violence and honor in southern culture to its primary source—the South's Celtic heritage.
8.   James Logan, *The Scottish Gael; or, Celtic Manners, as Preserved Among the Highlanders* . . . (rpr. 2 vols.; Edinburgh, 1976), I, 116–17. See also Alwyn Rees and Brinley Rees, *Celtic Heritage: Ancient Tradition in Ireland and Wales* (London, 1961), 122–23; Lloyd Laing, *Celtic Britain* (New York, 1979), 148; Barry Cunliffe, *The Celtic World* (New York, 1979), 42–59; Gerald of Wales, *The Journey Through Wales and the Description of Wales*, trans. Lewis Thorpe (New York, 1978), 233–74; Anne Ross, *Everyday Life of the Pagan Celts* (London, 1970), 56. Some of the other similarities between Celtic and southern culture are discussed in Grady McWhiney and Forrest McDonald, "The Celtic Origins of Southern Herding Practices," *Journal of Southern History*, LI (1985), 165–82; Grady McWhiney and Forrest McDonald, "Celtic Names in the Southern United States," *Names*, XXXI (1983), 89–102; Grady McWhiney, "Education in the Old South: A Reexamination," in Walter J. Fraser, Jr., and Winfred B. Moore, Jr. (eds.), *Southern Enigma: Essays on Race, Class, and Folk Culture* (Westport, Conn., 1983), 169–88; Forrest McDonald and Grady McWhiney, "The South from Self-Sufficiency to Peonage: An Interpretation," *American Historical Review*, LXXXV (1980), 1095–118; Forrest McDonald and Ellen Shapiro McDonald, "The Ethnic Origins of the American People, 1790," *William and Mary Quarterly*, 3rd ser., XXXVII (1980), 179–99; and Forrest McDonald and Grady McWhiney, "The Antebellum Southern Herdsman: A Reinterpretation," *Journal of Southern History*, XLI (1975), 147–66.

Scotland's history, as an Englishman noted, was "characterised by violence of a scale and of an intensity unknown in England." Clansmen went everywhere armed, and their accoutrements included a knife, pistols, a sword, and often a gun as well. "Every person wishes to be thought a soldier," noted an eighteenth-century Scot, who insisted that the popular poetry of the country "might, with great propriety, be termed pastorals for warriors. And great was their influence upon . . . both sexes, from the highest to the lowest. Their poetical tales, breathing a warlike spirit, were well calculated to inspire the men with an ardent desire of imitating, on some future occasion, their ancient worthies. The women, too, who were passionately fond of them, regarded the martial virtues as essential in a son or a lover."[9]

Conflicts and feuds were customary. "The Highlanders, before they were disarmed," observed Dr. Samuel Johnson, "were so addicted to quarrels, that the boys used to follow any publick procession or ceremony, however festive, or however solemn, in expectation of the battle, which was sure to happen before the company dispersed." An English officer reported that the people of Inverness had small windows with heavy shutters on the ground floor of their houses because "in their Clan-Quarrels, several had been shot from the opposite Side of the Way, when they were in their Chamber, and by these Shutters they were concealed and in safety."[10]

A careful observer described the Irish as "a barbarous and . . . a warlike people," with a "romantic sense of honour"; inordinately proud; "wild and unruly"; "with passions the most violent and sensitive." Such quarrelsome people were always ready to fight foreigners—or each other. Travelers agreed that the Irish enjoyed fights

9. Walter Allen, *The British Isles* (London, 1965), 21; Thomas Kirk and Ralph Thoresby, *Tours in Scotland, 1677 & 1681*, ed. P. Hume Brown (Edinburgh, 1892), 29; John Ramsay, *Scotland and Scotsmen in the Eighteenth Century, from the MSS. of John Ramsay, Esq. of Ochtertyre*, ed. Alexander Allardyce (2 vols.; Edinburgh, 1888), II, 408, 409; see also Logan, *The Scottish Gael*, I, 328; Eve Begley, *On Scottish Ways* (New York, 1978), 55–57, 61–62, 100–101.

10. R. W. Chapman (ed.), *Johnson's Journey to the Western Islands of Scotland and Boswell's Journal of a Tour to the Hebrides with Samuel Johnson, LL.D.* (Oxford, 1970), 40; Edward Burt, *Burt's Letters from the North of Scotland*, ed. R. Jamieson (1730; rpr. 2 vols.; Edinburgh, 1974), I, 61. On Scottish violence, see also John Prebble, *Culloden* (Harmondsworth, England, 1967), 32–53, 300.

and feuds. "It is not unusual with them to meet in clans or factions, for the avowed purpose of a battle," wrote an Englishman. And a German visitor noted "the sudden and continual wild quarrels and national pitched battles with the shillelah (a murderous sort of stick which every man keeps hidden under his rags), in which hundreds take part in a minute, and do not resist till several are left dead or wounded on the field; the frightful war-whoop which they set up on these occasions; the revenge for an affront or injury, which is cherished and inherited by whole villages."[11]

Duels, as late as the eighteenth century, "were an everyday occurrence in their lives," wrote a distinguished Irish historian, "and the results were often fatal." An Irish judge recalled: "Our elections were more prolific in duels than any other public meetings: they very seldom originated at a horse-race, cock-fight, hunt, or at any place of amusement: folks then had pleasure in view, and 'something else to do' than to quarrel; but at all elections, or at assizes, or, in fact, at any place of business, almost every man, without any very particular reason, immediately became a violent partisan, and frequently a furious enemy to somebody else; and gentlemen often got themselves shot before they could tell what they were fighting about." This judge also observed: "It is incredible what a singular passion the Irish gentlemen, though in general excellent-tempered fellows, formerly had for fighting each other"—this from a man who remembered 227 "memorable and official duels" fought during what he called "my grand climacteric."[12]

Another Irishman stated that the "universal practice of duelling

11.   Thomas Crofton Croker, *Researches in the South of Ireland [1812–1822]* . . . (rpr. New York, 1969), 2, 4, 13, 224–25, 231; William Shaw Mason (ed.), *A Statistical Account or Parochial Survey of Ireland, Drawn Up from the Communications of the Clergy* (3 vols.; Dublin, 1814–19), III, 471; [Hermann Ludwig Heinrich], *Tour in England, Ireland, and France in the Years 1826, 1827, 1828, and 1829* (Philadelphia, 1833), 348–49. See also Mason (ed.), *A Statistical Account of Ireland*, II, 97, 364–65, 455–56, III, 72–73.
12.   Edward MacLysaght, *Irish Life in the Seventeenth Century* (rpr. Dublin, 1979), 91; Sir Jonah Barrington, *Personal Sketches of His Own Times*, ed. Townsend Young (3rd ed., 2 vols.; London, 1869), I, 285, 272–73. See also Charles Topham Bowden, *A Tour Through Ireland* (Dublin, 1791), 25–26; De Latocnaye, *A Frenchman's Walk Through Ireland, 1796–7*, trans. and ed. John Stevenson (Belfast, 1917), 120–21.

[in eighteenth-century Ireland] . . . contributed not a little to the disturbed and ferocious state of society." He pointed out that dueling clubs existed throughout the country; in fact, no gentleman could take "his proper station in life till he had 'smelt powder,' as it was called; no barrister could go circuit till he had obtained a reputation in this way; no election, and scarcely an assizes, passed without a number of duels; and many men of the bar . . . owed their eminence, not to powers of eloquence or to legal ability, but to a daring spirit and the number of duels they had fought." A dueling "code of laws and regulations were drawn up as a standard, to refer to on all points of honour." Irish laws prohibited dueling, "but such was the spirit of the times, that they remained a dead letter. No prosecution ensued, or even if it did, no conviction would follow."[13]

When South Carolinians "talked of the duello, and of famous hands with the pistol in these parts," a native of Ireland noted, their "conversation had altogether very much the tone which would have probably characterised the talk of a group of Tory Irish gentlemen over their wine some sixty years ago." Indeed, the eighteenth-century Irish gentlemen who so vigorously favored dueling were known as "Fire-Eaters," and the *Irish code of honor* was the model for South Carolina's own dueling code.[14]

Violence was also a significant part of the culture of the Celtic fringe of England and Wales. The "reiver" tradition of the English-Scottish border country prevailed in Cumberland even into the nineteenth century, and an Englishman noted that many of the "inhabitants . . . are descendants of the borderers, who yet retain much of their native fierceness and savage courage." The Welsh, who loved combat so much that they would "fight without protection against men clad in iron, unarmed against those bearing weapons, on foot against mounted cavalry," enjoyed the sport of "purring" in which

13. John Edward Walsh, *Sketches of Ireland Sixty Years Ago* (Dublin, 1847), 18, 22–23, 30. See also Daniel Corkery, *The Hidden Ireland: A Study of Gaelic Munster in the Eighteenth Century* (rpr. Dublin, 1975), 57.

14. William Howard Russell, *My Diary North and South* (2 vols.; London, 1863), I, 188; Barrington, *Personal Sketches*, I, 270 (his chapter on dueling is entitled "The Fire-Eaters"); Jack K. Williams, *Dueling in the Old South: Vignettes of Social History* (College Station, Tex., 1980), 40–41, 100.

two opponents grasped each other firmly by the shoulders. At the starting signal, they began kicking each other in the shins (their shoes had toeplates). The first man to release his grip was declared the loser.[15]

In describing the violent ways of antebellum southerners, observers often used the same terms employed in descriptions of other Celts and sometimes even compared southerners to Celts. The first trial in Williamsburg County, South Carolina, was held in 1806, and the four men—at least three with Irish surnames—who were charged with assault and battery reportedly said they had "held a good old Irish discussion with sticks, pleaded guilty, paid their fines, and considered the money well spent." In 1861 an observer found Irishmen living in the South as eager as native southerners to fight Yankees. In fact, an Englishman stated, the Old South "appears to resemble Ireland, or what Ireland was 60 years ago. One hears of bowie-knives and revolvers continually, and I was assured that nine-tenths of the party carried them in their pockets." In a Montgomery, Alabama, hotel in May, 1861, British reporter William H. Russell noted the same phenomenon: "One of our party comes in to say that he could scarce get down to the [hotel lobby] . . . on account of the crowd, and all the people who passed him had very sharp bones. He remarks thereupon to the clerk at the bar, who tells [him] that the particular projections he alludes to are implements of defence or offence, as the case may be, and adds, 'I suppose you and your [English] friends are the only people in the house who haven't a bowie-knife, or a six-shooter, or Derringer about them.'" Furthermore, southerners were as willing as any other Celts to use the weapons they carried. One sightseer declared that a southerner would challenge anyone to a duel, "no matter whether he be his best friend or his worst enemy. He acts on the impulse of the moment, and puts no restraint on his passions. When provoked he gives way to the feeling of revenge, and as all classes go armed, he attacks the object of his hatred. . . . The only

15.   George MacDonald Fraser, *The Steel Bonnets* (New York, 1972); James Dugdale, *The New British Traveller; or, Modern Panorama of England and Wales . . .* (4 vols.; London, 1819), I, 621; Gerald of Wales, *The Journey Through Wales*, 234; Bruce Felton and Mark Fowler, *Felton's & Fowler's More Best, Worst and Most Unusual* (New York, 1976), 86.

security for life . . . is the belief that every one is armed and ready to use his weapons in an instant."[16]

In their violent attitudes and practices Celts and southerners were vastly different from the peaceful professions and habits of Englishmen and Yankees, who boasted that they were and always had been less violent and more civilized than their neighbors. "More robberies and murders are committed in Virginia, than in all England," stated an Englishman visiting the South. "There are fewer capital crimes committed in New England since its settlement than in any other country on the globe . . . in proportion to the number of its inhabitants," claimed the president of Yale College. "During the last fourteen years," he declared shortly before his death in 1817, "I have traveled . . . twelve thousand miles, chiefly in New England and New York, and in this extensive progress have never seen two men employed in fighting. Nor do I remember more than one instance of this nature which fell under my own eye during my life."[17]

Duels, which were so popular with Celts and southerners, were much rarer in England and in the North. English gentlemen denounced dueling as early as the seventeenth century, and a Frenchman wrote in the eighteenth century: "It may be said with entire justice that Englishmen are very brave [but] . . . very few are partisans of duelling." The English frequently denounced and lampooned dueling. As for New England, Timothy Dwight claimed that since its settlement, five duels had been fought there and only two involved residents.[18]

16.   Mary R. Reid, "Williamsburg County [South Carolina] Court House," *Three Rivers Chronicle*, I (1981), 2; Russell, *My Diary North and South*, I, 411, 238; Robert Everest, *A Journey Through the United States and Parts of Canada* (London, 1855), 91; James Logan, *Notes of a Journey . . .* (Edinburgh, 1838), 178.
17.   Faux, *Memorable Days in America*, 127; Timothy Dwight, *Travels in New England and New York*, ed. Barbara Miller Solomon (4 vols.; Cambridge, Mass., 1969), I, 123.
18.   Donna Andrew, "The Code of Honour and Its Critics: The Opposition to Duelling in England, 1700–1850," *Social History*, V (1980), 409–34; Marcia Valle, *The Gentleman's Recreations: Accomplishments and Pastimes of the English Gentleman, 1580–1630* (Cambridge, England, 1977), 65; Ceasar de Saussure, *A Foreign View of England in the Reigns of George I & George II: The Letters of Monsieur Ceasar de Saussure to His Family*, trans. and ed. Madame Van Muyden (London, 1902), 179; Dwight, *Trav-*

Southerners, who scorned such pacifism, considered Yankees and Englishmen too business-minded and dishonorable to fight. An Englishman reported that southerners held the English in "contempt" because they "believe that we, too [like Yankees], have had the canker of peace upon us. One evidence of this, according to Southern men, is the abolition of duelling. This practice, according to them, is highly wholesome and meritorious." But others regarded these affairs of honor as deplorable atrocities. "Cruel horrid custom thus to butcher & destroy men for the false code of honor," admonished a Yankee. "Honor! It is a vague idea the duelist has of honor." Dr. Samuel Johnson, who denounced dueling, insisted that in contrast to what happened in Celtic areas, there was never a "case in England where one or other of the combatants *must* die: if you have overcome your adversary by disarming him, that is sufficient[;] . . . you should not kill him; your honour, or the honour of your family, is restored, as much as it can be by a duel." Shocked by bloody southern encounters, an Englishman wrote: "The barbarous baseness and cruelty of public opinion [in the South] dooms young men, when challenged, to fight. They must fight, kill or be killed, and that for some petty offence beneath the notice of the law. Established names only . . . may refuse to fight, but this is rarely done; to refuse is a stain and high dishonor." An Englishwoman stated: "Very often fathers will go . . . with their sons—quite boys—to see them fight. . . . There is a recklessness and carelessness about these Southerners which I did not think the Anglo-Saxon race could attain under any circumstances." Her mistake, of course, was thinking that the South's cultural heritage was Anglo-Saxon.[19]

Southern ways simply were too foreign for most Yankee and En-

---

els in New England and New York, I, 123. On the lack of violent crime in Puritan New England, see David T. Konig, *Law and Society in Puritan Massachusetts: Essex County, 1629–1692* (Chapel Hill, 1979); David H. Flaherty, "Crime and Social Control in Provincial Massachusetts," *Historical Journal*, XXIV (1981), 339–60; and Eli Faber, "Puritan Criminals: The Economic, Social, and Intellectual Background of Crime in Seventeenth-Century Massachusetts," *Perspectives in American History*, XI (1977–78), 83–114.

19.   Russell, *My Diary North and South*, I, 93; Whipple, *Southern Diary*, 29; Chapman (ed.), *Johnson's Journey*, 313–14; Faux, *Memorable Days in America*, 187; Barbara Leigh Smith Bodichon, *An American Diary, 1857–8*, ed. Joseph W. Reed, Jr. (London, 1972), 64. See also Williams, *Dueling in the Old South*, 75.

glish observers to understand or appreciate. One northerner was appalled that a southern woman would have her brother's marble monument inscribed "Micajah Green Lewis who fell in a duel." But southern women, like traditional Celtic women, often supported dueling. After all, an Englishman acknowledged, the South was a violent place, "the land of Lynch law and bowie knives . . . [as] barba-rous as a jungle inhabited by wild beasts." Even the literature written by southerners, a northerner declared, was "atrocious"—full of "gouging, biting, and horse-play which form the body of their humour"—and "valuable only to the moralist as expressive of the sort of savage spirit which slavery could breed in people."[20]

To blame southern violence on slavery rather than the South's cultural heritage was typical, even though most Yankees regarded southerners with fully as much contempt as Englishmen regarded Celts. A northerner advised Yankees to "mingle freely" with southern-ers "and . . . strive to bring up their habits, by a successful example, to the New England standard." When that proved impossible, stronger measures were recommended. "I believe," announced a saintly north-erner, "that the great conception of a Christian society, which was in the minds of the Pilgrims of the Mayflower . . . is to displace and blot out the foul [South] . . . with all its heaven-offending enormities." Many Massachusetts soldiers in the Civil War favored a policy of geno-cide toward southerners. "I would exterminate them root and branch," wrote one Yankee just after the war. "They have often said they pre-ferred it before subjugation, and, with the help of God, I would give it them. I am only saying what thousands say every day."[21]

20. Welcome Arnold Green, *The Journal of Welcome Arnold Green: Journeys in the South, 1822–1824*, ed. Alice E. Smith (Madison, Wis., 1957), 116–17; Williams, *Dueling in the Old South*, 19; Russell, *My Diary North and South*, II, 9, 11; William Dean Howells, "American Letter: The Southern States in Recent American Literature," *Literature*, No. 47 (London, September 10, 1898), 231. See also Philo Tower, *Slavery Unmasked: Being a Truthful Narrative of Three Years' Residence and Journeying in Eleven Southern States . . .* (Rochester, N.Y., 1856), 386; Murray, *Lands of the Slave and the Free*, I, 247; J. Benwell, *An Englishman's Travels in America: His Observations of Life and Manners in the Free and Slave States* (London, 1853), 106, 115; and John Henry Vessey, *Mr. Vessey of England: Being the Incidents and Reminiscences of Travel in a Twelve Weeks' Tour Through the United States and Canada in the Year 1859*, ed. Brian Waters (New York, 1956), 103.
21. Abner D. Jones, *Illinois and the West* (Boston, 1838), 157; Julian M. Sturtevant,

In calls to exterminate southerners and their "odious ways," northerners sounded much like Englishmen who advocated the obliteration of their "barbarian" Celtic neighbors. It may be no coincidence that the Irish-born reporter William H. Russell described Federal Secretary of War Edwin Stanton as "excessively vain . . . a rude, rough, vigorous Oliver Cromwell sort of man." Typically, Yankees referred to southerners as dirty and ignorant, just as the English had spoken of the Irish, the Welsh, and the Scots. A Connecticut soldier informed his sister that the "Rebels are Barbarians and savages."[22]

In support of these charges of barbarism, several Yankees reported that some Confederates beheaded their enemies. A Massachusetts soldier claimed that in May, 1862, he discovered in an abandoned Rebel camp five neatly polished skulls inscribed with the words "Five Zouaves' Coconuts killed at Bull Run by Southern lead." Another Yankee insisted that Confederates had used the skulls of slain Federals as soup bowls, and a Minnesotan reported that he found in an abandoned Confederate campsite the cranium of a Union soldier that had been "used by the Rebs for a soap dish."[23]

Such claims may have been true. Although the practice of decapitating an enemy and saving his head appears to have been uncommon in the Confederacy, it was not unprecedented in Celtic history or in the Old 'South. "They cut off the heads of enemies slain in battle and attach them to the necks of their horses," explained Diodorus of the ancient Celts. "The bloodstained spoils they . . . carry off as booty, while striking up a paean and singing a song of victory; and they nail up these first fruits upon their houses." Livy, writing in the third century B.C., mentioned "Gallic horsemen . . . with heads hanging at their horses' breasts, or fixed on their lances, and singing their customary songs of triumph." He also stated that Celts beheaded the Roman consul-elect Lucius Postumius, "cleaned out the head . . . and gilded the skull, which thereafter served them . . . as a drinking cup."[24]

An Address in Behalf of the Society for the Promotion of Theological Education in the West (New York, 1853), 568–69; Bell I. Wiley, *The Life of Billy Yank: The Common Soldier of the Union* (Indianapolis, 1951), 346.

22.   Russell, *My Diary North and South*, II, 433; Prebble, *Culloden*, 231–300; Wiley, *The Life of Billy Yank*, 349.

23.   Wiley, *The Life of Billy Yank*, 347.

24.   Ross, *Everyday Life of the Pagan Celts*, 73; Cunliffe, *The Celtic World*, 83–86.

Lest these accounts be dismissed as hyperbole, it should be remembered that beheading enemies is a recurring theme in Irish and Welsh literature. Cú Chulainn, the famous Celtic folk hero, collected many heads; indeed, he once displayed twelve that he had taken in combat. A judge recalled a contest between two Irish gentlemen who "in the presence of the archbishop and all the chief authorities and ladies of rank" fought with broadswords and large knives until one beheaded the other "very expertly with his knife . . . and . . . handed it to the lords-justices . . . by whom the head and neck was most graciously received." Scots often beheaded their enemies, especially those who aroused their hatred, and decapitation also was practiced in the antebellum South. When Kentuckians captured outlaw Micajah Harpe, for example, they not only cut off his head but Squire Silas McBee rode home with it attached to his saddle and stuck the trophy on a tree "as a warning to other outlaws." A few years later the head of Samuel Mason was exhibited in Natchez, and the heads of Wiley Harpe and James May were stuck on poles by a Mississippi roadside as "warnings to highwaymen." Late in the antebellum period a Yankee visitor in the South saw a sight, he wrote, "which makes my very blood run cold as I think of it . . . a human head stuck on a pole." An outlawed runaway slave had been killed and his severed head "put upon the highway, as a terror to deter other slaves from following in his footsteps."[25]

Violent deaths were far more frequent in the South than in other parts of the country. In a sparsely populated region of Georgia a visitor learned that "about as many men died by being *killed*, as in any other way; there being a man in jail for murder, in each of five contiguous counties." "The South has the unenviable distinction of having slain a greater number of their fellow men with murderous hands than all the other States, including California, put together," announced a Mississippi preacher in 1855. During the preceding year,

25.   T. G. E. Powell, *The Celts* (New York, 1958), 108; Ross, *Everyday Life of the Pagan Celts*, 72–74; Cunliffe, *The Celtic World*, 82–87; Mary McGarry (comp.), *Great Folk Tales of Old Ireland* (New York, 1972), 74, 91; Jeremiah Curtin, *Myths and Folk-Lore of Ireland* (rpr. New York, 1975), 309–26; Barrington, *Personal Sketches*, I, 271; Wallace Notestein, *The Scots in History* (repr. Westport, Conn., 1970), 36; James Hall, *Letters from the West; Containing Sketches of Scenery, Manners, and Customs . . .* (rpr. Gainesville, 1967), 265–82; Paul I. Wellman, *Spawn of Evil* (New York, 1965), 80–100, 120–35; Tower, *Slavery Unmasked*, 144.

he pointed out, more men died violently in Mississippi alone than in all the six New England states, though those states had an aggregate population five times as great as that of Mississippi. "The reckless manner in which the sixth commandment, which forbids murder, is disregarded in this community, is truly alarming," proclaimed this minister, who insisted that if "these murders were committed by vagabonds and the scum of society . . . [the] moral effect would not be so injurious to society. But . . . [too often] men of fair standing in society, received and regarded as gentlemen, are the perpetrators of the butcheries!"[26]

Visitors noticed the excessive violence in southern society and how unconcerned most southerners were about it, as well as how often crimes of violence went unpunished. "The law is not duly enforced," complained an observer, who charged that "legalized duelling . . . and deliberate assassination" were all too common. Other peripatetics stated that men literally got away with murder in the Old South. As one Yankee insisted, "The administration of justice throughout the South is far more imperfect and partial than in the North."[27]

Neither southern courts nor lawmen paid much attention to violence. "Public fights" in the South, when "gentlemen descend to the common bully," remarked a Yankee, were abundant. "Witnessed a laughable trial today of one judge . . . for having whipped another judge," wrote this same observer, who also noted that "there are six indictments against individuals for fights at this session of court." But none of these was regarded as a serious offense. "During the recess of court," explained this northerner, "one of the . . . jury men came below & found his hopeful son of some 8 or 9 years of age fighting with another boy. The father looked coolly on until it was ended and then said, 'Now you little devil, if you catch him down again bite him, chaw his lip or you never'll be a man.' Really a singular character to guard over the peace & well being of the country but only one of the

26.   [Jeremiah Evarts], *Through the South and the West with Jeremiah Evarts in 1826*, ed. J. Orin Oliphant (Lewisburg, Pa., 1956), 105; the Reverend James A. Lyon quoted in the Columbus (Miss.) *Eagle*, June 1, 1855.
27.   William Charles Macready, *The Diaries . . . 1833–1851*, ed. William Toynbee (2 vols.; London, 1912), II, 246; Whipple, *Southern Diary*, 128–29; Josiah Quincy, "A Journal, 1773," in *Josiah Quincy (1772–1864), Memoir of the Life of Josiah Quincy . . .*, ed. Eliza Susan Quincy (Boston, 1875), 89, 95; Parsons, *Inside View of Slavery*, 139.

numerous specimens of this fighting spirit only to be found in the South."[28]

Just how ineffective southern lawmen were in suppressing violence is illustrated in the account of a foreigner who saw two young North Carolinians fighting "in front of the house and in the presence of the Justice of the Peace. Women, children, and blacks gathered around." Several times the justice calmly asked the fighters to stop. When they ignored him, he stepped back to enjoy the combat. His wife, "outraged at the disobedience," rushed up and "repeated the commands of her husband, but was received with derision. Finally, the antagonists cooled, shook hands by the fighting code, and each rode on his way." At that point the puzzled foreigner asked the justice: "By the law, must they not give obedience to your commands, and abstain from their squabbling in your presence?" His answer was: "They should." And when asked if he could not bring the men into court and have them punished for their behavior, he replied: "I could." But it was clear to the foreigner that this "good-natured Justice, who seemed to make far less of the matter than his indignant wife, and was of the opinion that it was more in keeping with his official worth to pass over an apparent slight, instead of taking the proud revenge which an injured self-love might demand."[29]

Another reason why the justice may have been reluctant to enforce the law, which apparently the foreigner failed to perceive, was that it would have been dangerous to do so. A lawman who was too diligent, or who offended the wrong man or family, could get himself injured or killed. Southern families, like those of their Celtic ancestors, were extended and clannish, and family feuds in the Old South were as easy to start and as difficult to stop as they were in premodern Scotland and Ireland. Southerners tended to protect family members from the law and to take revenge against family enemies just as their forefathers had done. In 1830, rather than allow a deputy sheriff to serve a writ on one of their kinsmen, some rural Alabamians imprisoned the deputy beneath a grocery store until he promised to leave the area and never come back. When several feuding Kentucky families met at a funeral they opened fire on each other re-

28. Whipple, *Southern Diary*, 24–25.
29. Johann David Schopf, *Travels in the Confederation [1783–1784]*, trans. and ed. Alfred J. Morrison (rpr. 2 vols.; New York, 1968), II, 123.

gardless of the crowd. "These occurrences are so common in this State," claimed an Englishman, "that little excitement was produced, and no attempt was made to arrest the parties."[30]

Such actions had Celtic models. In 1730 an English officer observed that Scots were inclined to excuse the crimes of their fellow clansmen. Jail keepers often allowed "Murderers and other notorious Villains" to escape, insisted an Englishman, who claimed that "the greatest Part of these Escapes have been the Consequences, either of Clan-Interest or Clannish Terror. As for Example, if one of the Magistrates were a Cameron (for the Purpose), the Criminal (Cameron) must not suffer, if the Clan be desirous he should be saved." "If keeping the peace in Scotland had depended on the justices," wrote a scholar, "Scotland would have been overrun with rioters and foreign invaders. It is quite possible to read the justice of the peace minutes and not be aware that general peacekeeping was one of their duties." And in Ireland as late as 1778, a justice of the peace who issued a summons for a gentleman would be virtually forced into a duel because he had insulted that person.[31]

Life for a lawman was as hazardous in the Old South as in Ireland. In 1861 a southerner admitted to a visitor that "the law is nearly powerless [to stop] shootings and stabbings" because the perpetrators "are so reckless, they have things their own way." A sojourner in South Carolina told of a young colonel, with the Celtic surname of McKinnon, who threatened to kill both a family friend and a hotel owner when neither would extend him additional credit. He tried "to shoot the landlord, and then attempted to shoot himself, but had no prime. He then begged round for prime, but could get none. I endeavoured to reason with him," reported the frightened visitor, "but with as much effect as with a woman possessed with seven devils. 'I have a right, sir,' said he, 'to do as Brutus did. What Cato did,

30. Harris, "Rowdyism, Public Drunkenness, and Bloody Encounters in Early Perry County," 20; Henry Arthur Bright, *Happy Country This America: The Travel Diary of Henry Arthur Bright [1852]*, ed. Anne Henry Ehrenpreis (Columbus, Ohio, 1978), 236–37. See also William Gilpin, *Observations . . . Made in the Year 1776, on Several Parts of Great Britain . . .* (2 vols.; London, 1789), I, 211.
31. Burt, *Burt's Letters*, I, 46–47; Anne E. Whetstone, *Scottish County Government in the Eighteenth and Nineteenth Centuries* (Edinburgh, 1981), 48; Frank O'Connor (ed.), *A Book of Ireland* (Glasgow, 1980), 264–65.

and Addison approved, cannot be wrong.'" This dangerous and independent-minded young man, described as "naturally witty and highly gifted," at age twenty-two had "abandoned three wives [and] killed several men."[32]

An Englishwoman noted that when southerners "engaged in a dispute, however violent may be the discussion, the courtesy of the 'sir' is never omitted. On the contrary it is repeated at every third word, and mixed up as it is with the oaths and denunciations, with which they always interlard their discourse, the effect is curious enough."[33]

Southerners knew that the words they used as well as their tone of voice could prevent or start a fight; they also knew that custom sanctioned their violent ways. Even if they were taken to court, their chances of escaping punishment were excellent. Men often killed and went free in the South just as in earlier times they had in Ireland and Scotland. As one observer in the South noted, enemies would meet, exchange insults, and one would shoot the other down, professing that he had acted in self-defense because he believed the victim was armed. When such a story was told in court, "in a community where it is not a strange thing for men to carry about their persons deadly weapons, [each member of the jury] feels that he would have done the same thing under similar circumstances so that in condemning him they would but condemn themselves." Consequently, they free the slayer, "and a hundred others, our sons and half grown lads amongst them, resolve in their hearts, that since every man may go armed, and every one is therefore justifiable in slaying his enemy, they will do likewise." In Alabama a lawyer reportedly told a visitor: "We have more cases on the docket in this county now, for murder, than can be tried during the next ten years." And a Mississippian complained that "while we were trying a man for murder at the last court at Starkville, the next county seat above, two murders were committed within gunshot of that court house."[34]

32. Russell, *My Diary North and South*, II, 44; Faux, *Memorable Days in America*, 47–48.
33. Matilda Charlotte (Jesse) Fraser Houstoun, *Texas and the Gulf . . .* (Philadelphia, 1845), 191.
34. Kevin Danaher, *Gentle Places and Simple Things: Irish Customs and Beliefs* (Dublin, 1979), 31–36; MacLysaght, *Irish Life*, 271–77; L. M. Cullen, *Life in Ireland*

The actions of southern courts often amazed outsiders. An Englishman described how in Augusta, Georgia, in 1834 the mayor presided "at a court for the trial of petty offences. . . . The Aldermen sat as a jury & they were trying a man for fighting in the market, there was as little ceremony or distinction as can be imagined, the offender with his accuser & witnesses stood together side by side, & the Mayor was so polite as to Mister them all, even the dirty scroundrell who had been making a riot." The mayor explained to the anxious Englishman how local justice worked. "There is no apprehending before the trial," said the mayor; "we just serve them with a summons to appear, & if they neglect it we fine them, & should they escape by leaving the state, we are very glad to get rid of them; the principle may be bad, but we cant undertake to prosecute rogues for our neighbours, it is enough if we rid ourselves of them." A northerner reported that in the South the "classification of crimes is singular. Manslaughter, bigamy and falsely packing cotton are under one head. Murder here costs about 2 years imprisonment or $1000 fine. . . . Such juries as they have here are beyond any man's control."[35]

The meeting of these "uncontrollable" juries on court days in the various county seats often provided entertainment to southerners. The courtrooms were the stage on which dramas of real life—murder, assault, slander, and other crimes—were played before appreciative audiences. During a single session a Carroll County, Georgia, grand jury indicted one man for keeping drunken and disorderly company about his place, allowing "fiddling and dancing" and whiskey making on Sunday, and for "menacing voters"; indicted another man "for assaulting and violently beating Absalom Adams on election day [and] for threatening to beat . . . Thomas Wynn and having pistols and rocks to annoy the good people"; required two more men to stand trial "for fire hunting at night to the great annoyance of their

---

(London, 1979), 44, 57, 107–109; Ian Whyte, *Agriculture and Society in Seventeenth-Century Scotland* (Edinburgh, 1979), 14–16; Thomas Pennant, *A Tour in Scotland, MDCCLXIX* . . . (rpr. Perth, 1979), 205; Sir John Sinclair (ed.), *The Statistical Account of Scotland, 1791–1799* (rpr. 20 vols.; East Ardsley, Wakefield, England, 1981), XVII, 153, 215; Prebble, *Culloden*, 32–53; the Reverend James A. Lyon quoted in the Columbus (Miss.) *Eagle,* June 1, 1855; Parsons, *Inside View of Slavery*, 142, 144.

35.   George Townsend Fox American Journal, December 4, 1834 (MS in Public Libraries, South Shields, Durham, England); Whipple, *Southern Diary*, 24.

neighborhood"; and indicted still another man for keeping "a gambling house at the Villa Rica gold mines."[36]

People sometimes traveled many miles to attend court; to exchange news and gossip; to buy and sell things; and to drink, gamble, dance, and socialize with their friends. A carnival mood often prevailed in ordinarily sleepy county seats on court days just as had been the custom in Scotland and Ireland. A New Englander reported that southerners "seem to look upon law as a species of amusement, and to regard 'court-week' [as a festival]." Some southerners regularly let their children miss school when court was in session, and one judge twice adjourned court to attend horse races at which, said a contemporary, "he officiated with more appropriateness than on the bench."[37]

With such a variety of judges in the South, one visitor pointed out, "there is but little certainty of right & justice being properly meted out. . . . The judge has great power & can exercise a great influence," yet his will could be frustrated in various ways. A traveler remarked: "Mrs. Reid told me of an amusing revenge the 'crackers' had

36. James C. Bonner, *Georgia's Last Frontier: The Development of Carroll County* (Athens, Ga., 1971), 34.

37. Charles S. Sydnor, *The Development of Southern Sectionalism, 1819–1848* (Baton Rouge, 1948), 34; Eugene L. Schwaab (ed.), *Travels in the Old South: Selected from Periodicals of the Times* (2 vols.; Lexington, Ky., 1973), II, 439. On southern county courts, see Ralph A. Wooster, *The People in Power: Courthouse and Statehouse in the Lower South* (Knoxville, 1969), and *Politicians, Planters, and Plain Folk: Courthouse and Statehouse in the Upper South, 1850–1860* (Knoxville, 1975); Robert M. Ireland, *The County Courts in Antebellum Kentucky* (Lexington, Ky., 1972). On court days in Ireland and Scotland, see Barrington, *Personal Sketches*, I, 285; Mason (ed.), *A Statistical Account of Ireland*, II, 82–83, 364–65; Constantia Maxwell, *Country and Town in Ireland Under the Georges* (Dundalk, 1949), 48–56, 156–58; Charles Rogers, *Social Life in Scotland: From Early to Recent Times* (1884; rpr. 2 vols.; Port Washington, N.Y., 1971), II, 308–11, 333–35; Sinclair (ed.), *The Statistical Account of Scotland*, XVII, 4, 273; George Gunn (trans.) and Clement B. Gunn (ed.), *Records of the Baron Court of Stitchill, 1655–1807* (Edinburgh, 1905), xxxi–xxxvii; Whetstone, *Scottish County Government*, 1–3, 27–31, 116–17; I. F. Grant, *Highland Folk Ways* (London, 1961), 353; Rosalind Mitchison, *Life in Scotland* (London, 1978), 19; Whyte, *Agriculture and Society in Seventeenth-Century Scotland*, 44–47; Sarah Witherspoon (Ervin) McIver Diary, March 24, 1854 (MS in Southern Historical Collection, University of North Carolina, Chapel Hill); Everett Dick, *The Dixie Frontier: A Social History of the Southern Frontier from the First Transmontane Beginnings to the Civil War* (rpr. New York, 1964), 229.

on her husband by sending him to Congress to get rid of him as judge."[38]

Other than violent acts, the crime that most often came before judges and juries was theft. Some southerners, it was charged, would rather steal than work. One man called such people "the poorest and the idlest of the human race—averse to labor, and impatient of the restraints of law and the courtesies of civilized society." A Texan, cursing his neighbors for stealing hogs, told a visitor: "If ever were any hog-thieves anywhere, it's here." He claimed that several families in the county "ostensibly had a little patch of land to attend to, but . . . really . . . derived their whole lazy subsistence from their richer neighbors' hog droves."[39]

What most observers failed to understand was that the stealing of livestock was a long and honored Celtic tradition. The greatest of all Celtic folk tales, *The Cattle-Raid of Cooley*, features the exploits of Cú Chulainn, the heroic Ulster warrior and cattle stealer. Irishmen continued the practice of livestock raids into modern times, as did the Highland Scots. A traveler in eighteenth-century Scotland wrote: "The Highlanders . . . esteemed the open theft of cattle . . . by no means dishonorable." Southerners expected and tolerated a certain amount of livestock stealing, but when it became excessive and blatant they reacted violently. In 1832 a group of Georgians rounded up a gang of horse thieves, whipped them, and ran them out of the county. This appears to have been standard procedure throughout the antebellum South. A visitor recounted how it was customary for notorious livestock thieves to be "tied to a tree, lashed without mercy, and ordered to leave the county within a given time."[40]

Aside from livestock poaching and some minor pilferage, theft probably was as uncommon in the rural South as in the Scottish Highlands. An Englishman reported from the South in 1855: "There is such a sense of security in this country, that doors and windows are as often left open as closed." A wayfarer in Scotland noted in the eighteenth century "that crimes were few, remarkably few, among

38. Whipple, *Southern Diary*, 45–56.
39. Hall, *Letters from the West*, 271–72; Olmsted, *A Journey Through Texas*, 66.
40. MacLysaght, *Irish Life*, 276; Whyte, *Agriculture and Society in Seventeenth-Century Scotland*, 14; Pennant, *A Tour in Scotland*, 205; Bonner, *Georgia's Last Frontier*, 33; Hall, *Letters from the West*, 291–92.

the Highlanders. That they fought fiercely with men of another sept on occasion; that they 'lifted' cattle from a hostile clan or made a foray on an alien Lowlander with placid conscience is true . . . but it is said that cases of theft from dwelling-houses seldom occurred, highway robberies were unknown, the people lived with their property safe without bolts or bars . . . and in many a mansion not a door was locked." Between 1655 and 1807 the Scottish Baron Court of Stitchill recorded only a single case of housebreaking.[41]

Southerners worried little about burglary, yet the punishment for crimes against property in the Old South was often more severe than that for certain crimes of violence. "A man may, here, murder . . . almost with impunity, or by paying a paltry fine to the state," exclaimed an English visitor in the South, "but if he steals . . . he must be hanged for it." The situation was similar in eighteenth-century Ireland. A traveler remarked that "the criminal law of Ireland is the same as that of England, but in the execution it is so different, as scarcely to be known. I believe it is a fact," he continued, "that no man was ever hanged in Ireland for killing another in a duel: the security is such that nobody ever thought of removing out of the way of justice, yet there have been deaths of that sort, which had no more to do with honour than stabbing in the dark."[42]

Most southerners believed just as did their Celtic ancestors that under certain circumstances to kill was honorable; to steal, except perhaps a stray cow or hog, was dishonorable. William H. Russell found southerners to be remarkably honest even when they had the need and the opportunity to steal. Another man discovered that nu-

41. Murray, *Lands of the Slave and the Free,* I, 225–26; Henry Grey Graham, *The Social Life of Scotland in the Eighteenth Century* (2 vols.; London, 1900), II, 235–36; Gunn (trans.) and Gunn (ed.), *Records of the Baron Court of Stitchill,* 215. David J. Bodenhamer, "Law and Disorder in the Old South: The Situation in Georgia, 1830–1860," in Walter J. Fraser, Jr., and Winfred B. Moore, Jr. (eds.), *From the Old South to the New: Essays on the Transitional South* (Westport, Conn., 1981), 109–99, concludes that more crimes, especially violent ones, took place in southern towns than in the countryside, but that the "theft of livestock was more common in predominantly rural areas."
42. Faux, *Memorable Days in America,* 49; Ayers, *Vengeance and Justice,* 111; Arthur Young, "A Tour in Ireland; With General Observations on the Present State of the Kingdom in . . . 1776, 1777, and 1778," in *A General Collection of . . . Voyages and Travels,* ed. John Pinkerton (10 vols.; London, 1809), III, 875.

merous Texans "had fled from justice, or as they chose to call it, from law, in their own country." But most of these men had committed only crimes of violence and were thus considered honest citizens. "I saw at the breakfast table one morning, among those who were seated with me, four murderers who had sought safety in this country; and a gentleman assured me, that on one occasion, he had sat down with eleven," claimed this traveler, who nevertheless believed that "from evidence of general honesty and confidence between man and man, I should think money would be as safe here without lock and key as in our own country. I am confident that if stores were left in some part of the United States without a watch and exposed as many are in Texas, they would be robbed one of the first nights."[43]

Antebellum southerners and their Celtic ancestors, besides being more violent than Yankees and Englishmen, were less materialistic. "We do not understand shares and stocks, the use of money to make money," boasted a southerner. Irishmen could say the same about themselves; they were too hospitable and generous, too fond of drinking, gambling, and fighting to be successful money-makers. Highlanders were no different. An English officer once reported that Highland clansmen "chose to live sparingly, and be accounted a Martial People, rather than submit themselves to low and mercenary Employments." Antebellum southerners were much like other Celts—according to a proverb, "A Southerner never sells what he can eat, and a Northerner never eats what he can sell."[44]

Southerners and other Celts were also alike in their attitude toward law enforcement and what acts they condoned. They consistently ignored laws designed to control their movement and independent actions such as the making and drinking of whiskey and traffic regulations. Even today southerners and Irishmen are partial to what they both call moonshine—and the attraction, one suspects, has something to do with its being illegal. The Irish disregard traffic laws and stoplights; they drive and stop and park and walk anytime and

43.   Russell, *My Diary North and South*, II, 47–48; *Visit to Texas: Being the Journal of a Traveller . . .* (New York, 1834), 214–16.

44.   Ben Robertson, *Red Hills and Cotton: An Upcountry Memoir* (New York, 1942), 106; Everest, *A Journey Through the United States*, 100–101; MacLysaght, *Irish Life*, 42; Burt, *Burt's Letters*, I, 50–51; Owen S. Adams, "Traditional Proverbs and Sayings from California," *Western Folklore*, VI (1947), 63.

anywhere they please, just as southerners tend to do. (One indication
that Dallas may be losing some of its southernness is the current vigorous enforcement of the city's ordinance against jaywalking.) "Less
than ten years ago," a visitor to Ireland wrote in 1972, "there were no
speed limits in Dublin, and parking meters, which have been in-
stalled only recently, are blatantly ignored." Today Highland Scots are
more Anglicized, but they were not always so—as we have seen.[45]

The types of combativeness and selective lawlessness found in
the Old South were precisely those found in the premodern Celtic
areas of the British Isles, and antebellum southerners were just as
martial and prideful, just as combative and touchy about their honor
as were their Celtic ancestors. A Mississippian told a Yankee woman
that "he could say what few other Southerners could say, that he, *a
native of the South, had never thrown a card, been on a race track,
or fought a duel.*" She considered him an "honor to any mother, to
any State," but to most southerners, men and women, he was a
"sissy." The culture demanded that "real" southern men be quick to
take offense and ready to avenge by physical force any insults or
wrongs they suffered. The slightest breach of courtesy or any unfair-
ness in business was sufficient reason for a challenge. Southerners almost never considered duelists as criminals or enforced laws against
dueling. Nearly all southerners were willing to fight to protect their
pride and honor, including planters, politicians (the governor of
South Carolina wrote a standard text on dueling), and plain folk;
even preachers dueled.[46]

45. Derek A. C. Davies, *Ireland* (Tokyo, 1972), 9–10; see also MacLysaght, *Irish Life*, 78, 37, 54, 68, 73, 162, 255, 287, 291, 299, 308; Cullen, *Life in Ireland*, 44–45, 87, 96–97. On moonshining in the South, see William F. Holmes, "Moonshining and Col-
lective Violence: Georgia, 1889–1895," *Journal of American History*, LXVII (1980), 589–611; William F. Holmes, "Whitecapping: Agrarian Violence in Mississippi, 1902–1906," *Journal of Southern History*, XXXV (1969), 165–85, and "Whitecapping in Georgia: Carroll and Houston Counties, 1893," *Georgia Historical Quarterly*, XLIV (1980), 388–404; and Ayers, *Vengeance and Justice*, 260–64.
46. Schwaab (ed.), *Travels in the Old South*, II, 340; Williams, *Dueling in the Old South*, 13, 23, 60, 66–67, 40, 76, 34; Bodichon, *An American Diary*, 97; Henry Herz, *My Travels in America [1846–1851]*, trans. Henry Bertram Hill (Madison, Wis., 1963), 93; J. F. H. Claiborne, "A Trip Through the Piney Woods," *Publications of the Mississippi Historical Society*, IX (1906), 512; Timothy Flint, *Recollections of the Last Ten Years*, ed. C. Hartley Grattan (1826; rpr. New York, 1932), 324.

It was characteristic of Celts and southerners to settle their personal disputes, especially those related to their honor, outside the courtroom. "Questions affecting personal character were rarely referred to courts of law," noted a Tennessee lawyer. "To carry a personal grievance into a court of law degraded the plaintiff in the estimation of his peers and put the whole case beneath the notice of society." Southerners were just as ready to protect their honor or that of their kin as was the Scot who knew no English but, while standing protectively behind his clan chief's chair during a banquet, mistook the whiskey-stimulated conversation for a quarrel between his leader and an English officer. This loyal clansman "took it into his head that his master was insulted, and, without farther ceremony, drawing a pistol from his belt, snapped it at the head of the English officer, who would have been a dead man, if the pistol had not providentially missed fire." The ease with which southerners justified violence is typified in a letter from an Alabamian to a kinsman in 1834: "Dr Withers shot a Mr Stolingworth . . . who very improperly attempted to horsewhip him in the streets for some remark on his character." [47]

The mother of Andrew Jackson reportedly told her son: "Never tell a lie, nor take what is not your own, nor sue anybody for slander or assault and battery. *Always settle them cases yourself!*" Jackson not only followed his mother's advice; he followed his Celtic and southern heritage: he fought several duels and engaged in what a contemporary called another "one hundred fights or *violent and abusive* quarrels." [48]

Whether fights in the Old South were formal duels or simply rough-and-tumble contests, they were an intrinsic part of a culture that was as violent as its Celtic progenitor and—what is highly significant—just as unrepentant of its combativeness. Southerners, like other Celts, were proud of their violent ways. An Irishman might as readily have been describing the antebellum South when he observed that near the end of the eighteenth century, "the *Fire-eaters* were in great repute in Ireland. No young fellow could finish his education

47. Williams, *Dueling in the Old South*, 25; Louis Simond, *Journal of a Tour and Residence in Great Britain, During the Years 1810 and 1811* (2 vols.; Edinburgh, 1817), I, 413–14; George M. Johnston to Charles W. Johnston, August 22, 1834 [copy], in George Doherty Johnston Papers, University of Alabama, Tuscaloosa.
48. Williams, *Dueling in the Old South*, 5, 18.

till he had exchanged shots with some of his acquaintances. The first two questions always asked as to a young man's respectability and qualifications, particularly when he proposed for a lady, were,— 'What family is he of?'—'Did he ever blaze [*i.e.*, engage in a duel]?'" It certainly was no coincidence that the Old South's "best-known and most feared duelist" was of Celtic descent—Alexander Keith McClung.[49]

The combative tradition of Celtic Britain and the Old South doubtless encouraged some men to bully others, but Celts and southerners believed that it also promoted courtesy and the careful weighing of words before speaking. South Carolinian Benjamin F. Perry, who killed a man in a duel, said: "When a man knows that he is to be held accountable for his want of courtesy, he is not so apt to indulge in abuse. In this way dueling produces a greater courtesy in society and a higher refinement." The rash and the insolent in the Old South as well as in premodern Scotland, Ireland, and Wales rarely died in bed, unless put there by a mortal wound. Whether fights were formal duels or less structured contests, they prepared men to defend themselves and their society. Antebellum southerners, unlike their Yankee neighbors, never claimed to be lovers of peace. In March, 1861, Louis T. Wigfall of Texas promised his northern colleagues in the United States Senate: "If the Republican Senators . . . can get the backbone . . . into their President-elect . . . we shall . . . fight." The views of southerners and of all other Celts—that combat was the surest and the best way to protect their rights and their honor—were captured in the words of an early Welsh poet: "Turn peace away, for honour perishes with peace."[50]

49. Barrington, *Personal Sketches*, I, 273; Williams, *Dueling in the Old South*, 37.
50. Lillian A. Kibler, *Benjamin F. Perry, South Carolina Unionist* (Durham, 1946), 135; *Congressional Globe*, 36th Cong., 2nd sess., 1399; Gerald of Wales, *The Journey Through Wales*, 233.

Family, Kinship, and Neighborhood in an Antebellum Southern Community

Robert C. Kenzer

The history of Orange County, North Carolina, is a history not of individuals but of families. During the 1740s and 1750s the first permanent settlers came to Orange, primarily from Pennsylvania and Virginia. Their descendants were still residing in the same settlements a century later. By 1850, these settlements had evolved into tightly knit, rural neighborhoods, each tied together by an extensive network of kinship. This pattern of family structure was not confined to the white community; blacks developed a separate but parallel network of families. In Orange County, families lived close to each other and people looked to their relatives and neighbors for assistance and security. This interlocking kinship network gave the county a remarkably stable social order prior to the Civil War.

Orange County was established in 1752 in response to the needs of the growing population of North Carolina's Piedmont. When formed, it was rectangular in shape and stretched south from the Virginia border. It encompassed an enormous area, approximately 3,500 square miles, that within a century was carved into ten other counties. Although some white settlers had come to this area of North Carolina as early as 1740, it was not until the early 1750s that the population began to grow rapidly. Only 20 residents paid taxes in 1748; 1,113 paid in 1752. By 1767, Orange had the largest population of any county in North Carolina.[1]

Most of the settlers were Scotch-Irish and German immigrants from Pennsylvania who came to North Carolina's Piedmont in search of less expensive land. Many of them had in common not only the experience of migration but also their ancestry. Often groups of them had lived in the same village in Europe and crossed the Atlantic on

1. Ruth Blackwelder, *The Age of Orange: Political and Intellectual Leadership in North Carolina, 1752–1861* (Charlotte, N.C., 1961), 9.

the same vessel. Once they settled on the Carolina frontier, these families quickly forged their lives together. For instance, to the Hawfields settlement, located along the Haw River in the center of what would become Orange County, came the Blackwoods, Craigs, Freelands, Kirklands, Johnstons, and Strayhorns. (See Map 1.) Four of these families, the Blackwoods, Craigs, Freelands, and Kirklands, may have lived near one another in county Londonderry in northern Ireland before boarding the same ship to the colonies.[2] These families arrived in America around 1741 and settled in Paxtang Township, along the Susquehanna River in Dauphin County, Pennsylvania. Here they probably met the Johnston family, who, after coming from Ireland in 1732, had also settled in Dauphin. Sometime between 1743 and 1745, these five families and Gilbert Strayhorn, who had just returned from North Carolina, made the trip down the Shenandoah Valley on the "Great Wagon Road" and settled near the Haw River.[3]

The land these people settled was composed of gently rolling hills and valleys. The area generally ranged from only 250 to 600 feet above sea level. The most fertile soil was in the bottomlands. Most of the land was blanketed by huge pine and hardwood forests. These trees provided excellent building material for cabins and fences and a source of fuel, but they also necessitated painstaking work, since there could be no farming until the land was cleared. The numerous rivers and creeks meant water for the settlers and their livestock, but they also separated groups from one another.

Intending to stay, the settlers promptly established a Presbyterian church, which they called Hawfields. But within a few years,

2. See Robert W. Ramsey, *Carolina Cradle: Settlement of the Northwest Carolina Frontier, 1747–1762* (Chapel Hill, 1964), 3–50; Harry Roy Merrens, *Colonial North Carolina in the Eighteenth Century: A Study in Historical Geography* (Chapel Hill, 1964), 3–31; David I. Craig, *A Historical Sketch of the New Hope Church, in Orange County, North Carolina* (Reidsville, N.C., 1886), 5–10; and Luther M. Sharpe Genealogy, in Luther M. Sharpe Papers, William R. Perkins Library, Duke University, Durham. The genealogy indicates that John Freeland was born in county Londonderry, the probable residence of the other families in northern Ireland.

3. Craig, *Historical Sketch of New Hope*, 16–17, 7–10; Henry Poellnitz Johnston, *The Gentle Johnstons and Their Kin* (Birmingham, Ala., 1966), 86; Herbert Snipes Turner, *Church in the Old Fields: Hawfields Presbyterian Church and Community in North Carolina* (Chapel Hill, 1962), 34–36. Turner believes that both Gilbert Strayhorn and William Craig first went to the Hawfields and marked the area.

Map 1
Orange County, *ca.* 1752

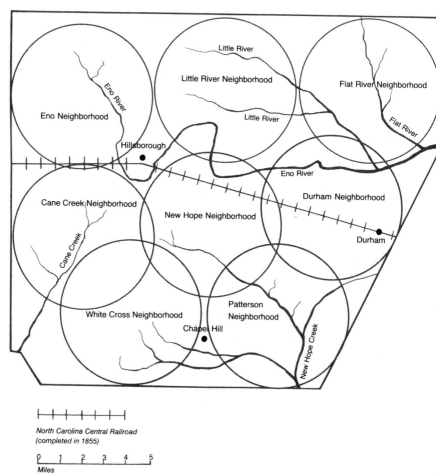

Little River

Little River Neighborhood

Flat River Neighborhood

Eno River

Eno Neighborhood

Little River

Hillsborough

Eno River

Durham Neighborhood

Cane Creek Neighborhood

New Hope Neighborhood

Cane Creek

Durham

Patterson
Neighborhood

White Cross Neighborhood

Chapel Hill

New Hope Creek

North Carolina Central Railroad
(completed in 1855)

0 1 2 3 4 5
Miles

Note that the circles only
approximate the borders.

rumors began to spread about the validity of the land titles they had received from the agents of the Earl of Granville, the lord proprietor of the land. Rather than defending their titles, all six of the original families of Hawfields moved about ten miles to the east, settled along a creek of the Haw River, and purchased this new land directly from the Earl of Granville. (See Map 1.) Trusting that their difficulties were past and their future secure, they named the creek New Hope and established another Presbyterian church in 1756.[4]

In 1754 the county seat of Orange was located on four hundred acres five miles north of the New Hope Presbyterian Church. First called Corbin Town and then Childsburg, the town's name was changed in 1756 for the final time to Hillsborough, to honor the Earl of Hillsborough, the British secretary of state for the colonies. Hillsborough was the commercial as well as the administrative and judicial center for Orange County for over a century. By the 1770s, the town, an observer recalled, "was a small village, which contained thirty or forty inhabitants, with two or three small stores and two or three ordinary taverns, but it was an improving village." Although the town grew during the next eighty years, it remained modest in size.[5]

Other rural settlements similar to New Hope began to dot the countryside as the appeal of cheap and abundant land attracted other people to Orange. Eight miles northwest of Hillsborough another group of Scotch-Irish from the counties west of Philadelphia established themselves on the Eno River in 1755 and organized the Eno Presbyterian Church. Within six years, some of them founded a new settlement and church a few miles to the east on the Little River.[6] Such settlements never developed into villages or towns, nor were they ever formally recognized as administrative, civil, or judicial districts. Rather, they were rural settlements that were largely self-sufficient; most residents rarely found it necessary to leave. But borders often overlapped, and residents living near the edge of one settlement might have a close relationship with those living nearby in another.

4. Craig, *Historical Sketch of New Hope*, 9–11; Turner, *Church in the Old Fields*, 22.
5. Blackwelder, *The Age of Orange*, 11–12; "Autobiography of Col. William Few of Georgia," *Magazine of American History*, VIII (November, 1881), 344.
6. Francis Nash, "The History of Orange County—Part I," *North Carolina Booklet*, XI (October, 1916), 63–68.

At the same time the Scotch-Irish were settling the lands south and north of Hillsborough, Virginians were coming from the area between the Potomac and James rivers, their soil exhausted from over a century of cultivation. They chose the land along the Flat River about twelve miles northeast of Hillsborough and along the New Hope and its tributaries. With the passing of time, these neighborhoods became known as Flat River and Patterson, the latter in honor of John T. Patterson, the first man to build a mill on the lower New Hope Creek.[7]

Not all settlers had such distinctive ethnic or geographic origins. Some Quakers came to Orange in these early years, probably from both Pennsylvania and eastern North Carolina, and lived in the area stretching from Cane Creek to northeast of Hillsborough. But many of the Quakers moved west to Guilford County when it was formed in 1770; others who resided in the vicinity of the Eno and Little River settlements joined the Presbyterian churches there. By the mid nineteenth century, the Quakers' influence had disappeared.[8]

Another settlement grew up on Cane Creek, where the Cateses, the most prominent family, were probably Germans from Pennsylvania. Although some of the other families had German surnames, what seems to have united these people was the establishment of the Cane Creek Baptist Church in 1789.[9] To the southeast was a group dominated by the largest family, the Lloyds; by the mid nineteenth century, this settlement was called White Cross. Still other settlers lived between the Flat River and the Patterson settlements, a fairly level area with few rivers or creeks to impede movement, so that its residents had a great deal of contact with their neighbors to the north, south, and west. This was thus the least distinctive of all the settlements. The small village of Durham emerged in the area during the 1850s.

7. See Merrens, *Colonial North Carolina*, 61–69; Ruth Herndon Shields *et al.* (comps.), *A Study of the Barbee Families of Chatham, Orange, and Wake Counties in North Carolina* (Boulder, 1971), 10, copy in the North Carolina Collection, University of North Carolina, Chapel Hill.
8. Nash, "The History of Orange County," 69–70; L. J. Phipps, "The Churches of Orange County," in Hugh Lefler and Paul Wager (eds.), *Orange County, 1752–1952* (Chapel Hill, 1953), 290–92; interview with Mrs. Alfred Engstrom, an expert on the Quakers in Orange County, June 21, 1980.
9. Phipps, "The Churches of Orange County," in Lefler and Wager (eds.), *Orange County*, 300. Most of the Germans from Pennsylvania settled west of the Haw River.

In the mid nineteenth century, many of the residents were descendants of the families who had settled the county during its early years. Specifically, forty-nine of the sixty most common surnames in 1850 were recorded on the county's 1779 tax list. Because the county lost four-fifths of its area through five divisions—the last taking place in 1849—and because a substantial number of people moved west, some of these families were more numerous at one time than another. Nevertheless, what stands out is the continuity of surnames over a century.[10]

There are no maps of Orange County from the 1850s to indicate where these families resided. Further, because this was a rural society, there were no street addresses. The only source that provides a hint is the federal manuscript census, the ledgers in which census takers recorded their handwritten tabulations, entering the names of all the free inhabitants of the county. If one assumes that the numbering reflects the order in which the households were visited, so that families with consecutive or close numbers were likely to live next to or near each other, then a general residential pattern can be reconstructed. The manuscript census reveals that by 1850 the descendants of the original settlers were residing in the same eight settlements, which by then should be termed neighborhoods, that their ancestors had established. (See Map 2.) Each of these neighborhoods contained approximately 250 households and covered 80 square miles, or about 3 households to a square mile. Therefore, there was 1 family for every 200 acres, but residents lived much closer than these figures might suggest because many tended to cluster along creeks and rivers.[11]

The Lloyds, residents of the White Cross neighborhood, are representative. The founder of the family in Orange, Thomas Lloyd, came from Virginia in the 1750s. Settling between nine and ten miles south of Hillsborough, Lloyd was appointed a justice of the peace in 1757 and served as a member of the North Carolina General Assembly for a number of terms between 1761 and 1768. Lloyd fathered three sons, two of whom stayed in Orange for the remainder of their lives, and by 1850, there were nineteen grandsons and great-grandsons of Thomas Lloyd in Orange who bore his surname, headed

10. See Robert C. Kenzer, "Portrait of a Southern Community, 1849–1881: Family, Kinship, and Neighborhood in Orange County, North Carolina" (Ph.D. dissertation, Harvard University, 1982), 11–13.
11. See *ibid.*, 184–88.

Map 2
Rural Neighborhoods of Orange County, 1850s

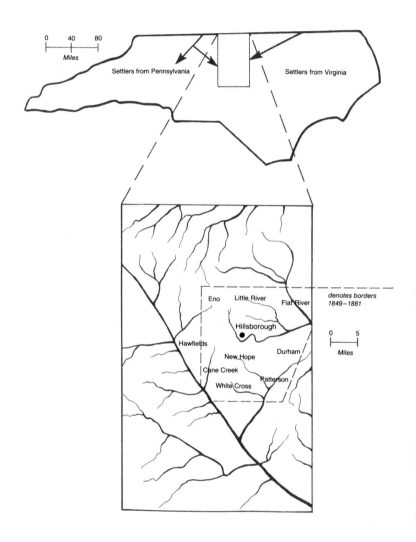

households, and lived near where he originally settled. After Thomas Lloyd's land was divided among his children, they tended to live close to one another, often on adjacent land. In turn, when this property was inherited by his grandchildren, they continued to live side by side. Cousins also resided in the same general area, though they dwelled farther apart.[12]

This pattern of close kin residences was partly an outgrowth of geography and the lack of transportation. In 1772, Governor Josiah Martin commented to the Earl of Hillsborough on the "extreme badness of the roads" in Orange; eighty years later, they were not much better. Until 1855, when the North Carolina Central Railroad linked Hillsborough and Durham, a horse or carriage hobbled along the thirteen-mile dirt path "at a rate of not much better than three miles per hour." Other roads in the county were similarly jolting and slow—and practically impassable after rain or snow. Residents of one neighborhood consequently had little social or commercial intercourse with those of other communities. Children had only a limited number of acquaintances. Even after the beginning of a common school system in 1839, the pattern of local isolation was unbroken. School districts were drawn to prevent children from having to cross creeks or rivers, often the borders of neighborhoods.[13]

12. The genealogical papers for the Lloyds were more complete than for any other family in the county. Robert Bruce Cooke, "The Thomas Lloyds of North Carolina" (1926) (Mimeographed copy in North Carolina Collection). For genealogical charts identifying all of the Lloyd households in 1850 and 1860, see Kenzer, "Portrait of a Southern Historical Collection, University of North Carolina Library, Chapel Hill); Minutes of the Orange County Board of Commissioners, December 17, 1868, in North Carolina Division of Archives and History, Raleigh; hereinafter cited as NCDAH. Although this concern for children's safety was not expressed in writing until after the Civil War, it was evident prior to 1860 in the borders laid out for school districts.
13. William L. Saunders (ed.), *Colonial Records of North Carolina* (10 vols.; Raleigh, 1866–90), IX, 311; Hillsborough *Recorder*, January 6, 1855; Adolphus Williamson Mangum Diary, June 24, 1852, February 8, 1857 (MS in Mangum Family Papers, Southern Historical Collection, University of North Carolina Library, Chapel Hill); Minutes of the Orange County Board of Commissioners, December 17, 1868, in North Carolina Division of Archives and History, Raleigh; hereinafter cited as NCDAH. Although this concern for children's safety was not expressed in writing until after the Civil War, it was evident prior to 1860 in the borders laid out for school districts.

The church, probably the most important social institution in the lives of Orange's families, also seems to have been affected by these residential patterns. For instance, between 1823 and 1860 the Little River Presbyterian Church had a large number of members, but more than three-fourths of them accounted for over one-third of the surnames. Those with the most common surnames, the Woodses, Halls, Allisons, and Rays, all could trace their ancestry in Orange as far back as 1761, when both the Little River settlement and church were established.[14]

The church played an important role in preserving the bonds between families and promoting cohesion in the neighborhood. For example, two sisters-in-law in the Little River Presbyterian Church were called before the church elders for "living a very unhappy life" because they "had a fight" with one another. Apparently the elders soothed the women's differences, for the church's records note the two "agreed to become reconciled to each other & to endeavor to live in the future as Christians should do."[15]

The church regulated behavior and encouraged conformity to the norms of morality of the neighborhood. One student of southern evangelicalism has given this process the appropriate title "To Set in Order the Things That Are Wanting." Between 1823 and 1860 the Little River Presbyterian Church called members before the elders fourteen times for such infractions as intoxication, gambling, and profanity. Only in three cases did the elders find that excommunication was necessary, and that because the members refused to come before the elders, often over a period of a year, answer the charges,

14. Of the 42 different surnames of white male members of the Little River Presbyterian Church from 1823 to 1860, the 16 most common ones (38.1 percent of all surnames) belong to 89 out of 115 members (77.4 percent of members). An examination of the rural churches throughout the county demonstrates the same pattern. For the Eno Presbyterian Church (1822–1860) the percentages are 34.8 and 70.9; for the Cane Creek Baptist Church (1856), 33.3 and 66.3; for the New Hope Presbyterian Church (1820–1851), 34.6 and 60.6; for the Mount Moriah Baptist Church (1840–1867), 33.3 and 60.5. Little River Presbyterian Church Session Books, I–II, Little River Presbyterian Church, Caldwell, N.C.; Eno Presbyterian Church Session Minutes, 1822–1874, Cane Creek Baptist Church Roll, 1829–1856, New Hope Presbyterian Church Register and Session Minutes, 1816–1950 (Microfilm copies in NCDAH); Charles Edward Maddry, "History of Mount Moriah Church" (MS in Southern Historical Collection).

15. Little River Presbyterian Church Session Books, I, July 18, September 17, 1847.

and show signs of repentance.[16] By their defiance of church authority, these three had in fact removed themselves from the church, and the excommunication merely acknowledged the situation. This defiance could not have been the result of fear of punishment. The elders, realizing that the relatives of guilty members might be forced into an uncomfortable position, demonstrated a high degree of tolerance. They even permitted a fellow elder charged with swindling and forgery to be readmitted into the church once he displayed repentance. That many did so repent is indicative of the powerful role that the church must have played in their lives.[17]

These isolated, self-contained, rural neighborhoods were cemented together by a distinctive pattern of marriages. Since family connections were so intimate and so important, young people contemplating marriage had to consider not only their own preferences but also the wishes of their relatives and friends in the neighborhood. Writing in 1857, one young man cautioned his bride-to-be that "before matters go too far with us, I would like us to consult some of our nearest and dearest friends relative to the subject [marriage] between us to see if it would be agreeable or not with the majority of them." He later suggested that a grandmother who favored the marriage might help secure parental consent. "You stated," he acknowledged to his fiancée, "that you had talked to your grandma about it and that she seemed very willing to it. . . . She also told you that she talked to your parents about [it]—but seems as if they had not desided [*sic*] yet." And if couples received parental consent and got married, as newlyweds they still sought the blessings of other relatives. They would spend days, as one groom termed it, "visiting *kinfolks.*" The round of visits might go on at length—he explained, "I think it will take us [from summer] until Christmas to get around seeing all; we are well blessed with kin."[18]

16.   Donald G. Matthews, *Religion in the Old South* (Chicago, 1977), Chap. 2. This low rate of excommunication was similar to that for other denominations in North Carolina. See Cortland Victor Smith, "Church Organization as an Agency of Social Control: Church Discipline in North Carolina, 1800–1860" (Ph.D. dissertation, University of North Carolina, Chapel Hill, 1966).

17.   Matthews, *Religion in the Old South*, 40–46, points out how discipline was used to preserve the bonds of the community (rather than to drive out members) and how "sincere repentance" usually prevented permanent excommunication.

18.   Lambert W. Hall to Frances N. Bennett, September 14, November 18, 1857, both

Ordinarily young people found their spouses among nearby neighbors. Between 1850 and 1859, half the brides and grooms lived less than one hundred households apart—about one to three miles—before their marriage. In a sample of the fifty-eight marriages in which the groom and bride's parents could be identified, 36.2 percent lived between one hundred and five hundred households apart. In only a few cases (13.8 percent) did spouses come from homes listed in the census as over five hundred households apart, or from two different neighborhoods.[19]

No neighborhood better represented the pattern of marriages between nearby residents than did New Hope. The marriage between John Kirkland and Mary Jane Strayhorn in 1851 is illustrative. (See Table 1.) They both had strong connections with the Blackwoods, Craigs, and Johnstons. Further enhancing their common ancestry is the fact that William Craig's sister Elizabeth had married William Blackwood and William Blackwood's sister Margaret had married William Craig. The only one of the six original New Hope families not represented in their genealogy is the Freelands, but both John and Mary Jane had numerous ties with the Freelands through marriages of their aunts, uncles, and siblings.[20]

Marriages further unified the neighborhoods because the newlyweds established their new households near their parents. (See Table 2.) In nearly six out of ten marriages the bride and groom established

---

in Frances N. Bennett Papers, Perkins Library, Duke University. Few letters of this type exist from this period because, as will be discussed shortly, fiancés rarely lived far enough from one another to make corresponding necessary. This woman, however, lived just across the county border in Caswell County and apparently did not often see her fiancé. Dr. Benjamin F. Mebane to Frances L. Kerr, August 22, 1857, in Mebane Family Papers, Southern Historical Collection.

19.   U.S. 1850 MS census, Orange County, Schedule I; *Orange County Marriage Bonds to 1868* (Salt Lake City, n.d.), copy in NCDAH; Kenzer, "Portrait of a Southern Community," 188–89. There were also several marriages between residents of White Cross and neighboring Cane Creek. This was probably the case because the Lloyds and many of the other residents of White Cross were, like most of the families of Cane Creek, Baptists. Therefore, many of the people who lived on the northern border of the White Cross neighborhood resided as close to the Cane Creek Baptist Church as to the Bethel Baptist Church in White Cross. Further, since preachers would hold services in one rural church one week and another church the next week, those members who resided within traveling distance of the two churches could attend services at both.

20.   Sharpe Genealogy.

Table 1

Genealogy of John Kirkland and Mary Jane Strayhorn of New Hope

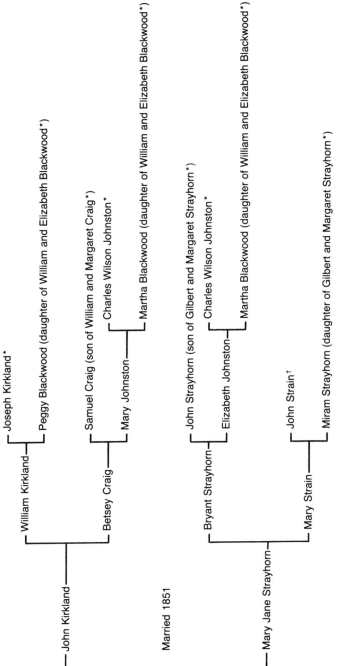

SOURCES: Craig, *Historical Sketch of New Hope Church*, 12–19; Sharpe Genealogy; Johnston, *The Gentle Johnstons and Their Kin*.

*Denotes an original settler of New Hope.

†"Strain" and "Strayhorn" refer to the same family (see Johnston, *The Gentle Johnstons and Their Kin*, 119).

Table 2

Newlyweds' and Parents' Households, 1860
(Distance in Households)

Distance	5 or Less	Under 100	100–499	500+
From Groom's Parents	34.1%	60.2%	27.3%	12.5%
	(N = 30)	(53)	(24)	(11)
From Bride's Parents	13.2%	39.6%	32.1%	28.3%
	(N = 7)	(21)	(17)	(15)
From Closer of Parents	31.0%	58.4%	28.3%	13.3%
	(N = 35)	(66)	(32)	(15)

SOURCES: U.S. 1850 and 1860 MS census, Orange County, Schedule I; *Orange County Marriage Bonds to 1868*; for methodology, see Kenzer, "Portrait of a Southern Community," 189–90.

their new household less than one hundred houses—under three miles—from one or the other's parents. This was clearly dictated by the agrarian nature of the economy. Therefore, marriage meant not a dramatic separation from but continued close association with both sets of parents.[21]

This pattern of marriage and residence bonded together a number of households in the neighborhood which, even though headed by people with different surnames, nevertheless had a common ancestry. For example, a list of the households from the manuscript census for the White Cross neighborhood immediately bordering the household of Stephen Lloyd II, one of Thomas Lloyd's grandsons,

21. The close parent-child residence was not the result of early marriages. During the 1850s in Orange, the mean age at marriage for grooms was 27.1 years and for brides 22.8 years. For a distribution of the age at marriage and the methodology used to calculate the age, see Kenzer, "Portrait of a Southern Community," 26, 190. Although there has not been a great amount of research done on the age at marriage for whites in mid-nineteenth-century America, the age at marriage for males in Orange seems to be much higher than for other American communities. For New Jersey in this period, Thomas P. Monahan has calculated that the age at first marriage for native-born white males was 25.3 years (*Pattern of Age at Marriage in the United States* [2 vols.; Philadelphia, 1951], II, 253). For the various regions of Alabama, William L. Barney has found age at marriage for white males to range from 21.5 to 26.2 years ("Patterns of Crisis: Alabama White Families and Social Change, 1850–1870," *Sociology and Social Research*, LXIII [1979], 540n).

demonstrates the bonds of kinship shared by neighbors in 1850 and 1860. (See Table 3.)

In the neighborhoods, children in one family frequently married siblings in another family. Thus two of the six sons and three of the five daughters of Henry Lloyd (Stephen II's cousin and another of Thomas' grandsons) chose spouses with the surname King. Forms of leviratic marriage, though not common, strengthened these neighborhood bonds. For example, William Brewer, following the death of his wife, Nancy Lloyd Brewer, married her sister, Sally. He had two sons by each sister.

The neighborhood structure made it unnecessary for someone to write to a relative or close friend who lived nearby. By the time a letter was written, mailed, and received, the sender and the recipient would have seen one another. This lack of correspondence makes the diary of Adolphus Williamson Mangum especially important. He gives us a firsthand account of what it was like to reside in these neighborhoods in Orange County during the 1850s. Adolphus proved to be a very careful observer of his neighborhood, Flat River:

> I passed my childhood scenes & had my reminiscences of childhood recalled to my view. . . . I crossed the fence below the old schoolhouse spring & here . . . were the trees that I used to climb with my supposed agility, the old spring around which we used to meet & indulge in mirthful glee; and at which I used to slake my "often-returning thirst." . . . I passed by the old steep bank higher up old Dials [Creek] to the washing hole where the striplings of the neighborhood used to meet on Sunday mornings & play & wash in the water. So pleasant were the hours that I spent there that I never shall forget the spot while I walk these mortal shores. The sandybank, the old oak logs, the peculiar shape of the hole of water & the overshadowing trees strange as it may seem have an unchanging home in the memory. Oh scenes of my childhood, how dear, how unequalled, how long remembered!!!

For Adolphus and for many others who could trace their ancestry back for a century in the neighborhood, time, place, and person were interwoven and could never be separated.[22]

22. Mangum Diary, July 9, 1852. For this relationship between people and place, though in an earlier period, see Rhys Isaac, "Dramatizing the Ideology of Revolution: Popular Mobilization in Virginia, 1774 to 1776," *William and Mary Quarterly*, 3rd ser., XXXIII (1976), 357–85, esp. 364–65.

Table 3

Relationship of Head of Household to Stephen Lloyd II

Household Number in 1850 Census	Household Head	Relationship
542	Lloyd, Stephen, III	son
543	Lloyd, Henry B.	son
544	Lloyd, Manly	son
545	Lloyd, Stephen, II	
546	Lloyd, Chesley	son
547	Andrews, Henry C.	grandson
548	Suit, Jourdan	not identifiable*
549	Reeves, John	not identifiable
550	Poe, Hasting	cousin's husband
551	Durham, Mebane	niece's husband
552	Lloyd, William	cousin
553	Brewer, William	son-in-law
554	Lloyd, Dilly	sister-in-law

Household Number in 1860 Census	Household Head	Relationship
1576	Andrews, William	cousin's husband
1577	McCauley, Elizabeth	cousin
1578	Poe, William	not identifiable
1579	King, Matthew	niece's husband
1580	Pearson, Presley	not identifiable
1581	Brewer, Merideth	grandson
1582	Brewer, William	son-in-law
1583	Lloyd, Stephen, III	son
1584	Andrews, George	son-in-law
1585	Lloyd, Stephen, II	
1586	Lloyd, Manly	son
1587	Lloyd, Henry B.	son
1588	Strowd, Andrew	not identifiable
1589	Lloyd, Chesley	son
1590	Lloyd, Sidney	cousin
1591	Strowd, Alfred P.	niece's husband's brother

SOURCE: U.S. 1850 and 1860 MS census, Orange County, Schedule I; Thomas Lloyd Papers, in Perkins Library, Duke University; Eugene Suggs, "Sketches of Major General Thomas Lloyd of Orange County, North Carolina" (MS in North Carolina Collection). For a discussion of why households are not always listed as neighbors in consecutive censuses, see Kenzer, "Portrait of a Southern Community," 184–87.

*Many of those listed as not identifiable were probably related to Stephen but the exact relationship is not yet clear.

Adolphus also described the neighborhood general store, which rivaled the church as a focal point for the residents. They would gather at the store not only to purchase salt, sugar, cloth, and gunpowder, goods that could not be produced locally, but to meet their friends and relatives. At the store of Adolphus' father, where he frequently found himself "*pro tem*" clerk, often he and "several others had a long 'chat' on matters and things in general." At the general store, which served as a post office, neighbors read copies of such publications as the Hillsborough *Recorder*, the *Christian Advocate*, and the *National Intelligencer*. Political meetings and temperance society gatherings also took place at the store.[23]

Much of Adolphus' diary is primarily a log of his and his relatives' visits to each other. His cousins—the Parkers, Laws, Cozarts, Moizes, Carringtons, Lockharts, Harrisses, and Mangums—frequently came to his home for conversation and stayed to share meals. Although these kinsmen lived but a short distance away, often they would choose to stay overnight at the Mangums' house. One series of visits that Adolphus made was to his great-aunt, Dicey Mangum, who, though in her seventies, lived alone. On one occasion he brought her some game he had hunted. Such assistance between the generations was particularly important in Orange, where in 1860 more than 80 percent of the men aged seventy or older still headed their own households. Support of family and relatives was also important for the almost 17 percent of the households in Orange that were headed by women. Twenty-four percent of the elderly men and 17 percent of the women who headed households resided next door to someone with the same surname as their own. Many more of them lived equally close to kin with a different surname.[24]

Relatives assumed a high degree of responsibility for each other not only out of love but also out of fear of what neighbors would think or say about intentional maltreatment or even neglect. When a

23. Mangum Diary, July 2, 1852, October 19, 1854, August 3, 1852; Hillsborough *Recorder*, May 19, 1852, November 2, 1853, May 16, 1860.

24. Mangum Diary, June 24, 27, July 9, 20, 26, August 8, 9, 11, 15, 1852; U.S. 1860 MS census, Orange County, Schedule I. Of the 2,215 white household heads in 1860, 357 (16.8 percent) were women. Of the 1,768 white male household heads in 1860, 106 (6.0 percent) were men age seventy or older. Of these groups, 60 women (16.8 percent) and 25 men (23.6 percent) resided next door to someone with the same surname.

seventy-eight-year-old mother insisted on heading her own household, her sons worried. "She might fall & be seriously hurt for life," one brother warned another. "Is it not a duty we owe ourselves & our mother[?] . . . Heretofore we have held our peace, let anything happen to her & we will be held responsible, let us therefore advise her, if she does not choose to act upon the advise [*sic*] given, we are to some extent clear." The mother seems to have had the final word in the matter. Seven years later, she lived next door to one son and continued to head her own household.[25]

Protection and assistance to kin extended to children in this era when disease often swept through the region and struck down parents. In more than 40 percent of the cases when both parents were lost, the court awarded custody of the orphan to a relative with whom the child shared a surname. Also, aid was frequently provided by a relative with a different surname but who lived in the neighborhood. For instance, in 1852, Bryant Strayhorn of New Hope became the guardian for his niece and nephew, Elizabeth and Joseph Craig.[26]

In dealing with the highly fluid population of the United States in this era, demographers often speak of the rate of persistence—the percentage of the population that remained in the same locality from one decennial census to another. In several southern and western communities, only 30 to 40 percent of the population stayed on through the 1850s. But in Orange County, the rate of persistence was much higher. (See Table 4.) More than 50 percent of the white men in 1850 still resided in the county ten years later.[27]

25. Patterson H. McDade to John A. McDade, December 5, 1853, in John A. McDade Letters and Papers, Southern Historical Collection.
26. Orange County Court Minutes, 1850–1854, in NCDAH. In twenty-three out of fifty-two cases (44.2 percent), the guardian had the same name as the orphan.
27. It is difficult to compare rates of persistence because various writers have used different groups to calculate this measurement. Two writers, however, have selected groups similar to the one here. For Clarke County, Georgia, Frank J. Huffman, Jr., found that 41.2 percent of the men age twenty and over persisted during the 1850s ("Old South, New South: Continuity and Change in a Georgia County, 1850–1880" [Ph.D. dissertation, Yale University, 1974], 35). William L. Barney found rates of persistence for this group ranging from 24.5 percent to 36.6 percent depending on the region investigated in Alabama ("Patterns of Crisis," 532). See also Mildred Throne, "A Population Study of an Iowa County in 1850," *Iowa Journal of History*, XXVII (1959), 305–30; Don Harrison Doyle, *The Social Order of a Frontier Community: Jacksonville, Illinois, 1825–1870* (Urbana, 1978), 261.

Table 4

Rate of Persistence in Orange County, 1850–1860

Ages	White Male Household Heads (%)	White Male Non–Household Heads (%)	Total (%)
20–29	48.4	45.5	46.6
30–39[a]	61.4	37.6	57.6
40–49	66.0	43.3	64.3
50–59	57.0	46.2	56.5
60–69	49.4	35.3	48.0
70†	17.0	11.1	16.0
	55.9*	43.2†	52.2‡

SOURCES: U.S. 1850 and 1860 MS census, Orange County, Schedule I.
NOTE: Students attending the University of North Carolina were excluded.
[a]For the combined age group 20–39, the percentages are 56.4, 44.3, and 51.20
*939 out of 1,679 persisted.
†295 out of 683 persisted.
‡1,234 out of 2,362 persisted.

The rate of persistence varied with age. Men in their twenties were the least persistent; as a man approached middle age, he became more likely to remain in Orange. It is harder to calculate how many older men stayed in the county because during a decade, some would have died. But it is evident that the vast majority stayed in Orange for a decade.[28]

Whether a man was a household head also affected his decision

28. Death as a factor in rate of persistence can be removed if one calculates the survival rates for the age cohorts. One such study is Michael B. Katz et al., "Migration and the Social Order in Erie County, New York: 1855," *Journal of Interdisciplinary History*, VIII (1978), 678. Thus the rates of persistence are as follows:

Ages	White Male Household Heads(%)	All White Males (%)
20–29	52.6	50.7
30–39	69.0	65.0
40–49	79.8	77.7
50–59	80.7	80.0
60–69	100.0	98.8
70+	93.8	85.0
	71.8	64.7

to stay in the county or to move elsewhere. At all age levels, men who did not head households—who therefore probably were not married—were less persistent than those who did. The emigration of young men in their twenties produced less social disruption in the neighborhoods than did the removal of middle-aged men who had families. Men who had kinsmen in the neighborhood were less likely to emigrate than those who had none. Indeed, the more relatives a man had, despite real estate and slaveownership, the more likely he was to remain in the county. For men who shared surnames with seven or more male household heads, for example, the rate of persistence was 60.9 percent.[29]

In Orange County as a whole during the 1850s, this high rate can be explained in part by the predominantly rural population; farmers were less likely to emigrate than were city dwellers. Equally important, the overwhelming majority of the population was native-born. By 1860, almost every head of household in Orange had not only been born in the United States but within North Carolina. In contrast, recently arrived Irish and German immigrants, who moved more frequently, lowered the rate of persistence in the northern states.[30]

This higher rate of persistence in Orange County also suggests

29.   U.S. 1850 and 1860 MS census, Orange County, Schedules I, II, IV. The overall rate of persistence by shared surname was 52.9 percent (1,158 out of 2,190) instead of 52.2 percent as noted in Table 4. This difference results from excluding 8 surnames (172 household heads) because the census takers often spelled the names differently (as was the case for 2) and because some were so common (Brown, Davis, Jones, Smith, Williams, and Wilson) that kin connections could only be assumed. Further, students attending the University of North Carolina were excluded as well.

For male household heads who owned slaves, the rate of persistence was 58.4 percent, compared to 51.5 percent for nonslaveholders. Another indication that there was no significant link between the rate of persistence and ownership of real estate and slaves is found by comparing the wealth of the most persistent men, white male household heads in 1850 who shared their surname with seven or more other household heads, with the wealth of all white male household heads in 1850. For the former group, the rate was 64.1 percent; for the latter, 55.9 percent. If we consider those who owned no real estate in 1850, the percentages are 37.1 and 40.0, and for those who owned no slaves, the percentages are 70.4 percent and 67.4 percent.

30.   Many town residents were in fact farmers and planters and therefore should not be considered as true urban dwellers. Of the 11,395 whites in 1860, 567 lived in Hillsborough, about 250 lived in Chapel Hill, and fewer than 100 in Durham. See Hillsborough *Recorder*, October 24, 1860; and William Kenneth Boyd, *The Story of Durham: City of the New South* (Durham, 1925), 97. In 1860, the distribution of heads of household in Orange by place of birth was 97.1 percent born in North Carolina, 2.5

that the few newcomers to the area were assimilated into the rural neighborhoods. A man who purchased property, joined the local church, and married a woman with one of the common surnames was likely to remain in Orange. His sons would be even more likely to stay since through their mother's family they had a number of kin connections in the neighborhood.

Although most inhabitants remained in Orange, something needs to be said about those who left. Family genealogies do not present the traditional picture of people forced to break family ties when they migrated to the frontier. Rather, those who left Orange seem to have been fairly successful in transplanting the kinship network to their new locations.[31] One of the best examples can be found among the descendants of the Johnston family of the New Hope neighborhood. Three of the seven children of George Johnston, son of Charles Wilson Johnston, an original settler of New Hope, left Orange and migrated during the 1830s to Greene County, Alabama. In addition, three of George's married granddaughters, children of the four siblings who remained in Orange, made their way to Greene. A son of George's sister, Mary, who married a Samuel Craig, also migrated to Greene. There, these emigrant families from Orange continued to intermarry. In so doing, they were only repeating the actions of their ancestors who had left Ireland with their relatives and neighbors, initially settled in Pennsylvania, and then moved to Orange.[32]

---

percent born in the United States but not North Carolina, and .4 percent foreign-born. On the impact of the foreign-born population, see Merle Curti, *The Making of an American Community: A Case Study of Democracy in a Frontier Community* (Stanford, 1959), 72–73; Katz et al., "Migration and the Social Order," 682–93; and Peter R. Knights, *The Plain People of Boston, 1830–1860* (New York, 1971), 63. For a comparison of the regional structure of the native-born population, see *Eighth Census, 1860*, 622–23.

31. By "traditional" is meant the interpretation by Frederick Jackson Turner, who attempted to draw a distinction between the liberating quality of the frontier, where, he believed, every family was a "self-sufficing" unit, and the tradition-bound structure of society to the east (*The Frontier in American History* [New York, 1920], 153–54). For a much different interpretation, one which is similar to my findings for Orange, see Doyle, *The Social Order of a Frontier Community*, 92–118.

32. Johnston, *The Gentle Johnstons and Their Kin*, 107–19, 138–42, 152, 172–75, 216–22, 235–46. For examples of relatives moving to the same type of communities in the border states and in the Midwest, see Florence (Ray) Lewis and William A. Ray, "The Rays (Raes) Down Through the Years" (Copy in Hillsborough Public Library, Hillsborough, N.C.), 1–10.

Kinship thus played an important role in promoting continuity. Within Orange this continuity was expressed by high rates of persistence. The kin network, however, was not limited to Orange's borders but extended beyond them to the frontier, where it encouraged a more stable transition from the older communities of the East to the younger communities of the West.

In Orange County, one-third of the population consisted of blacks, the vast majority being slaves. The same forces that so significantly shaped the relations among whites also affected those among blacks. The tax list for Orange in 1755 recorded that 8 percent of the white families owned slaves. During the second half of the eighteenth century, the number of slaves grew at a rate similar to that of the white population, and by 1790, they composed 17 percent of the county's population. Throughout the first half of the nineteenth century, the slave population grew at an even faster rate than the white population and by 1860 stood near 33 percent.[33]

The experiences of slaves in Orange County varied. Some masters were provident and lenient; others were careless and harsh. One former slave from Orange County remembered Spartan conditions: "We did not know nothin' 'bout feather beds. Slaves like dat had bunks an' some slept on de floor. We went barefooted most of the time." In contrast, another slave fondly recalled: "When any of us niggers got sick Mis' Annie would come down to de cabin to see us. She brung de best wine, good chicken an' chicken soup an' everything else she had at de big house dat she thought we would like, an' she done everything else she could to get us well again."[34]

Slaves' perceptions of slavery differed depending on the size of their masters' holdings. In 1860, Paul C. Cameron, the owner of nearly five hundred slaves, was the largest slaveholder in Orange. Although these slaves were well treated, their sheer numbers forced them to live fairly regimented lives that included little contact with their master. This fact was noted by one of Cameron's former slaves who stated that "Marse Paul had a heap of nigrahs. . . . When he met

33. Blackwelder, *The Age of Orange*, 9–10. Of the 5,636 blacks, 5,108 (90.6 percent) were slaves.

34. George P. Rawick (ed.), *The American Slave: A Composite Autobiography, North Carolina Narratives* (17 vols.; Westport, Conn., 1972), XV, 313, XIV, 303.

dem in de road he wouldn' know dem an' when he axed who dey wus an' who dey belonged to, dey tell him dey belonged to Marse Paul Cameron an' den he would say dat wus all right for dem to go right on." In contrast, the majority of slaveholders owned few slaves and not only lived in close proximity to these slaves but often worked alongside them in the fields.[35]

Slave marriages were not recognized by law, and families faced the danger of separation. A former slave from Orange sadly recalled the difficulties and pains of the slave family: "I belonged to a man named Bob Hall. . . . He died when I was eight years old and I was put on the block and sold in Nelson Hall's yard by the son of Bob Hall. I saw my brother and sister sold on this same plantation. My mother belonged to the Halls, and father belonged to the Glenns. They sold me away from my father and mother and I was carried to the state of Kentucky." It is not surprising, then, that another former slave concluded that marriage and family life were "a joke in the days of slavery." He recalled: "The main thing in allowing any form of matrimony among the slaves was to raise slaves in the same sense and for the same purpose as stock raisers raise horses and mules, that is for work. A woman who could produce fast was in great demand."[36]

Despite all these problems, slaves sought to establish and preserve their families. Evidence of their success in maintaining stability comes from a questionnaire many completed after the Civil War. When required by law between 1866 and 1868 to declare how long they had lived together, black couples in Orange reported marital relations spanning a long period. Two-thirds said they had been married before the war.[37]

Just as geography limited the number of potential spouses for whites, the boundaries of even the largest plantation in the county severely restricted the choices for slaves. A slave could marry either another slave who also resided on the plantation or, if his master permitted it, one from a nearby plantation. The slaves of small slave-

35. U.S. 1860 MS census, Orange County, Schedules I, II; Rawick (ed.), *The American Slave*, XV, 35.

36. Guion Griffis Johnson, *Ante-bellum North Carolina: A Social History* (Chapel Hill, 1937), 538–39; Rawick (ed.), *The American Slave*, XIV, 329, 360.

37. Orange County Negro Cohabitation Certificates, 1866–1868, in NCDAH. Of 897 certificates noting the year of marriage, 588 (65.5 pecent) were before 1860.

holders, like their masters, rarely left the neighborhood. Therefore, for these slaves, selection of spouses was even more restricted. These restrictions resulted in the creation of a black community bonded together by a century of intermarriage in a manner quite similar to that of the white neighborhoods.[38]

Like Orange County whites, slaves mostly lived and died within the same community. When a master died, there was always a possibility that his slaves could be sold to an owner outside of the county, but in most cases they were parceled out among the master's children, nearly all of whom lived in the same rural neighborhood.[39] The kin-oriented structure of the white rural neighborhood, therefore, generally allowed the slaves to preserve their own network of kinship.

In Orange County the isolation after initial settlement, the continued rural nature of the region, the lack of foreign immigration, and the limited means of transportation all fostered a life largely shaped by the primary relations among kinfolk. Although close family residences did not always guarantee absolute harmony, they did encourage stability. By promoting cohesion and order, the network of kinship in Orange not only shaped the county's antebellum economic, social, administrative, and political structure, it also later defined the character of both the community's participation in and the impact of the Civil War.

38. Herbert G. Gutman, *The Black Family in Slavery and Freedom, 1750–1925* (New York, 1976), 169–90. Gutman focuses specifically on the Cameron plantation in Orange County.

39. An example of how these slaves chose spouses who lived nearby is shown in the testimony of former slave Robert Glenn, who noted that his mother belonged to Robert Hall and his father to the Glenns (probably the family of James S. Glenn, who resided in household 1640 in the 1860 census). In 1860, Robert Hall resided in the Little River neighborhood and his household in the census was number 1636. For Robert Glenn's testimony, see Rawick (ed.), *The American Slave*, XIV, 329. For a detailed analysis of slave inheritance patterns, see Kenzer, "Portrait of a Southern Community," 57–61.

The Ceremonies of Politics
Nineteenth-Century Rituals of National Affirmation

Jean H. Baker

So they march in percessions an' get up hooraws,
An' tramp through the mud fer the good o' the cause,
An' think they're a kind of fulfillin' prophecies,
W'en they're on'y jest changing the holder of offices.
James Russell Lowell, *The Biglow Papers*

After it was over, only the Republicans denied that the evening had been a success. Preparations had begun Saturday afternoon when Democrats gathered in their clubrooms throughout the city. Here they dressed in uniforms purchased from one of several New York firms specializing in such election paraphernalia. These outfits so closely resembled military garb that some Democrats simply wore their old army uniforms.[1] As they dressed, party regulars received their instructions. They must stay in line, keep in step, and not light their lanterns until told to do so by their officers. This last was especially important because in the past overenthusiastic marchers had used up their kerosene supply, leaving more than one Democratic army in darkness. Strong-shouldered club members were assigned to carry transparencies, and these silk banners—either purchased from J. Bromley's or stitched by female supporters—provided abbreviated versions of the central themes of this year's presidential election: "Little Mac, You're the One"; "Lincoln—the Coffin-Maker"; "No Draft for Free Men."

Meanwhile some Democrats worked to prepare the wagons on which party platforms were enacted. For years the Third Ward Club

1. The following description is based on accounts in the New York papers, especially the New York *World* and New York *Times*, October 29, 31, November 5, 1864; *Illustrated London News*, October 15, December 19, 1864. See also "Political Campaign Torches," *United States National Bulletin*, 1964; Minutes of the Democratic Club, Third Ward, New York City; Jean Baker, *Affairs of Party: The Political Culture of Northern Democrats* (Ithaca, 1983), 291–99. For other similar events, see New York *Times*, October 9, 1860.

had created the best of these displays, and for this occasion they had produced a thirty-foot wagon with a ship named the *Constitution* heading for the rocks under a Republican crew. Lincoln, of course, was the pilot. The Empire Club had also taken great pains with its representation of the Union: thirty-one women, each dressed in white and labeled with a state's name, reached out toward another woman bearing the sign "Confederate States of America." As always, some party officials made certain that the drifters who were paid a quarter for the evening did not disappear into nearby taverns.

Finally, it was seven o'clock and time to begin. Amid the shouts and cannon fire, few actually heard the pistol shots that signaled the procession's beginning. At the command of their officers they were under way, using the cadenced step so often practiced. Already the sulfur from cannon and firecrackers filled the air. So too did the staccato commands of officers who patrolled on horseback: "Keep in line there"; "Close up ranks"; "Onward to battle, Boys." Somewhere up the line Dodworth's Brass Band was playing the martial music that served for war and for politics.

As they approached Broadway other units appeared. Some had marched down Fifth Avenue past the hotel where their presidential candidate George B. McClellan was staying. Everywhere—from balconies, open windows (for the weather was still warm), and sidewalks—observers cheered. An occasional enemy tossed a rotten egg or anti-Democratic curse. But Democrats had been warned about such insults and the ranks held firm. Women wearing scarves and skirts printed with McClellan's name and face, some with huge party badges on their shawls, waved white handkerchiefs, and as a sign of support, Democrats along the line of march pulled back the curtains in their houses. On this evening it was safe to assume that a darkened building housed a Republican.

Along Broadway toward Union Square they came, marching slower now that they had formed, cotillionlike, into regiments and divisions. Some sixty thousand men and boys moved past Delmonico's, where well-fed leaders waved from the restaurant's open windows and balconies; past the elegant hotels and shops of upper Broadway and Fifth Avenue; and finally into the square. Here the blazing tar-barrels, kerosene torches, and illuminated mansions made it seem like daytime. Someone had rigged a powerful Drummond light to cast the image of the equestrian statue of George Washington onto the building behind, and no Democrat could miss the intended resemblance to McClellan. A reporter for the *Illustrated London News* (describing an earlier torchlight procession in October) had never seen anything like it:

> The square was broken into brilliant coruscations of light. Every platform was garlanded by the Chinese lanterns I have spoken of and gas lamps had, besides, been unscrewed from their posts and hung to the sides of the scaffolds—At eight o'clock artillery began to roar from the inclosures of the square. Many brass bands began to bray. The "Star-Spangled Banner" blended with the waltz from "Faust." A big eagle in gas suddenly spread his dazzling wings over the portal of (a restaurant)—from the corner of Fourteenth Street a blinding ray from a calcium-light apparatus shot across for many hundred feet—a bridge of radiance. There was a splendid display of fireworks before the procession of the "wards" entered the square.[2]

Once in the square, the men disbanded to watch the fireworks and listen to speeches. They would not march home, but they were under strict orders to return their uniforms and equipment promptly.[3] Although several stands decorated with red, white, and blue bunting had been erected, only a few Democrats could actually hear their leaders denounce Lincoln, the draft, and emancipation. Even reporters responsible for tomorrow's newspaper accounts could hardly catch the Democratic message above the din. For the thousands in Union Square, the significance of this evening was not what was said, but rather what was enacted and thus conveyed to those watching and participating.

Such torchlight parades were only one episode in an established nineteenth-century routine that began with ratification meetings after the nomination of the candidate, progressed during the late summer and fall with pole-raisings, serenades, barbecues, and mass rallies, and climaxed with the casting of the ballot on election day. Because they reveal little about election outcomes, these ceremonies of politics have been overlooked by both participants and historians. Partici-

---

2. *Illustrated London News*, October 15, 1864.
3. Some clubs required a deposit from those who wore uniforms. See *Lincoln Lore*, No. 1572 (February, 1969), 3.

pants preferred to write about leaders and what they perceived as the policy differences between parties, and until recently most historians followed the same track, organizing nineteenth-century politics into narrative episodes usually arranged in presidential blocs. Only in the 1960s did another generation of historians focus on the underlying aspects of nineteenth-century politics. Using new techniques and asking different questions about aggregate voting behavior, they transformed politics into social history.[4] Still none of these approaches considered the symbolic meanings of nineteenth-century campaigns and elections.

Although the ceremonies of politics do not lend themselves to either a social analysis of political history or popular techniques of quantification, they are worth examining. Like all rituals, these observances were cultural conventions that held only the loosest association with what anthropologists call rational-technical behavior. In purposeful activity aimed at some obvious result, there is a close deductive connection between means and ends that erases symbolic meanings. To some extent, of course, nineteenth-century politics was a rational, nonmagical enterprise of selecting candidates and enacting programs. Yet if we accept Richard P. McCormick's convincing argument that the similarity of campaign issues among parties extended to their public policies, then voting choices lose any relevance to political history.[5]

Certainly the ceremonies of campaigns fulfilled human designs quite different from rites of passage and communion services. Still they contained nonrational meanings. What makes nineteenth-century politics so provocative a field of study is the survival of ceremonial behaviors alongside more instrumental modern techniques of allocating power. There was, for example, no intrinsic connection

---

4. For the distinction between latent and manifest history, see Bernard Bailyn, "The Challenge of Modern Historiography," *American Historical Review*, LXXXVII (1982), 9.

5. For an analysis of ritual that makes this distinction between magical, noninstrumental ritual and modern man's rational behaviors, see Edmund Leach, "Ritualization in Man in Relation to Conceptual and Social Development," *Philosophical Transactions of the Royal Society of London*, 772, Ser. B (1966), 403. See also C. Raymond Firth, *Symbols: Public and Private* (Ithaca, 1973); Clifford Geertz, *Myth, Symbol and Culture* (New York, 1971); Richard P. McCormick, "The Party Period and Public Policy: An Exploratory Hypothesis," *Journal of American History*, LXVI (1979), 279–98.

between raising a one-hundred-foot pole decorated with a piece of satin and getting a lower tariff. Nor was there any necessary association among dressing in a uniform, setting off firecrackers, and electing James Buchanan.

Although the much-studied words of politics display party differences over policy leadership, the neglected ceremonies of politics showcase deeper structures of national thought. The rituals of politics touch on broad concerns about the delegation of power in a democratic society, the nature of the relationship between leaders and followers, the legitimacy of government, and the ways of establishing compliance to that government. These are matters that Lucien Pye, Sidney Verba, and many others have named political culture, or, in Verba's words, "the system of empirical beliefs, expressive symbols and values which defines the situation in which political action takes place."[6] Political culture assumes that societies produce civic arrangements that represent coherent patterns of public life and that are not random happenings. To discover these elements of our political system today, we use surveys and questionnaires. For the nineteenth century, there is no better avenue than dissecting election ceremonies.

Probably never as fully developed in the South as in the rest of the United States, nineteenth-century election ceremonies took place in rural communities as well as in large cities such as New York, Philadelphia, and Baltimore, where they are more easily studied because of newspaper coverage. Parties organized them in small towns, villages, and "hamlets." Frequently, processions in the country ended at courthouse squares while rallies were held on battlefields associated with the Revolution or the War of 1812.[7]

Never were either the forms or the places of celebration the private property of any one party. The need for consensus in a new republic transformed partisan festivals into national affairs shared by all. Language and symbols became interchangeable, and whatever modest innovation one party created, its opposition promptly appropriated. Thus the campaign techniques refined by Whigs during the

6. Lucien Pye and Sidney Verba, *Political Culture and Political Development* (Princeton, 1965), 513.
7. For an early example, see *Kentucky Gazette* (Lexington), November 3, 1836.

Harrison campaign of 1840 appeared almost immediately in Democratic celebrations.[8] Four years after the Republicans called their convention site a Wig-Wam, Democrats used the same name and design for their national convention. This mimetic style extended to party names. The two major organizations in the nineteenth century might have been called the Federalists, the Constitutionalists, the States' Rightists, the Americans, or even the Protestant party. In fact they divided the name Democratic-Republican, which had been used in the late eighteenth century.

Nowhere was the link between party and nation more evident than in political iconography. Nineteenth-century parties did not produce any special symbols; even election tickets provided no party logos other than the printed name of the party and candidate. Instead, they used representations that linked their organizations to the American Revolution.[9] Thus George Washington was the central figure for all nineteenth-century parties, as were the flag, the eagle, and the seal of the United States. Even in New York's ardently partisan Tammany Hall, a huge bust of George Washington presided over a meeting room decorated with a lugubrious eagle and the traditional red, white, and blue bunting. When Democrats assembled in this room, they sang national music including "Columbia" and "The Red, White and Blue."[10]

Like all symbols, the forms of nineteenth-century ritual drew on the past and were historical, not accidental. Nearly every partisan representation from the naming of parties and the location of events to the raising of liberty poles, the appropriation of George Washington, and the language of electioneering originated with the American Revolution. Created by a postmillennial generation which had the imposing task of keeping the Republic, these affairs of party were a natural response to a critical problem. Nineteenth-century Americans were constantly exhorting each other "to acquit ourselves of the

8. See Robert Gunderson, *The Log-Cabin Campaign* (Lexington, Ky., 1957).
9. The exception here is the Democrats' emphasis on Andrew Jackson. Somehow Thomas Jefferson became a national symbol, but efforts to do the same for Andrew Jackson failed. Note, for example, the unsuccessful struggle to make Jackson's birthday a national holiday.
10. *Tammany Society or the Columbian Order, Annual Celebration, July 4, 1863* (New York, 1863).

high trust which Providence has devolved upon us"—or in Henry Clay's words in 1832, "It belongs to you and to the young men of your age to decide whether the great blessings of Liberty and Union shall be defended and preserved. The responsibility which attaches to you is immense."[11]

This task, as George Forgie and Rush Welter have shown, was both a psychological and a political burden. To adhere to the "Christian Sparta" demanded by the founders of the Republic and to maintain a virtuous citizenry who intuited the public good was never easy. But amid the unrestrained individualism of the nineteenth century it had become more difficult than it had been during the collective enterprise of making a new republic. And even then, the eighteenth-century formulators of republican doctrine had depended on militarism for regeneration. During the Revolution, Benjamin Rush explained to John Adams that "several more military campaigns were needed if Americans were to purge away the monarchical impurity we contracted by laying so long on the lap of Great Britain." In the view of this generation, the Revolution would cleanse the American soul of its impurities, and thus from its national beginnings, American liberty depended on the discipline of war to create the requisite characteristics of a virtuous and prudent citizenry.[12]

By the nineteenth century, Americans not only needed to justify the heresy of political parties which were, in theory, antithetical to the commonwealth ideal; they also had to connect themselves to a vital point in their national past. They accomplished both ends by using the iconography, themes, and symbols of the Revolution in their political life. As symbols always do, these representations helped to resolve the dilemma this generation faced—the need to be as self-sacrificing and heroic as they imagined their fathers had been and the indulgent circumstances of their own age. The bipartisan imagery of their politics became one avenue to third-generation patriotism.

Nineteenth-century Americans who were exposed to this kind of

---

11. William Rives quoted in *Register of Congress*, 19th Cong., April 6, 1826; Clay quoted in Rush Welter, *The Mind of America, 1820–1860* (New York, 1975), 24.
12. George Forgie, *Patricide in the House Divided: A Psychological Interpretation of Lincoln and His Age* (New York, 1979), esp. 13–89; Welter, *The Mind of America*, 3–5, 70–71; Rush quoted in Gordon Wood, *The Creation of the American Republic* (Chapel Hill, 1969), 124.

politics came to understand parties as natural links between citizen and state. Ironically the very organizations that the founding generation of Americans feared would divide the Republic into special interest groups had become schools teaching seasonal courses in how to be Americans. Party activities were one of the best civics lessons the nineteenth century offered.

And these were indeed nineteenth-century occurrences. Under no party or person's special provenance, they developed during the early years of that century and were sufficiently in place by the Harrison–Van Buren presidential campaign of 1840 to be noticed, and then forgotten, by contemporaries and historians. By the 1850s, they were commonplace. Surviving nineteenth-century party systems, electoral realignments, and policy shifts, they became recurring rituals—what the anthropologist Victor Turner describes for the African Ndembu as "storage units" into which societies place symbolic commentary on their attitudes and expectations.[13] For the rest of the nineteenth century, election ceremonies brought Americans together in a highly stylized political drama that helped make their national life more coherent.

By World War I these affairs of party had largely disappeared. The popular song of the 1890s "Good-bye my Party Good-bye" forecast an end to partisan celebrations as well as voting patterns. The conversion to a less participatory style of politics did not mean that basic ideals about the legitimacy of government or the system of delegating power had changed.[14] Instead the conveyance of such political values through rituals of national affirmation was no longer necessary or appropriate. In the future, there would be more listening and less doing.

One reason for this was historical, the other technological. First, the system of delegating authority and removing governments by majority vote had survived the Civil War and the crisis of 1876. Twentieth-century Americans knew their roles, either as winners or

13.　Gunderson's study of the 1840 campaign, which is full of suggestive material on party rituals, was published in 1957 and has had no successor. Victor Turner, *The Drums of Affliction: A Study of Religious Processes Among the Ndembu of Zambia* (Oxford, 1968), 1.

14.　Robert Marcus, *Grand Old Party: Political Structure in the Golden Age, 1880–1896* (New York, 1971).

as members of an expectant loyal opposition. Having grown up in households where voting was a familiar activity, they needed less training in civic deportment. Furthermore, by 1900, automobiles, streetcar tracks, and even tighter municipal restrictions over parade permits ended the torchlight processions. Pole-raisings were impossible on cement sidewalks and lost their purpose if held too far out of town. New architectural standards provided fewer balconies from which leaders could salute the people. The primary system made ratification ceremonies superfluous, and the Australian ballot effectively destroyed the special amenities of election day. In time the radio rendered stump speeches redundant.

With the decline of ceremonial politics came a decrease in participation and what Walter Dean Burnham has labeled "the onward march of party decomposition." In the 1896 election between McKinley and Bryan, 80 percent of the eligible voters cast ballots; by 1920 the figure had dropped to less than 60 percent. It is impossible to make the end of ceremonial politics the single cause of lowered voting. Still the decline of party rituals depending on participation and the emergence of a "mercantilist" style of partisanship based on advertisement destroyed the sense of parties as patriotic bands— little republics of believers—en route to battle. And when this collegiality ended, so too did the nineteenth century's high turnouts.[15]

Like most rituals, election ceremonies involved a series of episodes that culminated in a special event—in this case, the casting of the ballot on election day. The routine began with ratification meetings held promptly after conventions had chosen a nominee who, if elected, would have to be accepted by all Americans. Usually these meetings were organized by a handful of party enthusiasts, and it was a self-selected group who recruited speakers and established a time and place for the assembly. In Illinois in 1856 a friend of the just-nominated Republican candidate for governor wrote that a crowd of two thousand had ratified the state convention's choice in Springfield. A few weeks later Lyman Trumbull, the United States

15.   Walter Dean Burnham, *Critical Elections and the Mainsprings of American Politics* (New York, 1970), 91; Richard J. Jensen, *Grass Roots Politics, Parties, Issues, and Voters* (Westport, Conn., 1983), 36–39.

senator from Illinois, received an invitation from the "Friends of Fremont" to speak "to a public meeting at the Tabernacle in New York to ratify the proceedings of the Republican Convention whose labors have just ceased in Philadelphia." Probably the largest ratification meeting in American history occurred in Baltimore after the Whigs nominated William Henry Harrison and twelve thousand enthusiasts met in Monument Square.[16]

Most ratification meetings, however, were small affairs with a formula for confirming the candidate. They began with speeches about the candidate, moved on to descriptions of the party's platform, and ended with resolutions for which the audience invariably shouted its support. Sometimes in their correspondence party leaders described these ceremonies as "going down to the People," and speakers always were on a stand, talking down to their followers. Voices carried better this way, but no matter what the practical reason, the setting dispelled any sense of political equality.

In symbolic terms the ratification meeting resolved the contradiction between the American ideal of government by all the people and the reality of governance by a few leaders chosen by party notables. By shouting their approval of resolutions supporting the nominee, the people confirmed what their leaders had already done. This, in turn, permitted the party to offer its candidate as the "People's Choice." Those who did not approve a specific candidate did not come to a ratification meeting, and as in the routine pause in Protestant marriage ceremonies for objectors, no one ever dissented. Instead, insurgents held their own conventions (as did Breckinridge Democrats in 1860 and Chase Republicans in 1864) and approved their own choices in a separate but parallel system.

In time the language of ratification meetings evolved into a set of bipartisan clichés. Followers must be "up and doing"; must "take to the hustings"; must "arise"; must "get the ball rolling." This last image was sometimes enacted by enthusiasts who sent huge party-labeled balls tumbling through the streets and courthouse squares. "As rolls the ball, so our enemy's reign doth fall," sang partisans.

16.   Thomas Quick to Lyman Trumbull, July 2, 1856, Peter Page to Lyman Trumbull, June 3, 1856, and Luman Sherwood *et al.* to Lyman Trumbull, June 19, 1856, all in Lyman Trumbull Papers, Microfilm; Baltimore *Sun*, May 5–9, 1840; *Niles' National Register*, VIII (May 9, 1840), 152–60.

Along with its intended demonstration of increasing power, the event engaged party members at an early stage of the campaign.[17]

One way to get the ball rolling was to raise a flagpole with a banner naming candidate and party. As with parties themselves, pole-raisings required an enemy who not only put up his own but also cut down that of his opponents. By the 1840s the ceremony was a set piece with party members marching to a prepared site, sometimes singing "Raising up the Liberty Pole" or the popular "Coming as the Winds Come." At a place where a deep hole had already been dug, usually on a prominent hill, party leaders gave short speeches in which they compared the raising of the pole to the lifting of the people through their votes for a special man identified with the cause. Then "the boys" (as they were often called by party leaders) used a team of horses to raise a huge pole. Often poles that measured seventy feet at the beginning of a campaign were no more than twenty by election time. The contrived passion of these events suggests that ritual deportment was involved. In Springfield, Illinois, a loyal partisan complained: "On Monday night some miserable infamous low-flung narrow-minded ungodly dirt-earting cut-throat hemp-deserving deep-died double-distilling concentrated miscreant of miscreants sinned against all honor and decency by sawing down two or three poles."[18]

Throughout the campaign, parties guarded their poles from opposition raids and at the same time tried to cut down those of their opponents. To go through the campaign with the tallest pole was to provide a concrete forecast of victory, and in some communities election-eve rallies took place on the site of a partisan pole. After the election, it was a common humiliation for the losers to pay off their bets by climbing a winner's pole.

Pole-raisings, like so many other aspects of party ceremony, originated in revolutionary times when liberty poles were visible signs of patriotic sentiment and, like the great liberty oak in Annapolis, meeting places for those who opposed the British. Certainly, Democrats played on the theme when they identified Andrew Jackson with hickory poles. As Kentucky Democrats sang:

17. Gunderson, *The Log-Cabin Campaign*, 130; "As Rolls the Ball," n.d., in Broadside Collection, Library of Congress; *Kentucky Gazette* (Lexington), March 5, 1837.
18. *Illinois State Journal*, August 4, 1860.

> Freeman, Cheer the Hickory Tree
> In storms its boughs have sheltered thee
> O'er freedom's land its branches wave
> 'Twas planted on the Lion's grave.

And as late as the 1870s, partisan poles were still referred to as liberty poles.[19]

Although most communities enjoyed the competition of pole-raisings, only a few held another sort of political ceremony—serenades. This was because the serenade required the candidate's presence, and given the nineteenth-century understanding that a nomination was a "gift" of the people, it was inappropriate for candidates to travel about, soliciting votes.[20] Most nineteenth-century candidates abided by this taboo, although there were some exceptions especially among those, like Stephen Douglas in 1860 and Horatio Seymour in 1868, whose chances of election were poor. But when a candidate did visit a community for whatever reason, loyalists usually raised a musical salute to their choice, who waved and smiled, but who did not say anything. In New York for an election-eve meeting with the "Delmonico set"—those New York leaders who raised money, set campaign strategy, and met at that restaurant—George B. McClellan spent several hours on the balcony of his father-in-law's Manhattan residence, listening to the partisan songs his candidacy had inspired.

> Hurrah for Little Mac,
> Millions of Volunteers, my boys,
> Our own George B. McC.
> Little Mac. First in Peace,
> First in War, First in the hearts of
>   his countrymen.

19. *Kentucky Gazette* (Lexington), May 17, 1834. See also A. M. Schlesinger, "The Liberty Tree: A Genealogy," *New England Quarterly*, XXV (1952), 435–38; Charles Lanman to George McClellan, October 8, 1864, in George G. McClellan Papers, Library of Congress; G. A. Hall to Charles Blake, July 11, 1860, in Trumbull Papers, Microfilm.
20. This is why candidates for the United States Senate were among the first to solicit votes personally. Because their election was accomplished in the legislature by state delegates, the process was indirect. In such circumstances they were removed from the people's balloting and therefore could campaign, as both Lincoln and Douglas did, for example, in Illinois. In time, of course, there was more direct campaigning by gubernatorial and congressional candidates themselves.

Four years later, Democratic presidential nominee Horatio Seymour enjoyed the same kind of occasion when fifty thousand New York Democrats turned out, along with Dodworth's Brass Band, to serenade him with party songs—among them "Seymour's March to the White House."[21]

These episodes enacted the expected relationship between leader and follower in a democratic society. As in military parades, party "soldiers" passed below their leaders, who looked down from balconies and second-story windows. Democrats, Republicans, Whigs, and Know-Nothings saluted those to whom they would shortly grant authority, just as soldiers did in their ceremonies. No one expected either McClellan or Seymour to speak on the issues any more than generals analyzed military tactics with their men on the eve of battle. Simulated here was deference but not servile submissiveness. Like soldiers who followed their commanders into battle, obedient partisans would support their standard-bearer to accomplish a mutual end.

Only in the last weeks of the campaign did parties organize the least expressive of all partisan events—the mass rally. In these ceremonies the purpose was to reach beyond the fraternity of believers and present the platform to all voters. Because the intention here was to turn elections into issue-preference affairs, it was essential that the people hear what party leaders said. Therefore, rallies were quieter, smaller affairs than were processions and parades. Frequently held on Saturday afternoons, they included two- to three-hour speeches delivered from separate stands by party notables who invariably concentrated on criticism of the opposition and nonspecific proposals for the future. Even the stands were set far apart, providing the kind of intimate setting depicted in George Caleb Bingham's painting *Stump Speaking*. There, the candidate engages his small audience, and they intently weigh his case and on election day will render their decision.

Often such affairs were followed by a barbecue, and sharing food became a bond among participants. In Kentucky in 1844, Whigs set up 100-yard-long tables alongside the barbecue pits where whole hogs, sheep, shoats, lambs, and several sides of beef were cooked.

21. Sidney Herbert, *McClellan Campaign Melodist* (Boston, 1864), 5; *New York World*, November 3, 1864; *Illustrated London News*, October 15, 1864; Charles Coleman, *The Election of 1868: The Democratic Effort to Regain Control* (New York, 1971), 261.

Nearby were huge kettles with a regional dish—the famed burgoo, or stew—as well as a good supply of Kentucky whiskey.[22]

Sometimes central committees recruited a team of party leaders who traveled throughout the state to speak at these rallies. Often politicians had to be convinced that they were not appearing at a torchlight procession where the opportunity for spreading the message was limited. When Lyman Trumbull questioned his hosts about what kind of affair he had been invited to, a Republican assured him that "each speech will be a campaign document. They will be correctly reported. . . . There will be no interruption of the meetings by music, processions or fireworks, nor will any [time] restrictions be imposed." Only when reassured that this was a "grand old-fashioned mass rally" followed by a barbecue where "the boys can cut up," did Trumbull accept.[23] Convinced that he was not competing with fireworks, cannon, and light shows, Trumbull became one member of a traveling caravan of Republican leaders who made appearances in county seats throughout Illinois in the fall of 1860.

Preelection ceremonies climaxed with the election-eve torchlight parade and grand procession. Unlike rallies with their high ratio of words to symbols, processions were full of nonverbal activity. They transmitted the sense of a disciplined and growing American army on its way to do battle with the enemy. Party followers wore uniforms; their torchlights looked like rifles; they were divided into regiments and divisions commanded by officers. Amid the rockets and firecrackers, processions even sounded and smelled like battlefields. To those who lined the streets and watched the paraders, the message was clear: Join our army. It will be the largest and best equipped with ballots, the political weapons of this campaign. The sense conveyed was one of mobilization for a battle undertaken not only as partisans but also, given the patriotic symbology of parties, as Americans.

Along with military images, light was central to these affairs. The huge bonfires, the flaming tar-barrels, the torchlights and kero-

22.   Baker, *Affairs of Party*, 278. See also William E. Gienapp, "Politics Seems to Enter into Everything: Political Culture in the North," in Stephen E. Maizlish and John J. Kushma (eds.), *Essays on American Antebellum Politics, 1840–1860* (College Station, Tex., 1982), 14–69; *Kentucky Gazette* (Lexington), July 22, 1844.

23.   Charles Ellis *et al.* to Lyman Trumbull, July 16, 1860, in Trumbull Papers, Microfilm.

sene lamps carried by participants, the fireworks, the illuminated houses, and calcium lights conveyed the sense of purification. Parties consciously played on the theme that they would rid the nation of the darkness of the opposition's corruption. "It has been dark but there is light ahead," predicted the New York *World*. "We will bring light to the hidden corners of our republic," the Baltimore *Clipper* insisted about the Know-Nothings. From their understanding of light as fire, nineteenth-century partisans drew another symbol. Their political movement would catch on and spread when they lit "the fires of popular support." "We will blaze up and catch the prairies on fire." "We have the light and fire of truth." The language of nineteenth-century political ceremonies reinforced the notion of an army of light. For those Americans who paid little attention to subtle programmatic differences between parties—and this was usually most of the electorate—the sense of an army of good on its way to do battle against an enemy was inescapable.[24]

Throughout the nineteenth century, Whigs, Know-Nothings, Republicans, and Democrats were exhorted "to close ranks and stand firm"; "to falter not before the enemy"; "to use your paper bullets tomorrow"; "to rally then with warm hearts, willing hands, and full ranks." "Come," sang regulars of all parties in a song used by organizations through the century:

> The foe is on his march again,
> Council fires aglow,
> Then rally now, my gallant band,
> To battle with the foe.

A defeated candidate was not a loser, but rather a casualty. The October congressional elections held in some states were not previews but rather skirmishes. In Wisconsin during the Civil War a volunteer found that he already knew the marching song of his regiment because he had learned it as a young Democrat:

> Come rally round the clarion sound
> The bugle blasts are sounding

24. New York *World*, November 9, 1864; *Illinois State Journal*, October 8, 1860; Henry Hayden to Lyman Trumbull, May 8, 1860, in Trumbull Papers, Microfilm; Baltimore *Clipper*, October 29, 1856.

The marshalling hosts are at their posts
The enemy surrounding.[25]

In the twentieth century we retain some of this language when we speak of election campaigns, tactics, and the rank and file. But without the accompanying rituals these metaphors have become clichés. In the nineteenth century the image of mobilizing an army of light to participate in a national battle inspired high voter turnouts and general interest in politics. Symbolically linked through the ceremonies of party politics, voting and patriotism were interconnected, underlying aspects of American civic life.

Occasionally, the understanding of fighting an enemy spilled over into election-day violence. In the mayoral election in Baltimore in 1857, for example, there were over one hundred casualties, including twenty dead. But with the exception of the eleven southern states in 1860, defeated partisans accepted the victors as holding legitimate power. Ironically the sense of a military mobilization that brought many to the polls helped defuse postelection antagonisms. Taught to believe that they were fighting a battle, Americans never confused this with a war. The nature of politics helped, for there was always another chance. So did the frequency of elections, which heightened the expectation that next time, with proper mobilization and leadership, their cause would triumph. Lincoln after his loss in 1858 said to a supporter who had written he felt "terrible" after the election, "Quit that. You will soon feel better. Another 'blow-up' is coming and we shall have fun again." The consoling words of the New York *World* to Democrats after McClellan's loss were also typical: "Never was fought a more gallant fight than did the loyal and true-hearted Democrats of the North. . . . We will take no delay in saying that four years from now the Democracy will vindicate its honor and patriotism alike."[26]

The practices of nineteenth-century voting further defused the

25. New York *Caucasian*, October 1, 1864; New York *Times*, October 13, 15, 1864; Newark *Journal*, October 8, 1864; *Kentucky Gazette* (Lexington), March 7, 1844; Clement L. Vallandigham, *Songbook: Songs for the Times* (Columbus, Ohio, 1863).
26. David Donald, "An Excess of Democracy," in *Lincoln Reconsidered: Essays on the Civil War Era* (rev. ed.; New York, 1961), 209–35; Roy P. Basler (ed.), *The Collected Works of Abraham Lincoln* (9 vols.; New Brunswick, N.J., 1953), III, 342; New York *World*, November 9, 1864.

preelection sense of mobilization and militarism. Sometimes local political parties did march to the polls as a group, gathering their supporters as they went along. There were no laws against this, but more often American men became accustomed to going to the polls as individuals. In any case, once there they stood in line as private citizens, on a first-come, first-served basis, severed from any collective affiliation—wheat farmers with small-town druggists and dry-goods merchants, rural farmers and renters; Republicans, Democrats, Whigs, and Know-Nothings; Lutherans, Methodists, and Catholics; rich and poor—the social and economic inequalities among them temporarily suspended. Ironically, in the act of fulfilling the intentions of the campaign, they lost their partisanship and became Americans.[27] Homogeneity was sexual, racial, and national. At the polls stood an assembly whose physical act of casting a ballot linked them to their government and at the same time sanctioned the winners.

The places chosen for this transference of authority from the sovereign people to the delegated leader were plebeian. Schools, stores, taverns, the verandas of hotels, and in the West, large homes served as polling places, and the sense of familiarity was reinforced by the simplicity of the affair. A hallowed ceremony, the act of voting was not a formal occasion. Within hours after the polls closed, the few accoutrements needed—ropes, wooden ballot boxes, tables, and chairs—had disappeared, and all had returned to normal.

Nineteenth-century voting procedures also displayed this lack of ceremony. By the 1850s, most communities had residency requirements, window-lists of preregistered voters, and public officials to supervise. Parties, of course, produced the printed ballots that voters handed to election judges. The latter ascertained the legality of the vote, although they wore no special clothes and had no symbol of authority. Yet the procedures of voting were still hierarchical. Ballot casting—the essential public act of American "freemen"—involved delivering a vote to a public official who served as a surrogate for future governors and who decided whether to place that vote in the simple wooden ballot box that at the end of the day contained the people's will.

27. For a romanticized rendering of nineteenth-century voting, see Bingham's *County Election* in the collection of the Boatmen's National Bank of St. Louis.

After the polls closed, most victory celebrations (and often there were none) were good-natured unorganized displays that dampened friction between winners and losers. Occasionally communities (rather than parties) held postelection suppers, where disenfranchised women were given a chance to participate. In Springfield, Illinois, after Lincoln's election in 1860, Republican women organized such an event, and many Democrats came to celebrate, not to contest, the results.[28] In earlier national elections, before the telegraph, no one knew who had won for days or even weeks. Moreover, the long gap between elections and the installation of new regimes (several months in the case of the president) further deflated partisan antagonism.

Thus the ceremonies of nineteenth-century politics taught Americans how to be just that—Americans. Through these symbolic rituals the sense of serving the nation, not just the party, was transmitted to generations of citizens. Parades conveyed the importance of mobilization and loyalty to the party, and their use of national symbols also diminished any notions of particularism. Serenades and ratification meetings explained in physical terms the ambivalent nature of leadership and governance by the few in a democracy. Pole-raisings linked Americans to their early history and gave a sense of continuity to an electoral system that otherwise was an array of episodes. And finally the lack of formal ceremonies on election day helped resolve the contradiction between the ideal of individual free choice and the reality of party control.

> Now, to keep all these glorious feeturs
> Thet characterize morril an' reasonin' creeturs,
> Thet give every paytriot all he can cram,
> Thet oust the untrustworthy Presidunt Flam,
> An' stick honest Presidunt Sham in his place,
> To the manifest gain o' the holl human race,
> An' to some indervidgewals on't in partickler,
> Who love Public Opinion an' know how to tickle her,—
> I say thet a party with gret aims like these
> Must stick jest ez close ez a hive full o' bees.[29]

28. *Illinois State Journal*, November, 1860.
29. James Russell Lowell, *The Biglow Papers*, 1st Ser. (De Kalb, Ill., 1977), 85.

Trent's *Simms*
The Making of a Biography
John McCardell

Charles Dudley Warner was a man who knew what he wanted and usually got it. Throughout his productive career as writer and editor, this native New Englander had earned a reputation, according to a biographer, for "natural shrewdness" and "old-time directness and charm." From early childhood, through his college years as a member of Hamilton's class of 1851, and later as an editor of the Hartford *Courant*, a collaborator with Mark Twain, and a penetrating critic of matters literary and political during America's Gilded Age, Warner had relentlessly pursued the art of clear expression through the writer's craft. "He saw clearly, he felt deeply, and he thought straight," wrote an admiring friend, and he had "learned that truth, though often strenuously enforced, is never so convincing as when stated in terms of beauty."[1]

In 1881, Warner desperately wanted to find the right man for an important assignment. He was then serving as general editor of the American Men of Letters Series, begun by Houghton, Mifflin, and Company of Boston in the 1870s. Most of the subjects, like most of the contributing authors, were well known: Oliver Wendell Holmes had written on Emerson, John Bach McMaster on Benjamin Franklin, Thomas Wentworth Higginson on Margaret Fuller, Warner himself on Washington Irving. The series aimed to provide a set of "biographies of distinguished American authors, having all the special interest of biography, and the larger interest and value of illustrating the different phases of American literature, the social, political, and moral influences which have moulded these authors and the generations to which they belonged."[2] But the series thus far lacked a vol-

1. Hamilton Wright Mabie, "Introduction," in Charles Dudley Warner, *Fashions in Literature and Other Literary and Social Essays and Addresses* (New York, 1902), viii, x, xii, xiv.
2. William Peterfield Trent, *William Gilmore Simms*, American Men of Letters Series, ed. Charles Dudley Warner (Boston, 1892), i.

ume on the literature of the antebellum South. Warner was determined to fill that gap, and he thought he knew how.

Without question, the leading man of letters in the Old South had been William Gilmore Simms of South Carolina. On virtually every issue of the period embraced by his life, from 1806 to 1870, Simms at one time or another had ventured an influential opinion. His astonishing literary productivity was unmatched—at least one volume a year (and frequently more) every year from 1832 to 1860—and his reputation during his lifetime had been national. Novelist, historian, editor, poet, critic, and man of affairs, Simms, his life and times, appeared to provide the ideal focus for a study of the mind of the Old South.[3]

Settling upon the proper subject, however, was much easier than choosing the author to execute the assignment. That had to be done with great care—in 1881, sentiments about the Old South and memories of the sectional conflict ran strong and deep. A biographer, whether northern or southern, with old-fashioned opinions about the plantation regime and the intellectual atmosphere fostered by it, would be unlikely to produce the kind of book Warner desired: a well-written book of enduring value, a book reflecting the critical outlook and sophistication of the late nineteenth century, and, most important, a book for a national readership yearning for sectional harmony. "The standard of literary judgment," Warner wrote, "is in certain immutable principles and qualities which have been slowly evolved during the long historical periods of literary criticism."[4] Simms's biographer, then, would face the task of placing his subject—and his subject's environment—in this broader, evolutionary context, showing the degree to which the subject and his society served to advance or retard the inevitable progress of civilization.

3. In addition to Trent, the best treatments of Simms's life and work may be found in Vernon L. Parrington, *Main Currents in American Thought*, Vol. II, *The Romantic Revolution, 1800–1860* (New York, 1927), 119–30; Jay B. Hubbell, *The South in American Literature, 1607–1900* (Durham, 1954), 572–601; William R. Taylor, *Cavalier and Yankee: The Old South and American National Character* (New York, 1957), 268–97; Joseph V. Ridgely, *William Gilmore Simms* (New York, 1962); Jon L. Wakelyn, *The Politics of a Literary Man* (Westport, Conn., 1973); and Keen Butterworth, "William Gilmore Simms," *Dictionary of Literary Biography*, III, 306–18.
4. Warner, *Fashions in Literature*, 16.

Such a condition summarily eliminated from Warner's consideration any candidate who retained an intellectual or emotional allegiance to the Old South. Far preferable would be a younger man, one who agreed with the postbellum tendency to view with some detachment and with a sharply critical eye the society of the old regime. Warner invited George W. Cable of New Orleans to undertake the Simms project. Cable's views of southern history were pronounced and wholly "reconstructed." He had written letters in the New Orleans papers condemning racial segregation in schools and on public transportation. He was a frequent critic of slavery at a time when most other, and older, southern writers were inclined to romanticize the antebellum past. His two early works, *Old Creole Days* (1879) and *The Grandissimes* (1880), had dared to question the system of race relations and the patterns of social behavior in old Louisiana. Denounced as a "Southern Yankee" by his neighbors, Cable found a sympathetic and influential northern readership. Warner well knew what kind of biography Cable was likely to produce, and he leaned heavily on the Louisianian. He flattered: "Our plan [is] to make some Southern author—and I suppose Sims [*sic*] is the best for the purpose—the center for a study of Southern literature in the old days, such as you can do better than any other man." He prophesied: "The volume from you is certain to be one of the best and perhaps the most important." And he compromised: "You could, in reason, take your own time in preparing your volume."[5]

When Warner's selection of Cable was announced, southern reaction was less than enthusiastic. As his other writing and lecturing activities before appreciative northern audiences continued to condemn the South, Cable came increasingly under attack. "The harm that fellow *Cable* has done to the South cannot be estimated," lamented Paul Hamilton Hayne of Charleston. "Good God! that our old friend's biography should fall into such hands!" Hayne's friend and frequent correspondent, the venerable Louisiana historian Charles A. Gayarré, concurred, more graphically still. "This pigmy author," he

5. The best discussion of postbellum southern literary attitudes remains Paul H. Buck, *The Road to Reunion* (Boston, 1937), esp. Chap. VII. Charles Dudley Warner to George W. Cable, July 4, July 24, 1881, both quoted in Kjell Ekstrom, *George Washington Cable: A Study of His Life and Early Work* (Cambridge, Mass., 1950), 20–21.

remarked, "seems to me afflicted with a mental disease which a physician would not hesitate to characterize as being 'diarrhea of words and a constipation of ideas.'"[6]

That such men as Hayne and Gayarré, both of whom had known Simms well and received professional support through his influence, should have considered Cable harmful and even mentally deranged suggested that much was at stake in the writing of the volume. For them, at least, much was. Probably no living writer in 1881 knew more about Simms than did Paul Hamilton Hayne. Like Simms, Hayne was a native Charlestonian, born in the City by the Sea in 1830. Simms had taken a paternal interest in the able young writer's intellectual development, and the younger man returned the compliment with affection and respect. During the 1850s, Simms and Hayne had been the most prominent among a group of Charleston literati who regularly met in the back room of Russell's bookstore to discuss books and ideas. As the two comrades struggled to rebuild their shattered lives and fortunes in the years after the war, their friendship, enriched by shared experiences and maintained by a candid correspondence, deepened. No man grieved more over Simms's passing in 1870 than did Hayne. "I cannot *make* him dead!" Hayne wrote. "So much *vitality* was there in the man, so vivid is his image before my mind's eye, that all attempts at a *realization* of his death utterly fail!"[7] For the remainder of his life, Hayne was jealously protective of his old friend's memory.

Like Hayne, Gayarré, born in 1805, held on as firmly as he could to the dead past. Like his better-known contemporaries Francis Parkman and William Prescott, Gayarré was a well-educated, independently wealthy scion of distinguished lineage. His fully researched and beautifully written volumes on Louisiana history won national praise. He too had been a loyal Confederate and had found himself,

6.   Paul Hamilton Hayne to Margaret J. Preston, January 22, 1885, Hayne to Charles Gayarré, May 8, September 25, 1885, Gayarré to Hayne, September 3, 1885, all in Rayburn S. Moore (ed.), *A Man of Letters in the Nineteenth-Century South: Selected Letters of Paul Hamilton Hayne* (Baton Rouge, 1982), 237, 262, 274, 276.
7.   The most recent treatments of Hayne are Rayburn S. Moore, *Paul Hamilton Hayne* (New York, 1972), and Moore (ed.), *A Man of Letters*. Paul Hamilton Hayne to Francis Peyre Porcher, July 9, 1870, [typescript], in Paul Hamilton Hayne Papers, South Caroliniana Library, University of South Carolina, Columbia.

by war's end, reduced to poverty. He lived until 1895, struggling to restore his lost fortune and to revive a reputation that had been certified before the war by no less a writer than George Bancroft, who had praised Gayarré's work as "an authentic history such as scarce any other [state] in the Union possesses."[8] But, embittered by war and Reconstruction, Gayarré recovered neither fame nor wealth and lived out his twilight years in sad and hostile musings over the fate of his beloved South.

For such men and others like them, who could never bring themselves to accept the defeat of the Confederacy, dispassionate critical judgment of new literary trends and ideas was scarcely possible. They found themselves fighting a rearguard action in their last years. The postwar South, the dominant idea of progress, held no charm. All that was good, all that was true had been lost in 1865. Physically enfeebled by advancing age and economically reduced by the devastation of war, they nevertheless devoted themselves wholly to memorializing the past. Skilled as they may have been as stylists and researchers, and committed to the preservation of old values as they surely were, they held views that were flawed by a critical sensibility that had become locked in time. It is arguable that Gayarré possessed a deeper familiarity and a defter touch with the Creoles of Louisiana than did Cable. It is likely that Hayne's intimate knowledge of Simms and the world of antebellum Charleston, displayed in a series of articles written for the *Southern Bivouac* in 1885, would have produced a distinguished biography. But there is no evidence to suggest that such men were ever considered by Charles Dudley Warner. And thus embittered, these relics of the past could only commiserate with each other when such a "pigmy" as Cable, who never acknowledged in print his genuine scholarly debts to Gayarré, won recognition as the latest flower of southern intellect.

Burdened by defeat, oppressed by debt, weakened by the years, these men, finally, suffered an acute attack of selective memory. For few southern writers had been more relentless or perceptive in viewing their native region than were these two men before the war. Not long after the collapse of *Russell's* in 1860, another in a long series of distinguished yet short-lived literary magazines, which Hayne had

8. Hubbell, *The South in American Literature*, 650–57.

edited, he attacked southern indifference toward works of the mind:
"The people are intensely provincial, narrow-minded, and I must
add—ignorant. . . . If the opportunity ever presents itself, I shall take
a final farewell of the South and 'pitch my tent' not far from 'Bunker
Hill.'" His volumes of poetry published in Boston had sold far better
and received far wider notice than had those published in Charleston.
Gayarré's view of the South was, like Hayne's in the antebellum years,
far from blindly worshipful. Leaving serious studies of history aside
for a time, Gayarré had published in 1854 a scathing political satire
denouncing the state of southern politics. "Drop entirely the garb,
manners, and the feelings of a gentleman," he wrote, perhaps recall-
ing his own difficulties in winning public office, "and you may have
the chance of a triumphant election." Feeling as unappreciated in
New Orleans as Hayne felt in Charleston, Gayarré once estimated
that his historical exertions had cost him upward of thirty thousand
dollars.[9]

These attitudes did not disappear after 1865, but they were re-
directed. Privately, and mostly to each other, Hayne and Gayarré continued to express their resentment. In 1886, Hayne promised to publish an article about Gayarré, giving "your Louisianians 'particular
hell' because of their conduct towards you." The feelings of neglect
persisted, but the basis had drastically changed. In public they expressed a level of blind affection for the old days that before 1861
would have been unthinkable. In 1885, Hayne observed that since
"the 'Old South' is being abused, undervalued, sneered at, right and
left, my being true to our Poets and our Traditions,—has shut the door
almost hermetically against further literary recognition." Gayarré,
meanwhile, contributed a series of articles to northern magazines, in
which he gently but firmly defended the Old South. Privately, however, with a sense of anguish, he viewed such work as "a prostitution
of the intellect . . . a profanation of the soul."[10]

Thus affected, writers of the older generation found it intolerable
that such a man as Cable, despite his proper sectional credentials—
New Orleans birth, Virginia ancestry, Confederate loyalty—should
dare publicly to suggest that the old order might have constituted

9. *Ibid.*, 746, 653, 652.
10. *Ibid.*, 655, 656.

something less than the best of all possible worlds. Such heresy was bad enough in the pages of the New Orleans *Picayune*, the newspaper for which Cable worked in the 1870s. Infinitely worse was its appearance in such prestigious national publications as *Scribner's* or the *Century*. Cable's decision to remove permanently to the North in 1885 merely confirmed their suspicions. And that such a man should have been asked to write the biography of their old friend Simms— "for the Yankee market, a book to *sell*," Hayne charged—was more than they could bear. "If *Cable does* wrong Simms' memory," Hayne promised, "I will *break every bone* in his (intellectual) carcass."[11]

There were others in the South who felt as strongly about Simms but were at least willing to give Cable a chance, none more so than Simms's eldest daughter Anna Augusta Singleton Simms Roach. Born in 1827, the only child of Simms's first marriage to the humble Anna Giles, who had died in 1832, Augusta had always had a special relationship with her father. She had accompanied him on his annual visits to the North; she had, as a child, been his favorite companion on long walks and, as an adult, been a pillar of support at moments of crisis and despair. To Simms's second wife, Chevillette Roach, Augusta had been more a sister than a daughter, and after her own marriage to Edward Roach, Chevillette's cousin, in 1858, her unique double attachment to the Simms family tree made her an especially authoritative source on family history. Later generations of Simms descendants, perhaps envious of her connection, remembered Augusta as "an iron sword in a rusty scabbard." Like her father, Augusta never knew her mother and thus took on many traits of her father. Like her father, she married a Roach. And after her father's death in 1870, Augusta's devotion to his memory became such an obsession that she could think of little else.[12]

Augusta was determined that Simms's life and work should not be forgotten. Because in her adoring eyes her father hadn't a single

11.   Paul Hamilton Hayne, "Ante-Bellum Charleston," *Southern Bivouac*, I (October, 1885), 257–68; Hayne to Gayarré, September 25, 1885, in Moore (ed.), *A Man of Letters*, 275.
12.   Biographical data on Augusta may be found in Mary C. Simms Oliphant *et al.* (eds.), *The Letters of William Gilmore Simms* (6 vols.; Columbia, S.C., 1952–56, 1981), I, cxlviii.

fault, even the slightest criticism of his work struck her as unwarranted and personally motivated, and she unhesitatingly accepted her mercurial father's occasional complaints that he was never truly accepted in Charleston. A biography, she believed, if carefully done by the right person, would fulfill Simms's deathbed prophecy that his native city and state would in time do him justice. Less than a year after Simms's death, Augusta approached the Reverend James W. Miles about editing her father's manuscripts, but the elderly clergyman was too ill to accept. She hoped—in vain, as it turned out—that one of Simms's erstwhile protégés, Dr. J. D. Bruns of New Orleans, might keep a promise to write Simms's life. She encouraged Hayne to attempt a biography and offered him unlimited access to her enormous collection of materials, but the aging and bitter poet was able to produce only a commemoration ode in 1877 and the *Southern Bivouac* pieces in 1885. "I grow weary of waiting for justice to be done to my dear Father," she lamented in 1877. When, finally, Cable was announced as the Men of Letters biographer, Augusta immediately forwarded to him a memorandum and selected documents to aid his research. By 1885, however, she had become so disillusioned by Cable's behavior that she demanded he return all the materials to her. "Mr. Cable is not the man to even attempt a Life of my father," she wrote Hayne. "From all I can see in print he has quite forgotten his allegiance to the South—& certainly could never write the life of one so truly and wholly Southern in all & everything as my father." It was doubtless with relief that she received the news that Cable, claiming other pressing responsibilities, had withdrawn from the assignment, even though that meant further delay in the preparation of a Simms biography.[13]

Warner, meanwhile, began to search for a suitable replacement for Cable. In the summer of 1889 he was invited to lecture at the University of the South at Sewanee, Tennessee, on the topic "Certain Diversities of American Life." "There is no place where I would choose to speak more plainly of our national situation today than in the South," Warner declared; "in the South because it is more plainly in a transition state, and at the University of the South, because it is

13. Augusta Simms Roach to Paul Hamilton Hayne, August 16, 1885, May 18, 23, 1871, December 19, 1877, July 27, 1885, all in Paul Hamilton Hayne Papers, William R. Perkins Library, Duke University, Durham.

here . . . that the question of the higher or lower plane of life in the South is to be determined." Warming to his subject, Warner tactfully surveyed the first century of national history, noting that although the South had "excelled in the production of statesmen, orators, trained politicians, great judges, and brilliant lawyers, it produced almost no literature." Meanwhile, he continued, during the antebellum years, there was in New England "awakening, investigation, questioning, doubt, [and] out of this free agitation sprang a literary product, great in quantity and to some degree distinguished in quality." Drawing the contrast gingerly but unmistakably, Warner pronounced: "New England . . . was alert and progressive because it kept its doors and windows open. It was hospitable in its intellectual freedom, both of trial and debate, to new ideas. It was in touch with the universal movement of humanity and of human thought and speculation. You lose some quiet by this attitude, some repose that is pleasant and even desirable perhaps, you entertain many errors . . . but you gain life and are in the way of better things. New England, whatever else we may say about it, was in the world." On the other hand, "isolation from the great historic stream of thought and agitation," such as characterized the Old South, produced "stagnation."

Yet, he concluded, these days were happily past. "As I travel the South and become acquainted with its magnificent resources and opportunities . . . I cannot but muse in a fond prophecy upon the brilliant part it is to play in the diversified life and the great future of the American Republic." Such institutions as Sewanee would be instrumental in this new phase of southern history, making "intelligent people awake to the great ideas that make life interesting."[14]

Seated among Warner's rapt audience that July day in 1889 was twenty-seven-year-old William Peterfield Trent. Trent had come to Sewanee the previous year with impeccable credentials, academic and otherwise, a young man's conviction about the world he lived in, and an ambition to match. A native of Richmond, Trent had attended the University of Virginia, where he received his A.B. in 1883 and his A.M. the next year. He then left Charlottesville to undertake graduate study in history under the direction of Herbert Baxter Adams at Johns Hopkins University. There, thoroughly modern historical training,

14. Warner, "Certain Diversities of American Life," in *Fashions in Literature*, 85–99, 113–14.

which emphasized the importance of man's environment in shaping his character, sharpened Trent's intellect and bolstered his confidence. It also made him an especially attractive job candidate, even though, at the time he came to Sewanee, he had not yet completed his doctoral work.[15] Doubtless the young professor was moved by Warner's speech, at least in part because it reinforced his own prejudices. He soon placed in the mail to Warner a pamphlet he had written, *The Constitution and the Churches*. Warner was impressed and promptly told Trent so. The young man was ecstatic. "You can hardly have forgotten," he bubbled, "how much a young writer can derive from the praise of his senior." Continuing, he expressed his hope that southerners would soon "wake up to the fact that we are doing good work" at Sewanee. This exchange convinced Warner that he had at last found the man to do the Simms biography. He met Trent in Richmond over the winter break of 1889–90 to discuss the project and invite Trent to undertake it. Trent accepted at once.[16]

Happily and swiftly Trent set to work. "The more I think of the subject, the more I am pleased with it," he wrote Warner in March, 1890. "And," he added disarmingly, "the more I hope to be able to keep you from feeling that your kind choice of me was a mistake." He cast a wide net in search of Simms materials, inquiring of friends in Charleston, Baltimore, and New York about Simms's acquaintances and papers, and delving into the antebellum periodicals with which Simms had been associated. Realizing, perhaps, the sensitivity of his likeliest sources, Trent was at pains in his letters of inquiry to dispel any fears about his intentions. To Mrs. Paul Hamilton Hayne, whose husband had died in 1886, Trent wrote reassuringly, "I have a great admiration for Mr. Simms, and a desire to do justice both to him and

15.   Franklin T. Walker, "W. P. Trent: A Critical Biography" (Ph.D. dissertation, George Peabody College, 1943), is the only full-scale life. Chapter 6 deals with the *Simms* episode. See also Bruce Clayton, *The Savage Ideal: Intolerance and Intellectual Leadership in the South, 1890–1914* (Baltimore, 1972), 63–76, for a brief discussion of Trent's career. Probably the best published treatment of Trent's life is Wendell H. Stephenson, "William P. Trent as a Historian of the South," *Journal of Southern History*, XV (1949), 151–77.
16.   W. P. Trent to Charles Dudley Warner, September 8, 1889, in Charles Dudley Warner Papers, Watkinson Library, Trinity College, Hartford, Conn.; Walker, "W. P. Trent," 128.

to the literature of my people—nor shall I make my book a vehicle for unsympathetic criticism of a people who, whatever their faults or misfortunes, have been and are essentially magnanimous and noble." Soon he had an outline, a research schedule—which included a trip to Charleston—and fond hopes of completing his manuscript by year's end.[17]

Trent's grueling pace, however, was difficult to sustain. Not only was he giving every free moment to Simms, he also was carrying a full classroom load of eighteen hours at Sewanee, where he was generally regarded as the best teacher on campus. As a result of such pressures, his health failed. In the summer of 1890 he contracted malarial fever, which forced him to revise his overly optimistic Simms timetable. Fearful lest this change of plans offend his editor, Trent dictated to his mother, for transmission to Warner, a pitiful account of his late misfortune, assuring Warner that he continued "conscientiously" to read Simms's works, apologizing for the delay, and needlessly adding, "I am sure that you do not wish hurried work." By the end of August he had recovered sufficiently to project completion of his volume in April of 1891; when he resumed his work, it was again at breakneck speed.[18]

A batch of letters supplied by Mrs. Hayne made a particularly vivid impression. The views expressed therein by her late husband and his correspondents, Trent later recalled, "illuminated what was in many respects a dreary work. I grew to have toward [Hayne] a *personal* regard such as one seldom has for a writer one never saw." The young scholar found himself attracted both to Hayne's barbed references to the Charleston elite that he believed had snubbed men of literary leanings and to the poet's candid, though confidential, assessment of Simms and his work. The former point so completely coincided with Trent's own sentiments (and Charles Dudley Warner's) that it informed much of his book's narrative. The latter point, however,

---

17.   Trent to Warner, March 26, 1890, in Warner Papers; Trent to Mrs. Paul Hamilton Hayne, October 11, 15, 1890, December 6, 1890, all in Hayne Papers, Duke University; Trent to Warner, April 8, 1890, in Warner Papers. The Sewanee calendar at this time provided for a three-month vacation in midwinter; its normal academic year ran from April through December. See Arthur B. Chitty, Jr., *Reconstruction at Sewanee* (Sewanee, 1954), 71.

18.   Trent to Warner, August 6, 21, 1890, both in Warner Papers.

so influenced Trent that he carefully transcribed it verbatim for later use: "Simms's genius *never had fair play*! Circumstances hampered him! Thus, the *man* was greater than his *works*. . . . A really *great author* (whether in *prose* or verse) *Simms emphatically was not*, and there is no use in maintaining so fulsome a proposition. But his *talents* were splendid, and his whole life seems to me *noble*, because of the 'grit,' the perseverance, the indomitable energy which it displayed. I've not the remotest idea that his *works* will endure. They were too carelessly written. They lack the '*labor limae*' to an extent which is distressing. Nevertheless Simms is worthy of *all honor*." These opinions, of course, expressed in private, diverged rather markedly from Hayne's public statements. For this reason, perhaps, Mrs. Hayne instructed Trent not to quote from any of these materials without first securing her permission. Trent may have made a mental note to comply, but under the pressures of research, he neglected, in returning the collection to her, to make such a request. Instead he simply thanked her for her "great assistance" and concluded, "If the letters in Mrs. Roach's possession are only as full, I do not despair of giving a fairly faithful picture of Mr. Simms in his private as well as his public relations." And in early December, he set out for Charleston.[19]

Probably no city in America was more demoralized in December, 1890, than Charleston. Physically and psychologically, the City by the Sea had yet to recover from the war. Everywhere one turned, one saw a city beleaguered. Touring the South for *Scribner's Monthly* in 1873, Edward King reported that, unlike other southern cities, "Charleston, with grim patience, awaits a turn in the tide of affairs." Seventeen years later, the prospects were hardly more pleasing. The economic and social elite, which had dominated Charleston before the war and which might have taken the lead in rebuilding the city, remained for many years in a state of economic paralysis and political impotence. Part of the problem was the immense physical damage wrought by the war. A related cause was the age-old antagonism between Charles-

19.   Trent to William H. Hayne, January 3, 1893, in Hayne Papers, Duke University; Paul Hamilton Hayne to Francis Peyre Porcher, August 4, 1870, in Hayne Papers, South Caroliniana Library; Trent, *William Gilmore Simms* (2nd ed., Boston, 1892), 322*n*; Trent to Mrs. Hayne, December 6, 1890, in Hayne Papers, Duke University.

ton and the South Carolina upcountry. Inherited prejudices on both
sides made a willingness either to lend or to receive assistance unlikely. Charleston remained in a state of relative decline for the rest of
the century, its population barely increasing, its tentative efforts in
the 1880s to join the railroad-building craze doomed to insolvency, its
shipping activity falling ever further behind that of competing ports.
Moreover, white Charlestonians, resentful of the more visible black
presence during Reconstruction, feared the social consequences of
economic development.[20]

A more important, though more subtle, cause of Charleston's
postwar ennui lay in the minds of many of its citizens: they refused to
surrender the shibboleths of the Old South. In this of course Charleston
was not alone, nor was every Charlestonian an unreconstructed curiosity. Nevertheless, a combination of economic, physical, and social
circumstances served both to heighten and to reinforce a state of
mind in Charleston that made its sensitivity to any form of innovation
acute and instantaneous.

That sensitivity crested in 1890 at almost the precise moment
that Trent arrived. On December 4, 1890, Benjamin Ryan Tillman
was inaugurated as governor of the Palmetto State, thereby apparently
signifying the final eclipse of Charleston. Tillman had mobilized a
political coalition wholly alien to the culture of old Charleston. But the
importance of Tillman's ascendancy lay more in the generational
than in the social makeup of his triumphant constituency. Had the
Tillman movement been merely another of the periodic rural upcountry revolts that had punctuated Carolina history, Charleston
could simply have waited, as it had in the past, for the passage of
time and the skill of lowcountry politicians to erode the strength of
the aggrieved masses. Tillman, however, made no effort to conceal
what he wanted and whom he represented. Too young to have fought
in the war, the farmer from Edgefield repeatedly attacked those who
continued to see the world "through ante-bellum spectacles." The

20. Edward King, *The Great South*, ed. W. Magruder Drake and Robert R. Jones
(Baton Rouge, 1972), 449; Francis Butler Simkins, *Pitchfork Ben Tillman, South Carolinian* (Baton Rouge, 1944), 78–79, 81; William J. Cooper, Jr., *The Conservative Regime: South Carolina, 1877–1890* (Baltimore, 1968), 128; C. Vann Woodward, *Origins
of the New South, 1877–1913* (Baton Rouge, 1951), 107, 125.

Tillmanites, who, according to the historian William J. Cooper, Jr., challenged "the sanctity of Confederate gray," represented in matters political what men like Cable represented in matters literary, a new generation of leadership. The tentative, stagnant, conservative regime of aging Confederates that had governed South Carolina, Tillman charged, "worship the past and march backwards when they march at all." For the "greedy old city of Charleston," symbol of that conservatism, he had no use. "You are the most self-idolatrous people in the world," he declaimed in the very shadow of St. Michael's. "I want to tell you that the sun doesn't rise and set in Charleston. . . . God have mercy on your pusillanimous souls." Now that man, supported by a coalition of young farmers and professional men for whom the past held little meaning, was governor.[21]

The Charleston to which Trent came, then, lingered, like so much of the South in so many ways in 1890, between two worlds, one dead, the other powerless to be born. Trent could not possibly have missed the sense of apprehension in the air, in the press, in daily conversation. Surely this tension was present at 34 Society Street when Trent called on Augusta Simms Roach. In 1890 she was sixty-three and in poor health, a semi-invalid. Her husband, at one time engaged in the shipping business, had been unemployed since 1877. For many years she had had to take in boarders. Life since 1865—and particularly since her father's death—had not been kind. Only that ever more distant past remained to cheer her, and now that past was under attack too, an attack led by the governor himself. Old, bitter, protective, and vulnerable, Augusta poured out her feelings to the young scholar from Sewanee, in whose work everything she cared about was at stake. Trent tactfully listened and made notes. "Mrs. Roach was very kind and furnished me with much information," he later reported, adding revealingly that "the chief result of my visit, however, was the securing of many of the first editions of works now out of print." By December 23, Trent was on his way to Richmond, there to complete his research, shape his thoughts, and draft his manuscript.[22]

21. Cooper, *The Conservative Regime*, 205–206; Simkins, *Pitchfork Ben Tillman*, 129, 153.
22. Augusta Simms Roach to Hayne, February 12, 1878, July 27, 1885, Trent to Mrs. Hayne, December 23, 1890, all in Hayne Papers, Duke University.

In Richmond during the winter of 1890–91 the disparate strands began to come together. As he read Simms's books, studied Simms's correspondence, and pondered his own earlier jottings, Trent began to see an interpretative framework for his biography taking shape. It was impossible, he discovered, to separate the man from his times. No biographer could discuss only Simms and his work without reference to the environment that produced them. Politics, therefore, had to be part of Trent's story. He reported to his old mentor Adams that "Simms practically confesses that the Secessionists must use the arts of *conspirators* . . . &⁹ if I mistake not, the letter will be *nuts* to some historians. My own comments," he carefully added, "shall be brief as I don't care to get into hot water." By the time he returned to Sewanee at the end of March, Trent believed he had a clear sense of his subject. Delightedly he wrote Adams, "I am certain that I have got hold of a fine subject in Simms, which is occupying all my thoughts." Through Simms, Trent would attempt "to weave into my narrative an impartial &⁹ as far as I can make it a philosophical account of the causes of the great differences between North &⁹ South which resulted in the war."[23]

Trent was, however, soon sobered by a letter from Houghton, Mifflin, urging him to get on with his book. His promise to have his volume completed in April simply could not be kept, but he assured his publisher that the twice-postponed manuscript would be "ready by midsummer" of 1891. Classes resumed in April, and once they were under control, Trent had seven weeks to write his book and keep his word. In that time, while teaching fifteen hours a week, he composed 850 pages of manuscript. For two additional weeks he edited his work, in the end delivering 700 typed pages to his publisher on the appointed day. "At the end of it all I was nearly dead," he recalled, "and now I look back on what I did with a kind of shuddering wonder." Early in 1892, *William Gilmore Simms*, at long last, was published.[24]

Readers of *Simms* found a book elegant in style, comprehensive in scope, vigorous in interpretation, and thoroughly reconstructed in sentiment—just the sort of volume that editor Warner had desired.

23.   Trent to Herbert Baxter Adams, March 5, April 17, 1891, both in Herbert Baxter Adams Papers, Milton S. Eisenhower Library, Johns Hopkins University, Baltimore.
24.   Trent to Warner, June 11, 1892, in Warner Papers; Walker, "W. P. Trent," 134.

Trent wasted no time in making his assumptions clear. In the book's preface, dated November 10, 1891, his twenty-ninth birthday, he wrote:

> A word must be said with regard to those portions of this book which are concerned with Simms's environment rather than with the romancer himself. It may seem at first sight that I have too frequently dropped the role of the biographer in order to assume that of the historian. . . . But I have an excuse for my offense—if offense it be—in the fact that Simms was a typical Southerner, and that it would have been impossible to convey a full idea of his character without constant reference to the history of the Southern people during the first seven decades of the century. . . . It is not for me to say how far I have succeeded in throwing light upon the subject, or in treating it with fairness; but I may say that the extended account I have given of Simms's political career was introduced with no desire to rake up dead issues or to say unpleasant things. I saw no way by which a conscientious biographer of Simms could avoid the mire of ante-bellum politics, so I waded in with very little hope that I should get through undraggled.

Trent's argument was simple, direct, and explosive. The environment of the Old South, he began, was shaped by slavery and feudalism. This environment included "not only Charleston and Carolina, but the whole South, for all Southern men were subjected to very much the same influences." All southerners "down to 1861 were living a primitive life" derived from "feudal notions" transplanted to the New World and made more "vigorous . . . from the moment that the first slave-ship made its appearance." As a result, slavery "helped feudalism and feudalism helped slavery, and the Southern people were largely the outcome of the interaction of these two formative principles." Life in the Old South, "though simple and picturesque, was nevertheless calculated to repress many of the best faculties and powers of our nature. It was a life affording few opportunities to talents that did not lie in certain beaten grooves. It was a life . . . that choked all thought and investigation that did not tend to conserve existing institutions and opinions, a life that rendered originality scarcely possible."[25]

Simms had no particular hereditary stake in the social order of the Old South, Trent wrote, but he sought, always unsuccessfully, ad-

25. Trent, *William Gilmore Simms* (2nd ed.), vi–vii, 21, 31, 37.

mission to it and recognition by it. It shaped him in spite of himself. Therein lay the central theme of Simms's life; therein, too, lay the central defect of virtually all of his writing: trying too hard to please a close-minded elite who "looked upon literature as the choice recreation of gentlemen." The life of Simms, then, took the form of a heroic struggle by one man against the heaviest of environmental odds, a struggle Simms was doomed to lose, albeit nobly, partly because he constantly longed to be a part of that environment but mostly because that environment stifled creativity and imagination and made even its most promising talents, in the end, second-raters. Thus Trent could accept without hesitation Simms's self-composed epitaph as the summary of a tragic life: "Here lies one who, after a reasonably long life, distinguished chiefly by unceasing labor, has left all his better works undone." Thus, too, Trent could accept with only slight and more charitable qualification Hayne's private and candid critical estimation of Simms, which, without Mrs. Hayne's permission, he reproduced in full.[26]

Trent's *Simms* was in fact a poignant, intensely human story, with a contemporary application that was all too clear. The author's unabashed affection for the New South permeated his book. "While chivalry was a good thing," he wrote, "modern civilization is a much higher thing." The study of southern history, he opined, reveals that "slavery was a much greater evil to the master than to the slave," for it made him "resist the course of development his country was taking [and become] day by day more conservative, more inert, more proud." These "evil effects, mental and moral, of overlordship—arrogance, contempt for inferiors, inertia of mind and body— [were common to] all the Southern people, and . . . they were just what might have been expected from a man living in [this] environment." These, "in the main, were the men whom Simms was destined to live with. . . . However clearly he might see their faults and failings, he could not escape from the fascination which their easy, pleasant life exerted."[27]

The Civil War, a necessary phase in the country's development, had removed this obstacle "that blocked the path which a great nation had to take. . . . No people," Trent wrote, "however brave and true, can wage an eventually successful war with advancing civiliza-

26. *Ibid.*, 20, 25, 326, 328, 332.
27. *Ibid.*, 36, 37, 39, 41, 42, 43.

tion." The victorious North was "the instrument by which the whole country, North and South, was finally saved for what we all believe will be a glorious future." Thus, "out of the ashes of the old South, a new and better South has arisen. A disintegrated and primitive people have become united among themselves and with their former foes, and are moving forward upon the path of progress." Simms's tragedy was that he did not live to be "cheered," as Trent was confident he would have been, "by the vision of the new order that was to be. . . . The energy and faith he had always shown were to become virtues of that new South which he was not permitted to see and rejoice over."[28]

That Simms would have been a hearty supporter of this new South—and, by implication, that his talents would have flourished—was of little doubt to Trent but of great doubt to unreconstructed reviewers who eviscerated his work in the southern press. Indeed, Trent's view of the Old South, more than his view of Simms and his writing, became the critics' focal point. First into the field was the Charleston *News and Courier*, that longtime defender of the Confederate heritage, which devoted two columns to a review whose headline divulged its content: "A Literary Caricature, Written Without Knowledge of the Subject—'A Very Small Coroner Sitting on a Very Large Body.'" From New Orleans the aged William Porcher Miles, a South Carolina fire-eating congressman in the 1850s and a friend of Simms, bestirred himself to condemn, in a public letter, Trent's "daring and outrageous misrepresentations." A Baltimore literary journal called the book an "abominable libel [and] an insult hard to be endured." A professor at the University of Virginia, Trent's alma mater, declared, "Indeed, no Southern man can read this book without feeling his blood boil within him at the injustice of the author, at the aspersions cast upon his people and their motives."[29]

Other responses were even less pleasing because they were more personal. On the streets of Trent's native Richmond, passersby refused even to speak to the biographer's mother. A prominent Charles-

28.   *Ibid.*, 274, 285–86, 287–88, 289, 290, 314.
29.   Charleston *News and Courier*, March 31, 1892; William Porcher Miles, "Letter to Mr. Simms' Daughter," *News and Courier*, May 30, 1892; Baltimore journal quoted in *News and Courier*, undated clipping in the possession of James Player, Florence, S.C.; Walker, "W. P. Trent," 151.

tonian was snubbed in his native city "for sending his son to Sewanee, since Trent, who had written such an offensive book, was on the faculty there." A *News and Courier* correspondent urged in 1892 that the Episcopal Diocese of South Carolina "make the retirement of Trent" from his teaching position at the church-supported institution "a condition of further contributions."[30]

Less vocal but no less disturbed was Augusta Simms Roach. As she perused the volume her disappointment mounted to anger. Taking pencil in hand, she began to jot her reactions in the book's margins. Simple check marks confirmed Trent's accuracy. Angry phrases revealed his errors of fact or judgment. Of these there were, Augusta believed, many. "Such society had no charms for him," she wrote in response to Trent's suggestion that Simms longed to be admitted to the inner circle of Charleston's elite. "No slavery there," she remarked when Trent acknowledged the early difficulties of the Boston literary community. Sarcastically reacting to Trent's opinion that Simms failed to remember that "a good artist is not called upon to exercise his powers upon subjects not proper to his art," Augusta wrote, "Good advice for Mr. Trent." There can be little doubt that by the time she had finished reading the book her despair was overwhelming.[31]

That feeling must have been made the more acute by the praise lavished on the book by reviewers outside the South. Evaluating the volume for readers of the *Atlantic Monthly*, Theodore Roosevelt declared that Trent "has added a noteworthy clearsightedness and impartiality of judgment which give his criticisms of men and events a permanent value." Brander Matthews praised the book in *Cosmopolitan*, Warner in *Harper's*. In some circles, at least, Trent was very much on the mark.[32]

Although the aftermath of *Simms* brought Trent some great difficulties, then, it also produced opportunities. His national reputation

30. Walker, "W P. Trent," 151; *News and Courier*, undated clipping, in the possession of James Player.
31. Augusta Simms Roach's personal copy of *Simms* (in the possession of James Player), 43, 56, 89.
32. Theodore Roosevelt, "Recent Biography," *Atlantic Monthly* LIX (June, 1892), 838; Walker, "W. P. Trent," 137–38; Brander Matthews, "Two Studies of the South," *Cosmopolitan*, XIV (1892), 322–23; Charles Dudley Warner, "Editor's Study," *Harper's Magazine*, LXXXV (1892), 153–54.

brought an inquiry from Woodrow Wilson about Trent's interest in a teaching position at Bryn Mawr. William A. Dunning, professor of political science at Columbia University, offered Trent a post at Barnard College, with the condition that he complete his doctoral work under Dunning's supervision. The invitation from Dunning carried with it the advice that "I should like to see you specializing in history and political science rather than running off after strange gods in the literary line." Doubtless attractive, both offers were nevertheless declined. For the moment, at least, Trent would remain at Sewanee and weather the storm.[33]

Trent's *Simms* and the reaction to it were part of a process of generational succession that would become much clearer with the passing of time. During the 1890s the remainder of the generation that had led the South during the war found itself challenged—in politics, in occupations, in the economy, in intellectual activity, in virtually every sphere of life—by a rising generation to whom the lost cause was distant, dim, and increasingly irrelevant. The elders reacted in ways that may at a distance seem irrational. But all that they held sacred was under attack, and they were determined to fight back. They would defend themselves, and they would, before departing the scene, attempt to erect a framework of law and custom which, if it endured, would perpetuate those bygone beliefs and values that had seemingly been lost at Appomattox. During the 1890s, that response took many forms and succeeded only in those areas, mostly racial, where the young and the old perceived a common self-interest.

For a young liberal caught in the cross fire, frustration could only mount. Although Sewanee's trustees resisted the considerable pressures brought to bear upon them to dismiss Trent, the young scholar grew more and more uncomfortable there. Privately he unburdened himself. "I have done the best I could," he wrote, "[and have] been baited . . . without the privilege a bear always has of giving a good hearty roar and occasionally mangling a hound." Continuing, he admitted "the many limitations of my book, but I do feel sure that I studied my subject diligently and that nothing was further

33. Walker, "W. P. Trent," 124.

from my thoughts than to take occasion to sneer. . . . And if I occasionally appear to rely too much on my small satirical and humorous powers, it must be remembered that Simms's biography might have been made deadly dull and that it is a man's duty to his readers not to be dull."[34]

As time passed, Trent refused to recant; he did, however, in a footnote in the second edition of *Simms*, apologize to Mrs. Hayne for failing to seek her permission to quote from her husband's letters. Speaking before the Vanderbilt Southern History Society in 1895, Trent noted that "if I do not know [Simms] as his descendants fancy him to have been, I have at any rate done my best to compass and fathom him. . . . I have not stultified myself, nor do I wish you to stultify yourselves." A year later he wrote that "much of the work that I have been called upon to do . . . has been done with the full consciousness that unless I reached certain conclusions it would be unacceptable to a majority of the people with whom my lot is cast."[35]

Nor could appointment as dean at Sewanee reduce either the enduring hostility toward him or his sensitivity to it. By 1898, Trent had concluded, "The South will only be regenerated by *time*. . . . I see clearly after 10 years that the Southern people will not be set right for more than one generation." At Sewanee, he said, "a considerable portion of the people around me consider me a traitor & don't like me & . . . I am continually made the object of prayers & other pietistic propaganda for my spiritual regeneration. I'm tired of it." When an invitation to join the English Department at Columbia University came in 1900, Trent promptly accepted.[36]

The passage of time outside the South, however, gave Trent's story a final, ironic twist. The longer he was in New York, the more ardently southern he became. To Professor Yates Snowden at the University of South Carolina, Trent confided in 1913, "I've abandoned a good many of the youthful notions I imbibed 20 years ago. . . . I am inclined to think I'm a better Southerner and Virginian than I ever

34. Trent to Brander Matthews, October 25, 1892, quoted in Walker, "W. P. Trent," 138–39, 151–52.
35. W. P. Trent, *The Study of Southern History* (Nashville, 1895), 20; W. P. Trent, *Southern Statesmen of the Old Regime* (New York, 1897), 260.
36. Trent to Adams, January 8, 1898, in Adams Papers.

was." Two years later, he wrote even more strongly to Snowden, "South Carolina makes me think of you and I wish I could have a good talk with you about books and the long ago. I'd apologize for all my shortcomings in 'Simms' and elsewhere." In 1924, again reflecting on *Simms* after a quarter century in New York and at the age of sixty-two, Trent wrote apologetically, "In the thirty-two years that have elapsed, I have learned, I hope, a great deal, and I am quite sure that I could make my points just as well as I did in 1892, without hurting the sensibilities of as many people as I did then. But, Lord bless me," he added, revealing a truth usually discovered only in time, "I was not quite thirty when the life of Simms was published, and you know that a young man, even though he may become something of a sage later, is always a bit of a fool." In 1935, an invalid, Trent finally closed the *Simms* case in a letter to the vice-chancellor at Sewanee who had supported him so stoutly. "At Sewanee," he recalled, "we had our little excitements, to which I am afraid I occasionally contributed more than my share. Looking back at it all . . . I can see that you gentlemen put up with a great deal from a fresh young man, for which he now desires to beg your pardon."[37]

At Trent's death in 1939, his *Simms* was still—and is today—the only full-scale biography of South Carolina's greatest writer. For this reason, despite numerous attempts to correct or revise one portion or another of Trent's analysis, his book remains, except among a small and exclusive circle of Simms specialists, the standard work on the subject. That this should be so is surprising in light of the almost constant drumbeat of criticism the book has received, at least in the South, since 1892. It is the more surprising given the growing interest in Simms. Since Trent's death, Simms scholarship has increased, spurred by the publication in the 1950s of five brilliantly edited volumes of his correspondence, itself a kind of raw biography, and the reissuance in the 1960s of many of his works, tediously thorough and prohibitively expensive, themselves an indication, however awk-

37.   Trent to Yates Snowden, May 6, 1913, March 23, 1915, both in Yates Snowden Collection, South Caroliniana Library; Trent to James Henry Rice, June 13, 1924, in James Henry Rice Papers, Perkins Library, Duke University; Trent to Thomas Frank Gailor, July 1, 1935, quoted in Walker, "W. P. Trent," 157.

ward, that Simms deserves serious examination. But the unpleasant fact remains that for almost one hundred years, Trent has had no measurable competition where it matters, in a full-scale biography published by a major press for a national audience.[38]

That, perhaps, is the ultimate consequence of the 1892 controversy. After Augusta's death in 1897, her stepbrother took her considerable collection of Simms material to his home in Barnwell, South Carolina. Perhaps hoping that their publication might balance Trent, he carried the papers to the New York office of G. P. Putnam, one of Simms's publishers. Putnam showed no interest but failed to return the material. Later another stepbrother, Charles Carroll Simms, went to recover the Simms papers, discovered them in an old trunk in a corner of Putnam's basement, and brought them back to Barnwell. He subsequently moved to Washington, D.C., where he died in 1930, and where the papers remained.[39]

Ten years later, in 1940, Furman University in Greenville, South Carolina, invited Simms's granddaughter, Mary C. Simms Oliphant, a Greenville resident, to prepare a new biography. It may have been only coincidental that the invitation came not long after Trent's death. From earliest childhood in the 1890s, she had borne an intense interest in her grandfather's life and work, an interest whetted by her own low opinion, as time went by, of Trent's book. "Mr. Trent set out to prove a thesis, not to write a biography," she wrote in 1942. "His own heredity and environment, the twisted age in which he developed, his immaturity at the time of the work, the hurried manner of his research . . . all were contributing factors." Then she added candidly, "Also, I have always felt that the Simms family were somewhat to blame. We all talk too much. We are great complainers. We are fiery and violent. Simms himself was fiery and violent—and he was a

38.   James B. Meriwether, "The Proposed Edition of William Gilmore Simms," *Mississippi Quarterly* XVI (1962), 100–12. Sixteen volumes were planned for the Centennial Edition. See John Caldwell Guilds, "General Preface to the Centennial Edition," *Voltmeier*, Vol. I of *The Writings of William Gilmore Simms* (Columbia, S.C., 1969), vi. As of 1984, Volumes I, III, V, and XVI have been published. Evidence of the proliferation of Simms scholarship may be found in Keen Butterworth and James E. Kibler, Jr. (eds.), *William Gilmore Simms: A Reference Guide* (Boston, 1980).
39.   John R. Welsh, "The Charles Carroll Simms Collection," *South Atlantic Bulletin,* XXXI (November, 1966), 1–3.

complainer too. . . . Mr. Trent talked with the children, heard their
wails, and with the burden of his thesis already heavy in his soul . . .
rushed headlong into print."[40]

Lest history repeat itself, Mary Simms Oliphant, representing the
family, would see to it that future treatments of Simms would be more
thorough and presumably less biased. To achieve the first objective,
she decided to postpone the writing of a biography herself in order
to collect and publish the magnificent *Letters of William Gilmore
Simms*. To achieve the second objective, the family engaged an "official" biographer. In 1947, after the South Caroliniana Library at the
University of South Carolina agreed to purchase, for $7,500, one col-
lection of Simms letters, the family presented the peripatetic Charles
Carroll Simms Papers to that repository. The family retained, however, control over access to the latter, in anticipation of the authorized
.biography. Access was later granted, in 1966, to the editors of the
standard edition of Simms's works. As of 1985, the "official" biography has yet to appear; the standard edition of Simms's works has suspended publication because of financial exigencies; and the Charles
Carroll Simms Papers remain off limits to researchers.[41]

"If biography is to have a useful function in the historical craft,"
David Herbert Donald remarked, "perhaps it is to steer us away from
cosmic and unanswerable questions toward the intricacies of reality."[42] To such a proposition all of the principal figures in this strange
tale—the Simms family, Cable, Trent, even Charles Dudley Warner—
could have readily subscribed, at least in the abstract. Yet for more
than a century since Simms's death, the cosmic and the unanswerable
have repeatedly gotten in the way of the intricacies and the actuality
of Simms's life. Studies of Simms continue for the most part to analyze
their subject within the framework erected in the troubled atmosphere of the 1890s, when every event seemed cosmic: was Simms socially accepted in Charleston? did the environment of the Old South

40.   Mary C. Simms [Mrs. A. D.] Oliphant, "William Gilmore Simms—Historical Artist," *University South Caroliniana Society: Report of the Secretary and Treasurer for
1942* (Columbia, S.C., 1943), 16; Mary C. Simms Oliphant to Franklin T. Walker, May
12, 1942, quoted in Walker, "W. P. Trent," 145–46.
41.   Welsh, "The Charles Carroll Simms Collection," 1.
42.   David Donald, *Charles Sumner and the Coming of the Civil War* (New York,
1960), x.

retard intellectual progress? to what extent did Charleston and the South influence Simms's literary status? To be sure, these questions were, and remain, important, but their persistence has been due only in part to Trent's perspicacity. That distant world still awaits description and analysis on its own terms. The intellectual life of the Old South has yet to be fully penetrated and discussed for what it was rather than for what it was not. From the roster of subjects treated in the Men of Letters Series, only Simms lacks a recent biography. Views forged in the passions of the 1890s, that crossroads of southern history, have proved surprisingly durable. The Simms family's guarded and deliberate quest for justice continues to direct and to limit the course of Simms scholarship; as an ironic result, Trent's judgments continue to carry weight. And all because Charles Dudley Warner was a man who knew what he wanted—and, with Trent's *Simms*, got it.

"Gotta Mind to Move, A Mind to Settle Down"
Afro-Americans and the Plantation Frontier

Sydney Nathans

Throughout the nineteenth century, the richness of the land of the Mississippi Delta drew people to it, though not all were drawn to it in exactly the same way. Some came in coaches, some came in wagons, some came in chains. The magnet for immigrants, free or forced, was the magnificent Delta soil—dark and deep alluvial topsoil, formed by deposits of river silt over the centuries. Opened to settlers in the 1830s, recognized at once as bottomland rich with promise for cotton crops and rife with danger from recurrent floods, the Delta began in northwest Mississippi just below Memphis and widened to the shape of a magnolia leaf as it stretched south for almost two hundred miles to Vicksburg. Bordered on the west by the Mississippi River and on the east by the state's central hills, the floodplain of swamp and forest at its widest point was eighty-five miles across. For the Afro-American before the Civil War, the Mississippi Delta was yet another extension of bondage. For the southern planter, it was the South's California— the California of slavery. With enough capital to buy the land, with enough labor to work it, the planter on this frontier could strike it rich, or multiply his riches.

All these motives and more impelled a North Carolina planter in 1856 to purchase about two thousand acres of land—only two hundred of which were cleared—in the northern part of the Delta. Paul Cameron was no Thomas Sutpen, scratching his way from obscurity to the portals of the planter gentry in one generation. Heir to a fortune accumulated by two generations on both sides of his family, Paul Cameron in the late 1850s was one of the largest slaveholders and richest men in his home state of North Carolina. In 1860 his holdings amounted to thirty thousand acres of land and almost a thousand slaves. Cameron had decided in the 1840s that his family should acquire a cotton plantation, and in 1844 he bought an established place in Greene County, Alabama. But within a month of the purchase, he was convinced that he had been duped into buying third-rate land.[1] When he decided to try again, Cameron sought land that was unquestionably rich, but still largely in cane and cypress. After searching for almost a decade, he bought two thousand acres and a fresh start in Tunica County, Mississippi. Located forty miles south of Memphis and three miles east of the river, Cameron's plantation was economically part of the frontier of plantation capitalism, the newest territory in the 1850s to be incorporated into the empire of cotton. But Tunica County was also literally, physically, palpably the frontier: the deeply forested and bounteous county from which the bears and panthers and parvenus of Faulkner's fiction were drawn. Paul Cameron would clear the Delta land, and reap its first profits, himself.[2]

Of course, the planter did not exactly clear the land himself. Rather, Cameron sent thirty-five young strong slaves to Mississippi from his Alabama plantation, where for a dozen years they had adjusted to the climate of the Deep South and the cultivation of cotton. They set out to work the two hundred acres already cleared for planting and to help open new parts of the land. An additional lot of slaves from Cameron's home plantation in North Carolina departed for Mississippi late in the autumn of 1860. They had arrived safely, the overseer reported in November of that year. Both the journey and the week had proved uneventful. He was right about the journey, wrong

1.   Charles Richard Sanders, *The Cameron Plantation in Central North Carolina (1776–1973) and Its Founder Richard Bennehan* (Durham, 1974), 5–6; Paul Cameron to Duncan Cameron, January 4, 1845, and James S. Ruffin to Duncan Cameron, January 5, 1845, both in Cameron Family Papers, Southern Historical Collection, University of North Carolina Library, Chapel Hill.

2.   Of the many letters detailing Cameron's long search for a new plantation in the Southwest, see Paul C. Cameron to Duncan Cameron, December 30, 1845, November 6, 1848, January 23, 1851; and for the negotiations that led to the purchase in Tunica County, see James M. Williamson to Paul C. Cameron, September 23, November 10, 24, 1856, and the enclosure, [early November, 1856], "Samuel Tate Proposes to Sell"; Andrew J. Polk to Paul C. Cameron, June 20, 1854, all in Cameron Family Papers. Land values in Tunica County rose from nine dollars per acre in 1850 to thirty-five dollars per acre in 1860. Tunica's land in 1860 was the second most expensive among counties in Mississippi and among the costliest in the South. See Thomas J. Pressly and William H. Scofield (eds.), *Farm Real Estate Values in the United States by Counties, 1850–1959* (Seattle, 1965), 55.

about the week. Days before the slaves arrived, Abraham Lincoln was elected president of the United States.[3]

In the tumultuous years that followed Lincoln's election, Civil War and emancipation changed forever the course of the South and the lives of Afro-Americans who dwelled there. The dimensions and limits of that change in the Delta are suggested by the fate of the black people who lived and worked on Paul Cameron's plantation after 1865. Against great odds, they sought to make the planter's frontier their own. As historians of the frontier and of the South have demonstrated, the obstacles to black attainment were enormous. Few historians today accept uncritically the thesis that the frontier was a great leveler. Even less do they think that the concept of a democratizing frontier ever applied well to the planter's South, or indeed to any region where the plantation took root. The prospect of a revived plantation society confronted all blacks in the Delta by the 1880s as planters and merchants, using debts and lien laws and force, fashioned a structure for renewed landlord rule. Yet decade after decade, notwithstanding immense disparities of wealth and power, blacks by the thousands migrated to the counties of northwest Mississippi. Paul Cameron's plantation correspondence, Tunica County deed and mortgage records, and interviews with descendants of those who labored on the Cameron land illuminate why blacks chose the Delta as a place to move and make a home.[4]

Of the many who struggled to make the planter's world a black frontier, only a handful ultimately succeeded. But for more than a

3. J. R. Webster to Paul C. Cameron, November 24, 1856; the itinerary and expenses for transporting forty-two slaves from North Carolina to Mississippi, November 10, 1860; W. T. Lamb to Paul C. Cameron, November 24, 1860, all in Cameron Family Papers.

4. Avery O. Craven, "The 'Turner Theories' and the South," *Journal of Southern History*, V (1939), 301–304; Todd M. Lieber, "The Significance of the Frontier in the Writing of Antebellum Southern History," *Mississippi Quarterly*, XXII (1969), 336–54; Malcolm J. Rohrbough, *The Trans-Appalachian Frontier: People, Societies, and Institutions, 1775–1850* (New York, 1978), 209, 217, 311–20; John Solomon Otto, "Slaveholding General Farmers in a 'Cotton County,'" *Agricultural History*, LV (1981), 170–71; Harold D. Woodman, "Post–Civil War Southern Agriculture and the Law," *Agricultural History*, LIII (1979), 319–37; Pete Daniel, "The Metamorphosis of Slavery, 1865–1900," *Journal of American History*, LXVI (1979), 88–99; Michael Wayne, *The Reshaping of Plantation Society: The Natchez District, 1860–1880* (Baton Rouge, 1983).

half century after emancipation, on the Cameron plantation and elsewhere in the northern Mississippi Delta, blacks sought to find refuge and resources sufficient to build an independent life. Black struggles during three periods in the history of the Cameron plantation encapsulate the aspirations and suggest the difficulties of those blacks who had a mind to settle down in the Delta. During the first twenty years after emancipation, a standoff prevailed on the plantation frontier. Conquest of the swamp came to a halt, control of labor remained uncertain, and blacks and whites competed for resources in an unsettled world. From the mid-1880s to the outbreak of World War I, the expansion of the plantation resumed and drew thousands of blacks to the Delta. Even as gulfs widened enormously between the races, blacks found ways to make gains. When both the physical and commercial frontiers of Tunica County closed in the aftermath of World War I, blacks confronted and coped with the constricted boundaries of a land where planter rule was again sovereign.

For two decades after emancipation, a standoff reigned in Tunica County and on the Cameron plantation. Unable to command the labor of freedmen as they had the labor of slaves, the planters had to face a dramatic slowdown in their conquest of the Delta's huge cypress forests. Much of the land on the Cameron place and in Tunica County remained in 1883 what it had been in 1863—a swamp.[5] In a world suspended between plantation and frontier, neither blacks nor whites possessed control.

The meaning of that deadlock for planters was personified in the career of Paul Cameron's son-in-law, George Collins, whom Cameron appointed manager of his Mississippi place in 1865. The son-in-law's tenure, which lasted until 1883, proved an abject failure. When cotton prices soared briefly after the war, his crops were short; when harvests were again abundant in the early 1870s, prices fell. By 1871 he wanted nothing more than to flee Mississippi forever. Unable to sell Cameron's land to whites or to relinquish it to blacks, Collins

5. Over three-quarters of Cameron's plantation was officially designated as "wild" by the Tunica tax assessor in 1860. In 1892, more than half of Cameron's land was still listed as "uncleared." See Tunica County Minutes of the Police Court, 1859–1860, pp. 106–107, and the Tunica County Land Roll, 1892, p. 16, both in Tunica County Courthouse, Tunica, Miss.

persisted another eleven years in the Delta, gradually losing his hair, his health, and his self-respect. Demoralized and destitute, Collins surrendered management of the plantation to two local merchants in 1883.[6]

Did the failure of Cameron's estate to thrive mean that on his and similar plantations, the El Dorado of slavery became a frontier for former slaves? If land is the measure, the answer seems to be no. The deed books of Tunica County reveal that blacks never acquired an inch of Paul Cameron's land, or the land of other large planters in this Delta county. Yet as Emilio Willems reminds us in his essay "Social Change on the Latin American Frontier," an "unsuccessful frontier" for the planter often became a haven for the "little man," who used the plantation's failure to better his own chances of survival. On the Cameron place after 1865, as in parts of Latin America, black workers found methods other than the acquisition of land to make the planter's resources their own. In part, blacks advanced themselves through keen survival skills. Although black workers were in poor condition, George Collins reported in 1877, "they become sharper every year." More exasperating to Collins were those blacks who accumulated mules and tools from their labor on his plantation, and then bargained for better contracts elsewhere. "Most of them I have built up but others offer them inducements and now and then one of them leaves." Black resourcefulness and black departures, Collins understood, had the same underlying aspiration. His workers sought to become "independent of me and each other."[7]

The "sharpness" of black workers grew quickly on the Cameron plantation, and eventually compelled the planter radically to alter his

6.   Paul C. Cameron "To all whom it May Concern," December 20, 1865; George P. Collins to Paul Cameron, January 19, 1871; Paul C. Cameron to [Mildred C. Cameron], November 11, 1873; Paul C. Cameron to Archibald Wright, November 17, 1873; George P. Collins to Paul Cameron, February 14, 1874, February 27, 1879; agreement between George P. Collins [for Paul Cameron] and R. W. Young, January 26, 1883, all in Cameron Family Papers; George P. Collins to Anne Cameron Collins, December 20, 1880, Paul C. Cameron to Anne Collins, January 22, 1883, both in Anne Cameron Collins Papers, Southern Historical Collection.
7.   Tunica County Deed Records, Vol. B-2, pp. 96–100, Vol. N-2, pp. 439–44; Emilio Willems, "Social Change on the Latin American Frontier," in David Harry Miller and Jerome O. Steffen (eds.), *The Frontier: Comparative Studies* (Norman, 1977), 260; George P. Collins to [Paul C. Cameron], March 6, 1877, in Cameron Family Papers.

goals. At the end of 1866, his cotton crop in the field and his work force short, Collins sent to North Carolina for additional laborers. Their arrival in late December helped him save the crop that winter. At settlement time in 1866 and at contract times in succeeding years, however, Collins found his hands tenacious in demanding an explanation of their accounts and excruciatingly slow in negotiating terms for the new year. By his own account, Collins became hesitant even to raise his voice to his workers, lest they pull up and leave. Because the blacks became sharper at negotiating contracts and settlements, and were willing to migrate short distances or the length of the South for better work, Collins found it impossible to control them.[8] A neighboring planter, Archibald Wright of Memphis, felt similarly trapped between unpredictable harvests and an uncertain work force. By 1873, both Wright and Collins were ready for a radical step. If they could find the "right kind" of black workers—those with their own mules and tools—they would rent them their cultivated lands. Both men stood ready to surrender the management and risks of their Delta plantations to black renters.[9]

Tunica county blacks who possessed mules and tools were quite interested in renting the planter's land—but on terms of their own. Most blacks of "the kind I want," Collins reported, were unwilling to rent the "improved" portion of the plantation, which produced the best cotton crop but also the greatest exposure to risks of fluctuating prices and harvests. Blacks sought instead the land not yet in cultivation. "I've fallen in" with some workers anxious to "get back there among the wolves & other wild things," Collins wrote in 1876. Some

8. Paul C. Cameron to George Mordecai, July 24, 1866, in George Mordecai Papers, Southern Historical Collection; Cameron to Collins, October 4, 1866, in Cameron Family Papers; Collins to Anne Collins, December 29, 1866, February 9, 1867, both in Collins Papers. In a provocative essay, David Herbert Donald suggests that George Collins' flaws—failure to discipline himself, inability to command others—afflicted an entire generation of young southerners after 1865 ("A Generation of Defeat," in Walter J. Fraser, Jr., and Winfred B. Moore, Jr. [eds.], *From the Old South to the New: Essays on the Transitional South* [Westport, Conn., 1981], 3–20).

9. Duncan Cameron to Paul C. Cameron, January 23, 1871; Archibald Wright to Cameron, July 13, 1873; George P. Collins to Cameron, December 6, 1873; on the willingness of Wright and Collins to sell their lands to black buyers, see Wright to Cameron, March 14, 1872, and Collins to Cameron, November 19, 1872, all in Cameron Family Papers.

were ready to rent the forested portion of Cameron's land; others looked to the "deadened" parts, where trees had been killed by girdling and the underbrush burned off. For black renters, this land offered important advantages. The rent was low, the distance from the planter was great, and the supervision was light. Another advantage was equally important. The "deadened" area that blacks preferred allowed them to exploit the special richness of burned-over land on the edge of the forest, where what ecologists call the edge effect operated. Deer came to graze at the edge of the forest and the new grasslands created by burning. Bear, as well as wolves, flocked to the area and made it rich for hunting game. On the land itself, ash from burned trees served as a natural fertilizer for the soil. With ease, black renters on the edge of the wild land and deadenings could reap a double harvest—that of the forest and that of the land. For a black with resources, interested in making money but also eager to be self-sufficient, the unimproved land provided an ideal place to practice the mixed economy of the yeoman farmer.[10]

The eagerness of black renters to "get back there among the wolves" helped catalyze a further shift in the landowner's strategy for making the plantation pay. Planters turned to new land as the way to increase the size of their crop and their incomes. Owners encouraged blacks to work unimproved land and let them have it for low rents, on the condition that they also help to clear the land for cultivation. Higher taxes on all his land provided a further spur for the planter to get unimproved land into production. Short-run gains would come to blacks; long-range profits would go to planters. The shift in strategy on the Cameron place widened the ways in which the plantation became a patchwork of options for black workers. Blacks with a mule team and tools rented, became the planter's temporary pioneers, and reaped the fruits of the forest and new clearings. Those without equipment worked for wages or a share of the crop, getting provisions, mules, and tools from the planter. Independent in different

10.   George P. Collins to Paul C. Cameron, February 7, 1876, in Cameron Family Papers. For an excellent discussion of the edge effect, see William Cronon, *Changes in the Land: Indians, Colonists, and the Ecology of New England* (New York, 1983), 50–52. The use of forest land by nineteenth-century white yeomen is analyzed in Steven Hahn, *The Roots of Southern Populism: Yeoman Farmers and the Transformation of the Georgia Upcountry, 1850–1890* (New York, 1983), 58–62, 248.

ways, they all obliged the planter to supply them with valuable re-sources and to "build them up."[11]

Collins wrote periodically about the fate of those who left the Cameron plantation to better their lot. From his perspective, most came to naught. But the case of one black who departed in the 1870s suggests the drive and potential of those able to use the plantation as a springboard for advancement. Robert Flagg had come out from North Carolina around 1870 and had impressed George Collins as an ideal worker. Collins was jolted, then, to discover in May of 1876 that "under a quiet demeanor [Flagg] stirs up others to mischief." Flagg had become involved in politics and planned to teach school on the plantation. Flagg's "great political aspirations," Collins concluded at once, "of course will unfit him for an agricultural laborer." Collins rid himself of Flagg as soon as the harvest was in.[12]

Expelled from the Cameron place, Robert Flagg moved to the land owned by his father-in-law, and demonstrated during the next half-century what an ambitious black man in the Delta could build from a fragment of the plantation system. During many of those years, Flagg taught in one-room country schools, where his strictness as a disciplinarian left indelible memories with his students. For the slightest slip—forgetting a lesson, failing a spelling test—he stung the legs of the girls with a switch or "knocked the socks off" the boys with a razor strop. Like most rural black teachers in Mississippi, Flagg taught only a few months of the year. He also worked in town for the owner of a Tunica cottonseed-oil press and learned from the owner how to keep books. Flagg ultimately inherited his father-in-law's land, added land of his own, and by the early twentieth century, had diversified his holdings. He owned a farm worked by several tenants, a large battery-powered generator to operate the

11. Archibald Wright to Paul C. Cameron, August 2, 1873, June 8, 1874, George P. Collins to Cameron, January 28, 1876, all in Cameron Family Papers; George P. Collins to Anne Collins, February 15, 1876, March 6, 1878, both in Collins Papers. For the diversity of Collins' arrangements with his plantation tenants and renters, see Tunica County Deed Records, Vol. J, pp. 589–613. For variation in tenant ownership of mules and equipment, see the Tunica County Personal Property Assessment Book, 1882, in the State Auditor's Files, Record Group 29, Box 564, Mississippi Department of Archives and History, Jackson.
12. George P. Collins to Anne Collins, February 13, 1874, February 15, 27, 1876, all in Collins Papers.

incubator for his chickens and provide electricity for the farm, a gristmill to grind corn, and cows to supply milk for his family and neighbors. Flagg also built a grocery store in the town of Tunica and a dance hall on its outskirts. Musicians from Memphis came down by train on a Saturday afternoon, got off at the Tunica depot, struck up the band, and marched the mile to Flagg's dance hall to promote the festivities of the evening. To keep abreast of his tenants, his crops, his store, and his dance hall receipts, Flagg kept elaborate ledgers. To Flagg's granddaughter, the long books were an emblem of the man. A "self-made educated man," a "fidgety businessman," Flagg always told his children and grandchildren, " 'If the house ever catches fire, first save yourselves, then save those records!' He was a *record* man." [13]

Blacks with similar ambitions joined Robert Flagg in his move to the plantation frontier after 1865, and others also bought little "forties" or "sixties" or eighty-acre tracts in the wild lands to start a farm of their own. But most blacks who came to Tunica remained landless, and in the 1870s they all discovered a narrowing of options. Blacks and whites alike suffered immensely from the panic of 1873, which brought a drastic fall in cotton prices and led to a halving of black incomes by 1878. By 1880, Collins found himself besieged by a surplus of laborers desperate for work and willing to serve on any terms he named. Even in desperation, however, blacks had not lost their resourcefulness. Rather than submit, many blacks left. By the end of 1882, Collins was back where he started on the plantation frontier in 1865: again, his crops were in the field; again, he was short of hands. Collins gave up and left Mississippi in 1883. [14]

The departures of George Collins and Robert Flagg from the Cameron place symbolized the standoff that characterized the plantation

13. Interview with Jesse Parker, April 27, 1981, in Tunica, Miss.; interview with James Flagg, May 1, 1981, in Lepanto, Ark.; interview with Bessie Rainey Gay, November 7, 1981, in Greenwood, Miss. Robert Flagg assumed the debt on his father-in-law's land. See Will of Robin Hall, Tunica County Wills and Letters Testamentary, Vol. 2, pp. 237–40. In 1920, Robert Flagg valued his estate at $25,000. See Will of Robert Flagg, Tunica County Will Record Books, Vol. 4, pp. 167–70. Flagg won widespread admiration as an educator in the county. See the obituary notice, Tunica *Times-Democrat*, January 10, 1929. Interview with Martin Bond, May 15, 1981, in Tunica, Miss. Bessie Rainey Gay vividly recalled the long ledgers that her grandfather instructed her to protect.
14. Blacks who worked on the Cameron-Collins plantation and who subsequently

frontier for two decades after emancipation. In the mid-1880s on the Cameron land and throughout the Delta, there was clear evidence of a renewed effort to complete the transformation of the physical frontier into commercial plantations. Black workers hammered down the first spikes for the railroad line that reached the Cameron plantation in 1883, and within months the first locomotive lumbered down from Memphis. The completion of the railroad prompted a Memphis mercantile firm to open a store in a black village four miles from the Cameron place, where they expected "to do a large business." Blacks on the Cameron place, as throughout the Delta, girdled and burned mile after mile of cypress forests and canebrakes, opening hundreds of fresh acres to cotton. They enclosed the newly opened farmland, first with wormwood fences and later with barbed wire. Fundamental to the conquest of the swamp was the building of a massive new levee system. Started in 1882 and completed in 1886, the levee drastically diminished the flooding which had recurrently wreaked havoc on the Delta's crops. With a railroad for easy transport, with a new levee to protect harvests and humans from the caprice of the river, the expanding Delta plantations hardly needed railroad agents or planters' promoters to entice recruits. Black workers themselves spread the word of crops "high as a man on horseback" and of plants so thick with cotton that a first-rate picker could bag five hundred pounds a day.[15]

One of those who got the word, and came to Tunica, was Mack Parker. "That old Mack Parker was the *devil!*" recalled his grandson. In moving to Tunica County, Mack Parker sought, as he had since slavery days, to keep the fruit of his own labor. Many times Mack Parker had recounted to his grandson Jesse the story of how, as a slave on an east Texas river plantation, he had struck a bargain with

---

purchased land in Tunica County included Augustus (Gus) Brown, Duncan Sears, and Adam Trice. See Tunica County Deed Records, Vol. N, pp. 304–305; Will of Duncan Sears, Tunica County Wills and Letters Testamentary, Vol. 2, pp. 496–97; Tunica County Deed Records, Vol. N, p. 333. Nell Irvin Painter, *Exodusters: Black Migration to Kansas After Reconstruction* (New York, 1976), 58; George P. Collins to Anne Collins, November 16, 1880, November 3, 1882, Anna Alexander Cameron to Anne Collins, April 19, 1883, all in Collins Papers.

15. R. W. Young to Paul C. Cameron, October 27, 1883, Duncan Cameron to Paul C. Cameron, November 17, 1883, both in Cameron Family Papers; Vernon Lane Wharton, *The Negro in Mississippi, 1865–1890* (Chapel Hill, 1947), 110–11; interview with Mirrie Hargrow, April 17, 1981, Robinsonville, Miss.

his owner. He could gather and chop wood on his day off and sell the wood to passing steamboats. But when the owner rode by and saw how much Mack Parker had cut and sold, he told his slave, "I can't let you have that—that's too much," and reduced the share to a third of what he sold. Mack Parker burned with resentment, but could do nothing. When the Civil War ended, Parker's owner gathered his slaves, told them they were free, and offered them wages to stay and work for him. Parker said nothing and then asked: "Is I really free?" Told yes, he exploded. "I'll be goddamned if I'll work for *you*." He moved elsewhere in Texas, then to Louisiana, and finally to the Mississippi Delta. Wherever his grandfather went, Jesse Parker recalled, he remained an angry man—"crazy, stubborn, just nuts, like a wild boar in the woods that gets so mad it runs up against a tree, grunt, grunt. He just bristle up all the time. Fight you, white or black. When Mack Parker got to be free, he shown the world!"[16]

Mack Parker was among the thousands of black immigrants who came to the Mississippi Delta in the years from 1880 to 1914. Like hundreds of thousands leaving Europe for the New World, like thousands leaving the East Coast for the Great Plains, Mack Parker moved "for betterment." The Delta was booming when Mack Parker came, not as a democratic frontier eager for settlers, but as a plantation country hungry for labor. Reclamation of the Delta from the swamp ultimately sealed its destiny as the domain of a planter oligarchy. Yet although their chances were drastically different, the planter and the black worker both saw an opportunity to make money during the years of expansion.[17]

On the Cameron plantation after 1882, black workers no longer had to labor for a former slaveowner. After George Collins' departure, a series of merchant-managers oversaw Cameron's Mississippi land. Young storekeepers, they lured tenants with "improvements" in houses and kept them with advances and extensions of credit for supplies. Tenants like Mack Parker knew full well that storekeepers made up in high prices what they conceded in self-supervision and

16. Interview with Jesse Parker, April 27, 1981.
17. *Negro Population, 1790–1915*, 130; W. E. B. Du Bois, "The Negro Farmer," in U.S. Bureau of the Census, *Negroes in the United States*, Bulletin No. 8 (1904), 98; R. H. Leavell, "Negro Migration from Mississippi," in U.S. Department of Labor, *Negro Migration in 1916–17* (1919), 16.

generous advances. The worst of them blatantly sought to substitute the "pencil" for the lash as a means of control and compulsion. They used debts and debtor laws to keep blacks bound to them.[18] Nonetheless the recurrent overextension and failure of storekeeper-managers on and around the Cameron place suggest that competition for labor led some whites to offer temporary economic advantages to their hands. They hoped to recover their money if renters produced good crops and if the market fetched decent prices.[19]

Like Robert Flagg, Mack Parker ultimately got land of his own, but not without a struggle that was symptomatic of the perils of the commercial frontier. Kept illiterate as a slave, Parker saw to it that his son went to school and later sent him to a nearby black college for two years. The drive of Mack Parker and the education of his son, Will, led to a confrontation with their plantation agent late in the century. Details of the episode have faded from the account passed down to Mack Parker's grandson. But the central issue remains clear enough—the manager sought to cheat Mack Parker, as had his slave-owner decades before. Parker sent for Will and, with characteristic belligerence, demanded that his son look at the books: "*That's* what I sent you to school for." Whether Will Parker saved that particular day is unclear, but he learned an enduring lesson. Always read before

18. Moore and Young to Paul C. Cameron, October 27, 1883; Duncan Cameron to Paul C. Cameron, November 22, 1883; Freeman & Bowdre to Duncan Cameron, August 13, 1886, all in Cameron Family Papers; interview with Jesse Parker, November 2, 1981. The power of the "pencil" to devour the black tenant's profit was well understood by blacks in the Delta, and was the subject of a Tunica County black folktale recorded in "dialect" in 1938 and entitled "De Wite man bown ter cut yer down." A white and black came upon two boxes at a crossroads. The black, "he spied it first," and "he run erhead and grab de *bigger* box an he speck he hab sumpin. Well, he opin hit and he fine picks en shubbles en hoes and de res ob hit, and den he turn erowun to see wot de Wite man got. Well de Wite man he got de little box and when he open hit dar war pens an pencils an paper an er big count book wat he keeps wat de niggars owes em in. And dats de way hits been eber since. De Niggar just caint outfigger de Wite man for he sure ter cut yer down." Story told by Mose Hamilton to H. C. Tinney, transcript in "Folklore and Customs," Materials for History of Tunica County, Works Progress Administration, Record Group 60, Box 119, Mississippi Department of Archives and History.
19. Archibald Wright to Paul C. Cameron, December 28, 1881, H. C. Warriner to Cameron, January 7, 1887, both in Cameron Family Papers; Du Bois, "The Negro Farmer," 80–81.

you sign anything, and keep count. Stubborn and vigilant, Mack Parker was able to reap the fruit of his labor on the Cameron plantation. Benefiting from the rise in cotton prices and farm incomes that began around 1899, he soon bought his own small farm.[20] His descendants held the land for eight decades of the twentieth century.

Most blacks, however, did not purchase land in Tunica County or elsewhere in the Delta. Although the number of black landowners increased each decade from 1880 through 1910, the number of black tenants increased far more, reaching 92 percent in 1910. Rising prices of land meant increasingly that land once passed over as marginal was eyed for cultivation and priced out of the reach of aspiring blacks.[21]

The landless black majority found other ways to make gains as plantations expanded rapidly in Tunica County and the Delta. From landlords who competed for their labor, black workers increasingly sought and won the chance to rent land rather than sharecrop it. The number of blacks renting twenty to thirty acres in the Delta grew to almost half the black work force by 1910. Blacks who rented the planter's land, unlike sharecroppers, took the risk that they would lose everything if the harvest was poor. But they also stood to gain if the crop grew and sold well. Renters had more acres to work, raised more provisions for themselves, and had a higher income and profit from the crop than did sharecroppers. Renters also had more success in resisting planter efforts to supervise their labor.[22]

There was a final way in which landless blacks of the Delta improved their lot. When the price of cotton finally began to rise in the late 1890s, so did black purchases of consumer goods. Much to the irritation of some planters, agents of midwestern mail-order houses crisscrossed Delta plantations, showing their catalogs and selling

20.   Interview with Jesse Parker, April 27, 1981; Robert L. Brandfon, *Cotton Kingdom in the New South: A History of the Yazoo Mississippi Delta from Reconstruction to the Twentieth Century* (Cambridge, Mass., 1967), 112–13.

21.   Only in 1900 did the census begin to identify farms by race in its report on agriculture. In 1900, there were 75 white landowners in Tunica County and 214 black landowners; in 1910, there were 76 white landowners and 246 black landowners (all figures include "Part owners"). *Twelfth Census, 1900: Agriculture*, 96–97; *Thirteenth Census, 1910: Agriculture*, 879.

22.   *Eleventh Census, 1890: Agriculture*, 159; *Negro Population, 1790–1915*, 733; E. A. Boeger and E. A. Goldenweiser, "Study of the Tenant Systems of Farming in the Yazoo-Mississippi Delta," U.S. Department of Agriculture, *Bulletin No. 337* (1916), 7–15.

their wares cash on delivery. Southern blacks sometimes bought from outsiders, and so circumvented the high prices and hungry "pencils" of the plantation commissary and local country store. Sometimes they bought from each other, and thus used their incomes to create a group economy that offered a few blacks the chance to make a living outside of the farm. For Delta and Black Belt plantation workers, as for industrial workers in the urban North, acquisition of personal property became an alternative to blocked social ascent.[23]

None of this, however, altered the fundamental reality of life in the Delta. In the river counties of northern Mississippi, where blacks outnumbered whites eight to one, a vast gulf separated black workers from white planters. That gulf grew in the boom-time years from 1900 through 1920. One reason for the widening disparity was simple—the consolidation of plantations among whites themselves. Planter families and large corporations bought up the best lands of the Delta, including the lands the Cameron family sold after Paul Cameron's death in 1891. The first purchaser of the Cameron plantation was a large Memphis mercantile and landholding company; the second owner was a European syndicate; the last buyer was a wealthy local white family which by 1921 owned thousands of acres in Tunica County. The growth and incorporation of plantations in Tunica meant that county land values soared, from $13 an acre in 1880 to $24 an acre in 1900 to $158 an acre in 1920. During the period of commercial expansion, Tunica and other Delta counties fulfilled the classic plantation pattern—fortunes for a few, remnants for the many.[24]

Yet there is no gainsaying the reality that for a brief time the intense demand for plantation labor allowed a minority of Delta blacks as well as a handful of whites to make gains. By 1900, black landowners in Tunica County outnumbered white landowners by almost three to one, and that margin of difference widened during the next decade. Unquestionably black-owned lands were the most marginal—"the backbone and the spare ribs"—and undoubtedly black gains were precarious. Still, as Manning Marable has noted, the cumulative black achievements in the first decade of the twentieth cen-

23. Alfred Holt Stone, *Studies in the American Race Problem* (New York, 1908), 190.
24. Tunica County Deed Records, Vol. B-2, pp. 96–100, Vol. N-2, pp. 439–44; Pressly and Scofield (eds.), *Farm Real Estate Values*, 55.

tury created a small rural black middle class. Perhaps it is no wonder that some still speak of that period as a heyday for blacks in Tunica County. "White people didn't own too much land years ago," recalled the Reverend Robert Grant. "Colored folks owned more land in Tunica County than white folks did." Legend exceeded reality, for though black landowners were more numerous than white, white farmers owned over 90 percent of the acreage of the county. Nonetheless, in the ownership of land, of their time, of their labor and its fruits, blacks in the early twentieth century had achieved hard-won advances during the plantation boom.[25]

A shattering blow to that moment of promise for blacks in the Delta came in 1914 with the outbreak of war in Europe. When the guns of August exploded that year, the largest cotton crop in the Delta's history was laid by in the field. Submarine warfare in the Atlantic stopped trade and brought a precipitate collapse of cotton prices. Within months, many of the members of the emerging black rural middle class were wiped out. Survivors learned anew the bitter lesson of the precariousness of their gains when they were dependent on white bankers for credit lines and worldwide markets for income. The agricultural census of 1925 showed that the number of black landowners in Tunica had stopped growing. The proportion of renters fell by 75 percent. The era of plantation expansion—and the marginal advantages it provided for blacks—was over.[26]

Long before the war, most of the thousands of blacks who lived in the Delta learned that the opportunities of the plantation frontier were not meant for them. Whether laborers, sharecroppers, or renters, most striving blacks before 1920 eventually confronted the reality expressed bluntly to one Tunica sharecropper when he protested that his settlement was short: "This plantation is a place for *me* to make the profit, not you." So although thousands streamed into Tunica County and the Delta in search of "betterment," thousands departed

---

25. *Twelfth Census, 1900: Agriculture*, 96–97; *Thirteenth Census, 1910: Agriculture*, 879; *Fourteenth Census, 1920: Agriculture*, 529; Manning Marable, "The Politics of Black Land Tenure, 1877–1915," *Agricultural History*, LIII (1979), 142, 147–48; interview with the Reverend Robert Grant, April 16, 1981, in Tunica, Miss.

26. Marable, "The Politics of Black Land Tenure," 142, 147–48; *United States Census of Agriculture, 1925*, 851.

as well. Many headed west for the farmlands of Arkansas and Texas. After 1910, many more left by train for Chicago and other northern cities. As historians Robert Brandfon and Robert Palmer put it, the Delta served blacks not as a promised land but rather as a "prolonged way station." What one Tunica County black resident said of the search for families from the old Cameron place applied to the region at large: "You're just not gonna find them folks you're looking for. This is a land of emigres." The tensions of a world without success found expression in a remarkable folk record. When a man felt like leaving Tunica County, recalled the Reverend Robert Grant, "you could tell. He sang the blues." From down the road, from across the field, he said, you could hear a voice at night, singing lyrics later immortalized by Muddy Waters. "If I feel tomorrow, the way I feel today, I'm gonna pack my bags and make my getaway." You knew that man was thinking about "slipping," about leaving his cabin and his crop and his debt behind, and finding another place to start again.[27]

But would a new plantation or a new county bring better fortune? Blues songs of the Delta, which appeared everywhere on plantations in the 1890s and which flourished on the old Cameron place and elsewhere well into the twentieth century, exposed the contradictions embedded in that question. Almost always the songs expressed a longing for escape, the hope of momentary release, and a gnawing worry that nothing would get better in the long run. In "over and over strains," that began slowly and built in tempo and tension, blues singers gave vent to contradictory thoughts of those whom endless plantation work had left afflicted with the "aching heart disease" and the "low down shaking chill" of a "good man feeling bad":

> Gotta mind to move,
> A mind to settle down.
> Gotta mind to move,
> A mind to settle down.

For some, escape was the only answer, and many of the lyrics of the "Big Road Blues" focused on flight, desertion, and reunion—the perils and dreams of black men and women on the move. Others

27. Brandfon, *Cotton Kingdom*, 136; Robert Palmer, *Deep Blues* (New York, 1981), 11; interview with O. Bodie, April 22, 1981, in Robinsonville, Miss.; interview with the Reverend Robert Grant, April 16, 1981.

chose to stay where they were, but served notice they would go "no lower down":

Goin' no higher,
Goin' no lower down.
Goin' no higher,
Goin' no lower down.

Gonna stay right here,
Gonna stay right here,
'Til they close me down.

For the black worker who chose to "settle down" on a plantation in the Delta after 1920, resigned to "goin' no higher," resolved to go "no lower down," how did he survive? Charley Thomas of Tunica County had reason to know the answer. Born on the old Cameron place in Mississippi in 1902, son of a father who had acquired land early in the twentieth century and then lost it, a Tunica County sharecropper for sixty of his eighty years, Charley Thomas glared at the outsider who asked him the question. "*You* know the answer to that. This is Mississippi. You see me? I'm alive. I learned to live here. I learned *how* to live here."[28]

Learning how to live in Tunica County meant in part learning how to endure in a world of lurking violence. "You know what it was like for the Indians, surrounded by fifty whites with rifles? Then you know what it was like in the Delta." The nine lynchings that occurred in Tunica County between 1890 and 1930—the highest number in the state—left no doubt that blacks who got out of line might meet their end on a lynch mob's rope. More endemic than lynching were other forms of violence. Jailed prisoners were flogged; levee marshals took sticks to workers' heads on the slightest provocation. Blacks who saw or suspected such violence "didn't hardly say anything," lest they be the next victims. "Back then, I tell you, white people mostly kept black people scary." A well-understood etiquette evolved to avoid danger. A black person did not "dispute" the white man's word; if he did, he sought to disguise the challenge by calling it a "confusion." Even with

28.   David Evans, *Big Road Blues: Tradition and Creativity in the Folk Blues* (Berkeley, 1982), 17–19, 28–29; interview with Johnny B. Henderson, November 14, 1981, in Robinsonville, Miss.; interview with Charley Thomas, April 23, 1981, in Robinsonville, Miss.

planters who sought to avoid force in dealing with workers, black workers remained ever alert to warning signs. A curse always meant trouble: "If a white man cursed you today, he might hit you tomorrow. Best thing to do was get away."[29]

But black ways of dealing with the closed world of the plantation went beyond knowing how to avoid or escape "confusions." Blacks sought and found resources beyond the cotton crop. "One way or another," recalled Charley Thomas, "you knew the planters was going to get that money from the crop." So he and others got themselves a "side trade." Thomas made some of his money as a barber. With any shade tree and orange-pop crate serving as his barber shop, Charley Thomas traveled all over to cut hair. More remunerative for Thomas was his second side trade. He was the agent for a Chicago mail-order house, the "Kostamatic" company. He showed his customers catalog pictures of ready-made suits and shoes, took sizes and a cash deposit, and ordered the goods, which arrived C.O.D. at a nearby rural post office. Other sharecroppers found resources in the remaining wild lands of the county. "My daddy was a scufflish man," Richard Jones recalled. He hunted and fished for the family's food; he trapped mink and sold the fur. Working his cotton crop brought in some money, but scuffling gave him his independence. "He carried $400 around in his pocket [and knew] he could get up and go anytime." The money and the mobility meant that he belonged to nobody.[30]

Through resourcefulness and what Ralph Ellison has termed sheer toughness of spirit, blacks learned how to live in the Delta.[31] They learned how to forge opportunities where there were few, to make a home out of what was only a workplace. With Robert Flagg, they struggled to make the planters' resources their own in the unsettled decades after emancipation. With Mack Parker, they sought to keep the fruits of their labor in the era of renewed plantation expan-

29. Interview with Charley Thomas, April 23, 1981; interview with Nathaniel Richardson, April 21, 1981, in Robinsonville, Miss.; interview with Richard Jones, November 15, 1981, in Tunica, Miss. See Charles S. Johnson (ed.), *Statistical Analysis of Southern Counties: Listing and Analysis of Socio-Economic Indices of 1104 Southern Counties* (Chapel Hill, 1941), 143.
30. Interviews with Charley Thomas, April 23, 1981, and with Richard Jones, November 15, 1981.
31. Ralph Ellison, *Shadow and Act* (New York, 1964), 64.

sion. With Charley Thomas, they scuffled within and around the plantation's limits through most of the twentieth century. At no point was Tunica County a California for Afro-Americans. But it was a place where, intermittently, the odds against them in the battle for "betterment" were less severe than they were elsewhere in the rural South. The land the blacks found, but more important their battle to make a better world within it, made the Cameron plantation and the Delta around it a "black frontier."

Jazz, Segregation, and Desegregation

Stanley P. Hirshson

Jazz and segregation came of age together. They often associated with one another, but they were hardly friends. Segregation dictated that blacks and whites exist separately. But jazz, though often yielding to segregation, frequently drew members of the races together. At times, jazz refused to dance Jim Crow.

Jazz drew its essential characteristics, as the music historian and critic Leonard Feather pointed out, not from "the Negro" but from "the segregated American Negro." Social not racial music, jazz emerged in the last years of the nineteenth century from the red-light district of New Orleans, where, "like gumbo, crinoline, and river-boats," music was a way of life. The creation of "dark" Negroes and light-skinned Creoles, jazz united these musicians who were segregated from whites. But as time went on, jazz—and the black musicians who played it—did much to break down the social system that had helped spawn the art.[1]

Jazz did not long remain hidden in New Orleans. It moved on to Kansas City and the Southwest, made its way to Chicago, and eventually reached New York, giving its name to the decade of the 1920s, known then and forever after as the Jazz Age. By the 1930s and 1940s, jazz and its offspring "swing" were, like segregation itself, a force throughout the United States.[2]

The early giants of jazz, those who inspired awe among both blacks and whites, were black men: Louis Armstrong on the trumpet; Lester Young and Coleman Hawkins on the saxophone; Art Tatum, Teddy Wilson, and the Harlem Triumvirate, James P. Johnson,

---

1. Leonard Feather, *The Book of Jazz, From Then Till Now* (New York, 1957), 8–9; Jack V. Buerkle and Danny Barker, *Bourbon Street Black: The New Orleans Black Jazzman* (New York, 1973), 19–21.
2. Ross Russell, *Jazz Style in Kansas City and the Southwest* (Berkeley, 1971), 1–6.

Thomas "Fats" Waller, and Willie "The Lion" Smith, on the piano; Chick Webb and Zutty Singleton on drums; and such bandleaders and arrangers as Duke Ellington, Fletcher Henderson, Don Redman, and Benny Carter. Harry "Sweets" Edison, who played trumpet in the black bands led by Count Basie and Lucky Millinder, best described the way jazz fans, regardless of race, lionized these innovators. "To me," he said, "the originator, like Coleman Hawkins, is just as great as Thomas Edison. To me he is because in his field he originated something on the tenor saxophone, you know. . . . Never been heard before. Louis Armstrong, he broke all the rules of trumpet. Duke, he broke all the rules of arranging. They said, you cannot play dissonant chords because it's displeasing to the ear. Duke played them and made everybody listen."[3]

Still, from the 1920s on, the black musicians who played jazz ran into racial troubles. After a dance in Florida in the early 1920s, Tom Howard had the distinction of having his entire orchestra, which included the noted jazz trombonist Vic Dickenson, beaten up by a gang of boisterous whites. Conditions were often bad in the North, but the South was much worse, and some black bands tried to avoid playing there. Fletcher Henderson's brother, Horace, once agreed to perform at a dance in a North Carolina warehouse. His band drove to the engagement in a bus that pulled right up to the warehouse door. The musicians spent their breaks in the vehicle and took off for home right after completing the job.[4]

Both whites and blacks frequently attended these southern dances. At some, a rope or wire down the center of the floor separated the members of each race. At others, the whites danced downstairs, and the blacks, who paid the same admission price, sat in the balcony, listening and watching.[5]

During the 1930s, the heyday of the big bands in America, dozens of black orchestras toured the country, trouble often accompany-

3. Harry "Sweets" Edison interview, May, 1981, Cassette 3, p. 11, Institute of Jazz Studies, Rutgers University, Newark. All other interviews cited can be found there.
4. *New Yorker*, September 7, 1981, p. 40; Horace Henderson interview, April 9–12, 1975, Pt. 2, pp. 23–24.
5. Stanley Dance, *The World of Swing* (New York, 1974), 73; John Simmons interview, June 29, 1976, Reels 1–4, p. 78.

ing them. "The one-night scene in the South was just simply terrible," recalled the bassist Milt Hinton, who played with several groups. With Cab Calloway, Hinton explained, they traveled first class:

> Cab would always retain a Pullman. We'd pull into one of those Southern towns and we slept in. . . . Cab had it easier because of his great popularity, so when you traveled with his band you were as comfortable as a member of a Negro band could be in the South. But it was still pretty bad. At dance halls people would insult us. . . . I'm telling you, some of those people came and paid their money just to heckle the Negro bands, like some people like to tease an animal, and we had no recourse. Did you know that in Miami, Florida, where we used to play, after nine o'clock at night, Negroes had to be off the streets unless they had a note saying something like: "This boy works for me"?

Calloway was famous and respected, his band having appeared in movies and on national radio, but even he ran into racial troubles. Adolphus "Doc" Cheatham, the trumpeter, spoke of a dance in Memphis where an admiring white girl came up to the bandstand to get Calloway's autograph. Leaning over to sign his name, the bandleader allowed his long black hair to touch the girl. And the result was chaos:

> The biggest fight started you ever saw in your life. . . . Chairs, bottles, everything, the biggest fight you ever saw in your life in the ballroom. Free-for-all, throwing at the band, fighting the band. Chairs, I got behind a table. . . . Cops came and hustled Cab out, took him out the back and put him in a car, and we didn't see Cab anymore until we got on the train. But they were fighting us all the way out of the ballroom, all the way . . . in the automobiles, on the highways . . . throwing bricks at the cars, everything, all the way till we got to the Pullman car.

Cheatham also described an incident in Florida:

> We were playing at a big place there, it was a white place, did not allow colored in it. So a couple of guys standing out in the front heckling the band, you know, and they—one called me, and I went over there 'cause I was a Southerner and I don't have problems with the Southerners. This guy had a big glass of corn whiskey and say have a drink. I says, I don't drink. He says, you gonna drink this. So I drank the whole glass of corn whiskey, and man I mean I was so drunk. I didn't know where I was. And at the end of that they just started throwing things. They

threw a bottle up there and it hit the drummer in the head, knocked a hole in his head. That was in Miami. We had to be hustled out of there.[6]

Episodes such as those involving the Calloway band often boiled down to prejudice. Others in the 1930s sprang from the need of musicians to fulfill human urges. Eating presented a problem. Quinn Wilson, who traveled with the Earl "Fatha" Hines band in the 1930s, remembered that in "most towns we had to eat out of the A & P or something. . . . No restaurants you could eat in, unless you run into a town where they had one side for colored and one side for white. They had those kind of restaurants in the big towns." Cheatham recalled a time the Calloway band's Pullman car stopped alongside an "old beat grease joint." A light-skinned musician left the car, went into the restaurant, and got served. Watching his successful companion, a darker band member tried to get something to eat. Realizing that he had served a black man, the restaurant owner threw both musicians out. Sandy Williams, who played trombone in Chick Webb's band, told of an unpleasant episode in Texas:

> We had one of those big Greyhound buses and we stopped for about seventy-five gallons of gas and seven or eight quarts of oil. . . . We all bought sandwiches and soda, but when you're thirsty after drinking you want water. Now there was a little, old, funny-looking woman had charge of this gas station.
>
> "Madam," I said to her, "would you mind giving me a glass of water, please?"
>
> "We don't give your kind no water down here," she said. "There's the river over there. Go help yourself."
>
> Chick laughed like hell. That was funny to him. . . . It burnt me up. . . . Look at the money we'd spent there. With the valets, road manager, bus driver, and all of us, there were about twenty guys altogether, and everybody bought two or three sandwiches. . . . But to Chick it was funny. I guess he thought I should have had more sense than to ask.[7]

A more violent incident involved Calloway's sister Blanche, herself a bandleader. In June, 1937, just outside of Yazoo City, Missis-

6. Nat Shapiro and Nat Hentoff (eds.), *Hear Me Talkin' to Ya* (New York, 1955), 326, 328; Adolphus "Doc" Cheatham interview, April, 1976, pp. 126–27, 128.
7. Quinn Wilson interview, December 3, 1977, Pt. 1, pp. 9–10; Cheatham interview, 129–30; Williams quoted in Dance, *The World of Swing*, 72.

sippi, she and the wife of one band member attempted to eat in a café. Within five minutes, two policemen pulled up to the band's bus and demanded to speak to the two women. Not hearing the policemen, Blanche's husband asked, "What did you say?" One of the officers answered by smashing the butt of his pistol against the black man's head, shouting: "We'll show you how to talk to a white man. You're in the South and we'll show you how we treat 'niggers' down here." For several hours, the three offenders were jailed. Pleading guilty to trespassing, each was fined $7.50 and released.[8]

Like finding a place to eat, locating a place to stay was sometimes difficult. "Economics and racism made it hard for many black musicians," Vic Dickenson said of the 1930s. "We were always on the road. Hotels wouldn't accommodate us, so we stayed in rooming houses, eating crackers and bologna for dinner." He added, "Those rooming houses weren't too hot either. A lot of places had a lot of bedbugs and things. Oh yes, you know, and that's no fun. I think hotels would have been better because all the guys would have been together. At rooming houses and things like that, guys were scattered all over. . . . The hotels wouldn't take no colored at that time, you know." Other black musicians offered similar accounts of their experiences. "Segregation," commented Jimmy Crawford, the drummer in Jimmie Lunceford's band during the 1930s, "we confronted that every night. When we wanted to go to a hotel, no, go to one of those cheap colored hotels. They were the only ones that would put us up. . . . There was some mean people back down South then, even right here in the North, very mean people." The trombonist Leo "Snub" Mosley agreed: "Many times we couldn't sleep in any hotel because the band was Black. We wound up sleeping on the bus. . . . That atmosphere is important to convey to people writing about the history of jazz."[9]

Such problems made black performers like Fats Waller reluctant to go south. "First time Fats went to Florida they offered him, oh, man, they offered him a mint to come," observed Herman Autrey, who played trumpet for Waller in the 1930s. "For he wouldn't take it.

8. *Amsterdam News* (New York), June 19, 1937.
9. New York *Times*, July 3, 1983; Vic Dickenson interview, July, 1976, pp. 46–47; Jimmy Crawford interview, August, 1978, Cassettes 3–4, pp. 37–39; comments of Leo "Snub" Mosley in Brochure, Oral History Project, Institute of Jazz Studies.

Fats had never been south in his life, and all he heard was stories, he didn't want any part of it. . . . He said, 'Forget it! I don't need it! Let them keep it!'" Persuaded by the members of his band to play in Miami, Waller found discrimination as well as fortune. Because Florida law prohibited blacks and whites from being under the same roof, his manager could not enter the dance hall. To keep track of the number of people attending the dance, the manager had to sit in the band's bus, which faced the hall, and count the entering patrons.[10]

Visiting the South, Autrey invariably asked around for a room:

> We had to go knock on doors, and say pardon me, Madam, would you, or do you happen to have a room that you would like to or care to rent? I'm here with the band, such and such a band, we're going to be here two nights, three nights, and need a place to stay. Yes, or no? No, but—I say well do you know of some place, and they say well go down the street by the old oak tree and make a left turn, and don't go in there, because that's a—they, you know, that—how you get those directions, and you finally—you hope—find some place.

There were, however, several rooming houses that became legendary. Nellie Lutcher, the pianist-singer, lavishly praised a boardinghouse in Lake Charles, Louisiana, her hometown. "Mrs. Cox's place was one of the nicest places," she observed. "I think Ellington and some of the larger bands that came through there stayed at this particular place in Lake Charles. She had a terrific place, and it was an old place, but she kept it up beautifully, it was nicely furnished, she had a restaurant, she had good food and it was just a class, a really nice, class spot." Other black boardinghouses in both the North and the South stood out—Mother Hadlow's in Philadelphia, Mom Sutton's in Atlanta, and the Palm Leaf Hotel in Birmingham. Rex Stewart, who played trumpet for Ellington and Fletcher Henderson, colorfully described the most famous of these establishments, Uncle Henry's in Cincinnati:

> As I look back to that table of Uncle Henry's, my taste buds water . . . mountains of mashed potatoes, platters of roast pork, fried chicken, flanked by corn on the cob, salad, hot rolls, hot biscuits, corn bread, and gravy. This kind of spread was an everyday affair with the gentleman, but to us ever-hungry bandsmen, it was a treat to play Cincinnati

10. Herman Autrey interview, May 1, 1975, Pt. 3, pp. 52–53, 58.

just so we could get the wrinkles out of our stomachs at Uncle Henry's. However, like all good things, it had to end somewhere, and after we had annihilated his table every day for a week, he finally said, "Sorry, fellows. I can't afford to feed you for fifty cents a meal. From now on, you will have to pay me double." Our pleas for leniency because of hardship fell on deaf ears.[11]

For touring black musicians, finding places to eat and sleep was an inescapable problem. So too was, as James "Trummy" Young, who played trombone and sang for Hines and Lunceford, put it, "getting to the bathroom. They didn't have that many bathrooms all the time for a big band, but it always worked out. There was always a way. . . . But you have to love music really to go through that then, you know." The most harrowing bathroom episode took place in the summer of 1937, when Snub Mosley and the saxophonist Theodore McRae toured the South with an orchestra led by Louis Armstrong's former wife, Lil. "It was a nice band," Mosley related, "but we didn't draw no people. Just didn't draw flies." Then:

> We finally got some money someplace, enough to get us back in the car, for gas and everything, and we were coming back through Tennessee and there was a little stand on the edge of the highway—just a little stand, not in the city, and the man was so happy we stopped there, because he didn't have no business and we bought hot dogs and hamburgers and soda and things like that, and all of a sudden I heard somebody cursing like hell and this guy opened his door to his bathroom and there was McRae on the stool and I never heard so much—this guy . . . he said, oh my God . . . oh Lord have mercy what am I going to do. . . . oh my God. I swear to God I'll blow your head off. . . . I went and grabbed McRae by the head and pulled him up. . . . It was an awful thing down there then.[12]

In both the North and the South, World War II and the postwar euphoria hardly ended the racial strife. Touring then with Louis Armstrong's band, the bassist John Simmons found conditions in the South deplorable. On a road near Macon, Georgia, the Armstrong

11. *Ibid.*, 52, 58–61; Nellie Lutcher interview, February 15, 1979, Reel 2, pp. 9–11; Teddy Wilson interview, March, 1980, Reel 1, pp. 32–33; Rex Stewart, *Jazz Masters of the Thirties* (New York, 1972), 175.
12. James "Trummy" Young interview, September 17, 18, 1976, Tapes 1–3, p. 97; Leo "Snub" Mosley interview, March 22, 1980, Tape 3, Side A, pp. 70–71.

group came across the truck carrying the belongings of Erskine Hawkins' black orchestra. There was only one man to guard it. Simmons said they went on to Macon. He later learned that the highway police had stopped and awakened the sleeping guard by shining a flashlight in his face. When he protested, he was dragged from the truck and beaten: "They pulled him out, say, 'Nigger, we've been watching you all day.' And they whipped him something awful. The highway police with those big-knobbed flashlights, long ones, billy clubs, blackjacks, they must have messed up his teeth, broke his nose, damn near put his eyes out. Both eyes is closed, ribs broken, arm broken, you know." Simmons also recalled what happend to Armstrong's band in Macon. They had played at a black dance, and afterward a white soldier named Norman Murphy, who had once played trumpet with Gene Krupa's orchestra, tried to see Simmons and some of the other black musicians. The Macon police stopped him and turned him over to the military police. "The M.P.'s beat hell out of him," Simmons recalled. "They beat him so he urinated on himself. . . . The city police joined in, with billy clubs. 'You Yankee son of a bitch. Didn't we tell you not to speak to no niggers down here?'" The more Murphy tried to explain that he knew the black musicians, the more viciously the police thrashed him. "He was adding to the injury, you know, and they almost killed him." [13]

Armstrong, fearing that if he were hit in the mouth he would never again be able to play his trumpet, stayed away from things. "First thing he'd do is put his hand up to his lips," Simmons said. "Everything that happened, he was guarding his lips all the time." Simmons remembered the events in Atlanta:

> They had chicken wire down through the middle of the auditorium. It was a dance. Whites on one side, blacks on the other. If the dance gets too good, the blacks got to leave, you know. If the music got too good, and some whites wanted to get in there, the blacks had to go. . . . Here's this [white] dude had been to New York several times, he's real hip, clean. He said, "Man, some of my best friends are colored." The first time I heard that expression, you know. That didn't rub me right. I'm waiting for him to say that magic word [nigger] so I can jump down his throat. He didn't come on with that. He says, "We had a colored mammy." I say, "Whew." "Yes," he said, "colored." 'Cause I'd have been

13. Simmons interview, 87–90.

on him like white on rice if he'd said that magic word. He says, "We nursed her breast." I said, "Well, man, you're a lucky S.O.B." He say, "What do you mean?" I say, "I was 21 years old before I sucked a Caucasian breast." And Louis said, "Oh," and held his mouth as though someone hit him in it. He said, "You're going to get us killed down here." I said, "Well, he asked for it." You know? He turned the color of your blouse. And he made a quick exit. . . . Just lucky that we were leaving the next morning.[14]

In the North, discrimination seldom led to violence, but it existed nonetheless. Trummy Young remembered that in the 1940s he, Teddy Wilson, and bassist Slam Stewart were refused a room in a Providence hotel because they were black. They complained to their boss, Benny Goodman, who replied unsympathetically: "I have problems too. I can't belong to this club or that one because I'm Jewish." Not, Young pointed out, that Goodman countenanced prejudice: "He just thought clarinet and that was it. . . . He didn't let anything else bother him." When the three black musicians threatened to walk out and go back to New York, Goodman finally sent someone to the front desk to correct things. Chicago too was a hotbed of prejudice. There, as in some other northern cities, white and black musicians had separate unions and could not appear on stage together. When Fatha Hines played piano with a white band in Chicago, the hotel manager placed a screen in front of him so the audience could hear but not see him.[15]

Becoming the only black member of Krupa's band in 1941, Roy Eldridge, the trumpeter whose nickname was Little Jazz, encountered Jim Crow both above and below the Mason-Dixon Line. Hotels in Los Angeles and Portland, Oregon, refused to accommodate him:

> By the time that kind of thing has happened night after night it begins to work on my mind; I can't think right, can't play right. When we finally got to the Palladium in Hollywood I had to watch who I could sit with. If they were movie stars who wanted to come over, that was all right; if they were just the jitterbugs, no dice. And all the time the bouncer with his eye on me, just watching for a chance.
>
> On top of that, I had to live way out in Los Angeles while the rest of the guys stayed in Hollywood. It was a lonely life; I'd never been that far

14. *Ibid.*, 88, 78–79.
15. Young interview, 92–94; Simmons interview, 21, 49, 54.

away from home before, and I didn't know anybody. I got to brooding. Then it happened. One night the tension got so bad I flipped. I could feel it right up to my neck while I was playing "Rockin' Chair"; I started trembling, ran off the stand and threw up. They carried me to the doctor's. I had a 105 fever; my nerves were shot.

In 1943, during the filming of *Ball of Fire*, in which Krupa's band appeared, Eldridge found himself pushed about. "I was refused a 'make-up' when others were readied for the camera, got switched from my regular position next to Krupa and his drums in the center of the bandstand to the end of the trumpet row where my five-foot-five frame wouldn't look 'too tall.'" In the completed film, "I wasn't in a single shot with the band. And in the one scene which I appeared for a brief four bars in a jam session I was made to look jet-black." Explaining these moves, Samuel Goldwyn, the producer, "gave me the same old malarkey Hollywood gives all Negroes who bid for straight roles in flicks"—the picture cost millions of dollars, and mixing the races would hurt business in the South. When the band moved on to Norfolk, Virginia, Eldridge was given an especially hard time. Barred from the musicians' bathroom, he was told to wash himself with a nearby bucket of water. He and Anita O'Day, the band's vocalist, were permitted to sing their hit songs together, but they had to appear on opposite sides of the stage. Attempting to ride with the other band members on the top deck of the Norfolk ferry, Eldridge was informed: "We don't allow no niggers up here." When his fellow musicians complained, the ferryboat captain told them: "Well, if you can stand him it's all right with me." It was, Eldridge moaned, "just as if I had leprosy." But his favorite observation came from a "white fellow" in a Nevada dance hall. "Thank you, Roy," the man stammered, "for playing that wonderful music. You know, there's nobody—no nobody—can play jazz like you colored people. I'd rather hear a Nigger—Oh! excuse me, Roy. I didn't mean that. But really I'd rather hear a Nigger play than anybody in the world."[16]

Black musicians often felt the sting of segregation, but the princes and princesses of jazz were among the first Negroes to dent the sys-

16.   Roy Eldridge, "Jim Crow Is Killing Jazz," *Negro Digest*, VIII (October, 1950), 44–49; Leonard Feather, "No More White Bands for Me, Says Little Jazz," *Down Beat*, May 18, 1951, pp. 1, 13.

tem. One of the earliest breakthroughs came in 1926, after a bellman at Dallas' finest hotel, the Adolphus, heard the black orchestra led by Alphonso Trent, often praised, because of his musicianship, as the Paul Whiteman of the South. The bellman raved to the hotel manager, who booked the band into the Adolphus for what was supposed to be two weeks. Trent's group stayed for a year and a half. "It was such a lily-white hotel," observed Snub Mosley, one of the band's stars, "when we went in there . . . we had to abide by the rules. We had to take the back elevator up and we had to take it out. . . . But we had a two-week contract and the guys were sensational. That was something too, we were the first ones to play for a white audience. . . . And it created such a sensation all around because nothing but the wealthy came to the Adolphus, but the poor class, especially some of the police department, they didn't like it and the Ku Klux Klan of course they didn't. They planned a little party for us one night." The hotel manager found out about it, "and he called up the right people and they took care of it."[17]

"The band was sensational," Mosley bragged. Across the street Don Bestor, later the orchestra leader on the Jack Benny radio program, was playing at another famous hotel, the Baker. But the people of Dallas preferred Trent's black to Bestor's white band. "When we finally finished our engagement at the Adolphus," Mosley related, "the Baker wanted to hire us to come over there." Trent's orchestra was also heard nightly over Dallas radio station WFAA. His musicians made the unheard-of salary of $150 a week, wore silk shirts and camel's hair coats, and drove Cadillacs. Touring the state, the band entertained at many famous colleges, including the opening of the new field house at the University of Texas at Austin. It played at the Governor's Ball and was booked into the all-white Houston Country Club. "I shall never forget the little town named Menard—Menard, Texas," commented Hayes Pillars, Trent's saxophonist. "We opened up a new hotel there. And that was rattlesnake country. They booked us out there and they had no place for us to eat, so we had to eat in the basement of the hotel. . . . But that was back in . . . a time of the century that you'd like to forget about." According to Pillars, the band always seemed to have white defenders. "We played for a guy named

17. Stanley Dance, *The World of Count Basie* (New York, 1980), 327–28; Mosley interview, Tape 1, pp. 13–14, 25.

Mike Hall, a millionaire in Texas—parties for him, and we played at this big hotel in Houston . . . and the Mexican waiters didn't want to wait on us." Hall thereupon "cursed the waiters out and told them if they wanted a job they'd better come on and wait on us, and so they served us right in the hotel dining room with his guests, only we had a different table."[18]

The most unpleasant post-Adolphus episode took place in a Texas dance hall. "We were broadcasting," said Mosley, "and the announcer was the owner and opening night he said, 'Ladies and gentlemen, I want you to hear the greatest nigger band you ever heard in your life,' and we all turned around and look, what is this? 'Just give me one more minute to tell you about these niggers. These niggers are from Texas, they played the Adolphus Hotel'—boy, he talked about us."[19]

In race relations, Trent broke barriers. But like several other Negro bandleaders, he quietly went out of his way to appease whites. Numerous black orchestra leaders, including Noble Sissle and Claude Hopkins, were extremely light and some of them shied away from dark musicians. Almost all of Trent's musicians were light, remembered Sweets Edison, who played trumpet for him, "most of them real light. I think Snub Mosley was the darkest guy in the band." In Chicago, Sammy Stewart refused to hire some exceptionally talented performers, including Hines and Armstrong, because he considered them too dark for his band.[20]

Possessing few peers as a jazz performer, Armstrong became the leading figure in a New Orleans episode that has long been misinterpreted. In 1931 he brought a band into the lily-white Suburban Gardens, a supper club overlooking the Mississippi River. Idolized by jazz fans, Armstrong signed to play there for four weeks. He and his band remained for four months. But, according to two of Armstrong's biographers, his stay was marred by a white announcer who broke off an introduction of Armstrong and said: "I just haven't the heart to announce that nigger on the radio." Zilner T. Randolph, the arranger

---

18. Mosley interview, Tape 1, pp. 16, 25; George T. Simon, *The Big Bands* (New York, 1971), 496; Hayes Pillars interview, September, 1977, pp. 9–11; Russell, *Jazz Style in Kansas City,* 61, 63.
19. Mosley interview, Tape 3, Side A, p. 2.
20. Edison interview, Cassette 2, p. 33.

and trumpeter who had hired each musician in the Armstrong band, swore that this incident never occurred. What got Armstrong into trouble with some whites was an innocent comment he made. He was so popular that during his stay in New Orleans the Pelicans, the baseball club in the all-white Southern Association, forgot about color and elected him an honorary member of the team. That night, during a radio broadcast, Armstrong spoke about the honor accorded him and said of the team's chances for success: "We're going to take them like Grant took Richmond." Letters of complaint poured in from irate Confederate sympathizers. After that, the owners of Suburban Gardens cautioned Armstrong to be more careful about what he said.[21]

A radical breakthrough came in 1935 and 1936, when Goodman, ignoring tradition, hired two black musicians, Teddy Wilson and vibraphonist Lionel Hampton, to play in his quartet, which traveled about the country. "It was a tremendous success," Wilson later said of the experiment. "As a matter of fact, it was an asset, racial mixing. The interest in the United States was tremendous, and the public was so for the thing that not one negative voice in any audience did we ever get. Just tremendous enthusiasm. This interracial thing was just wonderful." On tours Wilson and Hampton did their best to avoid trouble. "If we'd had to make a battle of that thing in every town on one-night stands, you couldn't ever get to work, making an issue of that. So Lionel and I generally would drive our cars and go into the Negro district of town and go to a Negro hotel. And we'd just go and do the job. . . . We went along with the tide the way it was, because we had opened up a door already, a giant crack, and there was no need of making a big fuss." The closest thing to an incident occurred in Dallas in 1937, when the Goodman quartet entertained during the Texas centennial. A policeman stopped one of Wilson's white friends, a University of Texas professor, from coming backstage to drink with the black performers. Wilson remembered:

> So the next day the police chief called all the policemen at the fair on the carpet and wanted to know what the trouble was. And the situation

21.   Max Jones and John Chilton, *Louis: The Louis Armstrong Story, 1900–1971* (Boston, 1971), 123; Robert Goffin, *Horn of Plenty: The Story of Louis Armstrong* (New York, 1947), 284–86; Zilner T. Randolph interview, February 20, 1977, Tapes 3–5, pp. 12–13.

was explained to him, what happened, and then the Dallas police chief asked for me and Lionel, had us in his office and he told us that he appreciated what we were doing and most of the people in the South were tired of the old handkerchief-head way of life, and the people appreciated performances like what we were doing in this mixed group. And he said, "And you boys will not have any trouble. If you have the slightest trouble at all, you come and let me know, because I'm the baddest man here." That's the police chief of Dallas, Texas, 1937, in his little speech to Lionel Hampton and me. "If anybody bothers y'all boys, just let me know, because I'm the baddest man here."[22]

One immensely popular musician who stood up to segregation in the late 1930s bore an unusual name: Bon Bon. One of the first blacks to perform regularly with a white orchestra, he sang with Jan Savitt's band. Indeed, Bon Bon was the band's prime attraction, singing on most of its hit records. In segregated hotels he usually got a room by posing as the band manager's valet. But one night, at a soda stand in a Kentucky ballroom at which the Savitt band was playing, Bon Bon was denied service. For two and half hours after that, he refused to come onstage, appearing only when the band played for a scheduled radio broadcast. Seeing him, the crowd cheered, but Bon Bon sang for the broadcast and then left. He would not entertain those who had insulted him.[23]

In 1941, Charlie Barnet, the wealthy white bandleader who loved the musical styles of Ellington and Basie, ran into the same racial problem as Savitt. In New York, Barnet's singers came down with laryngitis. Desperate, the bandleader called Clarence Robinson, the producer at Harlem's Apollo Theater, and asked if he knew of an available singer. Robinson responded by sending over a relatively obscure girl named Lena Horne. "She was an absolute gas," Barnet noted. But there were difficulties on the road:

> But the problems came, like the housing problems, see. So we used to have a gag we'd pull. The manager of the band would come in, and he'd say, "That'll be so many doubles," and he'd say, "And we want a single room for our Cuban vocalist." And he'd reel off a bunch of Spanish sounding words . . . and she'd say, "Si." And, oh that was all right. That was fine. As long as she was Cuban. And we overcame some of the

22.   Teddy Wilson interview, Reel 3, pp. 5–7.
23.   Simon, *The Big Bands*, 408–409.

problems that way, but—and then of course when we went into the deep South one time, we were down at the University of Alabama, I said, "Lena, I don't think you'd better make this trip because we've got to play some funny places, and I can't see you being—." So I said, "We'll pick you up in two weeks. You're still on salary, you know, don't worry about it." And of course I got to the University of Alabama and that Dean ate my butt out for not bringing her. I said, "Well, I hope you can understand. I can realize that probably here everything would have been fine. But you must realize, I mean, the places we have to play to get here and to leave here." And he was a very astute gentleman, and he said, "Well, I guess we'll just have to forego the pleasure of hearing Miss Horne."[24]

Another musician who challenged and sometimes bent the rules of segregation was Willie Smith, the alto saxophone player who looked white but whose father and mother were half black. For thirteen years, including much of the 1930s, Smith played with Lunceford's orchestra, which faced frequent discrimination in the South. "Travelling by train once," Smith told *Ebony* magazine in 1949, "a conductor came over to me and said I had to move into the white car. I couldn't sit back with the Lunceford band in the colored cars. He wouldn't believe I was colored. . . . When we played the University of Mississippi, the Lunceford band was a big hit. We went over so big they crowded us for our autographs. Then they told us we could eat in the kitchen." In one southern town a policeman who refused to believe Smith was black pulled him off the bandstand. "He had to carry his birth certificate around with him," said Trummy Young, who also played with Lunceford. "That's the only way he got to play with us." Young continued, "I remember one night we were going somewhere down Florida. And we go through a job and we got—we couldn't go nowhere to eat. So Willie Smith . . . we sent him in a place. Sure enough, he got a lot of sandwiches for us, about $30.00 worth of sandwiches. But we couldn't go into the place. So, you know, he went in and got it. Things were that bad, back there then."[25]

In 1944, after serving in the navy, Smith joined the all-white orchestra led by Harry James, a Texan. "On the band's Southern tours,"

24. Charlie Barnet interview, April 23, 1978, Reel 4, pp. 34–36.
25. "Willie Smith," *Ebony*, IV (June, 1949), 41, 43; Young interview, 90–92.

Ebony reported, "an unspoken truce seems to exist between Southern law enforcement officers and the James band. Despite the barrier against whites and Negroes performing together, objections are not raised when Willie appears on the tour." Still, Smith told of two episodes that occurred in the late 1940s. In one southern town some white officials told James: "We understand there's a nigger in this band." "Fine," James replied. "Find him." Try as they might, the authorities could not. Another time, when informed that Smith could not play, James pulled his band off the stage and canceled the engagement.[26]

Autrey spoke of another way black musicians quietly helped to overcome segregation. Traveling with several bands, he found that he and his friends were sometimes welcomed in southern restaurants that ordinarily refused to serve blacks. On occasion he and his hungry companions entered a white place, expecting something to happen:

> So anyway, and you go in, and you don't get it. And you're treated damn nice, and with a smile, well when are you fellows coming back through here? Be sure and stop now. We will be looking for you, and stop in and eat with us. . . . Instead of the guys looking at you, say don't come in here, that way, what you come in here for? What do you want? . . .
>
> So that happened a lot of times, and we came in, hi fellows, hey, they remembered two or three names. Come on over! Sit down! And the waitresses would be running, grabbing this, and grabbing that, and the managers, and the bosses and what not, everybody, you know. Sit down, be there. Be happy. What did you see? What do you like? Is the meat this and that?
>
> And you say, well confound, these people have changed, or something, or they think we're human after all. Anyway, it becomes delightful.[27]

The most publicized racial incident involving a black musician showed the underlying white sympathy for Negro performers. In April, 1956, six men rushed toward the stage of the Birmingham Municipal Auditorium, where Nat "King" Cole, the black pianist-singer,

26. "Willie Smith," 41; Barnet interview, Reel 3, pp. 24–25; Young interview, pp. 91–92. Another white bandleader with James's attitude was Boyd Raeburn. "Boyd was a beautiful man," said Young. "He'd fight. . . . He would say, well, they don't stay here, none of us stay here" (see Young interview, 92–94).
27. Autrey interview, 55–58.

was performing with a group that included such whites as singer June Christy and comedian Gary Morton. Also on the program was Ted Heath's white orchestra from England. Of the six attackers, only one reached the stage, the others being stopped by detectives in the audience. Except for a slight back injury, Cole, a native of Alabama, was unhurt. The next morning the performers were scheduled to leave Birmingham. "I would venture to guess over 100 people came to the airport apologizing," observed Cole's drummer, Lee Young, "saying how ashamed they were that this happened in their city . . . all white people."[28]

Thus did jazz—and the blacks who played it—help break down the barriers of segregation. For black musicians, traveling about the country often proved cruel. Surviving—finding places to eat and to sleep—added to the usual strains. Insults abounded. Small things like getting a glass of water sometimes became a chore. But over the years, jazz proved to be such an attraction that the musicians tended to obliterate what often seemed to be hard-and-fast rules. Proud of their accomplishments, Mosley, Crawford, Young, and the others agreed that the suffering was worth it. "I really believe," Horace Henderson said years later, "that the musicianship and the musicians had a lot to do with integration. . . . We demanded that. If we were good enough to entertain you, we were good enough to sit among you and talk—talk things over. And this is what gradually, I know, broke it down—helped to break down quite a bit of it. And I'm very happy now that we were instrumental—we were part of that."[29]

28. *New York Times*, February 16, 1965; Lee Young interview, November 10, 1977, Reel 4, pp. 38–41.
29. Henderson interview, Pt. 1, p. 46.

The "Long March Through the Institutions"

Movement for a Democratic Society and
the New University Conference

Irwin Unger

Historians, like other intellectuals, are influenced by the ideological climate of their formative professional years. This principle applies no less to scholars of the "Middle Period" than to others. We need only recall the prevalence of dualistic, class and economic interpretations of the Civil War during the radical 1930s and 1940s and their eclipse by pluralistic noneconomic approaches during the conservative 1950s to confirm the fact.

Today a new generation of scholars has come to the fore, armed with the apparatus of Marx, Lenin, and Antonio Gramschi to restore a dialectic perspective to the debates over the Middle Period. A few are middle-aged scholars who never ceased to voice their radical views even during the years of "consensus." Many, however, are young men and women who went to college in the early 1960s and took their graduate training in the last part of the decade or in the early 1970s.

These were times of enormous ideological stress when powerful currents of insurgency swept through the nation's campuses. In the early 1960s, many of these young men and women had been caught up in the movements for peace and nuclear disarmament, civil liberties, racial equality, and social justice. Many had belonged to Students for a Democratic Society (SDS), which was formed in 1960 as a youth extension of the social democratic League for Industrial Democracy.[1] At first hopeful about their country's capacity to reform itself, by mid-decade they felt frustrated by the slow pace of change and what they perceived as the increasing intractability of the "power structure." At this point many turned into militant radicals convinced that American "corporate capitalism," based on war and greed, must be superseded.

---

1. The best treatment of early SDS is Kirkpatrick Sale, *SDS* (New York, 1974), Chaps. 1–6.

Such radical convictions presented intellectual and personal dilemmas to young militants in the nation's graduate and professional schools. Should they stay in the university and prepare for professional careers, or should they leave and become full-time Movement workers? Either course raised the question of the role of middle-class people in the struggle for radical social change. Traditional Marxists had believed that only the proletariat could overthrow capitalism and make the revolution. Could professors, teachers, lawyers, and social workers make it instead? And if educated radicals chose the professional route, how should they function after completing their training? Should they seek primarily to undermine the conservative professional "establishments" that ultimately bolstered capitalism? Should their strategy be to use their professions as platforms to influence client and student opinion and their professional authority to alter the terms of the nation's political and ideological discourse? Should they devote their skills to the improvement of the lot of the underclass? How could they avoid being "co-opted" by the privileges and economic benefits of professional life in America? As the 1960s drew to a close, these issues became the focus of a major debate among young radicals that lasted until the early 1970s. During this five-year period, much of the discussion occurred within two professional organizations, Movement for a Democratic Society (MDS) and the New University Conference (NUC).

Both MDS and NUC were attempts to create alumni associations for first-generation New Leftists who had helped to establish SDS as the major embodiment of student insurgency and now, by the mid-1960s, with B.A.'s in hand, felt out of place in an undergraduate organization. SDS faced its first alumni crisis in 1963 when some of the "Old Guard" pioneers felt that they should move on and leave direction of the organization to younger people. This mood was responsible for ERAP, SDS's Economic Research and Action Project, which sponsored community-organizing, back-to-the-people projects in the white slums and black ghettos of a dozen northern cities during 1964 and 1965. ERAP never provided the satisfactions and the sense of useful political work for more than a handful of SDS postgrads, however, and at most served as a temporary perch for young men and women caught between school and careers.[2]

2. For ERAP, see *ibid.*, Chaps. 7–9.

Another outlet for SDS alumni was the anti–Vietnam War movement that erupted in early 1965 following President Johnson's order to bomb North Vietnam. SDS sponsored the first big antiwar rally in April, a march on Washington that drew 20,000 protestors. Discovered by the media and by the attorney general, SDS became famous overnight. Recruits poured in, pushing membership from about 2,500 in December, 1964, to 10,000 a year later.[3] For a while the antiwar-leadership role was an exhilarating experience but it created difficulties. SDS must not, its leaders felt, become a single-issue body like the Student Peace Union or the later Student Mobilization. Radicals must pursue change along a broad domestic and foreign front if they expected to transform the nation.[4]

As a stage for leadership, the civil rights movement, too, had its drawbacks. The struggle for equal rights for blacks had been a vital mobilizing force in the earliest New Left. In 1960, students on the activist campuses had picketed the local branches of the five-and-dime chain stores that had refused service to the black students during the sit-ins in Greensboro, North Carolina, and elsewhere in the South. For a while SDS had functioned largely as a white support group for the Student Non-Violent Coordinating Committee (SNCC), the organization that grew out of the sit-in demonstrations. SDS leaders like Tom Hayden and Barry Bluestone of VOICE, the University of Michigan SDS chapter, had gone to the South and been bloodied in defense of civil rights activists. But this arena, also, would not serve. By the mid-1960s it had been closed off to most SDS alumni by the advent of the black power movement within CORE and SNCC that insisted that blacks control their own organizations.[5]

3.   *Ibid.*, Chap. 11; Fred Halstead, *Out Now! A Participant's Account of the American Movement Against the Vietnam War* (New York, 1978), Chap. 2.

4.   The Student Peace Union was founded in April, 1959, by a coalition of young leftists associated with the Young People's Socialist League (YPSL) and a group of pacifists. Student Mobilization (Student Mobe) was founded at the end of 1966 by a combination of Trotskyists, Du Bois Clubbers, and SDSers. See George R. Vickers, *The Formation of the New Left: The Early Years* (Lexington, Mass., 1975), 505–55; Halstead, *Out Now!*, Chap. 9. On SDS's reluctance to lead the antiwar movement, see Irwin Unger, *The Movement: A History of the American New Left, 1959–1972* (New York, 1974), 84–88.

5.   August Meier and Elliot Rudwick, *CORE: A Study in the Civil Rights Movement, 1942–1968* (Urbana, 1975), Chap. 12; Clayborne Carson, *In Struggle: SNCC and the Black Awakening of the 1960s* (Cambridge, Mass., 1981), Chap. 13.

The alumni problem had become particularly acute by 1966. By this time the Old Guard SDS leadership felt besieged by a new class of student activists, many drawn to SDS by its sudden fame following the Washington march. The new people were often from the Midwest and the South; many were Texans. They came to be called collectively the Prairie Power people, though the name was not strictly accurate. Unlike their predecessors, often the children of Old Left parents whose radicalism was learned at home, the Prairie Power types had come to insurgency largely through a painful self-learning process that frequently involved a sharp break with their families.[6] In 1966 at SDS's Clear Lake National Convention and then the next year at its Ann Arbor meeting, the Prairie Power circle consolidated its hold on the SDS national office. The Old Guard was left stranded in the few remaining ERAP projects, SDS regional offices, and in the Radical Education Project (REP), set up in late 1965 as a haven for Al Haber, Paul Booth, Bob Ross, Barry Bluestone, and some of the more scholarly Old Guarders who believed that SDS might be kept from chaos and incoherence through better internal education.[7]

Many of the Old Guard leaders ceased to work directly with SDS but remained full-time activists in the broader Movement. Despite reservations, some attached themselves to the antiwar cause through such pacifist groups as the War Resisters League, the Committee for Non-Violent Action, or the Fellowship of Reconciliation. Some, including Carl Davidson and Tom Hayden, became regular contributors to established Left journals. A few became active in the underground press that had appeared in cities and college towns around the country after 1965.[8] Others, like Al Haber and Barbara Haber and Robb Burlage, found niches at the Institute for Policy Studies, a left-wing think tank in Washington, where they wrote papers and prepared proposals for social change under the patronage of Arthur Waskow, Marcus Raskin, and Richard Barnett.

A substantial contingent, however, cast their lot with the universities, though skeptical of what they perceived as rigidity, conformity, elitism, and, increasingly, "complicity" in the Vietnam War and self-

6. Sale, *SDS*, Chap. 15.
7. *Ibid.*, 288–89; *SDS Regional Newsletter* (Northern California), January 10, 1966.
8. *Old Mole*, in Boston, had on its staff two important SDS alumni from Swarthmore, Vernon Grizzard and Nick Egleson, both former national officers of SDS.

aggrandizing American foreign policy. As high academic achievers, they were attracted, reluctantly at times, to the intellectual life that at its best flourished in university corridors and classrooms. By 1967 or 1968, such young men as Todd Gitlin, Richard Flacks, Barry Bluestone, Bob Ross, Jesse Lemisch, and Staughton Lynd had either received Ph.D.'s or were earning them in history, sociology, economics, and other fields.

These young intellectuals were in their late twenties or older in 1967. But there was also a younger group of graduate students who had become radicalized in the course of Vietnam protest or the campus struggles that had erupted after 1964. Such young men and women, arriving in the graduate schools between, say, 1965 and 1968, encountered networks of older senior professors, most trained in the 1940s and 1950s. These seemed to the young dissenters to constitute "establishments" within the academic fields, cohesive oligarchies that controlled the academic marketplace and imposed on the disciplines implicitly conservative political and intellectual positions. By 1967 or 1968, the young militants were ready to take them on.

Although time and experience created a clientele for an adult academic Left organization, Neo-Marxism provided an appropriate ideology. From the outset SDS, and the student movement generally, had searched for an "agent of social change." To orthodox Marxists, of course, the revolutionary class had been the oppressed proletariat, and the "labor metaphysic" had informed the thinking of American Marxists of all varieties, Socialist, Trotskyist or Communist, before World War II.[9]

By the late 1950s the faith of Left intellectuals in the anticapitalist—or even the reformist—potential of the traditional working class had faded. Postwar prosperity had produced a degree of complacency among working people and their leaders that belied the hopes radical intellectuals had earlier reposed in them. The trade unions had lost whatever Left idealism they had possessed, the radicals believed, and had become solely instruments for extracting wages and hours benefits from management, which promptly passed the costs on to consumers, themselves often members of the working

9.   See C. Wright Mills, "Letter to the New Left," *New Left Review* (September-October, 1960).

class. Equally disillusioning, by the end of the first postwar decade the trade union leadership, without challenge from the rank and file, had become, many radicals felt, prime supporters of anticommunism and the cold war consensus that undergirded American foreign policy.[10]

The first of the radical intellectuals to abandon the traditional proletariat as hopelessly inert was C. Wright Mills, the maverick Columbia sociologist. As he looked around him in the late 1950s, Mills saw a political wasteland of "smug conservatives, tired liberals, and disillusioned radicals." The only hope as "a possible, immediate, radical agency of change" was the "young intelligentsia." Mills's ideas were borrowed by the New Left and incorporated into SDS's 1962 Port Huron Statement. Critical of organized labor as steeped in "bureaucracy, materialism [and] business ethics," its "social idealism waning," Port Huron declared that universities would be the leading edge of a Left revival. From the nation's "schools and colleges [a] militant left might awaken its allies and by beginning the process toward peace, civil rights and labor struggles reinsert theory and idealism where too often reign confusion and political barter." The "power of students and faculty united is not only potential; it had shown its actuality in the South, in the reform movements of the North." ERAP temporarily eclipsed the Port Huron vision but it did not represent a revival of faith in the proletariat. Rather, it was an attempt to find an "agent" in the underclass or the "lumpenproletariat."[11]

By 1966, with ERAP clearly a dead end, SDS theorists felt obliged to reconsider the agents problem once more. By this time the Free Speech movement at Berkeley, by mobilizing thousands of students against a paternalistic administration and compelling it to yield on campus-based political advocacy and recruiting, had revealed how powerful a force student revolt could be. By now, too, SDS and the student Left had broken with the liberals and become a frankly anticapitalist organization, though SDSers continued to use Aesopian language to describe their goals. But uncertainty over the political role and potential of students remained. As Greg Calvert, a Prairie

10.   Ronald Radosh, *American Labor and United States Foreign Policy* (New York, 1969), 304ff.
11.   Mills, "Letter to the New Left"; *Port Huron Statement* (Pamphlet in Tamiment Library, New York University).

Power leader, would later note, Port Huron notwithstanding, most SDSers were afflicted with anti-elitist, middle-class guilt and a propensity to romanticize the working class. This potent combination made it difficult for them to be fully comfortable with themselves as the chief vehicle for revolution.[12] At this point the SDS intellectuals encountered a model of social change assembled out of Marxist material by a group of post–World War II French thinkers that proved a godsend.

The French Neo-Marxists, like their counterparts all over the capitalist "First World," were confronted with the problem of the growing prosperity and declining numbers and militant class consciousness of the industrial proletariat. By the mid twentieth century in the "advanced capitalist" world, the traditional Marxist laws of "increasing misery" and accelerating class struggle seemed to have been repealed. But not only was the proletariat becoming complacent, everywhere in the advanced countries the proportion of factory workers, miners, and laborers in the work force was declining while that of the brainworkers was increasing. If revolution depended on the factory workers and miners, the revolution was in trouble. Could it be based on the new group? These technicians, bureaucrats, teachers, clerical and sales people were relatively well paid and well treated. How could they be expected to oppose the system? Had capitalism actually succeeded in canceling the social dialectic and rescuing itself from inevitable and deserved destruction?

At about this point the French thinkers discovered the Paris Economic and Philosophical Manuscripts, written by Marx as a young man. In this work (1844), the young university graduate was in a softer, more humane mood than he would be later. Marx deplored capitalism, not solely for its economic oppression of the workers, but also because it produced "alienation." Marx would later restrict use of the term *alienation* to the divorce of the worker from his product. But here it also had its present psychological and sociological meaning: the absence of strong ties among human beings and the personal and social pathologies that resulted therefrom. Capitalism not only separated man from his product, but man from his fellow man.[13]

12. Greg Calvert's remarks at the 1977 SDS "Reunion" at Port Huron (In the personal papers of Helen Garvy, Santa Cruz, Calif.).
13. Richard Schacht, *Alienation* (Garden City, N.Y., 1970), 65–111.

Alienation was a useful concept out of which to construct a Neo-Marxist theory suited to modern advanced capitalist reality. The new, and growing, armies of technicians, bureaucrats, teachers, and white collar workers were a New Working Class. Traditional Marxists considered them capitalist lackeys. The Neo-Marxists disagreed. True, they were not an impoverished proletariat, but they were alienated, estranged from their work, and without a sense of connection with fellow workers and other members of society. Capitalism sought to cover its social inadequacies by a barrage of advertising and a flood of shoddy consumer goods. Consumerism for a time could dazzle the public, but it ultimately could not conceal the basic emptiness and inhumanity of the system. Nor could it disguise the fact that under capitalism the New Workers had to subordinate their skills to the profit motive. Being unable to use those skills in the most socially beneficial way, they could expect little satisfaction in their work. These new discontents were sufficient to fuel a class-conscious insurgency. In the end the New Workers would find capitalism incompatible with their needs and desires and become a new revolutionary class.[14]

However strained, however off the mark in retrospect, the New Working Class analysis was eagerly seized on by a portion of the New Left as an answer to its dilemmas. The process of absorption was piecemeal, beginning at the SDS Clear Lake convention in August, 1966. There, Carl Davidson, a former philosophy graduate student at Penn State, attacked the universities for their role as servants of the "corporate liberal" society. They provided, he charged, the trained and educated personnel vital to that society. In effect, though he did not use the term, universities created the New Working Class, and if they could be forced, through student protest, to abandon their channeling and socializing functions, the corporate liberal society could be derailed from its evil course. What, he asked pointedly, if "the military found itself without ROTC students; the CIA found itself without recruits; paternalistic welfare departments found themselves without social workers; and the Democratic Party found itself without young liberal apologists and campus workers?"[15]

14. Arthur Hirsh, *The French New Left: An Intellectual History from Sartre to Gorz* (Boston, 1981), 71ff.
15. Carl Davidson, "Toward a Student Syndicalist Movement: Or University Reform Revisited," in SDS Papers, Microfilm, Reel 36.

Davidson's position paper, "Toward a Student Syndicalist Movement," provided the rationale for the student power movement that
would soon sweep through the campuses and at times make FSM at
Berkeley seem a high-spirited campus pep rally. Davidson's targets
were the programs on campus that produced the "servants of power":
war research, CIA recruiting, the paternalistic approach of social
work departments to welfare clients. His formula did not extend beyond the campus gates. But soon after, Martin Oppenheimer, a young
sociology instructor at Vassar in a talk to the Vassar SDS on Davidson's
syndicalism paper, showed how student power could affect the larger
society.

The student Left, Oppenheimer declared, must regard the university environment as a school for "professional cadres who [would]
be able to act in a revolutionary way in the milieus in which they
would find themselves after graduation." SDS must "permeate American social institutions with organizers using the campus as recruiting
and training ground." The graduate schools, he noted, were especially
important. It was there that young people were trained as faculty for
other colleges and it was their graduates who, through professional
associations, religious bodies, unions, and community organizations,
would help to influence attitudes and create an insurgent consciousness. In effect, radicals must treat the universities as crucibles for
creating a revolutionary professional class that would ultimately gain
access to influence and power. The process that Oppenheimer was
describing would soon be labeled by Rudi Dutschke, a German student radical, as the "long march through the institutions."[16]

The New Working Class analysis in fully developed form was introduced to SDS through two Middle Period SDS leaders, Calvert and
Robert Gottlieb. Both young men had spent time in France and had
been in contact with the French Left, Calvert pursuing research as a
graduate student at Cornell in French history, and Gottlieb as a visitor
to France before beginning college at Reed in Portland. Gottlieb, a
classic "red diaper baby," whose father had been a Communist party
official, had been especially influenced by the Situationists, a Neo-
Marxist group that believed that capitalism's most effective weapon

16. Martin Oppenheimer, "Some Comments on a 'Student Syndicalist Movement,'"
New Left Notes, October 14, 1966.

was its power to create through "consumerism" and advertising a revolution-dampening "spectacle," a false consciousness, among the masses.[17]

In 1965, Gottlieb came to New York to do graduate work at the New School and devote his political energies to the New York at-large SDS chapter. There, in collaboration with two other New School graduate students, Dave Gilbert and Jerry Tenney, he wrote "Toward a Theory of Social Change," a paper that brought together all the strands in the new analysis. The essay first appeared in abbreviated form in SDS's *New Left Notes* in February, 1967, and then, soon after, was presented in a much fuller version to an REP-sponsored conference at Princeton. Written in New York by New Yorkers, it came to be jocularly called the Port Authority Statement.

In their paper, Gottlieb and his colleagues described the growing social importance of students as the role of scientific knowledge and technical innovation expanded at a logarithmic rate. Professional and technical workers in training, students constituted "the structurally relevant and necessary components of the productive processes of modern American capitalism." As members of the New Working Class, they would not be content. Technology under capitalism led to a growing waste and a sense among the New Workers that they could not control its use. This impotence would give them "an immediate stake in radical social change." The authors warned of the possibility of the New Workers being "co-opted" by, instead of alienated from, the system around them; the new alienation, they noted, might only produce reformism. But they ended their analysis on a note of hope. The discontents of the New Workers, if joined with those of the underclass, contained "the seeds of a total revolutionary praxis with the potential for transforming American society from top to bottom."[18]

At the Princeton conference, Calvert, current SDS national secretary, fit the New Working Class into the program of the student Left. True radicalism, he said, meant struggling for one's own liberation; it was the liberals who wanted to free someone else. This raised the

17. Interview with Greg Calvert, November, 1980, in Austin; interview with Robert Gottlieb, February, 1981, in New York. On the Situationists, see Hirsh, *The French New Left*, 144–46.

18. The short version of this paper will be found in *New Left Notes*, February 13, 1967.

question whether students could be radical since on the face of it they were a privileged group. But now Gottlieb and his associates, he stated, had provided the answer. Students were not members of the exploiter bourgeoisie in the classic Marxist sense. They belonged to a new proletariat. This view was not only valid; it was necessary. If the student Left could not find "a constituency . . . an agent of social transformation, [a] revolutionary class" at home, then SDS's only hope lay "with external agencies, with revolutionary development in the Third World."[19]

The New Working Class theory held an immense appeal for many New Left intellectuals. It offered hope for radical change in a society that had produced material abundance and seemed capable of spreading at least some of it even to the blue collar workers. It also explained the puzzling fact that they themselves, the children of the privileged, were the most radical part of society. Material abundance and middle-class privilege were not enough; alienation remained. Capitalism, for all its success as a wealth-producing machine, created hollow men and women without satisfaction in their work, without connections to some larger community. Such dissatisfactions could fuel a revolution. Besides providing answers to a puzzling set of social problems, the New Working Class analysis was convenient. ERAP had shown how difficult it was to "organize" the poor when the organizers were graduates of Michigan, Chicago, Harvard, and Swarthmore. It was much easier to cultivate the congenial campus environs than the ghettos and slums of Chicago, Cleveland, and Newark. Some SDSers saw the self-serving quality of the analysis and would have nothing to do with it. Yet for a while it would powerfully affect the thinking of the young men and women seeking a way to combine careers with radical politics.

Armed with a new theory, eager to continue radical vocations into adult professional lives, and certain that ever-expanding economic growth permitted taking career risks, many young adult radicals began to consider forming radical professional bodies. The impulse culminated in a major conference held at Ann Arbor in July, 1967, under REP auspices and dedicated to "radicals in the profes-

19. "In White America: Radical Consciousness and Social Change," *National Guardian*, March 25, 1967, pp. 3–4.

sions." Two hundred fifty people, mostly schoolteachers, health professionals, academics, lawyers, social workers, city planners, and journalists, came for a round of speeches, workshops, and plenary sessions. Many delegates were senior campus activitists; a larger contingent included young adult radicals already plying their professions. All were deeply concerned about how to function as radicals in the workaday world.[20]

Many participants were also undergoing personal crises. Committed to changing the world, they also had jobs to do, families to support, and personal ambitions to fulfill. As Al Haber and Barbara Haber would write, people in this position faced three possible choices: they could abandon traditional careers and become full-time Movement workers; they could become, or remain, conventional professionals and divert their political concerns into after-hours and weekend work; or they could try to combine careers with radical commitment in some sort of coherent way. Each choice, they declared, had its drawbacks and it was not clear which was the best way.[21]

Seventeen papers were presented at the conference, most of them accounts of the problems faced by radicals on the job or descriptions of recently formed radical professional "caucuses." But two were frank confessions of professional ambivalence that anticipated the later flight of many young radicals from career commitments. Both authors were dubious about the political scope available for professional workers. The social work profession was hopelessly subservient to society's needs to manipulate the poor, declared Ed Spannaus, a New York City social worker trained at Columbia University. It was a form of social control, not humanitarianism. "If you can afford to be a full time revolutionary, then fight for socialism elsewhere." Ken Cloke, a former Berkeley radical, now an executive of the left-wing National Lawyers Guild, denounced American law as "the rationalization of force, coercion, and murder, and the means by which obedience is exacted" from the masses. The radical lawyers could, by "stalling for time . . . using the press, treating the courtroom as a

20. "Radicals in the Professions Conference: People Who Attended," in Michael Davis Papers, State Historical Society of Wisconsin, Madison.
21. Al Haber and Barbara Haber, *Getting By with a Little Help from Our Friends* (REP pamphlet in Tamiment Library, NYU).

classroom . . . have an effect on the ability of those within the movement to continue their political work." But this role at best would be
brief. Harsh repression would soon occur, he predicted, and the law
would cease to be a fig leaf for capitalist America.[22]

The most interesting document inspired by the radicals at the
conference was a summary and overview written afterward by the
Habers, *Getting By with a Little Help from Our Friends*. The Habers
pleaded for a reasonable definition of what constituted a proper radical life and for a less critical attitude toward professional careers.
Some people in the Movement believed revolution imminent. If so,
this made professional careers irrelevant. Radicals should be out on
the barricades, not taking Ph.D.'s or law degrees. The Habers preferred, however, a model of social change that assumed that revolution was a long way off and likely to come in small increments. In this
case, radical professionals would have an important role. They would
have to expect hard, painstaking work, leading clients and students
beyond their subjective experience of discontent toward a radical
analysis and into struggles for "root change." The Habers were
clearly not among the firebrands of the revolutionary Left. But even
they rejected the conventional professional ethic. Careers must be
secondary to Movement work. Radicals, they wrote, must regard
their professional callings, their intellectual disciplines, as means to
ends, not ends in themselves. Radical professionals must learn to
share their money and must always use their influence to support
militant "action programs" and the radical positions within their
professional group in all evolving social conflicts. They must be willing to jeopardize their careers for the Movement, if necessary. They
could *not* put "the code of ethics and responsibility of their professions" before the cause. This meant, for example, that they "should
have no 'ethical' scruples about providing 'cover' to movement people,
using politics as a criterion in giving recommendations, references,
jobs." They would make "professional resources such as equipment,
supplies, travel funds, expense accounts, etc. available to movement
people under the guise of professional expense." They would "not respect the confidentiality of documents, meetings, privileged information, etc., if their contents would be valuable to the movement." This

22. Ed Spannaus, *Radicals in Social Work*, and Ken Cloke, *Law and the Radical
Lawyer* (REP pamphlets in Tamiment Library, NYU).

course, they admitted, presented "moral problems," but they believed that conscience could be assuaged if radical professionals were honest about their "politics and values."[23]

In the end, the Radicals in the Professions Conference produced rather meager results. Participants set up a tithing system to provide support for radical colleagues who needed funds for Movement work and established a newsletter with a staff at Ann Arbor to provide a communications network for radical professionals around the country. RIP did useful work as an educational center, but it never became a membership group with dues and meetings, chapters, and elected officers.[24]

Few of those associated with the adult radical organizing movement were content with such an unsubstantial embodiment of the new perspective and even before the Ann Arbor conference several activists in New York City, including Spannaus, Gottlieb, Ted Gold, Brian Glick, Naomi Jaffe, and a young writer, Marge Piercy, had begun to organize chapters of a new group, Movement for a Democratic Society, modeled after SDS.

At first the theoretical core of the MDS group was the New Working Class analysis with a particularly strong emphasis, through Gottlieb's inspiration, on the coercion and manipulation endemic to a capitalist consumer-oriented society. Although there would be a few weak MDS groups in Buffalo, Rochester, Austin, Lawrence, Kansas, and Los Angeles, MDS put down substantial roots only in New York City. In New York, MDS groups were mostly formed around specific professional interests, with chapters composed of teachers (Teachers for a Democratic Society), social workers (Caseworkers for a Democratic Society), city planners (The Urban Underground), and computer programmers (Meta Information Applications and Computer MDS). In addition, however, there were individual at-large MDS memberships and clusters of MDS people investigating the New York City courts and the corporate structure of Consolidated Edison and agitating for day-care centers for working mothers. Before its demise, MDS organizers would also create various "affinity groups" of art-

---

23. Haber and Haber, *Getting By*.
24. Mike Goldfield, "Report on the Conference" (Mimeograph in Davis Papers). REP survived until the end of 1969; or at least the *Newsletter* did, though under a different name.

ists, lawyers, publishing people, and health-care technicians and professionals.[25]

By late 1968, New York MDS had become a battleground between the New Working Class proponents around Gottlieb and a more militant group, primarily within Teachers for a Democratic Society, who saw themselves, in Calvert's terms, as cadres for someone else's revolution, a position that anticipated the Weatherman view that would tear SDS apart in the summer of 1969. The leaders of TDS, as teachers in the inner city schools, were deeply influenced by the rage and rebelliousness that gripped the black ghettos following the murder of Martin Luther King in April, 1968. Sharing the black community's militancy, they were outraged by the stand that the United Federation of Teachers, the city teachers' union, had taken against community school control in New York. The teachers' position in the Ocean Hill–Brownsville dispute seemed self-protective and confirmed the militant view that when the chips were down, the New Working Class was incapable of a truly radical consciousness.[26]

By early 1969, a group within TDS, including Ted Gold, who would die a year later in the explosion at a Greenwich Village townhouse, had caught the apocalyptic fever that was sweeping through the ghettos and had penetrated parts of the white Left. The city's schools, already wracked by mindless violence and disorder, a TDS manifesto concluded, were about to erupt in a major rebellion of the black, Hispanic, and other Third World students. TDS must do more than excuse the rebellions; it must "help them." Given the provocation by the oppressive society, the impending uprising would be entirely justified. It was the duty of the "more privileged (though still oppressed)," that is, the teachers, to support the revolt of the truly oppressed. TDS should not romanticize the uprisings when they came. They would probably have little overt political content and little stay-

25.   Dave Gilbert, Bob Gottlieb, and Susan Sutheim, "Consumption: Domestic Capitalism," in Massimo Teodori (ed.), *The New Left: A Documentary History* (Indianapolis, 1969), 425–37; Bob Gottlieb and Marge Piercy, "Beginning to Begin to Begin: Movement for a Democratic Society," *Radicals in the Professions Newsletter*, March, 1968; *MDS Newsletter*, November, 1968.

26.   Interview with Robert Gottlieb, February, 1981. On the Ocean Hill–Brownsville issue, see Dianne Ravitch, *The Great School Wars: New York City, 1805–1973* (New York, 1974), 312–78; Mike Josefowicz and Ted Gold, *Co-Option City, or Ford Has a Better Idea* (Pamphlet in Tamiment Library, NYU).

ing power. But the teachers could inject political content into them. The TDS manifesto concluded with a list of demands that the rebels could make of the city: no suspensions or expulsions from school for even the most disruptive students, "open admissions" of all Third World students into the city's public colleges, and an end of school "tracking systems" that were at heart racist schemes to hold minorities back.[27]

The extremism of the TDS militants shocked many MDSers. Gottlieb would later observe that they were prescribing nothing less than the destruction of the New York City schools in the name of revolution. The moderates denounced the TDS leaders for their nihilism and for placing all their faith in the revolutionary potential of Third World minorities. Accepting Calvert's formula, they declared, "We reject the idea of merely organizing people around someone else's revolution." Yet even the moderates had lost some of their faith in the revolutionary potential of the middle class. Whites could not be ignored when the great overthrow came, and revolutionaries must not disregard the spiritual discontents that came with relative affluence as a factor in revolt. But by the spring of 1969, even the Gottlieb faction admitted that the underclass would lead the rebellion with the New Workers at best as allies.[28]

MDS did not long survive the breakup of SDS in the summer of 1969. But by this time the New University Conference had been organized to take up the slack among the largest contingent of politicized professionals, the nation's university teachers and teacher-apprentices. The founders of NUC were groups of younger faculty and graduate students mostly from Chicago, New York, and Ann Arbor, and predominantly in the humanities and social sciences. The Chicago circle was led by Richard Flacks, a University of Chicago sociology instructor and an early SDS leader, and by several other young Chicago area faculty including Naomi Weisstein, an experimental psychologist at Loyola; Jesse Lemisch, a historian at Roosevelt; Marlene Dixon, another University of Chicago sociologist; Heather Tobis Booth, a radical feminist recently married to former SDS National Secretary Paul Booth; and Richard Rothstein, an SDS alumnus for-

27. "Spring," *Something Else!* (May, 1969).
28. Interview with Robert Gottlieb, February, 1981; *Political and Organizing Principles for MDS* (Pamphlet in Tamiment Library, NYU).

merly active in JOIN, the Chicago ERAP project. Also involved were several Chicago area graduate students: Sandra Brown and Mel Rothenberg and Marcia Rothenberg. The Ann Arbor group included SDS veteran Bob Ross of REP; the New York contingent was led by John McDermott, editor of the antiwar *Viet Report* and sometime philosophy instructor at Long Island University; Bart Myers, a psychologist at Brooklyn College; and Bertell Ollman, a political scientist at NYU. Affiliated loosely with the organizers in their founding effort was a small group of senior academics—the sociologist Norman Birnbaum of the New School; Louis Kampf of MIT's English Department; his MIT colleague, the linguistics expert Noam Chomsky; and Howard Zinn, the radical historian at Boston University. These senior men signed the initiating conference "call" and several attended the founding conference at the University of Chicago in March, 1968.[29]

Although they were there to consider a Left faculty organization, many of the 350 participants at Chicago remained uncertain about the role of radicals in academic life. They had invested heavily of time, money, and energy in academic careers. Many enjoyed the life of the mind; they were passionate about history, literature, sociology; they valued security and long vacations. People such as these wanted to believe that it was possible to be a professor and an effective agent of social change at the same time. On the other side were those who doubted that in the last analysis colleges and academic careers were compatible with revolution. Could being a college professor be anything but a cowardly evasion? By 1968 a sizable portion of the New Left had come to see American society as a depraved system, every part of which, including higher education, was deeply implicated in the exploitations, oppressions, and aggressions of the American "warfare state." And these offenses did not have to be deduced from Marxist theory, they noted. Recent revelations at the University of Pennsylvania, Michigan State, and elsewhere had shown that American colleges were closely tied to the Pentagon and partners in the "imperialist" ventures of the United States in Vietnam.[30]

29. Norman Birnbaum, "New University Conference: The Dilemmas of Resistance," *Nation*, April 22, 1968, pp. 535–36; *NUC Newsletter*, May 24, 1968; interview with Bertell Ollman, December, 1983, in New York.
30. New York *Times*, August 12, 1966; Warren Hinckle, "The University on the Make," *Ramparts*, April, 1966.

The two keynote speakers at the conference's opening session, Flacks and Staughton Lynd, exemplified these opposing views. Lynd, a peace activist, a Columbia Ph.D. in history, and a former instructor at Spelman College and Yale, denied the possibility of a full-time academic career for a dedicated radical. A recent victim of bruising tenure and appointment battles at Yale and Chicago State College, he had given up on universities. Where radicals were not actually excluded from universities by their politics, they were often co-opted by them. "Whatever our social origins," he noted, "the university is a marvelously effective instrument for making us middle-class men." Besides, thinking radical and teaching radical were no longer enough. Movement people concluded that universities might be crucibles for forging radicals who would then disperse and transform society. But the radical faculty who helped create radical students would remain behind, examples to their students, not of revolutionaries, but of timid souls who talked revolution but failed to practice it. Lynd was an intellectual and prized ideas. But he believed they came from experience not cogitation. Radical intellectuals must remain in close touch with the real world outside the academy. At most they might do part-time teaching, without the security of tenure. The question of income would have to be solved year by year. "Face the problem of livelihood together with your friends in the Movement, recognize that at times you may support them, at others they you, and that you can all take greater risks because of this assurance."[31]

Flacks, a conference organizer and New Working Class proponent, was far more hopeful. The industrial working class had disappointed the Left's expectations. On the other hand, "despite itself, the university and the educated middle class have been a major source for whatever alternatives to capitalist values have persisted in this society." Although universities were key institutions in the capitalist system, ever since Berkeley it had become clear that they remained capable of subversion. Whether they would continue to be insurgent centers would depend on whether the new academic radicals remained or abandoned them for full-time radical organizing in the community. Flacks told his audience that the purpose of the conference was to start radical intellectuals on the quest for their proper

31. *NUC Newsletter*, May 24, 1968.

historical role. This must be nothing less than "to turn the universities into a major arena of struggle against imperialism, against militarism, against capitalist culture and ideology, and for the creation of an alternative culture and ideology, and a new class to carry that alternative into the rest of society."[32]

Neither of the keynote speakers had addressed the problem of the intellectual enterprise itself. Both had merely presented alternative views of how to make the revolution. But some participants among the 350 were concerned about "doing" radical history, radical sociology, or radical anthropology. Their spokesman was Jesse Lemisch, who responded in writing to their neglect after the conference adjourned. In a brief piece in the *NUC Newsletter*, Lemisch defended radical scholarship as valuable to the Movement. Radicals required information; they needed to know how things worked and how they came to be. Lynd had questioned whether scholarship had contributed to activism and social change; for himself, Lemisch was more impressed with the question someone else had pointedly asked: what had *activism* contributed to social change? It was ultimately better, he concluded, "to master the world through reason," than to slash professors' tires.[33]

The three days of NUC meetings on the "university and society," "research and publication," the "wider movement," and the "structure of the professions" revealed a generation gap. Many of the graduate students took the same critical position as Lynd and gleefully reproached the older, professorial types for their careerism and timidity. Their skepticism of the academic enterprise was incorporated into a resolution, narrowly defeated, declaring that only students could change the university, that nothing could be expected from the faculty. However divided they were on the role of faculty and the university in the movement for change, the more moderate voices at the conference prevailed. The delegates voted to create the New University Conference and adopted a provisional charter laying out a structure and a tentative program. They also established a newsletter and selected a thirty-five-person group as an interim executive committee

32. *Ibid.*
33. Jesse Lemisch, "Who Will Write a Left History of Art While We Are All Putting Our Balls on the Line?" *NUC Newsletter*, May 24, 1968.

charged with designing a permanent organization and a program for NUC at future meetings.[34]

Over the next few months the provisional NUC executive committee met a number of times and took several important actions. It established a national office at Chicago with an interim staff headed by Bob Ross of REP, voted to sponsor radical caucuses within the academic professional associations, authorized black and women's caucuses within NUC itself, planned a series of regional conferences to encourage local chapter organizing, established a speakers' bureau, and set a date for a formal national convention in 1969 to write a permanent constitution and devise a permanent structure for NUC. By the time of the June meeting, NUC, however provisional, claimed 4 functioning local chapters with 350 members and anticipated another 11 to begin operation when the fall academic semester opened.[35]

The first official NUC national convention at Iowa City in June, 1969, made it clear that the new organization was afflicted with all the ills of SDS and several more besides. The convention preliminaries, like most of SDS's, were carelessly handled. Papers and resolutions that should have been submitted to the *Newsletter* in advance, so that delegates and members could prepare for discussion and debate, were never written or written too late to be used. This slowed business so much at Iowa City that a large part of the agenda had to be jettisoned. The convention also exhibited all the factionalism and ideological confusion that had beset SDS and was, almost at that very moment, tearing it apart. The national office leaders of NUC were radicals who would be proud when they succeeded in getting NUC to call itself "socialist" in the new constitution's preamble. NUC attracted liberals and welcomed them, but this was a matter of expediency. We must "keep reaching, involving, and holding new people," wrote Barbara Kessel, an NUC office worker at Chicago headquarters. But we "must keep these involved people moving lefter." To help this radicalizing process along, in September, 1969, NUC would es-

34. Birnbaum, "New University Conference," 537; *NUC Newsletter*, May 24, 1968.

35. Howard Ehrlich, "Opening Remarks to the New University Conference Organizing Committee, September 19, 1968," in National Committee and Conventions File, NUC Papers, State Historical Society of Wisconsin; Bob Ross, "New University Conference: National Director's Report," *Radicals in the Professions Newsletter*, September, 1968.

tablish an internal education committee equipped with Marxist-oriented pamphlets and reading lists for the membership, and the following year it would run a summer training camp to raise the political consciousness of NUC organizers.[36]

NUC radicalism came in several conflicting varieties, however. At Iowa City, there were Progressive Laborites, American Maoists who supported Chinese Communist positions; unreconstructed Stalinists of the Communist party; Young Socialist Alliance and Socialist Worker party followers of Trotsky; and Independent Socialists, descendants of the Schactmanite Third Camp Socialists of the 1950s. Each was Old Left; all were skeptical of New Working Class theories. The Stalinists, Maoists, and Trotskyists also believed that a vanguard party composed of dedicated and ideologically pure revolutionaries was indispensable to fundamental social transformation. All strove to bend NUC to their own ideological ends or to recruit new members from its ranks. A majority of the NUC leadership, however, though Marxists who analyzed American society in class terms and saw American foreign policy as the imperialist thrust of late capitalism, hoped to establish a broad, nonspecific, umbrella-type organization for radicals of all kinds and fought the attempt of the "sects" to impose their ideology on the organization. Most of the core leaders were adherents of the New Working Class analysis, though increasingly on the defensive as the political atmosphere became ever more feverish and apocalyptic. At Iowa City the leaders beat back the sectarians, but the ideological squabbling contributed to the postconvention sense of letdown among NUC's mainstream.[37]

Another divisive issue that first flared up at Iowa City was feminism. By 1969, feminism had become a powerful force within the Left, both student and adult. Formed after the appearance of the new

36.   Richard Rothstein, "The Next Convention," *NUC Newsletter*, August 15, 1969; Barbara Kessel to Neal and Betty Resnikoff, January 28, 1970, Modern Language Association File; Resolution on Internal Education Submitted to the National Committee, Meetings and Conventions File; Paul Lauter and Florence Howe to Victor Rabinowitz, April 28, 1970, Internal Education File, all in NUC Papers.

37.   For an example of Marxist analysis, Ruth [Misheloff] to Richard Rothstein, October 7, 1969, in Internal Education File, NUC Papers; Lucy Gadlin, "Convention Summary," *NUC Newsletter*, August 15, 1969; Bob Sayre to Bob [Ross], June 18, 1969, in Correspondence File, NUC Papers.

radical feminism, with no history of male domination, NUC was particularly sensitive to feminist issues and demands. Several of its founders—Naomi Weisstein, Heather Tobis Booth, Marlene Dixon, for example—were mature, articulate, professional women who had already proved their ability to take on the male world. At Iowa City, women represented about a third of the delegates and they used their numbers and skills to create a strong women's caucus and mandate that all future NUC executive bodies be made up half of women.[38]

Yet this amicable solution disguised a serious gender rift. On its face NUC was an exemplary body from a feminist perspective, regularly endorsing day-care facilities at universities, rushing to condemn academic sex discrimination, and issuing regular denunciations of male chauvinism in the society at large. Yet behind the scenes all was not so collegial. NUC women often found their male colleagues classic chauvinists. At one point in 1971, one woman NUCer, Fairinda West, called John McDermott a "PIG" for his "bad politics" on the women's question. McDermott, she said, was a hypocrite. He perceived the Women's Caucus "as a body not to be offended publicly but to be sneered at privately." Male NUCers, in turn, often saw feminism as a disruptive force within the organization. The radical feminists, replacing class exploitation with sexual oppression as the critical social evil, added still another voice to the ideological Babel. Bob Ross remembered from the perspective of 1980 that the Women's Caucus had been a serious impediment to NUC's effectiveness. It had fragmented NUC leadership by focusing attention on male elitism. It had also made every issue a test of sexism. "The women's question was absolutely necessary and inevitable," he declared. Nevertheless, "you literally couldn't have a meeting of NUC without turning it into a hassle about man-woman relations." Even more serious, perhaps, was the diversion of women NUCers' energies into feminism. Toward the end of NUC's brief life, Barbara Andrew reported that several chapters had disaffiliated because their women members had decided to devote all their time to the women's movement.[39]

38. Sara Evans, *Personal Politics: The Roots of Women's Liberation in the Civil Rights Movement and the New Left* (New York, 1979); Gadlin, "Convention Summary."
39. Rinda [West] to Ellen [?], May 17, 1971, in NUC Papers; Bret Eynon's interview with Bob Ross, December, 1980, in Dorcester, Mass. Reports from the National Com-

Despite the poor "prep" work and the internal friction, the 1969 Iowa City convention succeeded in writing a constitution for the new organization. But even this was a dubious accomplishment, for the structure was complicated. The National Committee would meet four times a year to consider NUC business and to name the national officers and choose the office staff at Chicago. The National Committee would be made up of the Executive Committee, the seven men and seven women elected at the annual national conventions, plus two delegates from each NUC local chapter. The Executive Committee would have the power to make decisions between the four-times-a-year meetings of the National Committee. Further, the convention authorized regional NUC bodies with their own staffs. The complexity of this apparatus was not accidental. Like SDS, NUC was plagued by a phobia against hierarchy and the exercise of power, and the net effect was an unwieldy structure, incapable of providing direction. Bob Ross blamed not only feminism for the failure of NUC but also the "anti-elitism, quasi-anarchism" of the NUC membership.[40]

Yet however flawed and divided, NUC would serve several useful functions for Left academics. During its first year or two, its job file, collected through the network of Left faculty around the country, in the spirit of the Habers' *Getting By with a Little Help from Our Friends* helped to place unemployed radical faculty in college departments. NUC also defended radical faculty fired from colleges or denied tenure. During 1968, though still provisional, it took up the cudgels for Steve Shapiro, an assistant professor of English at the University of California at Irvine, and Marlene Dixon, a junior member of the University of Chicago sociology faculty, both threatened by their institutions with dismissal. Both disliked their colleagues; neither wanted to conform to traditional scholarly requirements, though by all reports, they were effective and popular teachers. Thereafter it regularly urged *NUC Newsletter* readers to rally 'round radical colleagues who, in the editor's view, had fallen victim to conservative senior faculty and repressive administrators.[41]

---

mittee Meeting in Chicago, 1972, in National Committee Meetings and Conventions File, NUC Papers.

40. *NUC Newsletter*, August 15, 1969; Eynon's interview with Bob Ross, December, 1980.

41. Mike Ducey, NUC Job File and NUC "Defense" Correspondence File, in NUC Pa-

Within weeks of its Chicago founding convention, NUC had pledged to organize radical caucuses within the major academic disciplines. Its actual achievements here were modest, however, perhaps in part because NUC was more radical than most of the insurgent professionals within the academic associations. In the end most of the caucuses were independent creations owing little to NUC.

The radical caucus movement had appeared before NUC itself, and indeed NUC was more often the beneficiary than the instigator of the impulse among radical scholars to challenge the academic "establishments" and their "hegemonic" ideologies. At every major association convention from 1969 to 1972, an NUC information and literature table was ensconced in some prominent site, often near the job file, where interested faculty and graduate students could buy NUC and radical caucus buttons and pamphlets and sign membership cards. NUC often returned from these conventions with a bundle of cash and a promising list of new members.

But in two instances, the American Historical Association and the Modern Language Association, the NUC contribution was that of actual midwife to radical caucuses. NUC planned and helped mount the radical caucus campaign at the MLA meeting in New York in December, 1968, where NUCer Louis Kampf was elected second vice-president for the following year with a guarantee of becoming association president the year after that. In 1969, Arthur Waskow of the Washington-based Institute for Policy Studies and other NUC historians coordinated the radical caucus drive at the AHA Christmas meeting at the nation's capital. There, the Left historians failed to get Staughton Lynd elected president over the official nominee Robert

---

pers. Shapiro had told one of his colleagues at a public debate that it was impossible to teach literature because genuine literary values were "mocked by the life style of the professor, the grading system, and the general atomization of society." He submitted to his department as evidence of scholarly endeavor four chapters of a critical work that insisted that the only hope for humanity was the "revolutionary transformation of the capitalist world and the re-creation of exploratory communities." Marlene Dixon had not published anything, though she claimed that she had not given up on scholarship. She was also at war with the sociology "establishment" which she said had failed to understand "anything at all about the thrust of history in the 20th c." She had, she admitted, "cut herself off from the mainstream of sociology and divorced [herself] from the sociology produced at this university," that is, Chicago. See *NUC Newsletter*, January, 1969.

Palmer of Princeton, and were defeated when they proposed a radical "counter constitution" for the AHA. Shortly after the meeting, however, they rallied sufficiently to create a permanent radical caucus group affiliated with NUC that in later years would help shake up the association and alter practices the Left considered elitist or repressive.[42]

But NUC not only functioned to advance faculty interests; it also sought to shield student insurgents from the wrath of college administrators and public authorities. In 1969, NUC prepared a statement on the student rebellion that called on radical faculty to rally behind students protesting "racism, imperialism, lack of democratic controls, psychological and moral squalor, and [the] irrationality which characterizes our society." Faculty should support the right of student dissent on campus, "including the right to disrupt institutional processes." They should join student protest against corporate and military intrusion onto the campuses and student efforts to stop university involvement in war research and other "racist, military, and imperialist activities."[43]

NUC never entirely deserted its interest in student and faculty campus issues. But even in its first two years, its mainstream leaders always placed political ahead of professional commitment. In a 1969 letter to friends at Providence College in Rhode Island, Bob Ross of NUC's executive committee noted that the organization's objectives should be to "transform the self-identification of teachers from that of being 'professionals' who relate to other colleagues in a field to that of being politicals whose most important relationships are to comrades who may or may not be in their field. I think," he added, "we should avoid . . . the notion that here is a group of like-minded friends banded together to make their profession more relevant." Politics must always "remain in the fore."[44]

By mid-1970, following the Cambodia incursion disorders and

42.   Florence Howe, "What Success at the MLA?" in Professional Associations File, NUC Papers; New York *Times*, December 29, 1968, January 5, 1969; Ronald Radosh, "The Bare Knuckled Historians," *Nation*, February 2, 1970; Richard Rothstein to Arthur Waskow, December 4, 13, 1969; Arthur Waskow to "Fellow Historians, Fellow Radicals," November [?], 1969, all in Professional Associations File, NUC Papers.
43.   *The New University Conference: The Student Rebellion*, in "Papers of NUC" File, NUC Papers.
44.   Bob Ross to Betty and Neal [Resnikoff], April 8, 1969, in MLA File, NUC Papers.

the Kent State killings, even this degree of militancy seemed tepid. Before long the whole academic enterprise began to appear beside the point except as a base for revolutionary activity. This mood culminated in the adoption of the OUTS program by the 1970 Ann Arbor National Convention.

OUTS was an acronym for "open up the schools." It pointed in the same direction as the TDS manifesto on ghetto school rebellion: faculty must become professional organizers of the discontented and convert them into insurgents. The OUTS program focused on the schools, especially the junior colleges, with large proportions of white working class and Third World students. These should, in effect, become "people's colleges," open to the entire community, not just privileged students and faculty. Admission requirements should be abolished; there should be no grades; no one should flunk out. The schools' facilities and resources should be used for community, not ivory tower, purposes. They must be converted into bases for political forays into the larger community and become centers of struggle against the local power structure. Ultimately, OUTS must provide a "strategic basis for a sustained revolutionary movement in our schools." The rhetoric and style of the OUTS program, even for these overheated, final days of the New Left, were unexpected. It is not surprising to learn that OUTS was copied from the Red Guards' demands to Peking University during the notorious Chinese Cultural Revolution.[45]

NUC also sought to become a rallying point for the antiwar effort. For a while it pushed the "People's Peace Treaty," a document declaring "peace" between the American people and the NLF and North Vietnam. In 1970 it called its antiwar strategy "Moby Dick," a reference, apparently, to the despised American Leviathan that, like the "White Whale" of Melville's novel, was dangerous and must be destroyed. Moby Dick rejected electoral politics in 1970 as a way to end the war. That was the route of the liberals. Instead, it advised an action program to sabotage the power structure. The authorities should be "hassled, harassed, and otherwise annoyed." Moby Dick activists devised an ingenious program of antisystem actions: NUCers were advised to phone in reservations to "sexist night clubs and rul-

45. *Open Up The Schools: NUC Paper 3*; Tom Hecht, "An Overview of the Coming Months," *NUC Newsletter*, November, 1971.

ing class restaurants" to disrupt their operations; they should order washing machines and TV sets on credit to be delivered to "pig stations and the ruling class"; they should dump chemicals in the heating and air-conditioning systems of business firms, university administration buildings, and government offices to force evacuations. NUCers were also urged to create "liberated zones" on the campuses to serve as bases from which to launch other antiwar attacks on the "warfare state's" rulers.[46]

NUC's palmy days were brief. In the fall of 1970 it had about sixty chapters concentrated in California, the Northeast, and the Midwest, with few in the South or at the elite colleges. Dues-paying membership numbered about nine hundred, with graduate students more numerous than full-time faculty. During this peak year, fifteen hundred to two thousand people considered themselves members of NUC, though not all had sent in their ten-dollar annual fee to make them official members.[47]

Even at its zenith, NUC's organizational success seemed limited. At its founding, enthusiasts had hoped to make the conference into the adult SDS that had failed to appear. Even two thousand members meant that it had organized less than a fraction of 1 percent of college and university faculty. Recognition of this led to a hot debate over whether NUC should abandon its "membership" status and become a "cadre" organization of dedicated and ideologically disciplined activists who would help lead the masses to revolution.[48] It did not take long for the debate to become irrelevant.

By mid-1971, NUC began a swift decline. In part the downward course followed the trajectory of the entire New Left in the early 1970s. As the rest of the Left slid into chaos and sectarianism it pulled NUC down with it. But NUC had its own special problems. I have noted the damage of anti-elitism and the male-female and Old Left–New Left conflicts to its effectiveness and inner cohesion. By 1970 the ideological battles had become so heated that NUC, to keep from becom-

46. "To: Liaison and International Committee. From R[inda] W[est]: People's Peace Treaty, December 2, 1970," and "Moby Dick: A Proposal on Imperialism and the War," both in Anti-War and Anti-Imperialism File, NUC Papers.
47. Rinda West to Jerry Boyle, September 25, 1970, in Correspondence File, NUC Papers; Eynon's interview with Bob Ross, December, 1980.
48. *NUC Newsletter*, January 20, 1971.

ing a recruiting ground for Maoism, expelled Progressive Labor from the organization. But PL's departure did not end the ideological infighting. In the same year the "Long March Caucus," a violence-prone, street-fighting Weatherman group, demanded that the leadership endorse "armed struggle," and had to be contained.[49] At about this time, reflecting the heightened consciousness of sexual, as well as ethnic, minorities, a gay caucus appeared within NUC to demand its place in the organization's programs and a share of its limited resources. Finally, there was the generation gap. Bob Ross, who deplored the sexual rift, also believed that the divisions between the graduate students, young men and women first getting started, and the older radical faculty, with their "kids and mortgages and dogs and station wagons," had been damaging.[50]

These explanations ignored the critical point: NUC's fatal flaw was its abandonment of professional concerns and their almost complete replacement by radical activism. Such a course was possible, perhaps, in good times, but by 1971 or 1972, the 1960s boom was over. The decline would be a powerful inhibitor of student activism. When it was no longer clear that careers and jobs were disposable commodities, easily acquired, easily discarded, students pulled in their political horns and contracted their political expectations. The lowering economic horizon was an even more effective deterrent to political activism among college faculty and would-be faculty, who experienced earlier than most professional groups the end of 1960s prosperity. By late 1971 or early 1972 an ominous sense of decline in the job market had begun to invade NUC consciousness. Mike Ducey, who ran the job file, reported that it was getting harder and harder to place people and that all projections indicated that it would get still more difficult in the ensuing years. Soon, he wrote, only a third of those with Ph.D.'s would be able to find openings in colleges and NUC would have to drop "University" from its name.[51]

NUC responded to the job crunch by putting its limited re-

49. "Press Release: To Movement Press: Statement of the New University Conference, February 9, 1970," in Progressive Labor Party File, NUC Papers; *On Sabotage, Terrorism, and the Underground: NUC Paper 1; NUC Newsletter*, September 15, 1970.
50. See Resolution: NUC Gay Caucus, in Meetings and Conventions File, NUC Papers; Eynon's interview with Bob Ross, December, 1980.
51. Ducey, NUC Job File and NUC "Defense" Correspondence, in NUC Papers.

sources behind the growing trade union movement among college faculty. But this did little to help. Membership dwindled as fewer fresh Ph.D.'s came from the graduate schools and as young instructors diverted their energies into simply keeping their heads above water. NUC, like all "causes," took many evenings. That was fine when one had a job and a decent prospect of security. But now the evenings were better spent completing dissertations and books and sending out résumés. By 1971, membership began to drop off. In February, 1971, it was down to 675; a year later it had fallen to 330. At this point, there were only about 15 active chapters left and total monthly NUC income from dues, contributions, and literature sales had declined to $2,750, about half the amount needed to run the office. Whether NUC liked it or not, the organization had been reduced to a cadre body.[52]

The 1972 convention at Bloomington, Indiana, was NUC's last. By this time, OUTS was virtually dead and with it had gone its network of regional organizers. Many NUC leaders, including Paul Lauter, Florence Howe, Rinda West, and David Herreshoff, had left. NUC had diminished to a dozen or so local chapters and the small surviving staff in Chicago. To beef up attendance, the Bloomington meeting was planned as a general "outreach conference in education" that would attract radicals in the public schools as well as college faculty. But at the same time participants would also consider NUC's future. The convention opened on Thursday, June 8. On Saturday the delegates passed a motion to disband NUC entirely. To take care of remaining business and financial obligations, they appointed an interim committee of six. The committee was mandated to maintain the NUC mailing list for one year to make it available for other Movement groups that might want to use it.[53] NUC had gone the way of the New Left generally.

Neither MDS nor NUC can be considered a success. Both were destroyed by their members' inability to decide whether they were

52. *NUC Newsletter*, November, 1971; Ellen Kollegar, "History of Wright Chapter NUC," in Chapter Histories File, NUC Papers; Tom Hecht, "Where From Here?" *NUC Newsletter*, February, 1972.

53. To EC and Staff, From Tom and Barbara, in National Committee Meetings and Conventions File, NUC Papers; "Dear Comrades," June 12, 1972, in NUC Papers, Tamiment Library, NYU.

professionals or radicals first. Neither organization ever discovered a successful formula for combining a radical and a professional vocation.

Yet the mood that initially informed NUC and MDS left a legacy. Today, various radical caucuses, networks, and formal radical professional associations survive and flourish. Their members have altered the bureaucratic practices of mainstream professional associations, advanced the professional interests of women and nonwhites, and succeeded in making their presence felt in professional association affairs. In the humanities and social sciences, Marxists and other radicals have mounted major intellectual challenges to the mainstream approaches and the preconceptions in their disciplines, including those of older Middle Period scholars. There is a legacy of personnel as well. In the larger and more cosmopolitan universities, there are significant numbers of young faculty who passed through the Movement and NUC, and consider themselves radicals or "progressives." In American history, for a while, the University of Rochester History Department, under the leadership of Eugene D. Genovese, Herbert Gutman, Loren Baritz, and Christopher Lasch, proclaimed itself a center of radical and Marxist historiography.[54] In medicine and law too, in such organizations as Health PAC, a group formed by Robb Burlage in 1968 to expose what radicals perceived as the class abuses of American health care, and in the public interest law firms founded with Great Society environmentalist and legal services funds to represent the poor or the consumer, New Left postgraduates have found a haven. The New Left as such died a decade ago, but the men and women who launched NUC and MDS did indeed set in motion a "long march through the institutions."

54.   See Bertell Ollman and Edward Vernoff (eds.), *The Left Academy: Marxist Scholarship on American Campuses* (New York, 1982); interview with Professor Daniel Walkowitz of New York University, January, 1984, in New York.

The Principal Writings of David Herbert Donald
A Bibliography

The following bibliography includes books, edited works, edited series, articles and essays, and book reviews. Although we do not claim that this bibliography is definitive, especially the book reviews, it does contain Donald's principal writings and it does show the breadth of his work.

Books

Lincoln's Herndon. New York, 1948.

Divided We Fought: A Pictorial History of the War, 1861–1865. New York, 1952.

Lincoln Reconsidered: Essays on the Civil War Era. New York, 1956; rev. ed., 1961.

Charles Sumner and the Coming of the Civil War. New York, 1960.

The Civil War and Reconstruction (with J. G. Randall). Boston, 1961; rev. ed., 1969.

The Divided Union (with J. G. Randall). Boston, 1961.

The Politics of Reconstruction, 1863–1867. Baton Rouge, 1965; rev. ed., Cambridge, Mass., 1984.

The Nation in Crisis, 1861–1877. New York, 1969.

Charles Sumner and the Rights of Man. New York, 1970.

The Great Republic: A History of the American People (with Bernard Bailyn, David Brion Davis, John L. Thomas, Gordon W. Wood, and Robert H. Wiebe). 2 vols. Lexington, Mass., 1977; 2nd rev. ed., 1981; 3rd rev. ed., 1984.

Liberty and Union: The Crisis of Popular Government, 1830–1890. Boston, 1978.

Edited Works (with introductions)

Inside Lincoln's Cabinet: The Civil War Diaries of Salmon P. Chase. New York, 1954.

George Cary Eggleston. *A Rebel's Recollections*. Bloomington, Ind., 1959.
Why the North Won the Civil War. Baton Rouge, 1960; rev. ed. 1961.
The Diary of Charles Francis Adams, January 1820–September 1829 (with Aïda Donald). 2 vols. Cambridge, Mass., 1964.
William A. Dunning. *Essays on the Civil War and Reconstruction*. New York, 1965.
Walter L. Fleming. *Documentary History of Reconstruction*. 2 vols. New York, 1966.
Sidney Andrews. *The South Since the War*. Boston, 1971.
Gone for a Soldier: The Civil War Memoirs of Alfred Bellard. Boston, 1975.
War Diary and Letters of Stephen Minot Weld, 1861–1865. Boston, 1979.

Edited Series

The Making of America. Hill and Wang.
  Clarence Ver Steeg. *The Formative Years, 1607–1763*. New York, 1964.
  Esmond Wright. *The Fabric of Freedom, 1763–1800*. New York, 1961; rev. ed., 1978.
  Charles M. Wiltse. *The New Nation, 1800–1845*. New York, 1961; rev. ed., 1982 (with John Mayfield as new author).
  Roy F. Nichols. *The Stakes of Power, 1845–1877*. New York, 1961; rev. ed., 1982 (with Eugene H. Berwanger as co-author).
  Robert H. Wiebe. *The Search for Order, 1877–1920*. New York, 1967.
  George E. Mowry. *The Urban Nation, 1920–1980*. New York, 1965; rev. ed., 1981 (with Blaine A. Brownell as co-author).
A Documentary History of American Life. McGraw-Hill Book Company.
  Jack P. Greene, ed. *Settlements to Society, 1584–1763*. New York, 1966.
  Jack P. Greene, ed. *Colonies to Nation, 1763–1789*. New York, 1967.
  Robert W. Johannsen, ed. *Democracy on Trial, 1845–1877*. New York, 1966.

David A. Shannon, ed. *Progressivism and Postwar Disillusion-
ment, 1898–1928.* New York, 1966.
Alfred B. Rollins, Jr., ed. *Depression, Recovery, and War, 1929–
1945.* New York, 1966.
Ernest R. May, ed. *Anxiety and Affluence, 1945–1965.* New York,
1966.

Articles and Essays

"The Scalawag in Mississippi Reconstruction." *Journal of Southern
History,* X (1944), 447–60.
"Billy, You're Too Rampant." *Abraham Lincoln Quarterly,* III (1945),
375–407.
"The Folklore Lincoln." *Journal of the Illinois State Historical Society,* XL (1947), 377–96.
ed., "The Autobiography of James Hall, Western Literary Pioneer."
Ohio State Archeological and Historical Quarterly, LVI (1947),
295–304.
ed., "Lexington, Mississippi, in 1844." *Journal of Mississippi His-
tory,* IX (1947), 265–67.
"Toward a Western Literature, 1820–1860." *Mississippi Valley His-
torical Review,* XXXV (1948), 413–28 (in collaboration with F. A.
Palmer).
"The True Story of 'Herndon's Lincoln.'" *New Colophon,* I (1948),
221–34.
"Herndon and Mrs. Lincoln." *Books at Brown,* XII, Nos. 2–3 (1950).
"Getting Right with Lincoln." *Harper's Magazine,* CCII (April, 1951),
74–80.
"The Collected Works of Abraham Lincoln." *American Historical Re-
view,* LIX (1953), 142–49.
"Why They Impeached Andrew Johnson." *American Heritage,* VIII
(December, 1956), 20–25.
"The Great Emotion." In *The American Story,* edited by Earl S. Miers
(Great Neck, N.Y., 1956), 178–83.
"The Confederate as a Fighting Man." *Journal of Southern History,*
XXV (1959), 178–93.
"Lincoln as Politician." In *Abraham Lincoln: A New Portrait,* edited
by Henry B. Kranz (New York, 1959), 48–54.

"An Excess of Democracy." Inaugural address as Harmsworth Professor, published by Oxford University Press, 1960.

"Abraham Lincoln: Whig in the White House." In *The Enduring Lincoln*, edited by Norman A. Graebner (Urbana, 1959), 47–66.

"American Historians and the Causes of the Civil War." *South Atlantic Quarterly*, LIX (1960), 351–55.

"Abraham Lincoln: America's Unique Folk-Hero." In *Speaking of the Famous*, edited by A. F. Scott (London, 1962), 89–94.

"Lincoln Bibliography." In *The American Plutarch*, edited by Edward T. James (New York, 1964), 276–81.

"Devils Facing Zionwards." In *Grant, Lee, Lincoln and the Radicals*, edited by Grady McWhiney (Evanston, 1964), 72–91.

"The Quest for Motives." *Western Review*, III (1966), 55–60.

"The Grand Theme in American Historical Writing." *Journal of Historical Studies*, II (1969), 186–201.

"Black History." *Commentary*, XLIX (April, 1970), 85–88.

"Radical Historians on the Move." *New York Times Book Review*, July 19, 1970, pp. 1–2, 23–26.

"Reconstruction." In *Interpreting American History: Conversations with Historians*, edited by John A. Garraty (New York, 1970), I, 341–67.

"The Proslavery Argument Reconsidered." *Journal of Southern History*, XXXVII (1971), 3–18.

"Between Science and Art." *American Historical Review*, LXXVII (1972), 445–52.

"Between History and Psychology: Reflections on Psychobiography." *Scientific Proceedings . . . of the American Psychiatric Association* (1972), 59.

"Writing About the Past." *Commentary*, LIV (November, 1972), 96–99.

"The Republican Party, 1864–1877." In *History of U.S. Political Parties*. Vol. II, *1860–1910*, edited by Arthur M. Schlesinger, Jr. (New York, 1973), 1281–94.

"Promised Land or Paradise Lost: The South Beheld." *Georgia Review*, XXIX (1975), 184–87.

"Living Through a Civil War." In *We Americans*, edited by Daniel Boorstin (Washington, D.C., 1975), 201–21.

"The Southernization of America." New York *Times* (Op-ed feature), August 30, 1976, p. 23.

"Our Irrelevant History." New York *Times* (Op-ed feature), September 8, 1977, p. 37.

"James Garfield Randall." In *Dictionary of American Biography: Supplement Five, 1951–55* (New York, 1977), 556–58.

"In the Great Tradition." *Commentary*, LXVI (December, 1978), 74–77.

"A Generation of Defeat." In *From the Old South to the New: Essays on the Transitional South*, edited by Walter J. Fraser, Jr., and Winfred B. Moore, Jr. (Westport, Conn., 1981), 3–21.

Book Reviews

Meet Abraham Lincoln, by G. Lynn Sumner. *Journal of the Illinois State Historical Society*, XXXIX (1946), 276.

The Lincoln Papers, by David C. Mearns. *New York Herald Tribune Book Review*, October 31, 1948, p. 1.

Lincoln Under Enemy Fire, by John H. Cramer. *Mississippi Valley Historical Review*, XXXV (1949), 688–89.

Lincoln's Secretary, by Helen Nicolay. *Saturday Review*, April 9, 1949, p. 18.

Lincoln Runs for Congress, by Donald W. Riddle. *American Historical Review*, LIV (1949), 691–92.

The Lincoln Collector, by Carl Sandburg. *New York Times Book Review*, November 6, 1949, p. 4.

Uncollected Works of Abraham Lincoln, Vol. II, by Rufus R. Wilson. *American Historical Review*, LIV (1949), 889–90.

Lincoln's Vandalia, by William E. Baringer. *American Historical Review*, LV (1950), 382–83.

Horace Greeley: Voice of the People, by William Harlan Hale. *Nation*, November 11, 1950, pp. 442–43.

Two Friends of Man, by Ralph Korngold. *New York Herald Tribune Book Review*, January 22, 1950, p. 3.

The Custer Story, by Marguerite Marington. *Journal of Southern History*, XVI (1950), 550–51.

Theodore Weld, by Benjamin P. Thomas. *New York Herald Tribune Book Review*, November 12, 1950, p. 26.

Abraham Lincoln and the United States, by K. C. Wheare. *Mississippi Valley Historical Review*, XXXVI (1950), 720–21.

Tyrant of the Illinois: Uncle Joe Cannon's Experiment with Personal Power, by Blair Bolles. *Journal of the Illinois State Historical Society*, XLIV (1951), 358–59.

Lincoln and the Press, by Robert S. Harper. *New York Times Book Review*, February 25, 1951, 23.

Charles Sumner: An Essay, by Carl Schurz. *Saturday Review*, June 16, 1951, p. 46.

A Rail Splitter for President, by Wayne C. Williams. *American Historical Review*, LVII (1951), 246.

Glory Road: The Bloody Route from Fredericksburg to Gettysburg, by Bruce Catton. *New York Times Book Review*, March 16, 1952, p. 7.

Dred Scott's Case, by Vincent C. Hopkins. *Thought*, XXVII (1952), 150–52.

Mr. Lincoln's Contemporaries, by Roy Meredith. *Mississippi Valley Historical Review*, XXXVIII (1952), 716.

The Life of Billy Yank, by Bell I. Wiley. *New York Herald Tribune Book Review*, March 30, 1952, p. 5.

Lincoln and His Generals, by T. Harry Williams. *New York Herald Tribune Book Review*, February 24, 1952, p. 6.

Lincoln and the Russians, by Albert A. Woldman. *Saturday Review*, November 29, 1952, p. 20.

Origins of the New South, 1877–1913, by C. Vann Woodward. *Nation*, May 17, 1952, pp. 483–85.

Years of Madness, by W. E. Woodward. *New York Herald Tribune Book Review*, January 20, 1952, p. 13.

A Stillness at Appomattox, by Bruce Catton. *Nation*, November 28, 1953, p. 450.

Rendezvous with Destiny: A History of Modern American Reform, by Eric F. Goldman. *Key Reporter*, XVIII (1953), 4.

Lincoln and Greeley, by Harlan Hoyt Horner. *New-York Historical Society Quarterly*, XXXVII (1953), 284–85.

Foreigners in the Union Army and Navy, by Ella Lonn. *Wisconsin Magazine of History*, XXXVI (1953), 214–15.

Sheridan the Inevitable, by Richard O'Connor. *New York Herald Tribune Book Review*, August 30, 1953, p. 10.

Stanton: Lincoln's Secretary of War, by Fletcher M. Pratt. *New York Times Book Review*, October 25, 1953, p. 38.

By These Words: Great Documents of American Liberty, by Paul M. Angle. *New York Times Book Review*, October 31, 1954, p. 30.

A History of the Southern Confederacy, by Clement Eaton. *Journal of Southern History*, XX (1954), 554–57.

The Living Lincoln: The Man, His Mind, His Times, and the War He Fought, by Paul M. Angle and Earl S. Miers. *New York Times Book Review*, December 11, 1955, p. 7.

Rutherford B. Hayes and His America, by Harry Barnard. *New York Times Book Review*, January 2, 1955, p. 3.

The Day Lincoln Was Shot, by Jim Bishop. *New York Herald Tribune Book Review*, January 30, 1955, p. 1.

Daniel Webster and the Rise of National Conservatism, by Richard N. Current. *New York Times Book Review*, July 3, 1955, p. 4.

Spies for the Blue and the Gray, by Harnett Kane. *Louisiana Historical Quarterly*, XXXVII (1955), 96–98.

A Program for Conservatives, by Russell Kirk. *Georgetown Law Journal*, XLIII (1955), 705–10.

Memoirs of General William T. Sherman, edited by B. H. Liddell Hart, and *Numbers and Losses in the Civil War*, by Thomas L. Livermore. *New York Herald Tribune Book Review*, December 8, 1957, p. 4.

Justice Oliver Wendell Holmes: The Shaping Years, 1841–1870, by Mark DeWolfe Howe. *New England Quarterly*, XXX (1957), 526–29.

Eight Hours Before Richmond, by Virgil C. Jones. *New York Herald Tribune Book Review*, December 8, 1957, p. 5.

Fiction Fights the Civil War, by Robert A. Lively. *American Historical Review*, LXIII (1957), 140–42.

The Photographic History of the Civil War, by Francis T. Miller. *New York Herald Tribune Book Review*, June 16, 1957, p. 3.

Samuel Gridley Howe: Social Reformer, 1801–1826, by Harold Schwarz. *Mississippi Valley Historical Review*, XLIII (1957), 681–82.

Mighty Stonewall, by Frank E. Vandiver. *New York Herald Tribune Book Review*, May 5, 1957, p. 5.

Mr. Lincoln's Navy, by Richard S. West, Jr. *New York Times Book Review*, November 24, 1957, p. 6.

Private Elisha Stockwell, Jr., Sees the Civil War, edited by Byron R. Abernathy. *New York Herald Tribune Book Review*, June 15, 1958, p. 12.

Chronicle from the Nineteenth Century: Family Letters of Blanche Butler and Adelbert Ames, Married July 21st, 1870, compiled by Blanche Butler Ames. *New England Quarterly*, XXXI (1958), 278–81.

The Lincoln Nobody Knows, by Richard N. Current. *New York Herald Tribune Book Review*, November 30, 1958, p. 4.

Why the Civil War? by Otto Eisenschiml. *New York Times Book Review*, July 20, 1958, p. 6.

The Battle of Gettysburg, by Frank A. Haskell. *New York Herald Tribune Book Review*, June 15, 1958, p. 12.

A Rebel War Clerk's Diary, by John B. Jones. *New York Herald Tribune Book Review*, October 12, 1958, p. 4.

Crisis of the House Divided, by Harry V. Jaffa. *New York Herald Tribune Book Review*, October 4, 1959, p. 11.

George Perkins Marsh, Versatile Vermonter, by David Lowenthal. *Mississippi Valley Historical Review*, XLVI (1959), 150–51.

Slavery: A Problem in American Institutional and Intellectual Life, by Stanley M. Elkins. *American Historical Review*, LXV (1960), 921–22.

Andrew Johnson, by Milton Lomask. *New York Times Book Review*, November 20, 1960, p. 70.

Andrew Johnson and Reconstruction, by Eric L. McKitrick. *New York Herald Tribune Book Review*, September 25, 1960, p. 6.

Money, Class, and Party: An Economic Study of Civil War and Reconstruction, by Robert P. Sharkey. *American Historical Review*, LXV (1960), 928–29.

1861–1865: The Adventure of the Civil War Told with Pictures, by Irving Werstein. *Lincoln Herald*, LXII (1960), 190.

Lincoln Day by Day: A Chronology, 1809–1865. Vol. I, *1809–1848*; Vol. II, *1849–1860*, edited by William E. Baringer. *American Historical Review*, LXVI (1961), 535–36.

The Coming Fury, by Bruce Catton. *New York Times Book Review*, October 22, 1961, p. 1.

Charles Francis Adams, 1807–1886, by Martin B. Duberman. *New York Times Book Review*, March 26, 1961, p. 1.

The Bold Brahmins: New England's War Against Slavery, 1831–1863, by Lawrence Lader. *New York Times Book Review*, July 16, 1961, p. 7.

The Image of War: The Pictorial Reporting of the American Civil War, by Fletcher W. Thompson, Jr.; *1861–1865: The Adventure of the Civil War Told with Pictures*, by Irving Werstein; *The American Civil War: A Popular Illustrated History of the Years 1861–1865 as Seen by the Artist-Correspondents Who Were There*, by Earl S. Miers; *Centennial Album of the Civil War*, by Marvin H. Pakula; *Uniform and Dress of the Army and Navy of the Confederate States of America*, edited by Ray Riling; *Harpers Ferry in Pictures*, by Bruce Roberts; *Confederate City: Augusta, Georgia, 1860–1865*, by Florence Fleming Cotey; *Horsemen Blue and Gray*, by Hirst Dillon Milhollen, James Ralph Johnson, and Alfred H. Bill; and *After the Civil War: A Pictorial Profile of America from 1865–1900*, by John S. Blay. *New York Herald Tribune Book Review*, April 9, 1961, p. 30.

Jubal's Raid: General Early's Famous Attack on Washington in 1864, by Frank E. Vandiver; *The Night the War Was Lost*, by Charles L. Dufour; *Beefsteak Raid*, by Edward Boykin; *Reluctant General: The Life and Times of Albert Pike*, by Robert Lipscomb Duncan; *Rebellion in Missouri, 1861: Nathaniel Lyon and His Army of the West*, by Hans Christian Adamson; *Inferno at Petersburg*, by Henry Pleasants, Jr., and George H. Straley; *Confederate Strategy from Shiloh to Vicksburg*, by Archer Jones; *Storming of the Gateway: Chattanooga, 1863*, by Fairfax Downey; *The Wilderness Campaign*, by Edward Steere; *Lee's Last Campaign: The Story of Lee and His Men Against Grant—1864*, by Clifford Dowdey; and *Soldier Life in the Union and Confederate Armies*, edited by Philip Van Doren Stern. *New York Herald Tribune Book Review*, April 9, 1961, pp. 35–36.

The Burden of Southern History, by C. Vann Woodward. *Journal of Southern History*, XXVII (1961), 90–92.

Politics and the Crisis of 1860, by Stephen E. Baringer. *American Historical Review*, LXVII (1962), 155.

Walt Whitman's Memoranda During the War [&] Death of Abraham Lincoln, edited by Roy P. Basler. *Lincoln Herald*, LXIV (1962), 102.

Antislavery: The Crusade for Freedom in America and *A Bibliography of Antislavery in America*, by Dwight Lowell Dumond. *Political Science Quarterly*, LXXVII (1962), 273–76.

Largely Lincoln, by David C. Mearns. *American Historical Review*, LXVII (1962), 805–806.

Lincoln Day by Day: A Chronology, 1809–1865. Vol. III, *1861–1865*, edited by C. Percy Powell. *American Historical Review*, LXVII (1962), 441–42.

Patriotic Gore: Studies in the Literature of the American Civil War, by Edmund Wilson. *New York Herald Tribune Book Review*, April 29, 1962, p. 4.

Guide to Federal Archives Relating to the Civil War, by Henry P. Beers and Kenneth W. Munden. *American Historical Review*, LXVIII (1963), 830.

Terrible Swift Sword, by Bruce Catton. *Saturday Review*, November 16, 1963, pp. 42, 92.

The Civil War: Fredericksburg to Meridian, by Shelby Foote. *New York Times Book Review*, December 1, 1963, p. 36.

Washington: Capital City, 1879–1950, by Constance M. Green. *New York Herald Tribune*, December 29, 1963.

Manifest Destiny and Mission in American History, by Frederick Merk. *Journal of Southern History*, XXIX (1963), 527–28.

The Reconstruction: A Documentary History of the South After the War, 1865–1877, edited by James P. Shenton. *Washington Post*, April 30, 1963.

Antislavery and Disunion, 1858–1861: Studies in the Rhetoric of Compromise and Conflict, edited by J. Jeffery Auer. *Civil War History*, X (1964), 101–102.

An Historian and the Civil War, by Avery Craven. *Journal of American History*, LI (1964), 483–85.

Aboard the U.S.S. Monitor, edited by Robert W. Daly. Baltimore *Sunday Sun*, March 22, 1964.

The Meaning of History, by Erick Kahler. Baltimore *Sunday Sun*, May 31, 1964.

The Historian and History, by Page Smith. Baltimore *Sunday Sun*, May 31, 1964.

Inside Lincoln's Army, edited by David S. Sparks. Baltimore *Sunday Sun*, May 24, 1964.

Jefferson Davis, Tragic Hero: The Last Twenty-Five Years, 1864– 1889, by Hudson Strode. *New York Times Book Review*, September 27, 1964, p. 6.

The Idea of the South: Pursuit of a Central Theme, edited by Frank E. Vandiver. *Louisiana History*, V (1964), 457–59.

Never Call Retreat, by Bruce Catton. *Book Week*, September 5, 1965, pp. 1, 10.

Lee, by Clifford Dowdey. *New York Times Book Review*, November 28, 1965, pp. 58–60.

The Inner Civil War: Northern Intellectuals and the Crisis of the Union, by George M. Fredrickson. *Book Week*, October 10, 1965, p. 19.

The Papers of John C. Calhoun. Vol. II, *1817–18*, edited by W. Edwin Hemphill. *Manuscripts*, IX (1965), 120–22.

The Oxford History of the American People, by Samuel Eliot Morison. Washington *Post*, April 22, 1965.

Lincoln's Scapegoat General: The Life of Benjamin F. Butler, 1813– 1893, by Richard S. West, Jr. *New York Times Book Review*, April 11, 1965, p. 6.

Margaret Mitchell of Atlanta: The Author of Gone with the Wind, by Finis Farr. *Book Week*, January 23, 1966, pp. 5, 21–23.

Robert E. Lee: A Portrait, 1807–1861, by Margaret Sanborn. *New York Times Book Review*, December 11, 1966, p. 4.

Historical Interpretations and American Historianship, by Jennings B. Sanders. *Journal of Southern History*, XXXII (1966), 532–33.

The Era of Reconstruction, 1865–1877, by Kenneth M. Stampp. *American Historical Review*, LXXI (1966), 700–701.

Jefferson Davis: Private Letters, 1823–1889, edited by Hudson Strode. *New York Times Book Review*, October 16, 1966, p. 12.

Zeb Vance: Champion of Personal Freedom, by Glenn Tucker. *New York Times Book Review*, November 6, 1966, pp. 52–53.

Simon Cameron, Lincoln's Secretary of War: A Political Biography, by Erwin S. Bradley. *Civil War History*, XIII (1967), 84–86.

John C. Calhoun, by Richard Current. *American Historical Review*, LXXII (1967), 701–702.

The Problem of Slavery in Western Culture, by David Brion Davis. *American Quarterly*, XIX (1967), 265–68.

The Secret City: A History of Race Relations in the Nation's Capital, by Constance M. Green. *Book Week*, June 11, 1967, p. 12.

Democratic Politics and Sectionalism: The Wilmot Proviso Controversy, by Chaplain W. Morrison. *Journal of Southern History*, XXXIII (1967), 570–71.

The Reconstruction of the Nation, by Rembert W. Patrick. *Commentary*, XLIV (September, 1967), 94–98.

James Lusk Alcorn: Persistent Whig, by Lilian A. Pereyra. *American Historical Review*, LXXII (1967), 707–708.

Robert Toombs of Georgia, by William Y. Thompson. *American Historical Review*, LXXIII (1967), 235–36.

Towards a New Past: Dissenting Essays in American History, edited by Barton J. Bernstein. *American Historical Review*, LXXIV (1968), 531–33.

A Portion of That Field: The Centennial of the Burial of Lincoln, by Gwendolyn Brooks *et al. Canadian Journal of History*, III (1968), 109.

The Papers of Andrew Johnson. Vol. I, *1822–1851*, edited by LeRoy P. Graf and Ralph W. Haskins. *North Carolina Historical Review*, XLV (1968), 327–28.

Intellectual Origins of American Radicalism, by Staughton Lynd. *Commentary*, XLVI (August, 1968), 78–79.

The United States Army and Reconstruction, by James E. Sefton. *American Historical Review*, LXXIII (1968), 1649–50.

The Shrine of Party: Congressional Voting Behavior, 1841–1851, by Joel H. Silbey. *Political Science Quarterly*, LXXXIII (1968), 455–56.

The First President Johnson, by Lately Thomas. *Book World*, November 10, 1968, p. 17.

The Emergence of the New South, 1913–1945, by George B. Tindall. *Commentary*, XLV (March, 1968), 83–86.

Cotton Kingdom of the New South: A History of the Yazoo Mississippi Delta from Reconstruction to the Twentieth Century, by Robert L. Brandfon. *Agricultural History*, XLIII (1969), 312–13.

Grant Takes Command, by Bruce Catton. *National Observer*, May 29, 1969, p. 21.

Heard Round the World: The Impact Abroad of the Civil War, by Harold M. Hyman *et al. American Historical Review*, LXXV (1969), 215–16.

August Belmont: A Political Biography, by Irving Katz. *Journal of Southern History*, XXXV (1969), 265–66.

The Radical Republicans, by Hans L. Trefousse. Baltimore *Sunday Sun*, May 29, 1965.

Huey Long, by T. Harry Williams. *Book World*, November 9, 1969, p. 4.

Free Soil, Free Labor, Free Men: The Ideology of the Republican Party Before the Civil War, by Eric Foner. *New York Times Book Review*, October 18, 1970, p. 16.

Hannibal Hamlin of Maine: Lincoln's First Vice-President, by H. Draper Hunt. *Journal of Southern History*, XXXVI (1970), 283–84.

Industrial Slavery in the Old South, by Robert S. Starobin. *Wisconsin Magazine of History*, LIV (1970), 60–61.

The South and the Nation, by Pat Watters. *Commentary*, L (July, 1970), 67–68.

North of Reconstruction: Ohio Politics, 1865–1870, by Felice A. Bonadio. *Journal of American History*, LVIII (1971), 472–73.

The Papers of Andrew Johnson. Vol. II, *1852–1857*, edited by LeRoy P. Graf and Ralph W. Haskins. *North Carolina Historical Review*, XLVIII (1971), 207–209.

Irish: Charles G. Halpine in Civil War America, by William Hanchett. *Journal of American History*, LVIII (1971), 464–66.

A Rap on Race, by Margaret Mead and James Baldwin. *Virginia Quarterly Review*, XLIX (1971), 619–22.

The Letters of William Lloyd Garrison. Vol. I, *I Will Be Heard! 1822–1835*, edited by Walter M. Merrill. *Journal of American History*, LVIII (1971), 743–45.

America at 1750: A Social Portrait, by Richard Hofstadter. *Commentary*, LIII (March, 1972), 88–91.

The Dawn's Early Light, by Walter Lord. *Book World,* September 24, 1972, p. 4.

The Papers of Jefferson Davis. Vol. I, *1808–1840,* edited by Haskell M. Monroe, Jr., and James T. McIntosh. *American Historical Review,* LXXVII (1972), 1506–1508.

The Letters of William Lloyd Garrison. Vol. II, *A House Dividing Against Itself, 1836–1840,* edited by Louis Ruchames. *Journal of American History,* LIX (1972), 670–71.

The Diary of Edmund Ruffin. Vol. I, edited by William K. Scarborough. *New York Times Book Review,* September 24, 1972, pp. 2, 20.

Mary Todd Lincoln: Her Life and Letters, edited by Justin C. Turner and Linda Levitt Turner. *Book World,* September 24, 1972, p. 4.

The Psychoanalytic Interpretation of History, edited by Benjamin B. Wolman. *Journal of Southern History,* XXXVIII (1972), 111–12.

The Legend of John Brown, by Richard Boyer. Baltimore *Sunday Sun,* March 4, 1973.

Daniel Webster and the Trial of American Nationalism, 1843–1852, by Robert F. Dalzell. *New York Times Book Review,* February 4, 1973, p. 4.

Stephen A. Douglas, by Robert W. Johannsen. *Book World,* May 6, 1973, p. 4.

A History of Mississippi, by Richard Aubrey McLemore. *American Historical Review,* LXXVIII (1973), 1523–25.

The Idea of Fraternity in America, by W. C. McWilliams. *Commentary,* LVI (November, 1973), 78–79.

The Papers of Andrew Johnson. Vol. III, *1858–1859,* edited by LeRoy P. Graf and Ralph W. Haskins. *North Carolina Historical Review,* L (1973), 330–31.

The Disruption of the Solid South, by George B. Tindall. *Journal of Negro History,* LVIII (1973), 207–209.

The Americans: The Democratic Experience, by Daniel J. Boorstin. *Commentary,* LVII (April, 1974), 86–88.

Thomas Jefferson: An Intimate History, by Fawn Brodie. *Commentary,* LVII (July, 1974), 96–98.

A More Perfect Union: The Impact of the Civil War and Reconstruction on the Constitution, by Harold M. Hyman. *Journal of American History,* LX (1974), 1129–31.

A Compromise of Principle: Congressional Republicans and Reconstruction, 1863–1869, by Michael Les Benedict. Book World, September 7, 1975.

Breckinridge: Statesman, Soldier, Symbol, by William C. Davis. Journal of American History, LXII (1975), 699–701.

The Hofstadter Aegis, edited by Stanley Elkins and Eric McKitrick. American Scholar, XLIV (1975), 508–509.

Roll, Jordan, Roll, by Eugene Genovese. Commentary, LIX (January, 1975), 86–90.

Gentleman Boss: The Life of Chester Alan Arthur, by Thomas C. Reeves. Book World, March 15, 1975, p. 3.

Impeachment of a President: Andrew Johnson, the Blacks, and Reconstruction, by Hans L. Trefousse. Book World, September 7, 1975.

A Slave's Log Book: Or 20 Years Residence in Africa, by Theophilus Conneau. New York Times Book Review, November 14, 1976, p. 1.

Roots: The Saga of an American Family, by Alex Haley. Commentary, LXII (December, 1976), 70–74.

Jefferson's Nephews: A Frontier Tragedy, by Boynton Merrill. New York Times Book Review, December 12, 1976, p. 3.

The Papers of Andrew Johnson. Vol. IV, 1860–1861, edited by LeRoy P. Graf and Ralph W. Haskins. North Carolina Historical Review, LIV (1977), 427–29.

Black Odyssey: The Afro-American Ordeal in Slavery, by Nathan I. Huggins. New York Times Book Review, December 11, 1977, p. 10.

The Papers of Jefferson Davis. Vol. II, June 1841–July 1846, edited by James T. McIntosh. American Historical Review, LXXXIV (1977), 1329–30.

With Malice Toward None: The Life of Abraham Lincoln, by Stephen B. Oates. New York Times Book Review, March 13, 1977, p. 2.

Exodusters: Black Migration to Kansas After Reconstruction, by Nell I. Painter. New York Times Book Review, January 30, 1977, p. 7.

Ballots for Freedom: Antislavery Politics in the United States, 1837–1860, by Richard H. Sewell. Journal of American History, LXIV (1977), 797–98.

Lincoln and the War Democrats, by Christopher Dell. *Journal of Southern History*, XLIV (1978), 123–24.

John Brown's Journey: Notes and Reflections on His America and Mine, by Albert Fried. *New York Times Book Review*, April 2, 1978, pp. 12–13.

Protest at Selma: Martin Luther King, Jr., and the Voting Rights Act of 1965, by David J. Garrow. *New Republic*, November 4, 1978, pp. 48–50.

The Diary of Edmund Ruffin. Vol. II, edited by William K. Scarborough. *Journal of American History*, LXIV (1978), 1117–18.

Uncollected Stories of William Faulkner, edited by Joseph Blotner. *New Republic*, December 15, 1979, pp. 36–37.

The Dred Scott Case: Its Significance in American Law and Politics, by Don E. Fehrenbacher. *Chronicle of Higher Education*, January 22, 1979, pp. 6–7.

Been in the Storm So Long: The Aftermath of Slavery, by Leon F. Litwack. *New Republic*, June 9, 1979, pp. 32–34.

Aaron Burr: The Years from Princeton to Vice President, 1756–1805, by Milton Lomask, and *Alexander Hamilton: A Biography*, by Forrest McDonald. *New York Times Book Review*, September 23, 1979, pp. 11, 30.

James T. Rapier and Reconstruction, by Loren Schweninger. *Alabama Review*, XXXII (1979), 228–30.

Slave and Citizen: The Life of Frederick Douglass, by Nathan I. Huggins; *The Frederick Douglass Papers, Series One: Speeches, Debates and Interviews*. Vol. I, *1841–46*, edited by John W. Blassingame *et al.*; and *Moral Choices: Memory, Desire, and Imagination in Nineteenth-Century American Abolition*, by Peter F. Walker. *New Republic*, March 15, 1980, pp. 28–32.

A Southern Renaissance: The Cultural Awakening of the American South, 1930–1955, by Richard H. King. *New Republic*, May 17, 1980, pp. 35–36.

The Imperiled Union: Essays on the Background of the Civil War, by Kenneth M. Stampp. *New Republic*, August 23, 1980, pp. 31–33.

George Washington Carver: Scientist and Symbol, by Linda O. McMurry. *New Republic*, October 28, 1981, pp. 35–36.

The Papers of Frederick Law Olmsted. Vol. II, *Slavery and the South*

1852–1857, edited by Charles E. Beveridge *et al. New York Times Book Review*, June 28, 1981, pp. 11, 23.

Ethnic America: A History, by Thomas Sowell. *New York Times Book Review*, August 2, 1981, pp. 1, 20.

The West and Reconstruction, by Eugene H. Berwanger. *Western Historical Quarterly*, XIII (1982), 449–50.

The Years of Lyndon Johnson: The Path to Power, by Robert Caro. *New York Times Book Review*, November 21, 1982, p. 1.

No Place of Grace: Antimodernism and the Transformation of American Culture, 1880–1920, by T. J. Jackson Lear. *American Spectator*, XV (1982), 40.

The War Within: From Victorian to Modernist Thought in the South, 1919–1945, by Daniel J. Singal. *New York Times Book Review*, October 31, 1982, pp. 13, 37.

Richmond Redeemed: The Siege at Petersburg, by Richard J. Sommers. *Parameters*, XII (1982), 93–94.

The Imperiled Union: 1861–1865. Vol. I, *The Deep Waters of the Proud*, by William C. Davis. *Journal of American History*, LXX (1983), 154.

Southern Honor: Ethics and Behavior in the Old South, by Bertram Wyatt-Brown. *New York Times Book Review*, April 24, 1983, p. 8.

The Contributors

JEAN H. BAKER, professor of history at Goucher College, is the author of *Ambivalent Americans* (1977) and *Affairs of Party* (1983).

WILLIAM J. COOPER, JR., professor of history and dean of the Graduate School at Louisiana State University, is the author of *The South and the Politics of Slavery* (1978) and *Liberty and Slavery: Southern Politics to 1860* (1983).

STANLEY P. HIRSHSON, professor of history at Queens College, City University of New York, is the author of *Farewell to the Bloody Shirt* (1962) and *Lion of the Lord: A Biography of Brigham Young* (1969).

MICHAEL F. HOLT, professor of history at the University of Virginia, is the author of *Forging a Majority* (1969) and *The Political Crisis of the 1850s* (1978).

ARI HOOGENBOOM, professor of history at Brooklyn College, City University of New York, is the author of *Outlawing the Spoils* (1961) and *A History of the ICC* (1976).

ROBERT C. KENZER, assistant professor of history at Brigham Young University, is currently working on a study of Negro landowning families of North Carolina from 1860 to 1900.

PETER KOLCHIN, professor of history at the University of Delaware, is the author of *First Freedom* (1972) and "Reevaluating the Antebellum Slave Community," *Journal of American History* (1983).

JOHN MCCARDELL, associate professor of history at Middlebury College, is the author of *The Idea of a Southern Nation* (1979) and "William Gilmore Simms," in Michael O'Brien (ed.), *Intellectual Life in Antebellum Charleston* (1985).

GRADY MCWHINEY, Lyndon Baines Johnson Professor of American History at Texas Christian University, is the author of *Braxton Bragg and Confederate Defeat* (1969) and *Attack and Die: Civil War Military Tactics and the Southern Heritage* (1982).

Bragg and Confederate Defeat (1969) and *Attack and Die: Civil War Military Tactics and the Southern Heritage* (1982).

SYDNEY NATHANS, associate professor of history at Duke University, is the author of *Daniel Webster and Jacksonian Democracy* (1973) and *The Quest for Progress* (1983).

IRWIN UNGER, professor of history at New York University, is the author of *The Greenback Era* (1964) and *A History of the New Left* (1974).

Index

Trent, Alphonso, 233, 234
Trent, William Peterfield: background
of, 187–88; and biography of W. G.
Simms, 188–89, 192–93, 198–99,
200–201; post-*Simms* career of,
197–200
Trumbull, Lyman, 169–70, 174
Tunica County (Miss.): postbellum con-
ditions in, 205–22 *passim*
Tyler, John, 56, 57

Unger, Irwin, 1, 6, 7, 12
University of the South, 186, 187, 188,
189, 193, 197, 198, 199, 200

Van Buren, Martin, 16, 17, 22, 31, 32,
53n, 65
Venable, Abraham, 82
Verba, Sidney, 165
Vietnam War: opposition to, 242, 243,
244, 265–66
Violence, southern: against blacks,
220–21, 224–26, 230–31, 238–39;
during elections, 176; northern attitude toward, 123–24; origins of,
112–37 *passim*; southern justification
of, 136
Voting: 19th-century patterns of, 16–17,
18–19, 23, 27–28, 29–30; and economic conditions, 20, 26, 27, 33; decline of, 169; ethnocultural interpretation of, 24–25, 26, 27, 27n

Waller, Thomas "Fats," 224, 227–28
Warner, Charles Dudley: and biography
of W. G. Simms, 179–80, 181, 183,
189; on life in the South, 186–87, 188;
mentioned, 193, 197, 202, 203
Washington, George: as political icon,
166
Waskow, Arthur, 263
Waters, Muddy, 219
Watson, Harry L., 16, 19n

Webb, Chick, 224, 226
Webber, Thomas L., 94
Weed, Thurlow, 66, 83
Weisstein, Naomi, 255, 261
Welter, Rush, 167
West, Fairinda, 261, 268
Wharton, Vernon L., 1, 2
Whig party: and candidacy of Zachary
Taylor, 64–65; and economic issues,
17–18, 32, 36–40, 40n, 41–51,
52–53, 53n; and election of 1840,
pp. 16, 17, 18, 19, 20–21, 21n, 22, 29,
34–35, 36–40, 40n, 41–51, 53–56,
165–66; and Independent Treasury
bill, 31, 31n; and territorial question,
60, 61, 62–63, 64, 65–67, 71–72,
73–75, 77, 78–79, 80, 82, 83, 84, 85;
defection of voters from, 56–58; devel-
opment of, 17, 23; in Ohio, 27n; on
state level, 33–34; mentioned, 170,
173
Wigfall, Louis T., 137
Willems, Emilio, 208
Williams, Sandy, 226
Williams, T. Harry, 11, 12
Wilmot Proviso: and Polk, 66; and Whig
party, 60, 61, 62–63, 64, 65–66, 73,
74–75, 77–79, 80, 82, 83, 84, 85; debate over, 59, 60–61, 69, 80, 84, 86
Wilson, Quinn, 226
Wilson, Teddy, 223, 231, 235–36
Wilson, Woodrow, 198
World War I: and cotton boom, 218
Wright, Archibald, 209
Wright, Gavin, 102

Young, James "Trummy," 229, 231, 237,
239
Young, Lee, 239
Young, Lester, 223

Zinn, Howard, 256
Znaniecki, Florian, 13